Catch These Hands!

murata

3

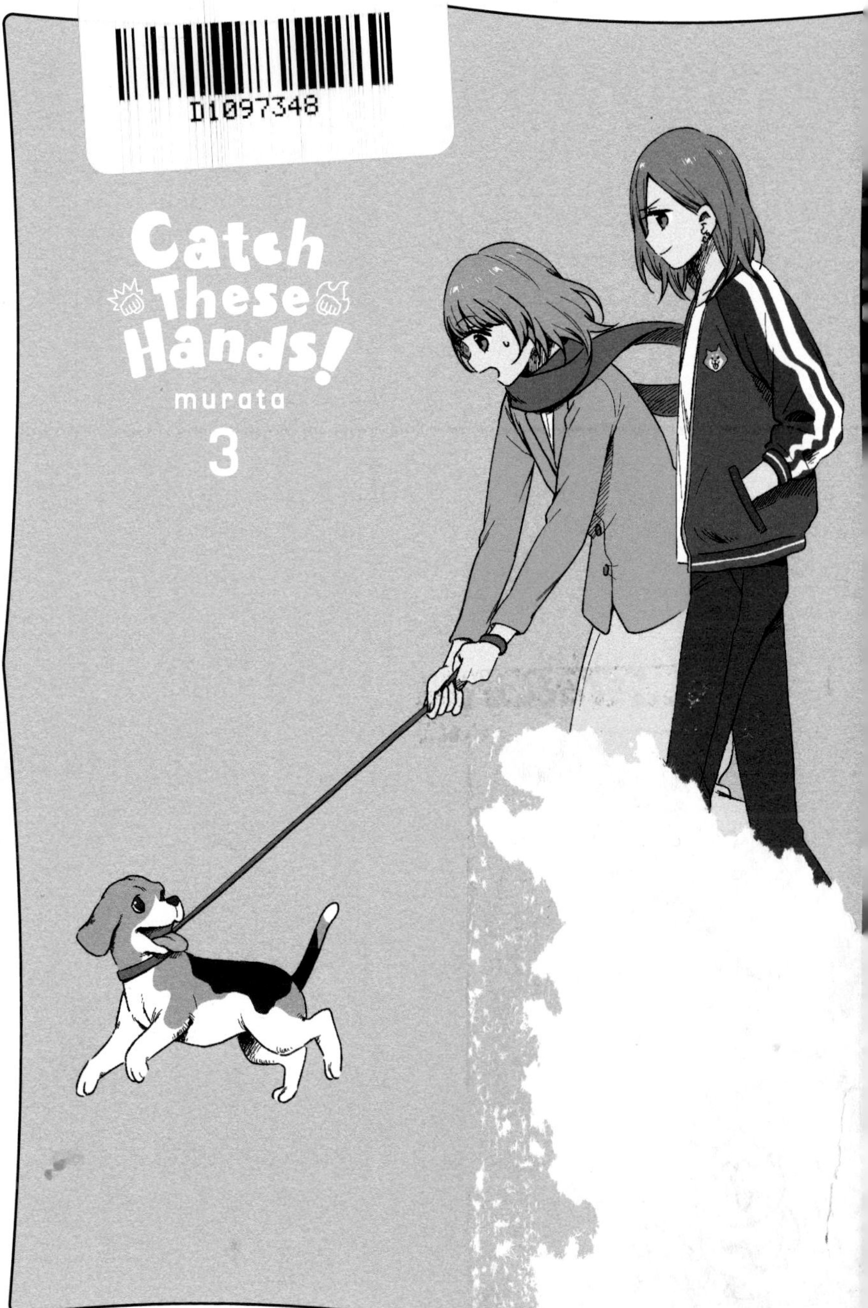

Contents

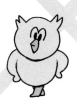

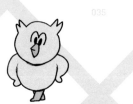

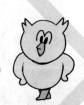

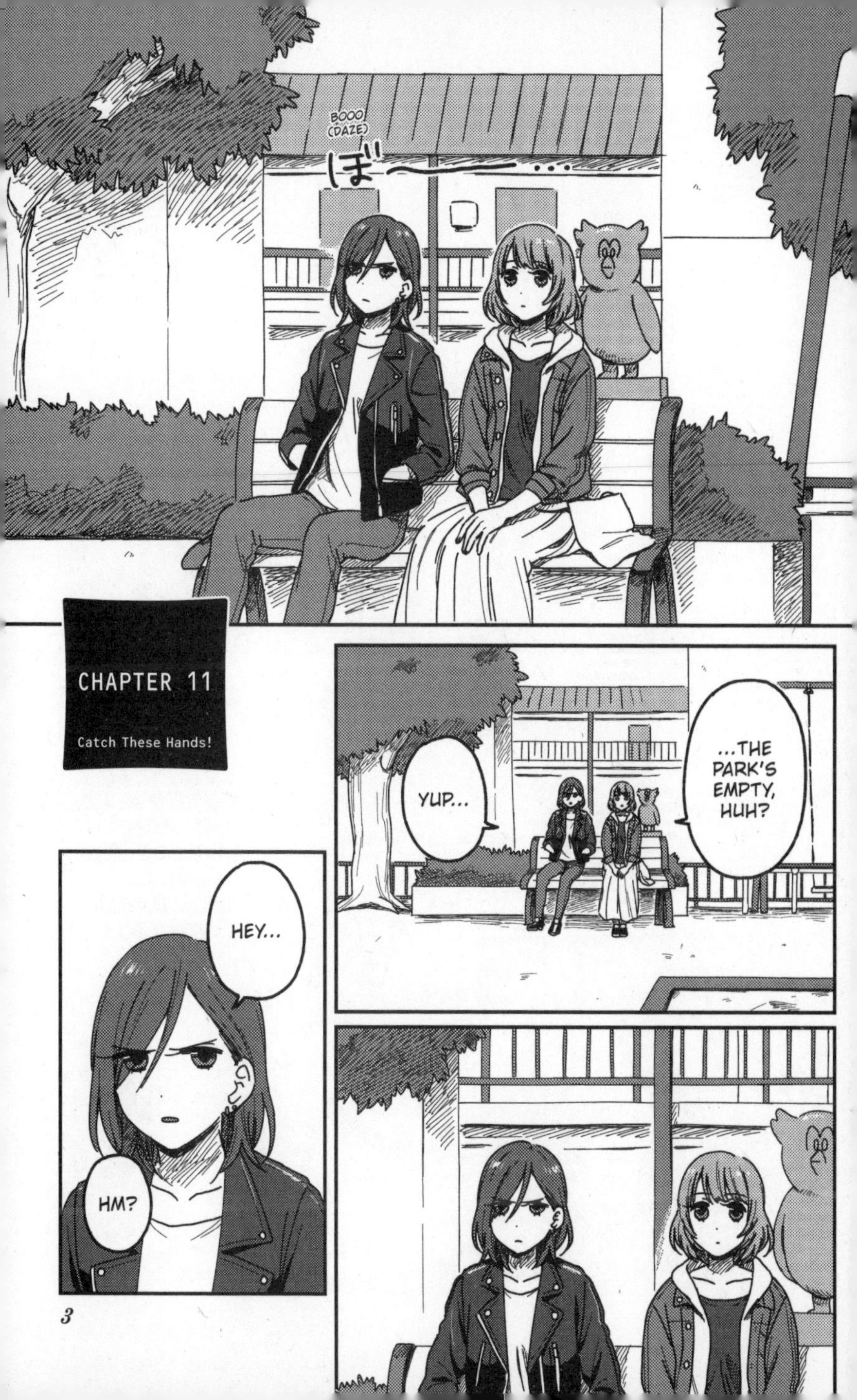
BOOO (DAZE)
ぼ～…
...THE PARK'S EMPTY, HUH?
YUP...
CHAPTER 11
Catch These Hands!
HEY...
HM?

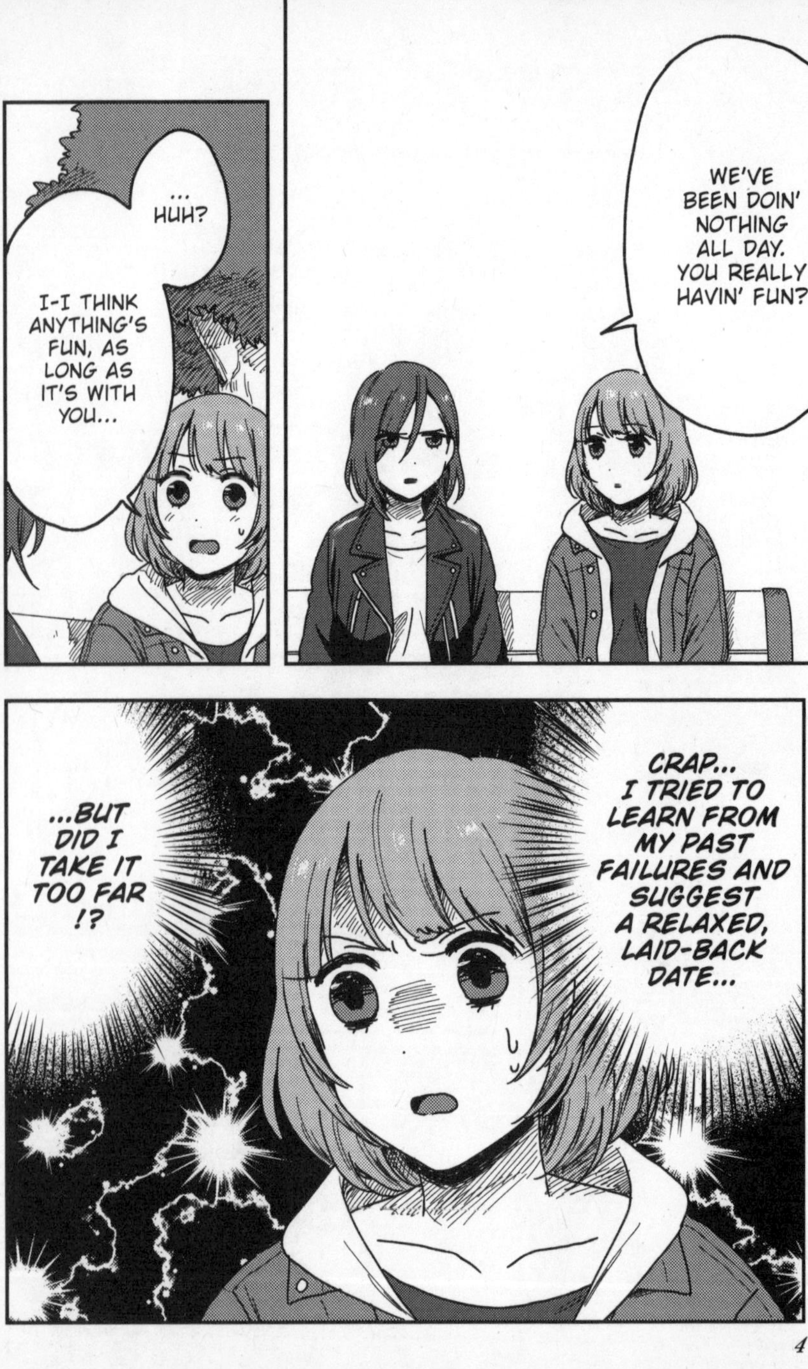
WE'VE BEEN DOIN' NOTHING ALL DAY. YOU REALLY HAVIN' FUN?
... HUH?
I-I THINK ANYTHING'S FUN, AS LONG AS IT'S WITH YOU...
CRAP... I TRIED TO LEARN FROM MY PAST FAILURES AND SUGGEST A RELAXED, LAID-BACK DATE...
...BUT DID I TAKE IT TOO FAR!?

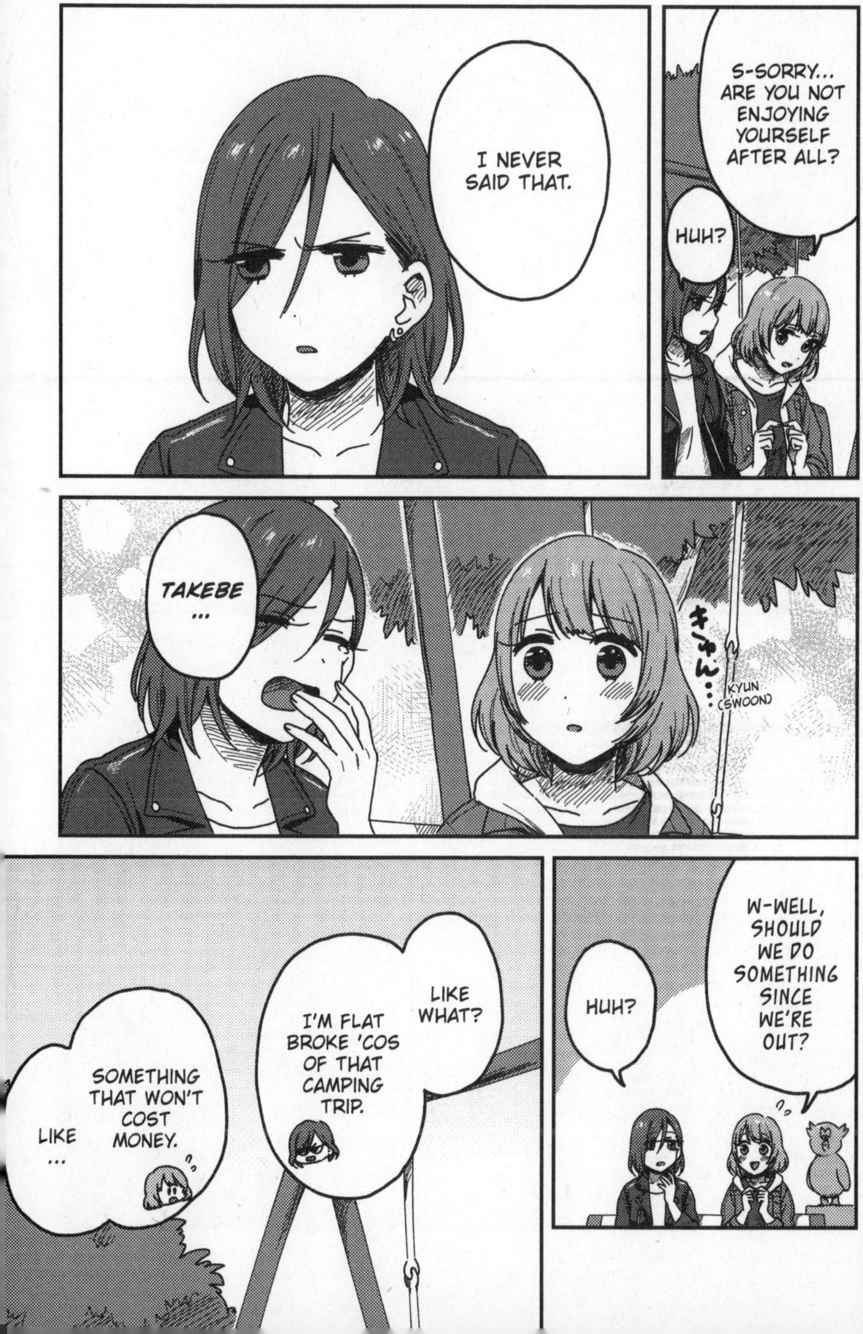
S-SORRY... ARE YOU NOT ENJOYING YOURSELF AFTER ALL?
HUH?
I NEVER SAID THAT.
きゅん…
KYUN (SWOON)
TAKEBE ...
W-WELL, SHOULD WE DO SOMETHING SINCE WE'RE OUT?
HUH?
LIKE WHAT?
I'M FLAT BROKE 'COS OF THAT CAMPING TRIP.
SOMETHING THAT WON'T COST MONEY.
LIKE ...

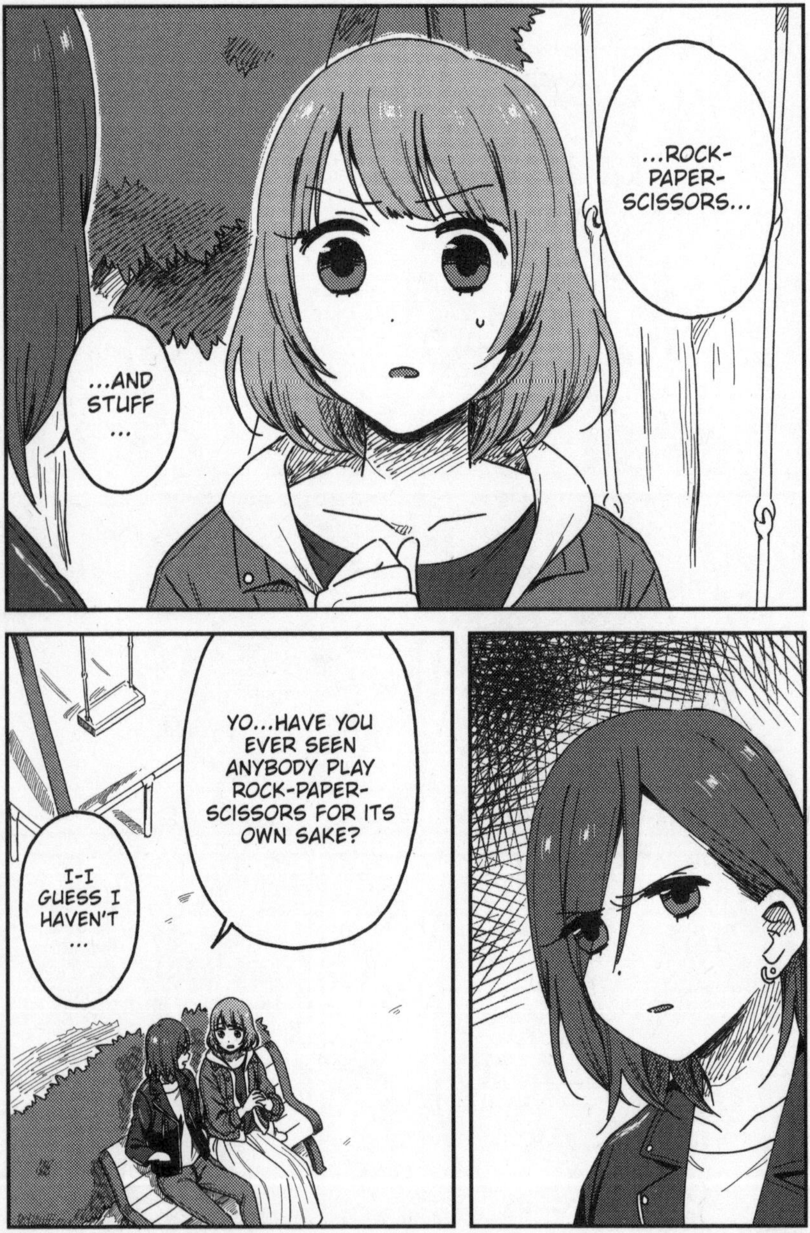
...ROCK-PAPER-SCISSORS...
...AND STUFF...
YO...HAVE YOU EVER SEEN ANYBODY PLAY ROCK-PAPER-SCISSORS FOR ITS OWN SAKE?
I-I GUESS I HAVEN'T...

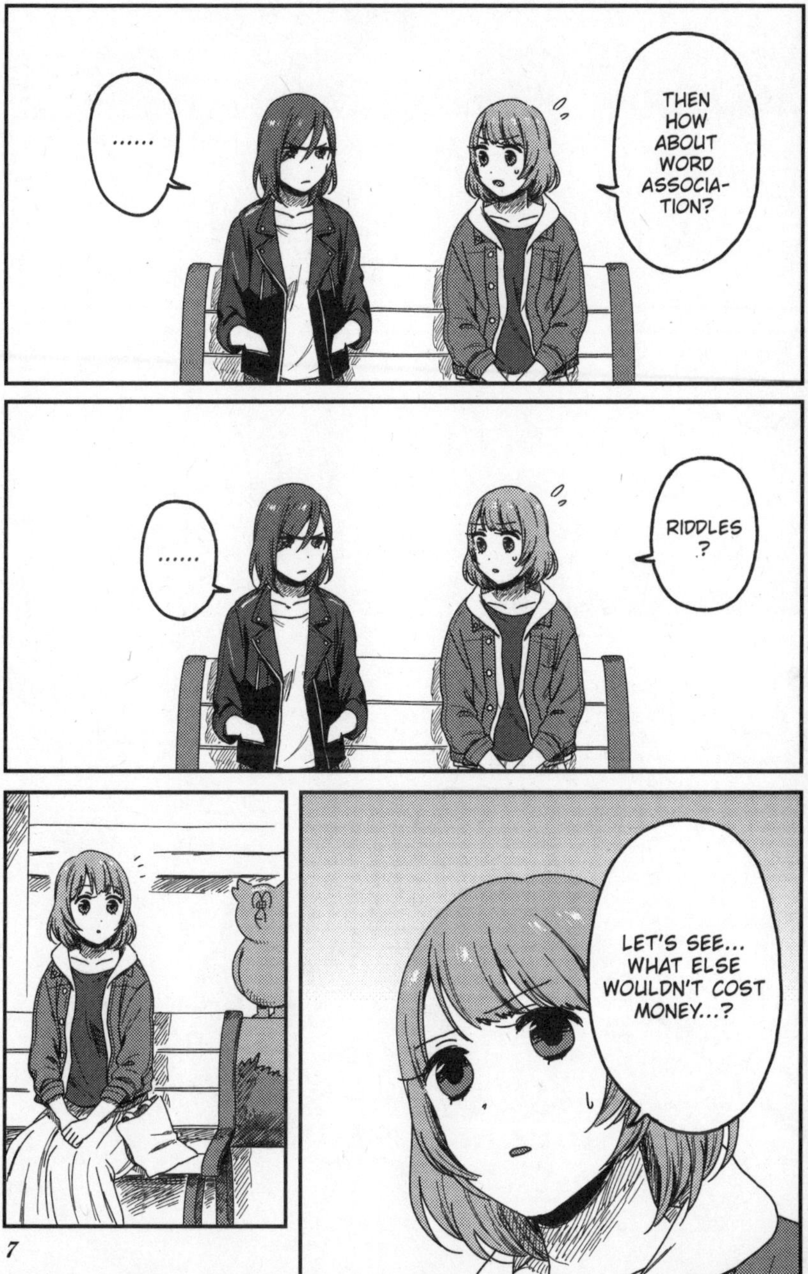
THEN HOW ABOUT WORD ASSOCIATION?
......
RIDDLES?
......
LET'S SEE... WHAT ELSE WOULDN'T COST MONEY...?

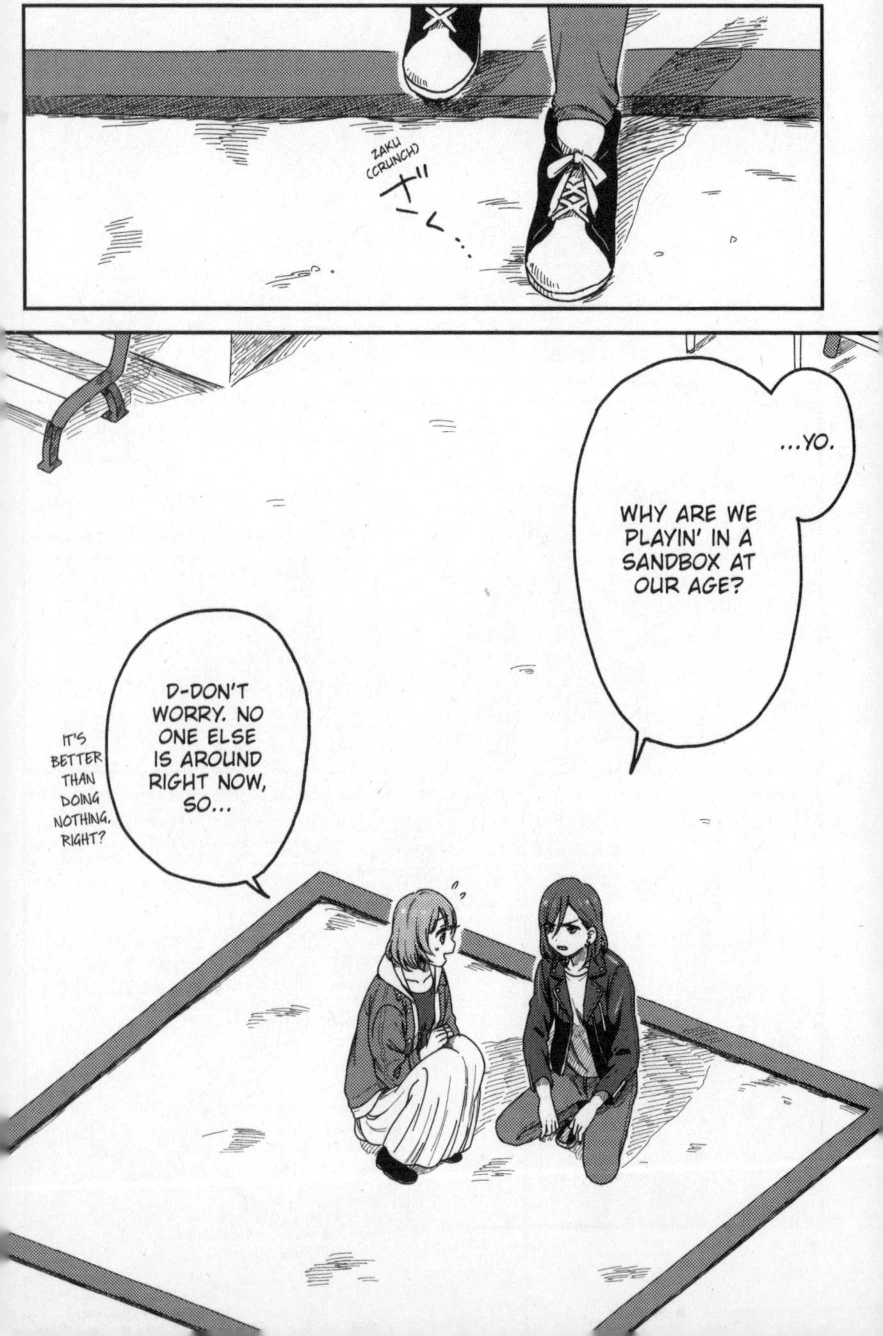
ZAKU (CRUNCH)
...YO.
WHY ARE WE PLAYIN' IN A SANDBOX AT OUR AGE?
D-DON'T WORRY. NO ONE ELSE IS AROUND RIGHT NOW, SO...
IT'S BETTER THAN DOING NOTHING, RIGHT?

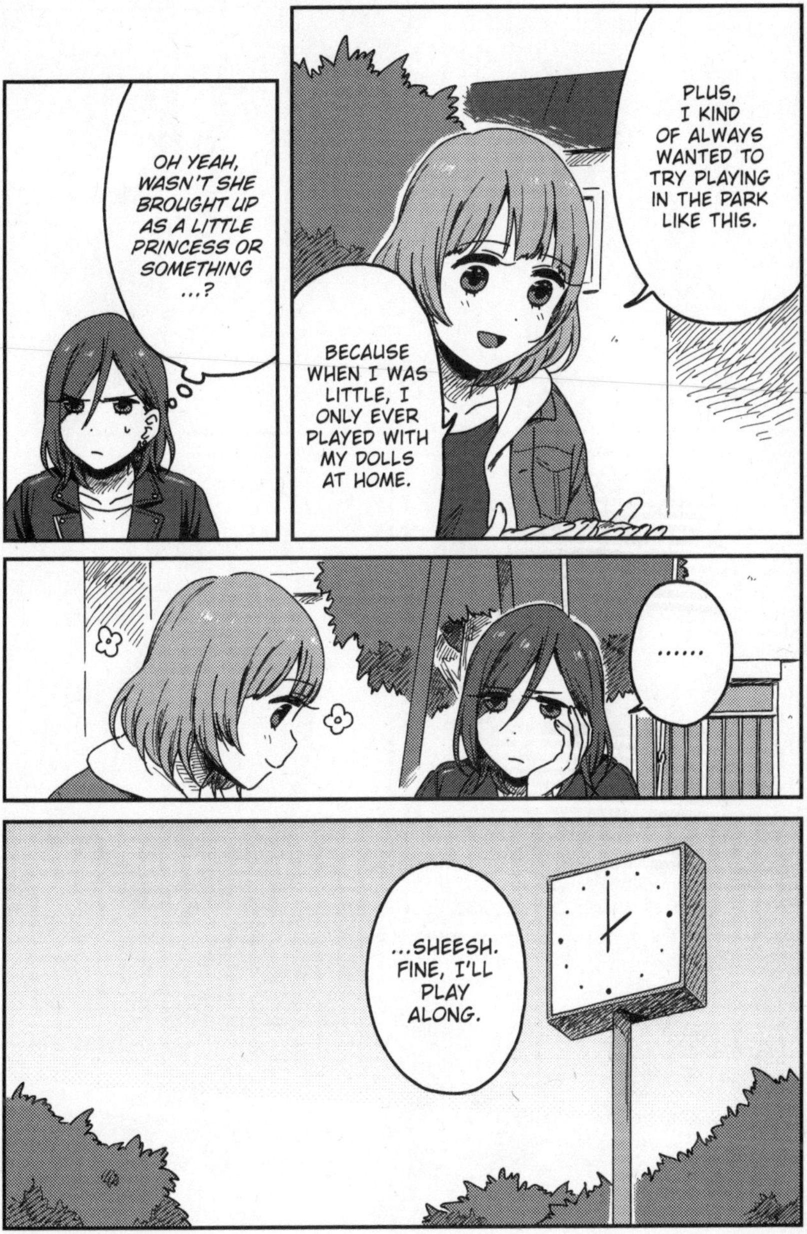
PLUS, I KIND OF ALWAYS WANTED TO TRY PLAYING IN THE PARK LIKE THIS.
BECAUSE WHEN I WAS LITTLE, I ONLY EVER PLAYED WITH MY DOLLS AT HOME.
OH YEAH, WASN'T SHE BROUGHT UP AS A LITTLE PRINCESS OR SOMETHING ...?
......
...SHEESH. FINE, I'LL PLAY ALONG.

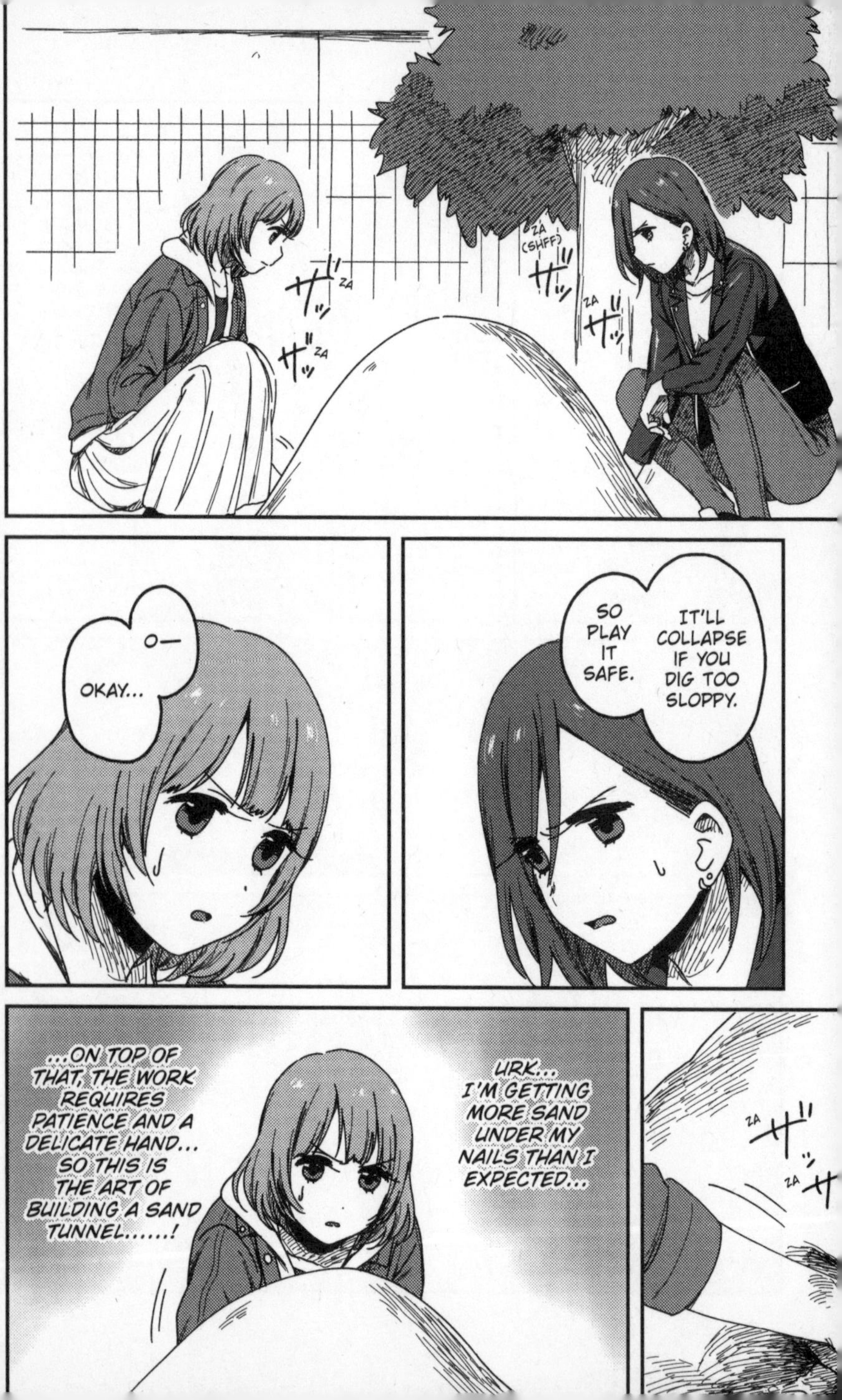

ZA (SHFF)
ZA
ZA
ZA
IT'LL COLLAPSE IF YOU DIG TOO SLOPPY.
SO PLAY IT SAFE.
O— OKAY...
ZA
ZA
URK... I'M GETTING MORE SAND UNDER MY NAILS THAN I EXPECTED...
...ON TOP OF THAT, THE WORK REQUIRES PATIENCE AND A DELICATE HAND... SO THIS IS THE ART OF BUILDING A SAND TUNNEL......!

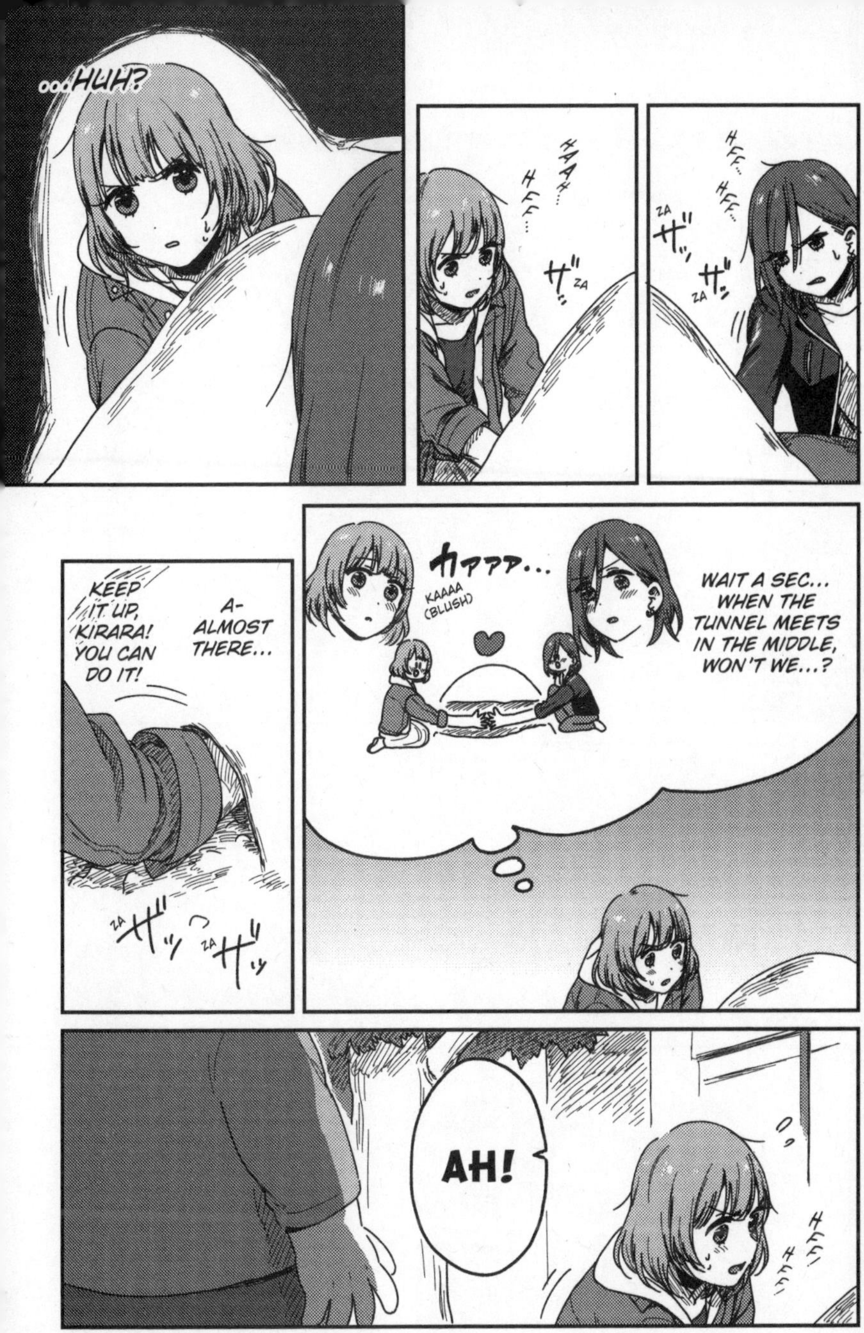
HFF... HFF...
ZA ザッ
ZA ザッ
HAAA... HFF...
ザッ ZA
...HUH?
WAIT A SEC... WHEN THE TUNNEL MEETS IN THE MIDDLE, WON'T WE...?
カァァァ...
KAAAA (BLUSH)
A-ALMOST THERE...
KEEP IT UP, KIRARA! YOU CAN DO IT!
ZA ザッ
ZA ザッ
HFF! HFF!
AH!

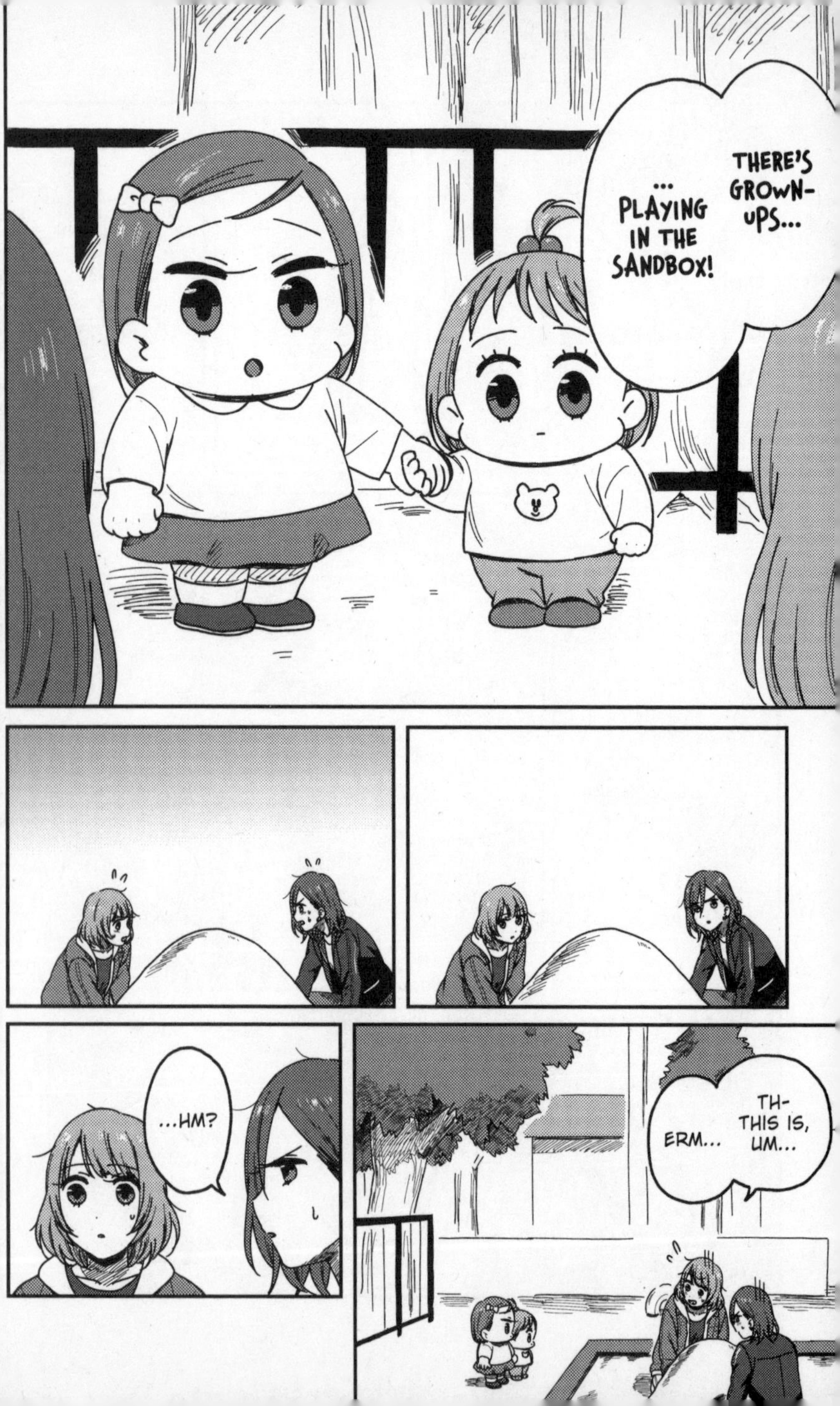
THERE'S GROWN-UPS...
...PLAYING IN THE SANDBOX!
TH-THIS IS, UM...
ERM...
...HM?

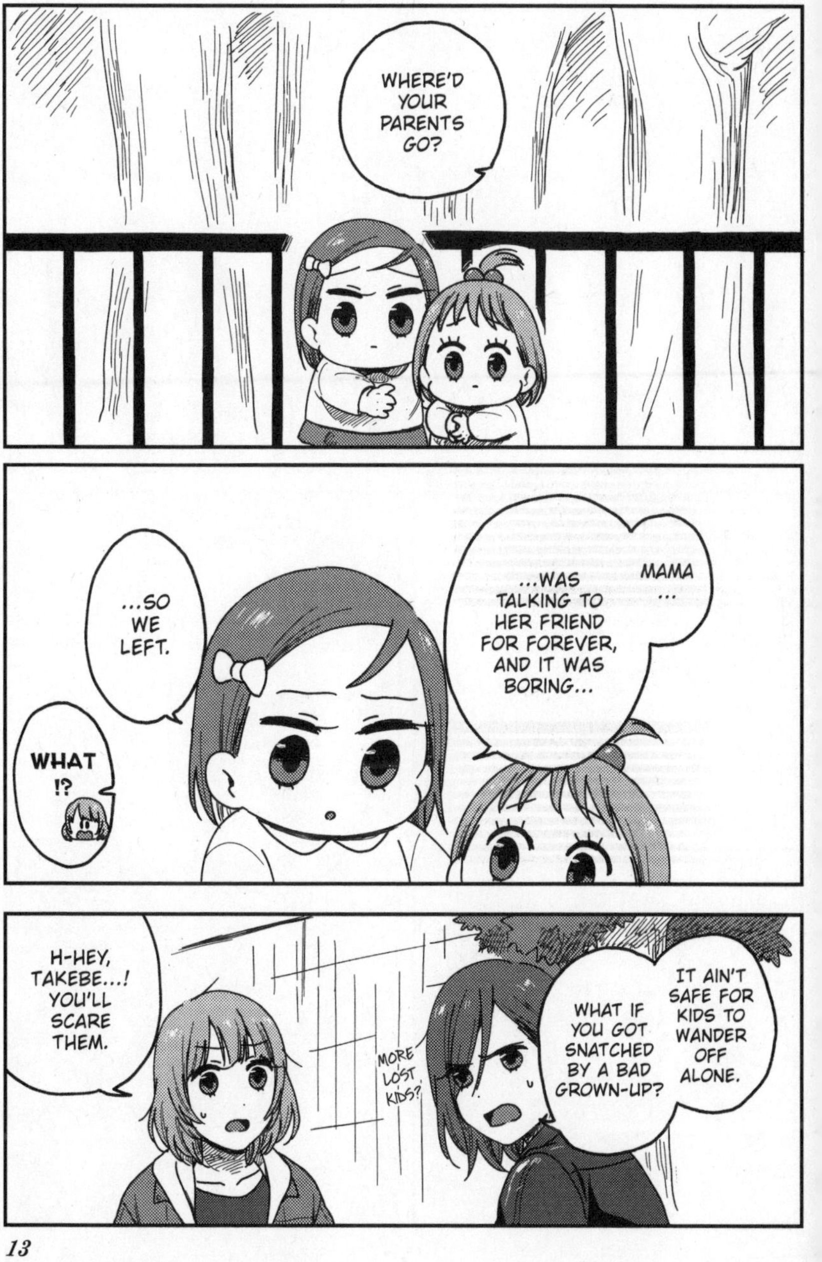
WHERE'D YOUR PARENTS GO?
MAMA...
...WAS TALKING TO HER FRIEND FOR FOREVER, AND IT WAS BORING...
...SO WE LEFT.
WHAT!?
IT AIN'T SAFE FOR KIDS TO WANDER OFF ALONE.
WHAT IF YOU GOT SNATCHED BY A BAD GROWN-UP?
MORE LOST KIDS?
H-HEY, TAKEBE...! YOU'LL SCARE THEM.

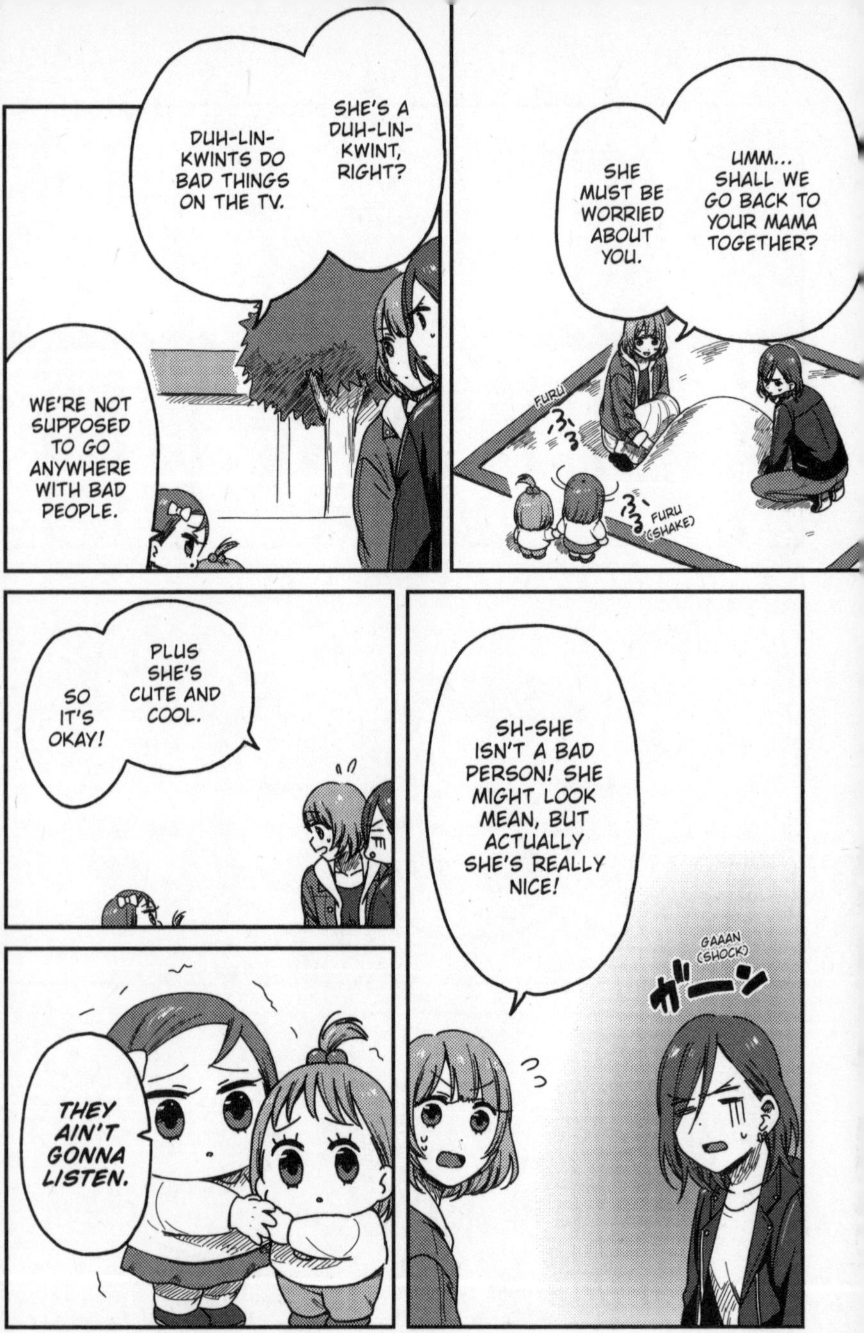
UMM... SHALL WE GO BACK TO YOUR MAMA TOGETHER?
SHE MUST BE WORRIED ABOUT YOU.
ふる FURU
ふる FURU (SHAKE)
SHE'S A DUH-LIN-KWINT, RIGHT?
DUH-LIN-KWINTS DO BAD THINGS ON THE TV.
WE'RE NOT SUPPOSED TO GO ANYWHERE WITH BAD PEOPLE.
SH-SHE ISN'T A BAD PERSON! SHE MIGHT LOOK MEAN, BUT ACTUALLY SHE'S REALLY NICE!
ガーン GAAAN (SHOCK)
PLUS SHE'S CUTE AND COOL.
SO IT'S OKAY!
THEY AIN'T GONNA LISTEN.

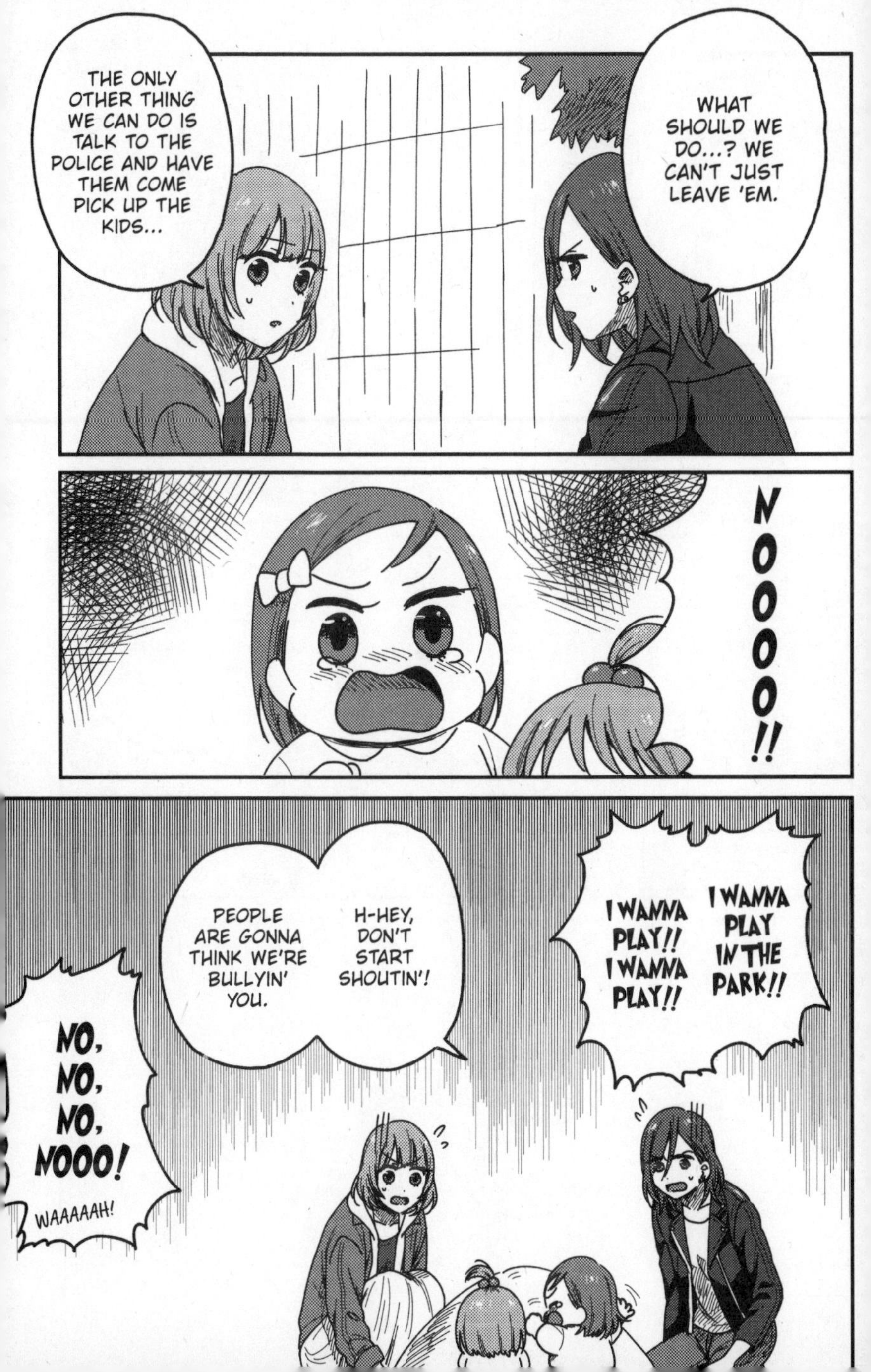
WHAT SHOULD WE DO...? WE CAN'T JUST LEAVE 'EM.
THE ONLY OTHER THING WE CAN DO IS TALK TO THE POLICE AND HAVE THEM COME PICK UP THE KIDS...
NOOOOO!!
I WANNA PLAY IN THE PARK!!
I WANNA PLAY!! I WANNA PLAY!!
H-HEY, DON'T START SHOUTIN'!
PEOPLE ARE GONNA THINK WE'RE BULLYIN' YOU.
NO, NO, NO, NOOO!
WAAAAAH!

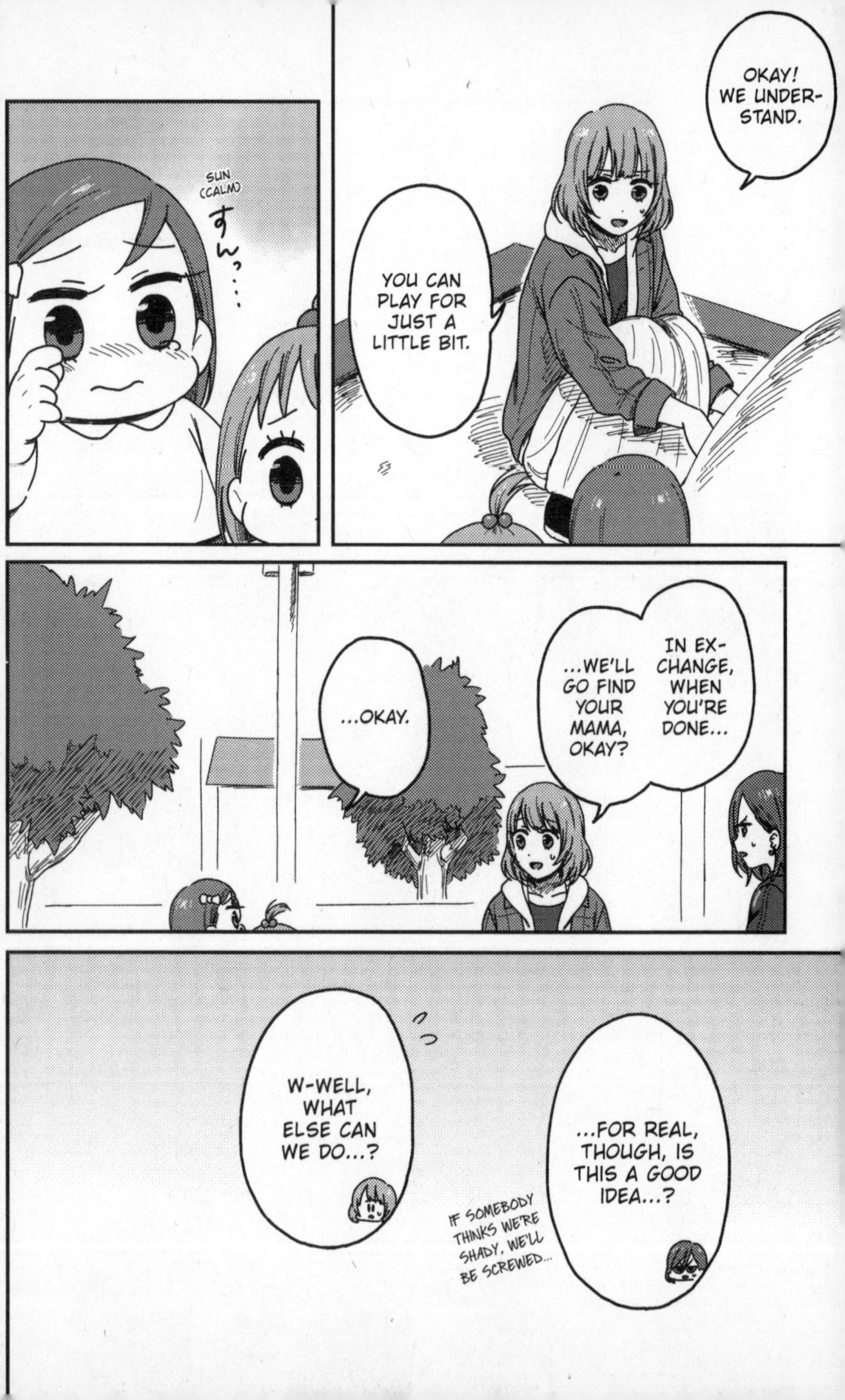
OKAY! WE UNDERSTAND.
YOU CAN PLAY FOR JUST A LITTLE BIT.
SUN (CALM)
すんっ…
IN EXCHANGE, WHEN YOU'RE DONE...
...WE'LL GO FIND YOUR MAMA, OKAY?
...OKAY.
...FOR REAL, THOUGH, IS THIS A GOOD IDEA...?
IF SOMEBODY THINKS WE'RE SHADY, WE'LL BE SCREWED...
W-WELL, WHAT ELSE CAN WE DO...?

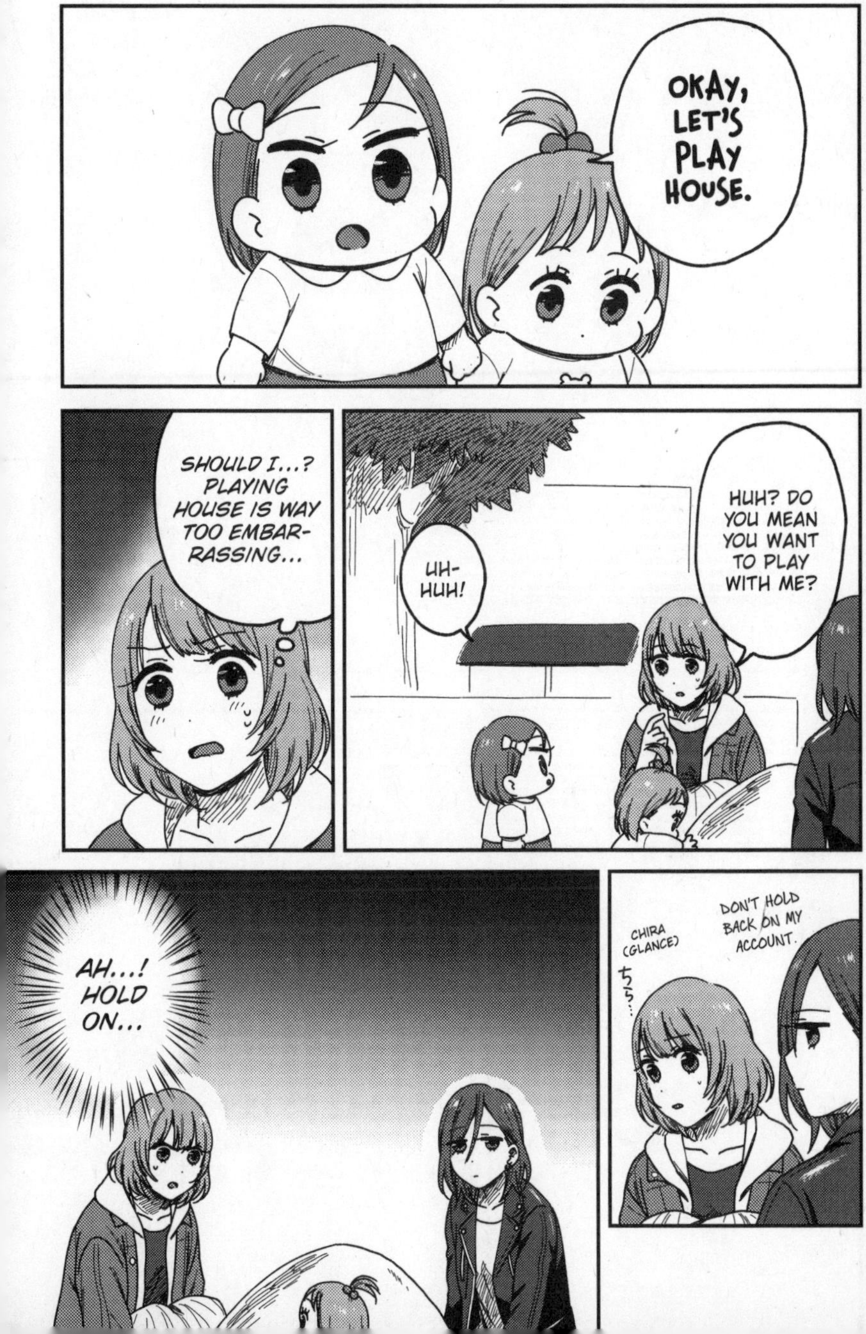
OKAY, LET'S PLAY HOUSE.
HUH? DO YOU MEAN YOU WANT TO PLAY WITH ME?
UH-HUH!
SHOULD I...? PLAYING HOUSE IS WAY TOO EMBARRASSING...
DON'T HOLD BACK ON MY ACCOUNT.
CHIRA (GLANCE)
ちら…
AH...! HOLD ON...

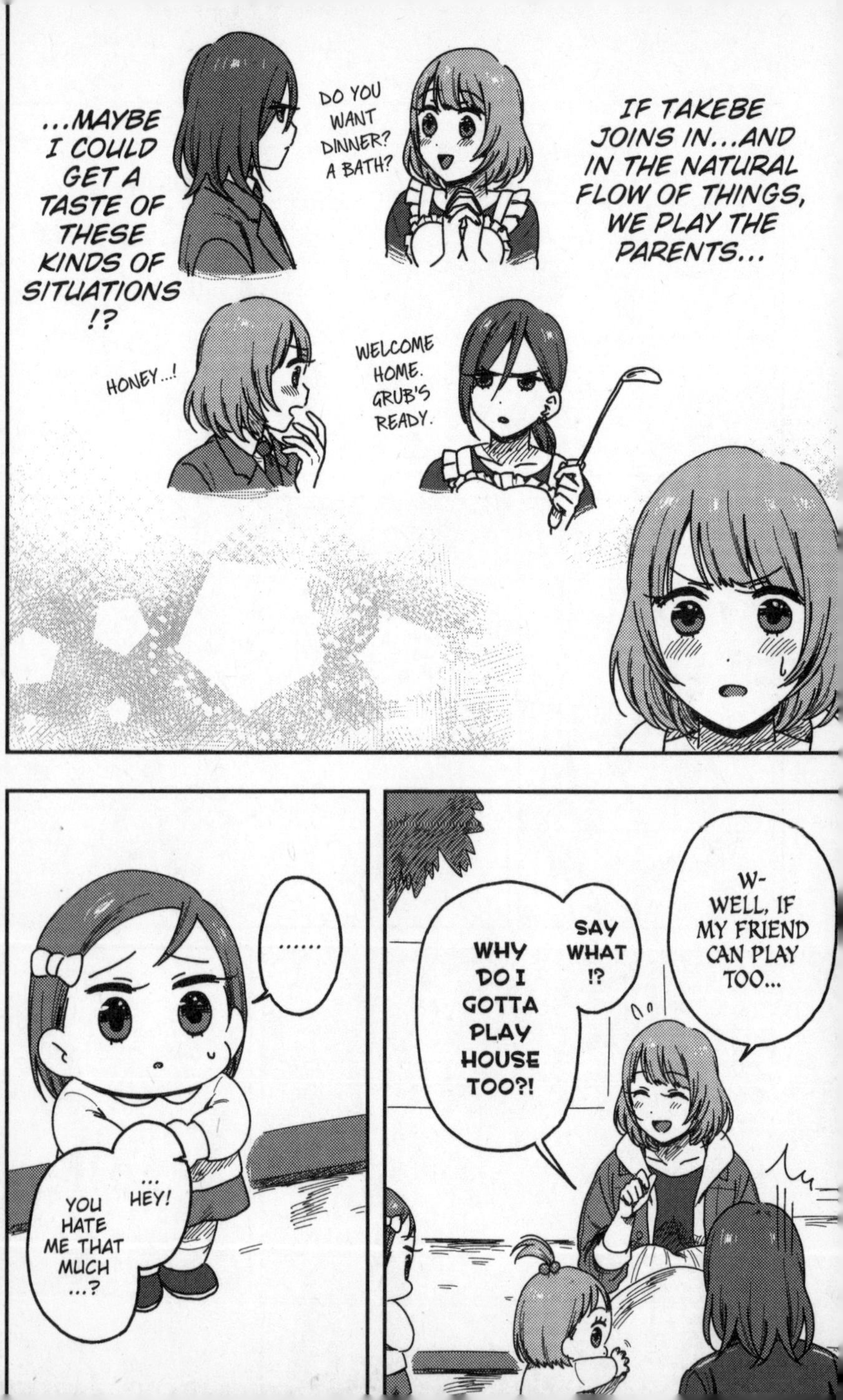
IF TAKEBE JOINS IN...AND IN THE NATURAL FLOW OF THINGS, WE PLAY THE PARENTS...
DO YOU WANT DINNER? A BATH?
...MAYBE I COULD GET A TASTE OF THESE KINDS OF SITUATIONS!?
WELCOME HOME. GRUB'S READY.
HONEY...!
W-WELL, IF MY FRIEND CAN PLAY TOO...
SAY WHAT!?
WHY DO I GOTTA PLAY HOUSE TOO?!
......
...HEY!
YOU HATE ME THAT MUCH...?

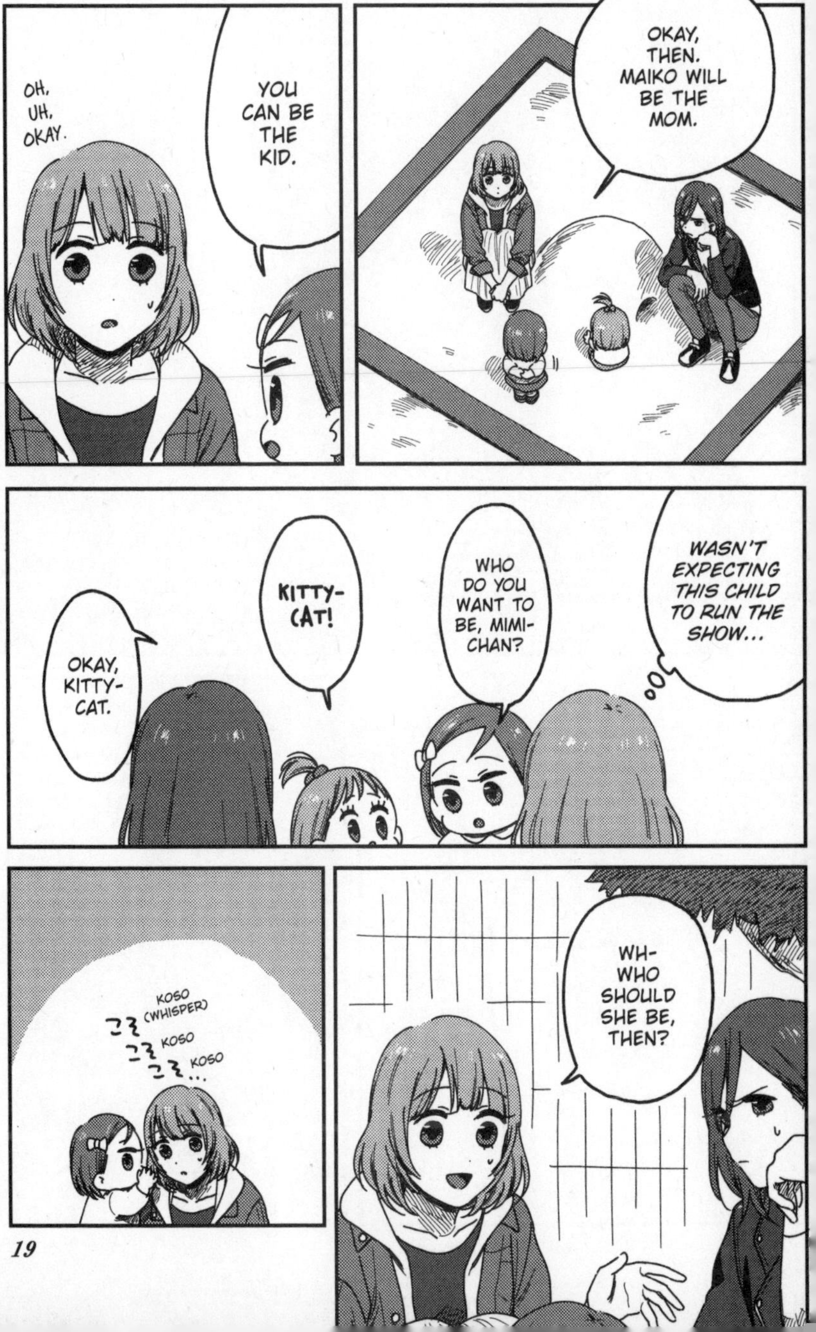
OKAY, THEN. MAIKO WILL BE THE MOM.
YOU CAN BE THE KID.
OH, UH, OKAY.
WASN'T EXPECTING THIS CHILD TO RUN THE SHOW...
WHO DO YOU WANT TO BE, MIMI-CHAN?
KITTY-CAT!
OKAY, KITTY-CAT.
WH-WHO SHOULD SHE BE, THEN?
KOSO (WHISPER)
KOSO
KOSO...

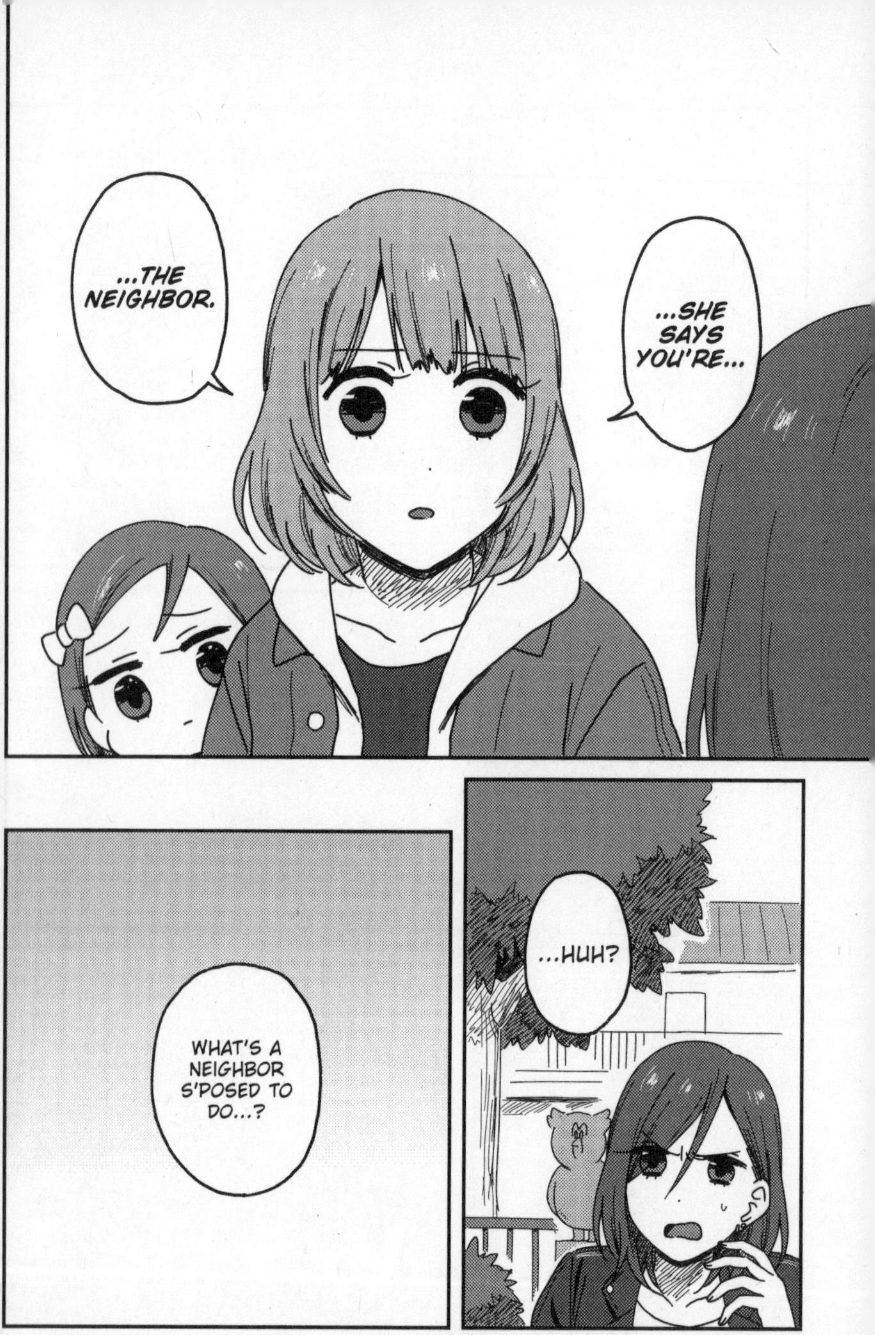
...SHE SAYS YOU'RE...
...THE NEIGHBOR.
...HUH?
WHAT'S A NEIGHBOR S'POSED TO DO...?

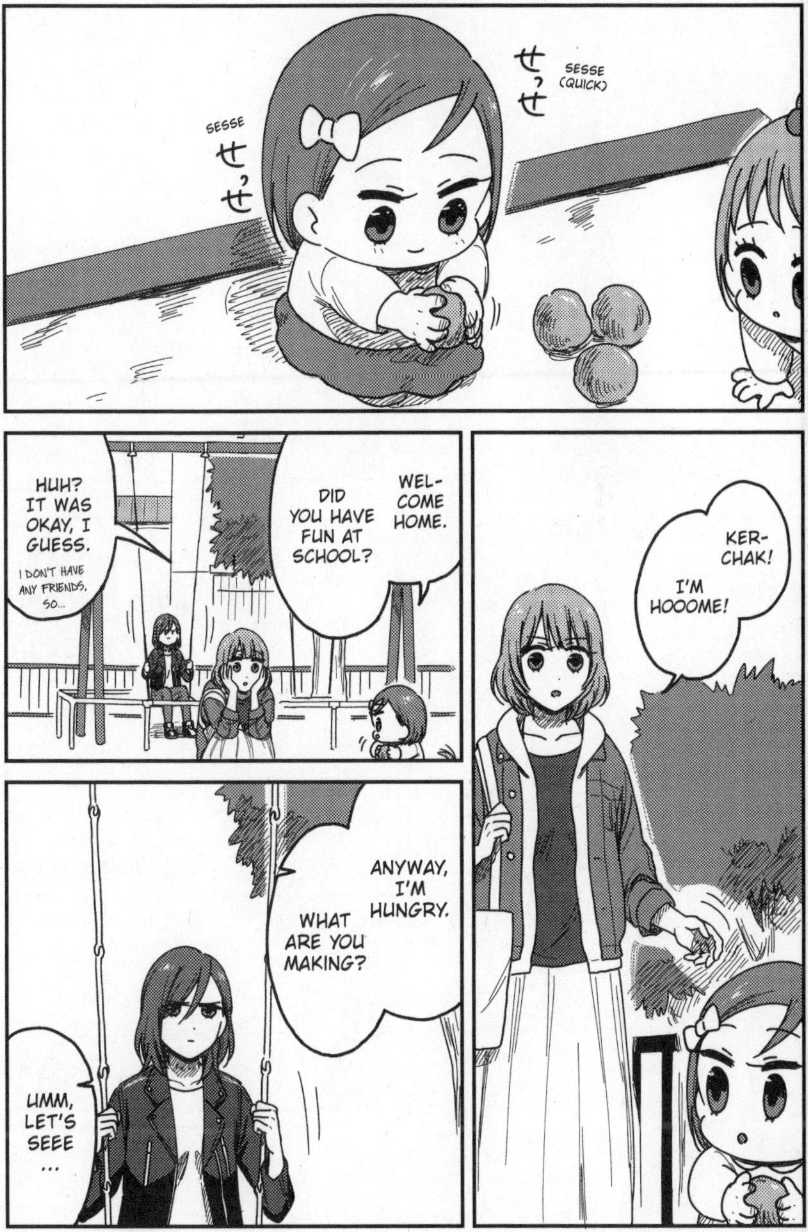

せっせ
SESSE (QUICK)
せっせ
SESSE
KER-CHAK!
I'M HOOOME!
WEL-COME HOME.
DID YOU HAVE FUN AT SCHOOL?
HUH? IT WAS OKAY, I GUESS.
I DON'T HAVE ANY FRIENDS, SO...
ANYWAY, I'M HUNGRY.
WHAT ARE YOU MAKING?
UMM, LET'S SEEE...

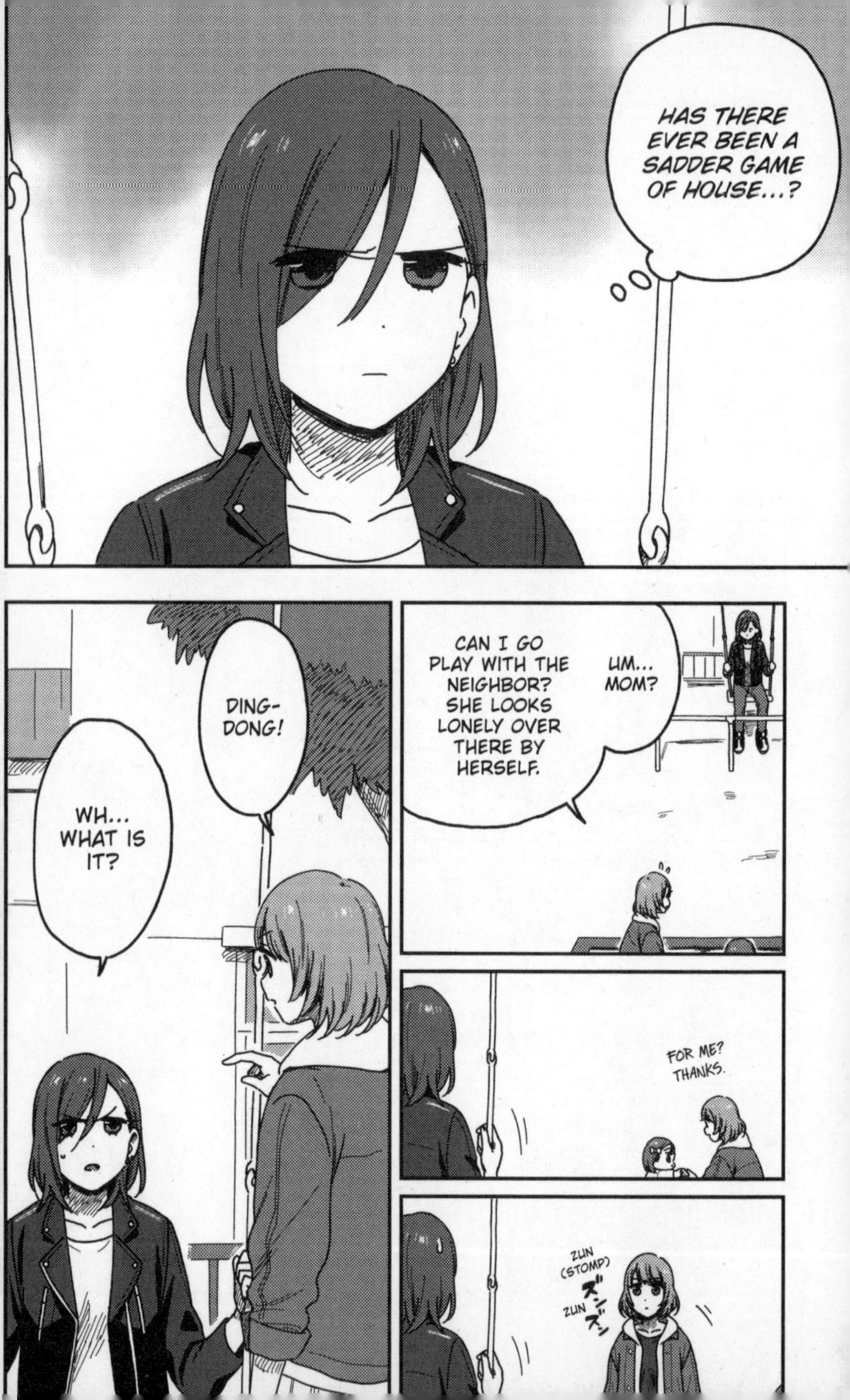
HAS THERE EVER BEEN A SADDER GAME OF HOUSE...?
UM... MOM?
CAN I GO PLAY WITH THE NEIGHBOR? SHE LOOKS LONELY OVER THERE BY HERSELF.
FOR ME? THANKS.
ZUN (STOMP)
ZUN
DING-DONG!
WH... WHAT IS IT?

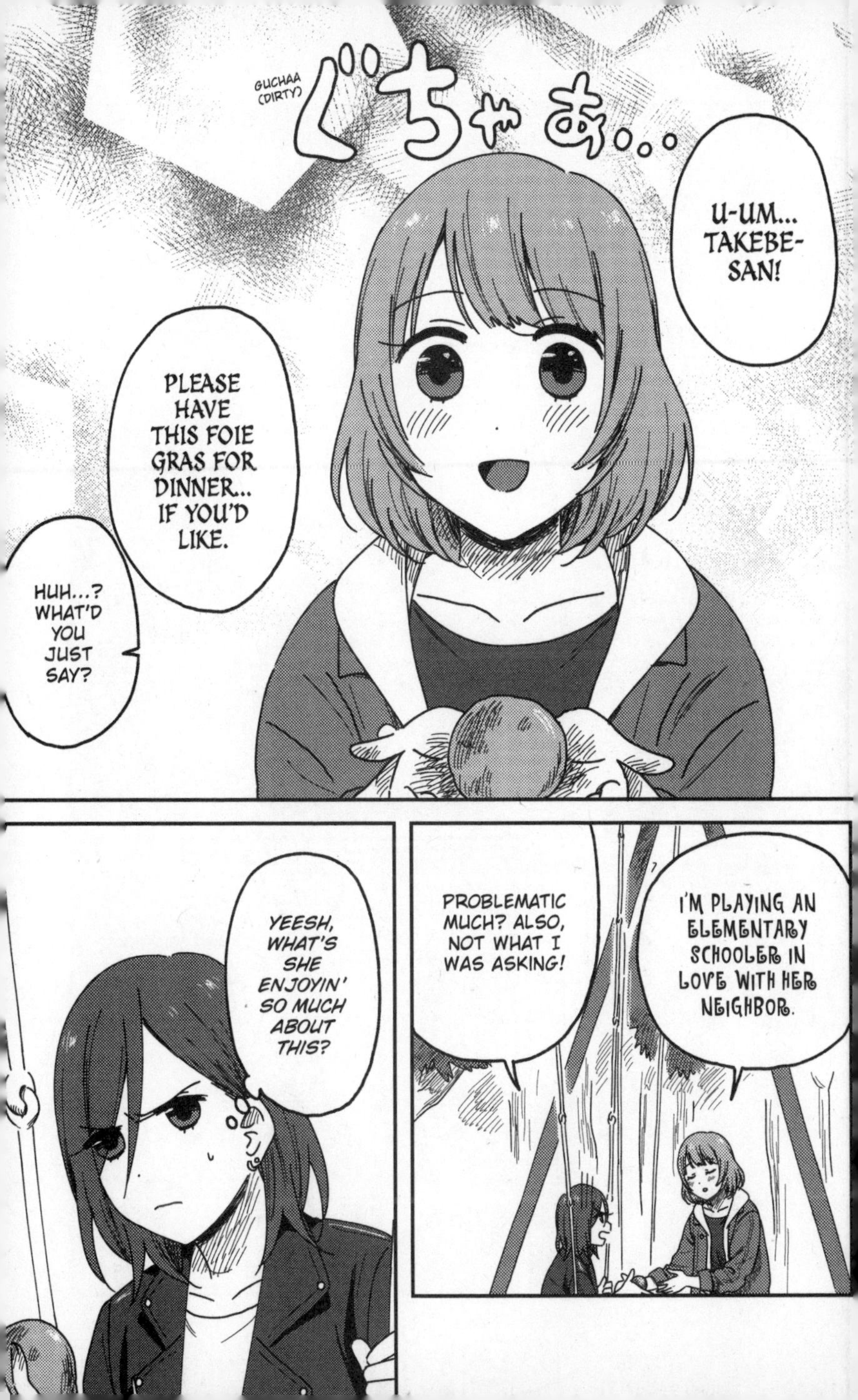
GUCHAA (DIRTY)
ぐちゃあ。。。
U-UM... TAKEBE-SAN!
PLEASE HAVE THIS FOIE GRAS FOR DINNER... IF YOU'D LIKE.
HUH...? WHAT'D YOU JUST SAY?
I'M PLAYING AN ELEMENTARY SCHOOLER IN LOVE WITH HER NEIGHBOR.
PROBLEMATIC MUCH? ALSO, NOT WHAT I WAS ASKING!
YEESH, WHAT'S SHE ENJOYIN' SO MUCH ABOUT THIS?

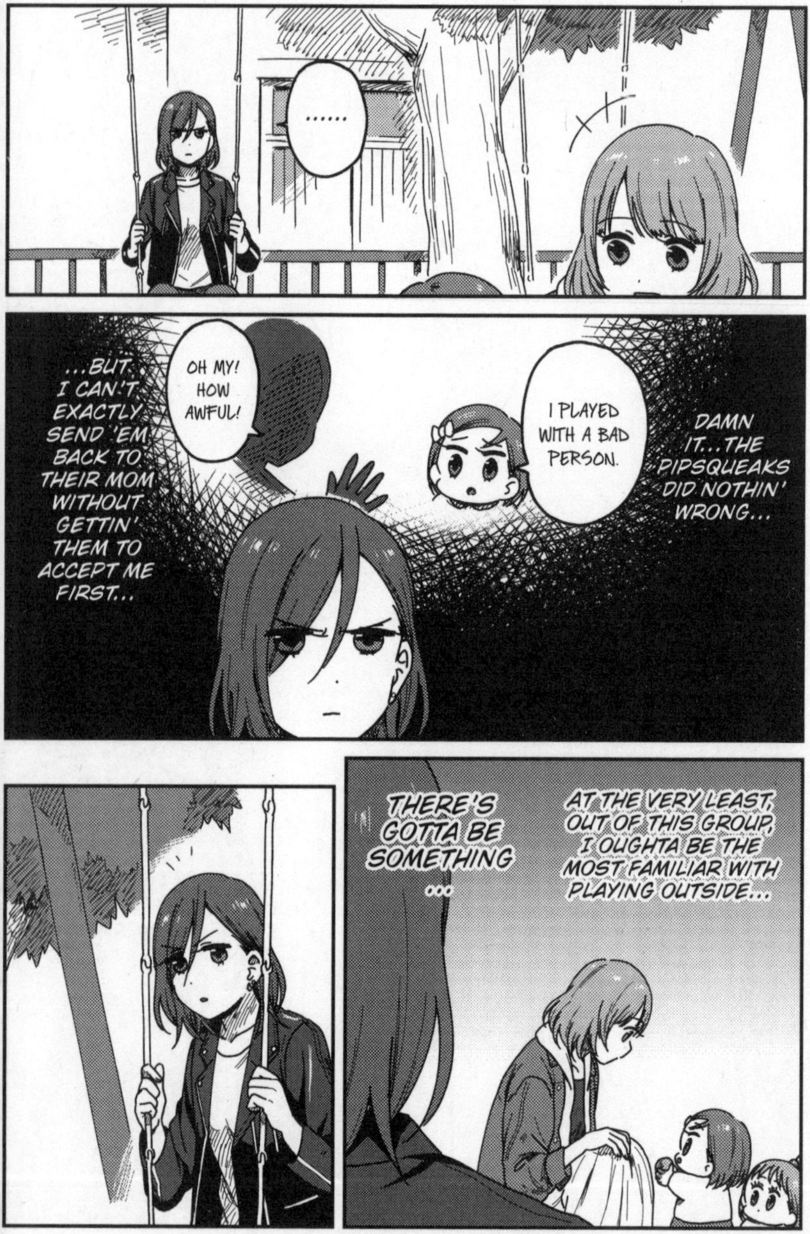
......
DAMN IT...THE PIPSQUEAKS DID NOTHIN' WRONG...
I PLAYED WITH A BAD PERSON.
OH MY! HOW AWFUL!
...BUT I CAN'T EXACTLY SEND 'EM BACK TO THEIR MOM WITHOUT GETTIN' THEM TO ACCEPT ME FIRST...
AT THE VERY LEAST, OUT OF THIS GROUP, I OUGHTA BE THE MOST FAMILIAR WITH PLAYING OUTSIDE...
THERE'S GOTTA BE SOMETHING ...

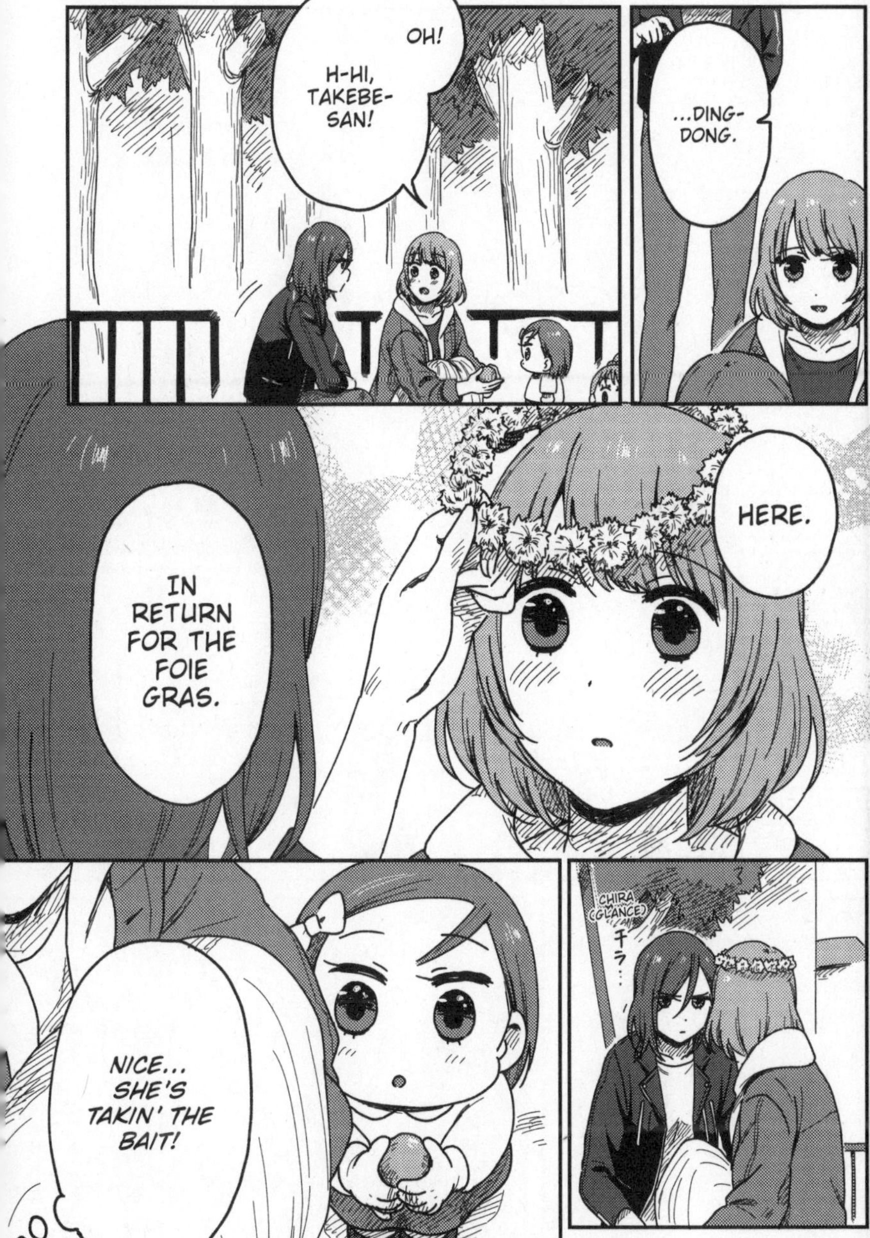
...DING-DONG.
OH!
H-HI, TAKEBE-SAN!
HERE.
IN RETURN FOR THE FOIE GRAS.
CHIRA (GLANCE)
チラ…
NICE... SHE'S TAKIN' THE BAIT!

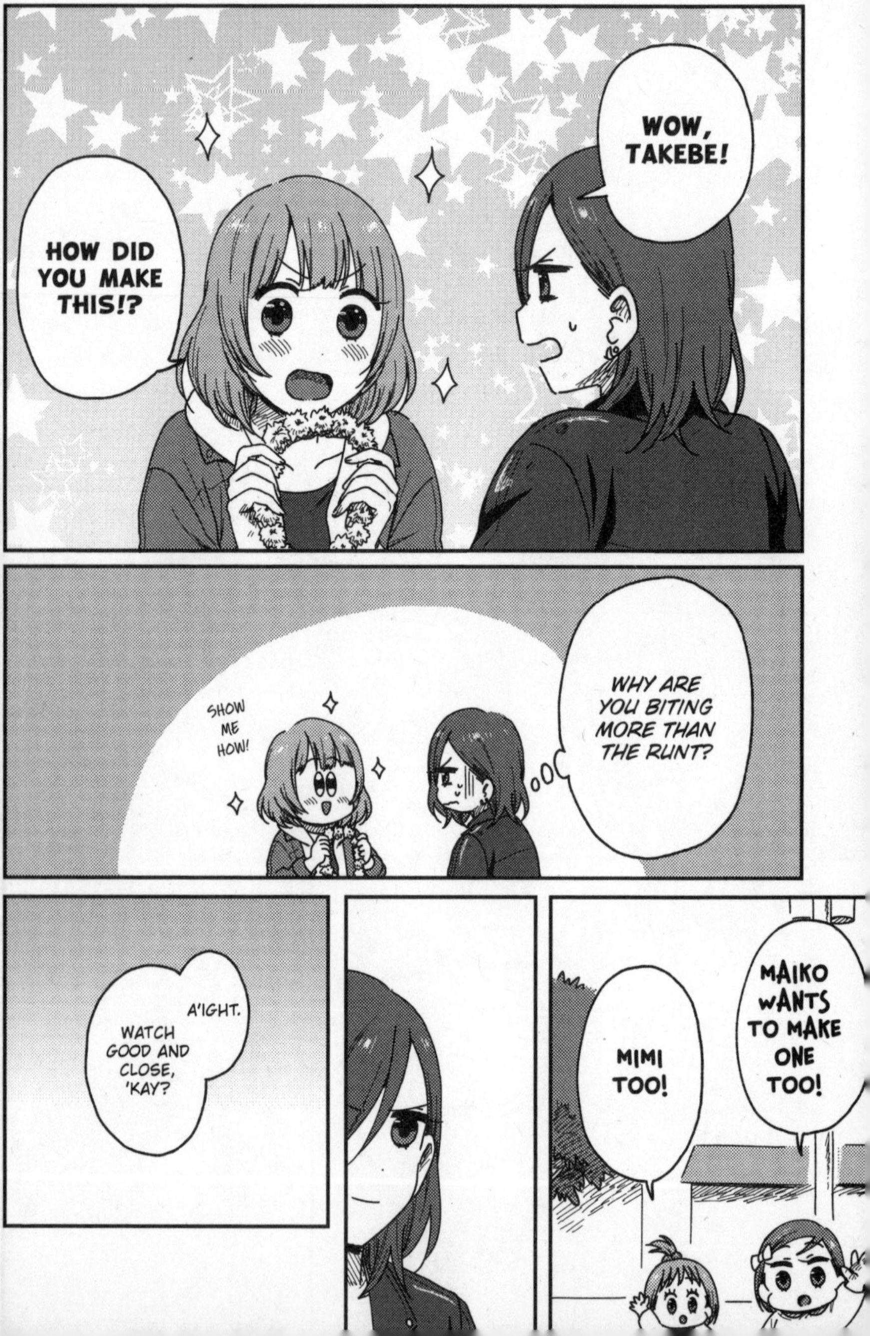
WOW, TAKEBE!
HOW DID YOU MAKE THIS!?
WHY ARE YOU BITING MORE THAN THE RUNT?
SHOW ME HOW!
MAIKO WANTS TO MAKE ONE TOO!
MIMI TOO!
A'IGHT. WATCH GOOD AND CLOSE, 'KAY?

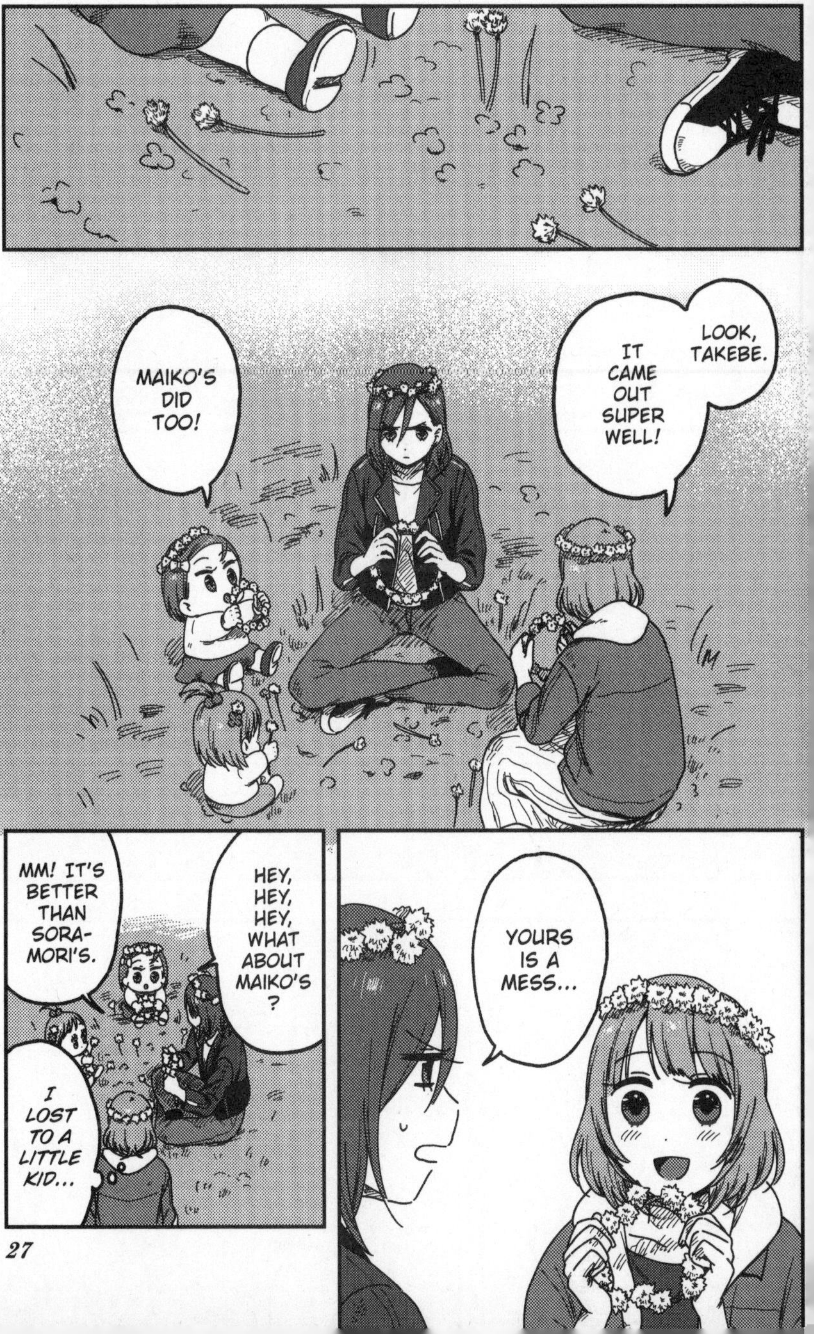
LOOK, TAKEBE.
IT CAME OUT SUPER WELL!
MAIKO'S DID TOO!
YOURS IS A MESS...
HEY, HEY, HEY, WHAT ABOUT MAIKO'S?
MM! IT'S BETTER THAN SORA-MORI'S.
I LOST TO A LITTLE KID...

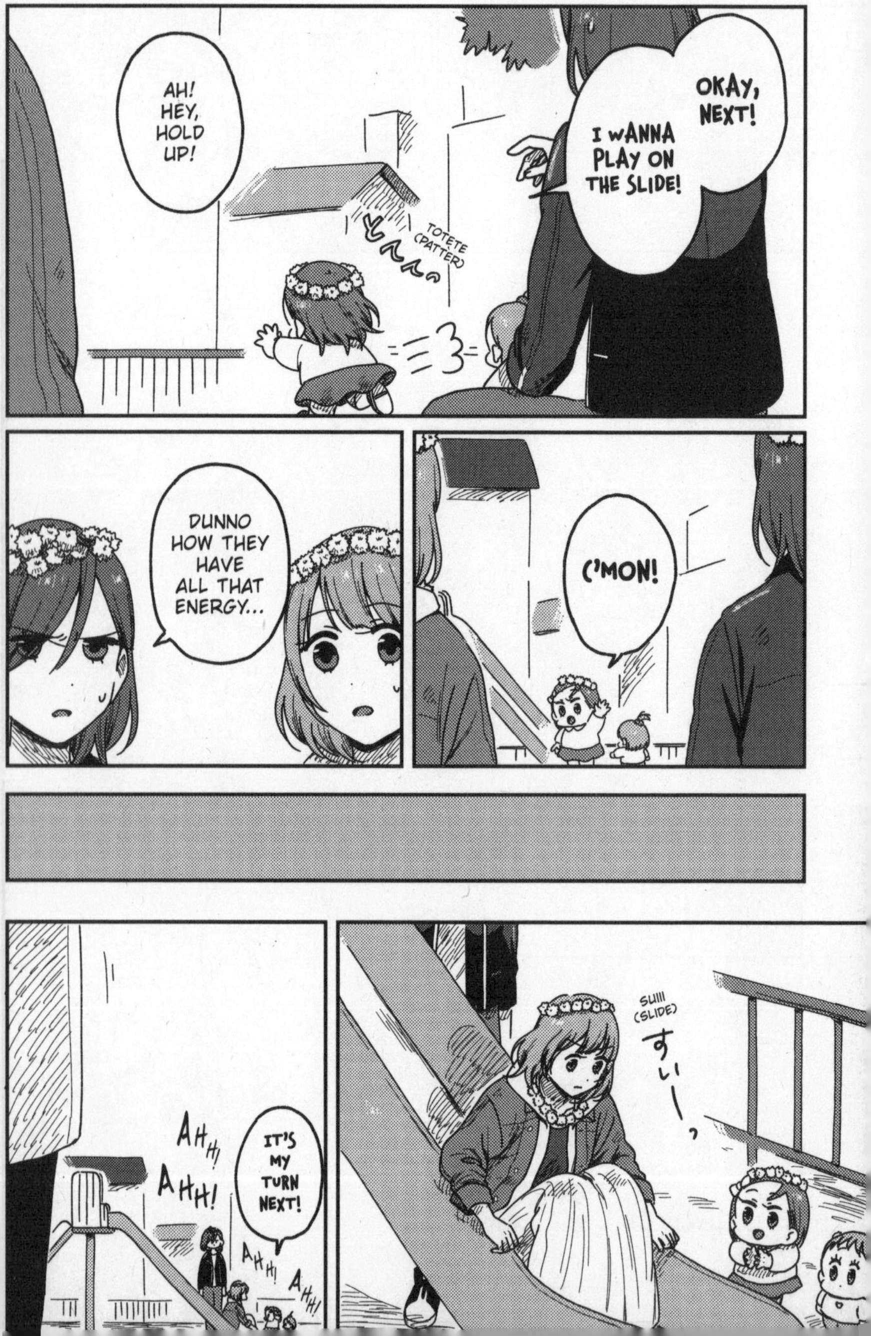
OKAY, NEXT! I wANNA PLAY ON THE SLIDE!
TOTETE (PATTER)
AH! HEY, HOLD UP!
C'MON!
DUNNO HOW THEY HAVE ALL THAT ENERGY...
SUIII (SLIDE)
すいーっ
IT'S MY TURN NEXT!
AHH! AHH!
AHH! AHH!

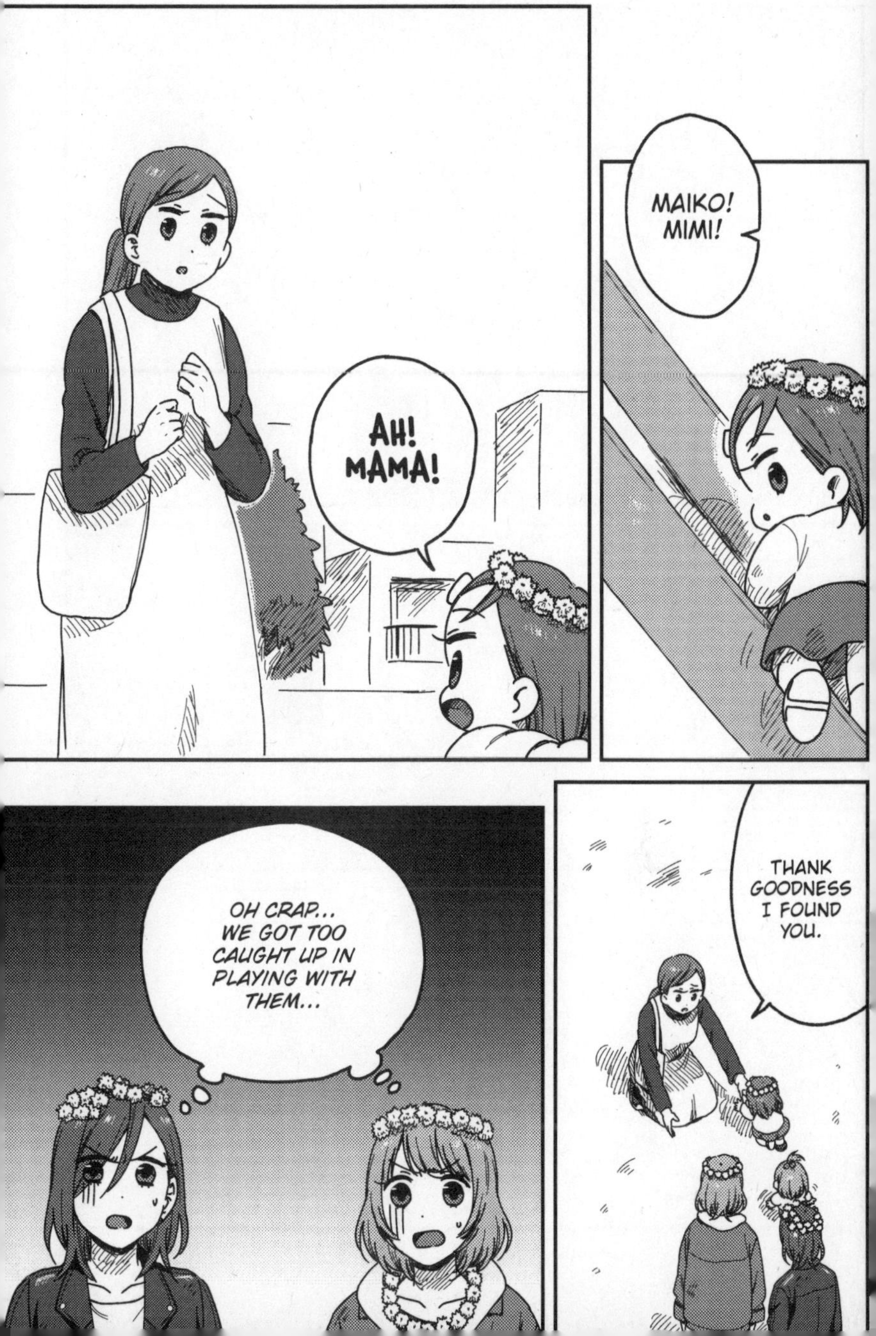
MAIKO! MIMI!
AH! MAMA!
THANK GOODNESS I FOUND YOU.
OH CRAP... WE GOT TOO CAUGHT UP IN PLAYING WITH THEM...

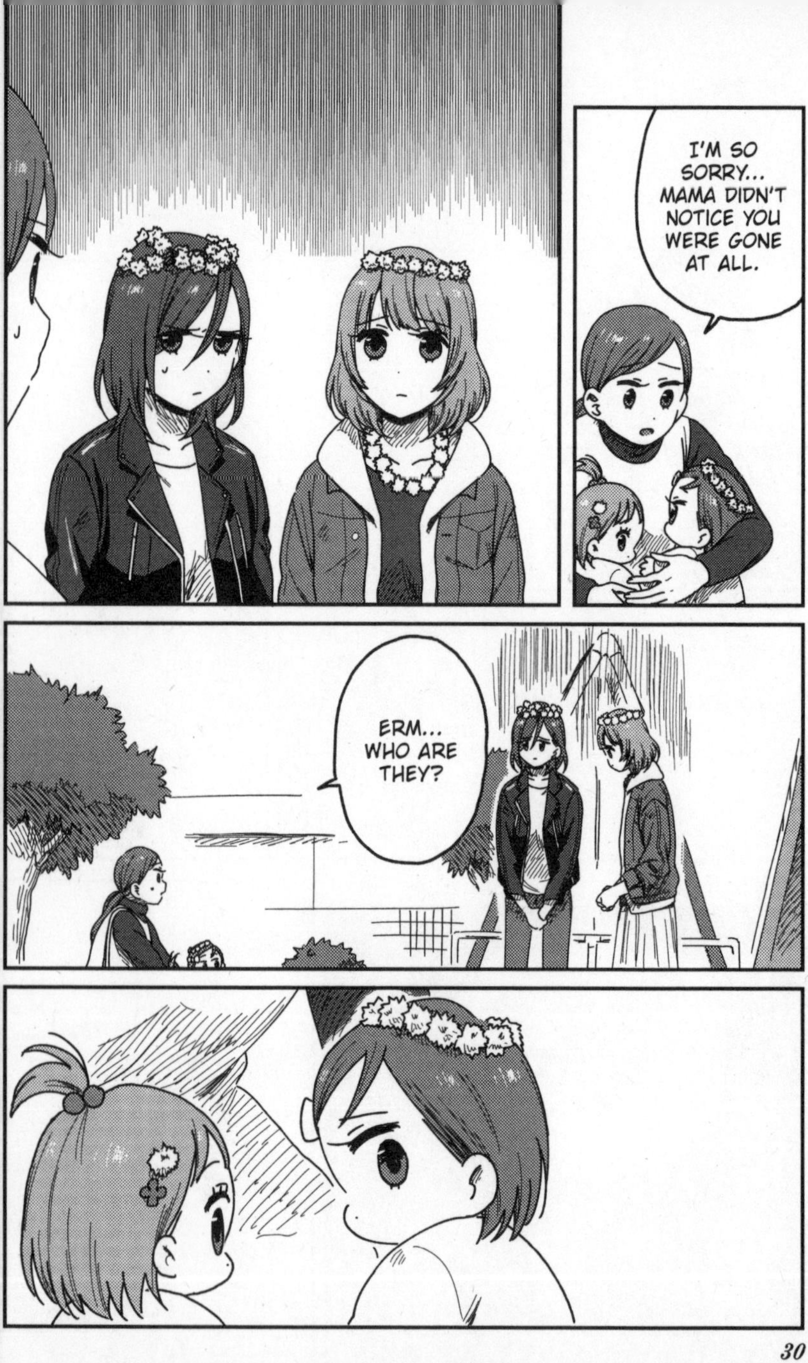
I'M SO SORRY... MAMA DIDN'T NOTICE YOU WERE GONE AT ALL.
ERM... WHO ARE THEY?

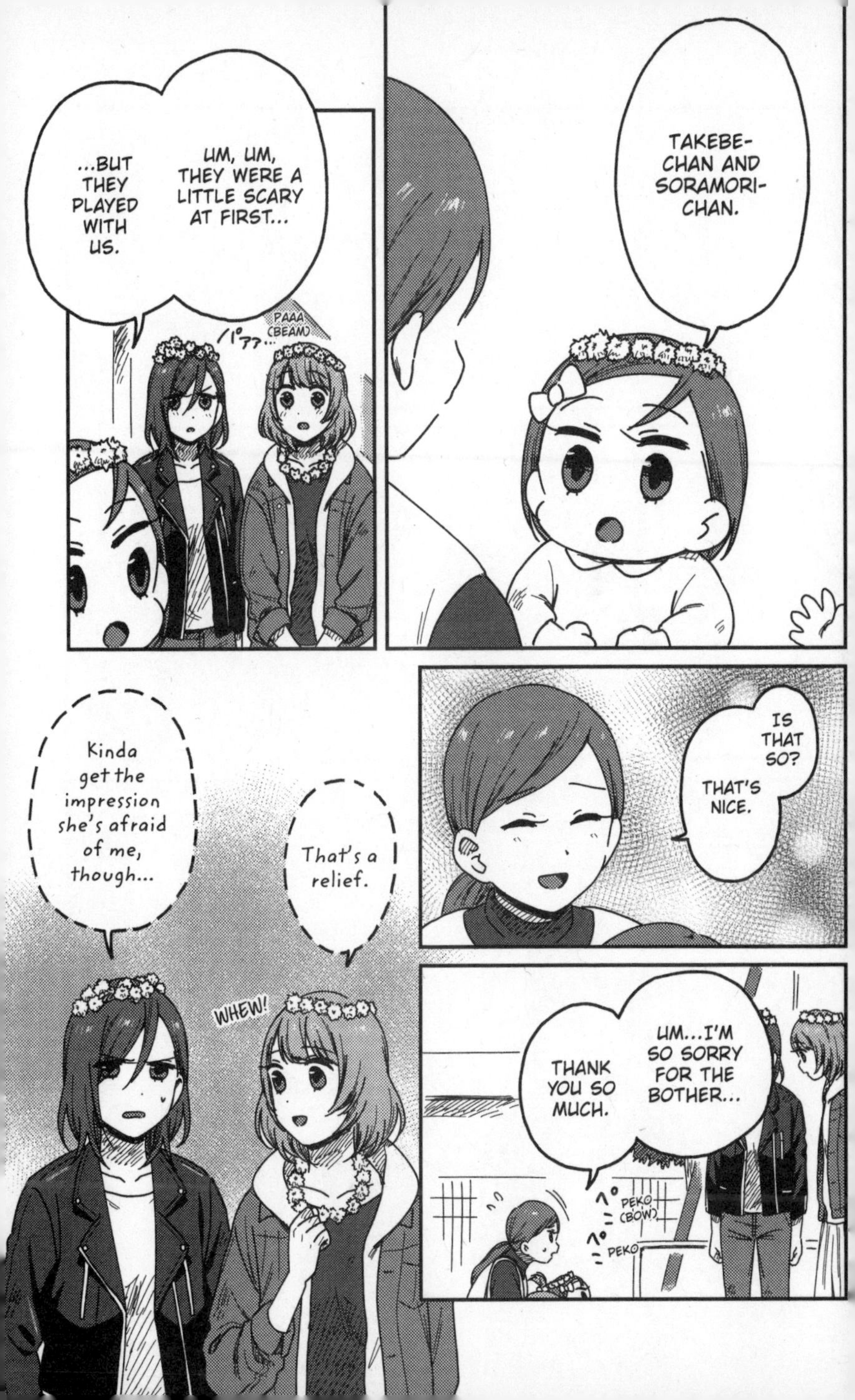
TAKEBE-CHAN AND SORAMORI-CHAN.
UM, UM, THEY WERE A LITTLE SCARY AT FIRST...
...BUT THEY PLAYED WITH US.
PAAA (BEAM)
IS THAT SO?
THAT'S NICE.
UM...I'M SO SORRY FOR THE BOTHER...
THANK YOU SO MUCH.
PEKO (BOW)
PEKO
That's a relief.
Kinda get the impression she's afraid of me, though...
WHEW!

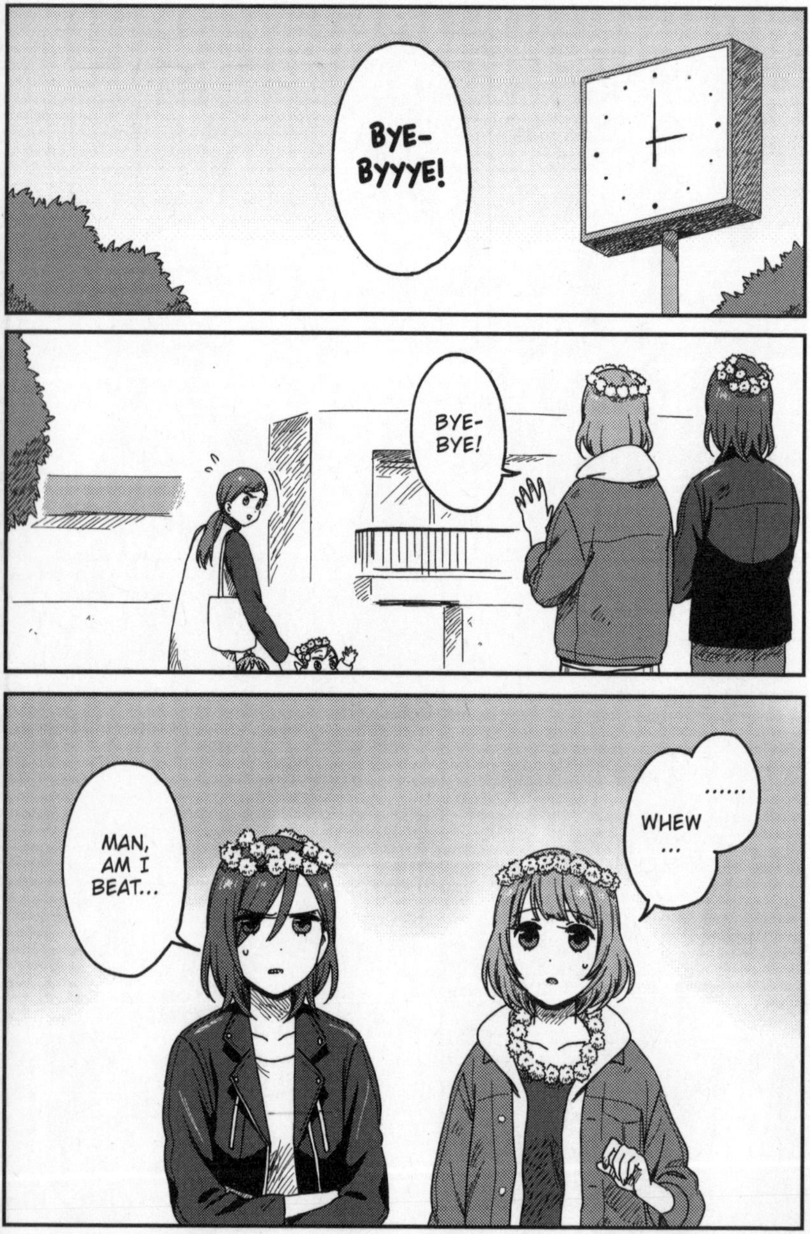
BYE-BYYYE!
BYE-BYE!
...... WHEW ...
MAN, AM I BEAT...

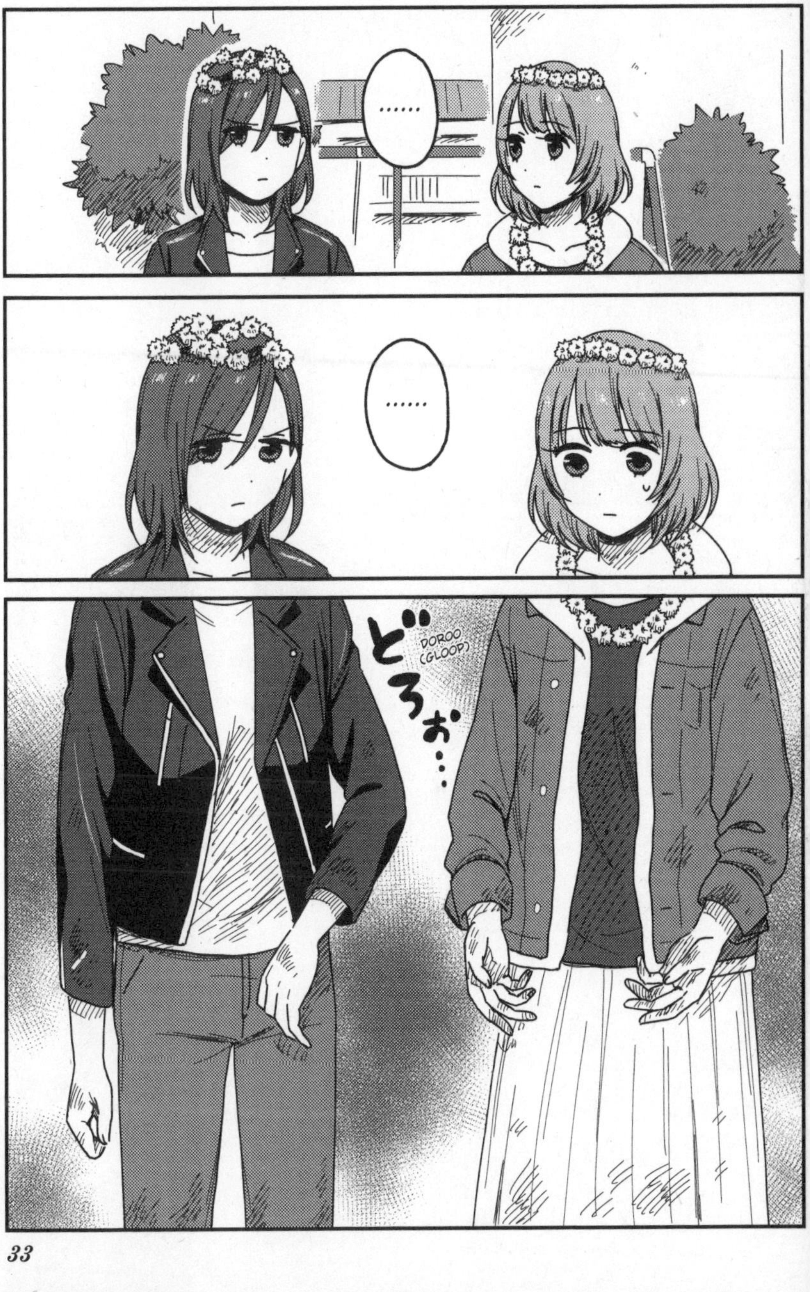
......
......
どろぉ…
DOROO (GLOOP)

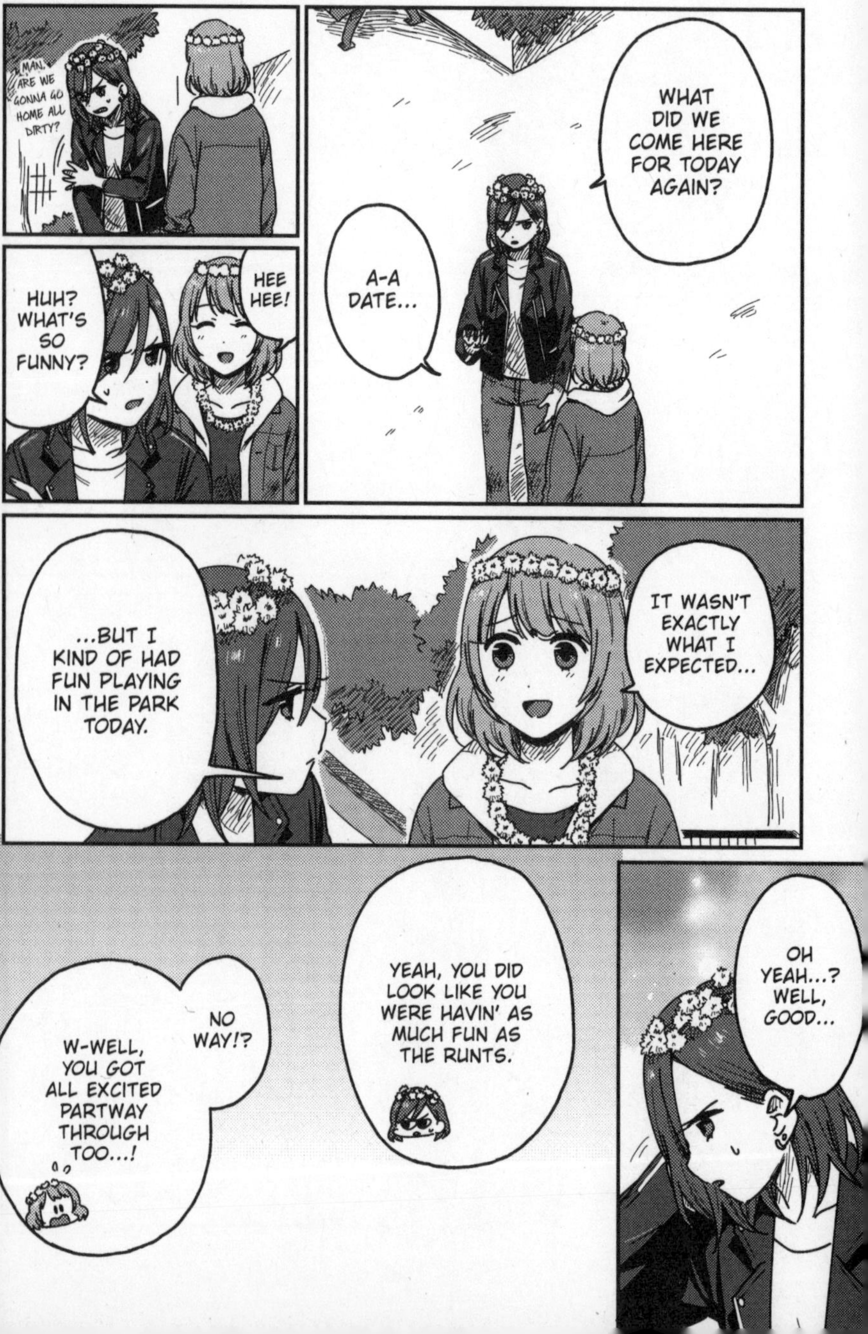
WHAT DID WE COME HERE FOR TODAY AGAIN?
A-A DATE...
MAN, ARE WE GONNA GO HOME ALL DIRTY?
HEE HEE!
HUH? WHAT'S SO FUNNY?
IT WASN'T EXACTLY WHAT I EXPECTED...
...BUT I KIND OF HAD FUN PLAYING IN THE PARK TODAY.
OH YEAH...? WELL, GOOD...
YEAH, YOU DID LOOK LIKE YOU WERE HAVIN' AS MUCH FUN AS THE RUNTS.
NO WAY!?
W-WELL, YOU GOT ALL EXCITED PARTWAY THROUGH TOO...!

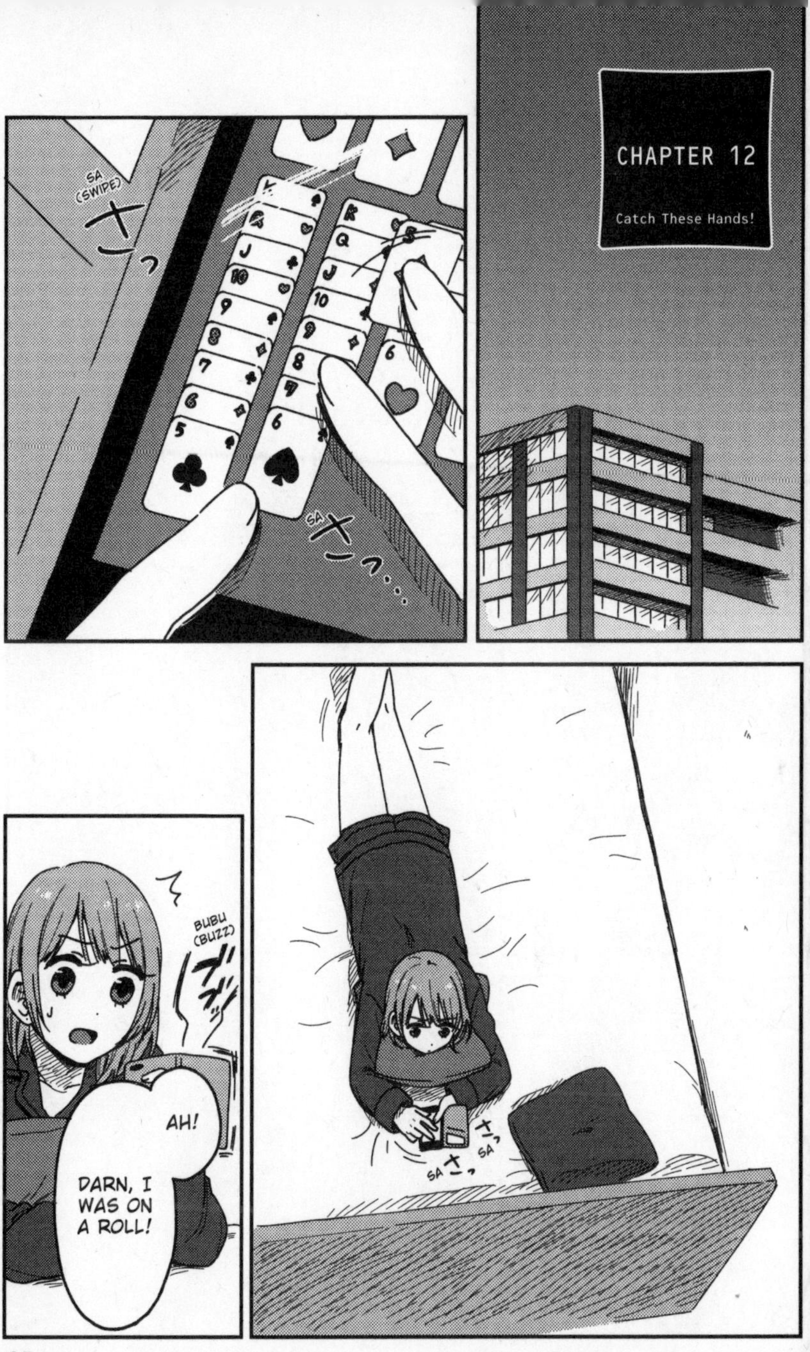

CHAPTER 12
Catch These Hands!
SA (SWIPE)
SA
SA
SA
BUBU (BUZZ)
AH!
DARN, I WAS ON A ROLL!

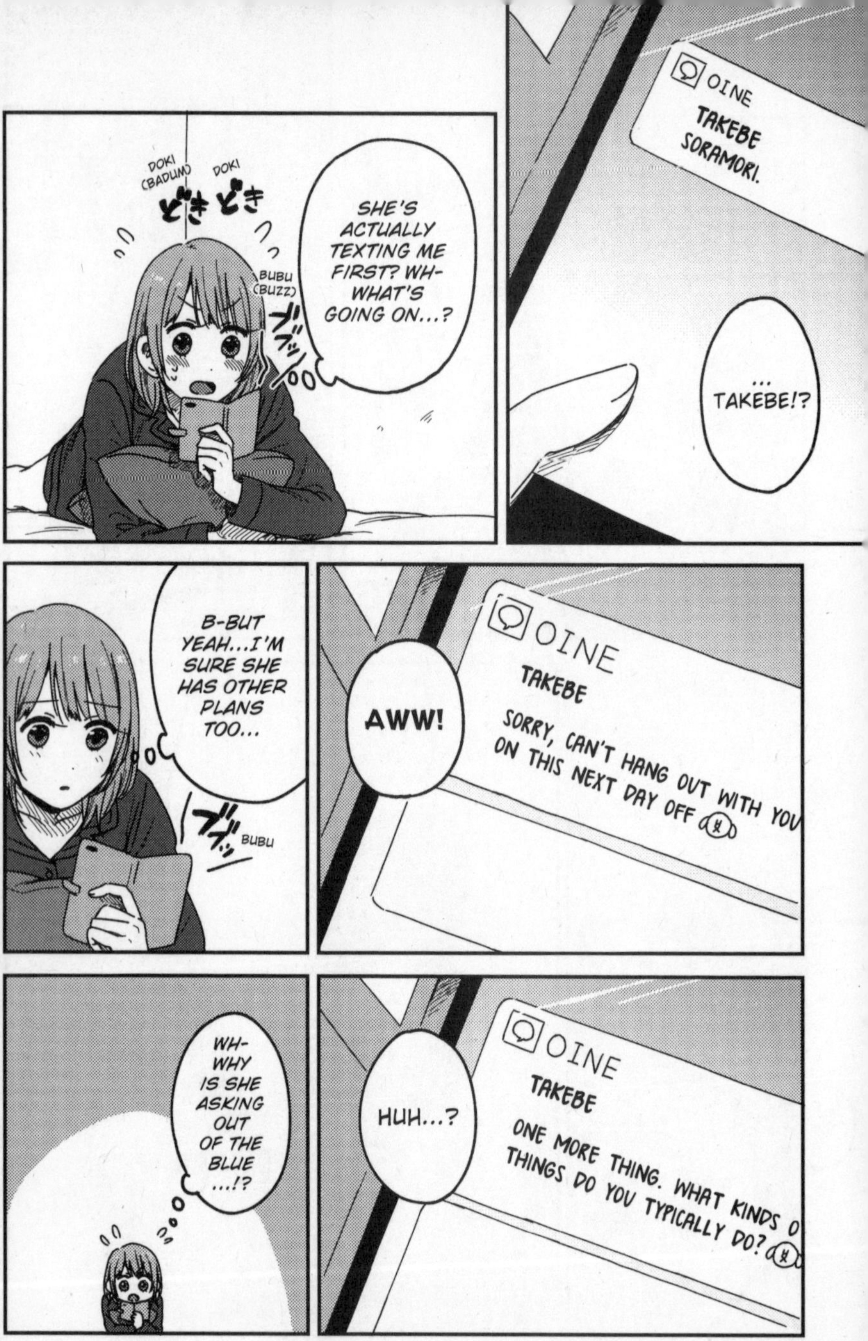
OINE
TAKEBE
SORAMORI.
... TAKEBE!?
DOKI (BADUM) DOKI
どきどき
SHE'S ACTUALLY TEXTING ME FIRST? WH-WHAT'S GOING ON...?
BUBU (BUZZ)
ブブッ
OINE
TAKEBE
SORRY, CAN'T HANG OUT WITH YOU ON THIS NEXT DAY OFF
AWW!
B-BUT YEAH...I'M SURE SHE HAS OTHER PLANS TOO...
ブブッ
BUBU
OINE
TAKEBE
ONE MORE THING. WHAT KINDS O THINGS DO YOU TYPICALLY DO?
HUH...?
WH-WHY IS SHE ASKING OUT OF THE BLUE ...!?

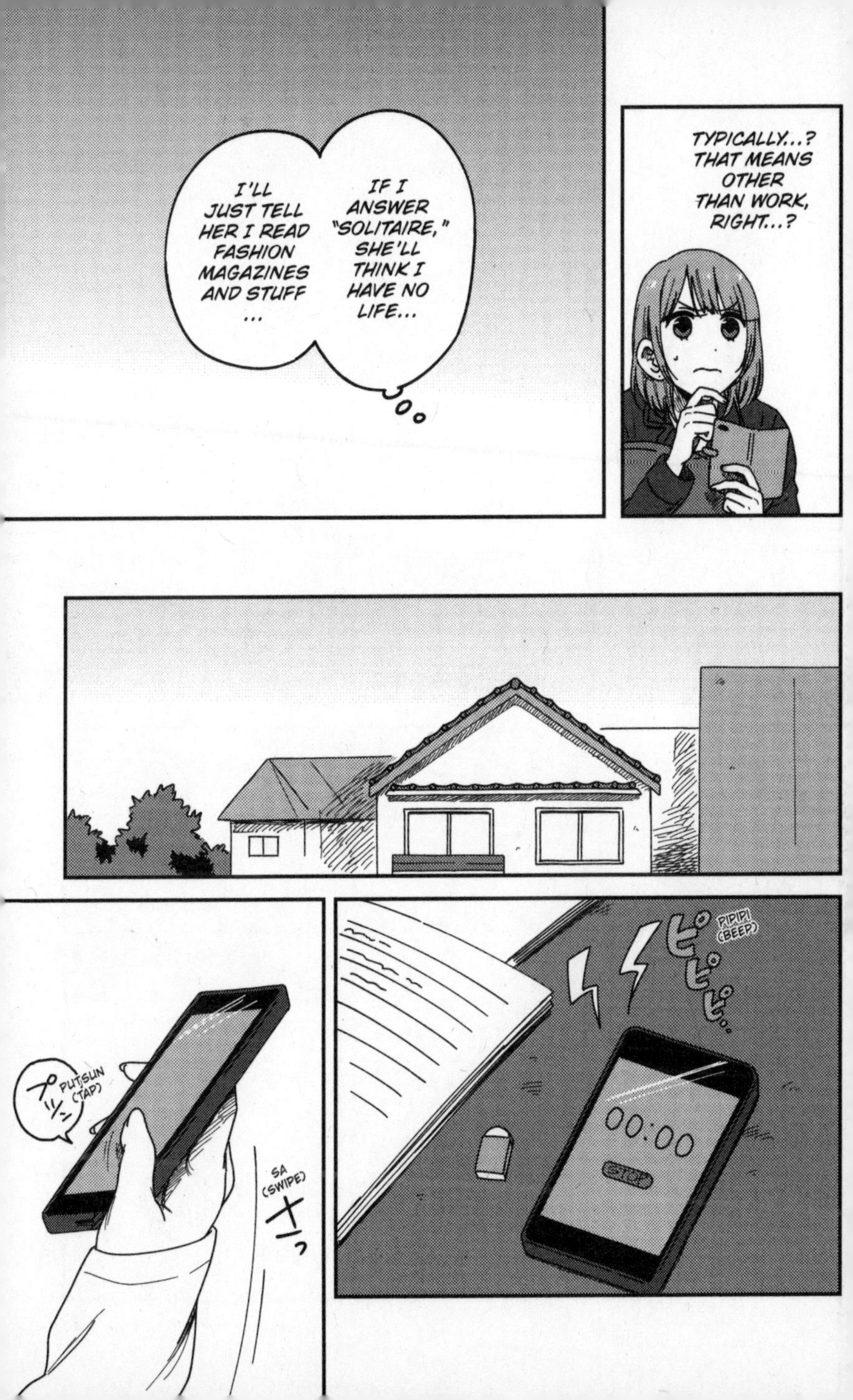
TYPICALLY...? THAT MEANS OTHER THAN WORK, RIGHT...?
IF I ANSWER "SOLITAIRE," SHE'LL THINK I HAVE NO LIFE...
I'LL JUST TELL HER I READ FASHION MAGAZINES AND STUFF...
PIPIPI (BEEP)
00:00
STOP
PUTSUN (TAP)
SA (SWIPE)

ふっ

ど

DOFU
(WHUMP)

UUUUGH.
STUDYING
IS, LIKE...

...SUCH A
DRAG, FOR
REAL...

ピンポーン

PINPOOON
(DING-DONG)

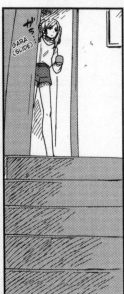

ガラ

GARA
(SLIDE)

......

38

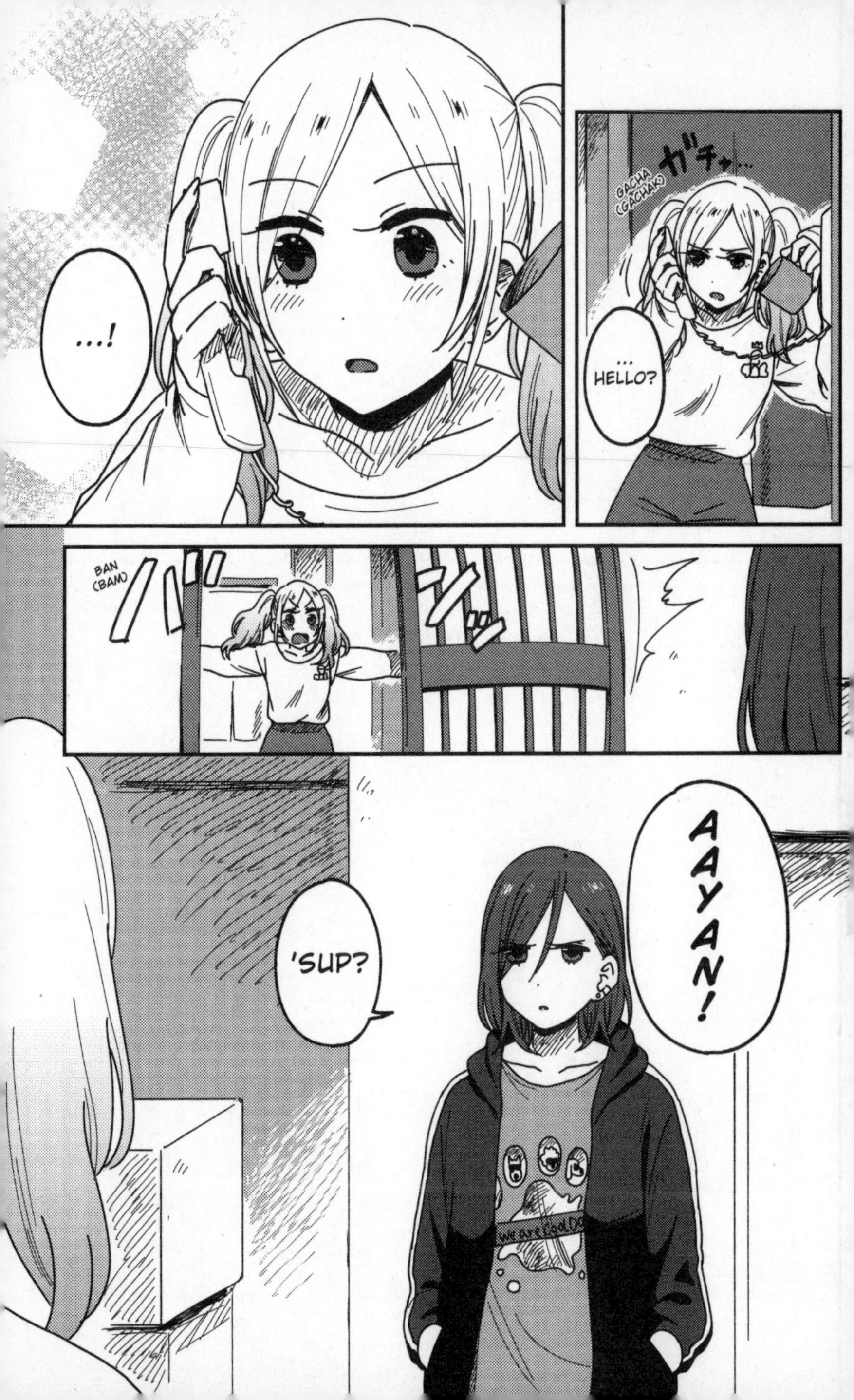
GACHA (GACHAK)
ガチャ…
… HELLO?
…!
BAN (BAM)
AAYAN!
'SUP?

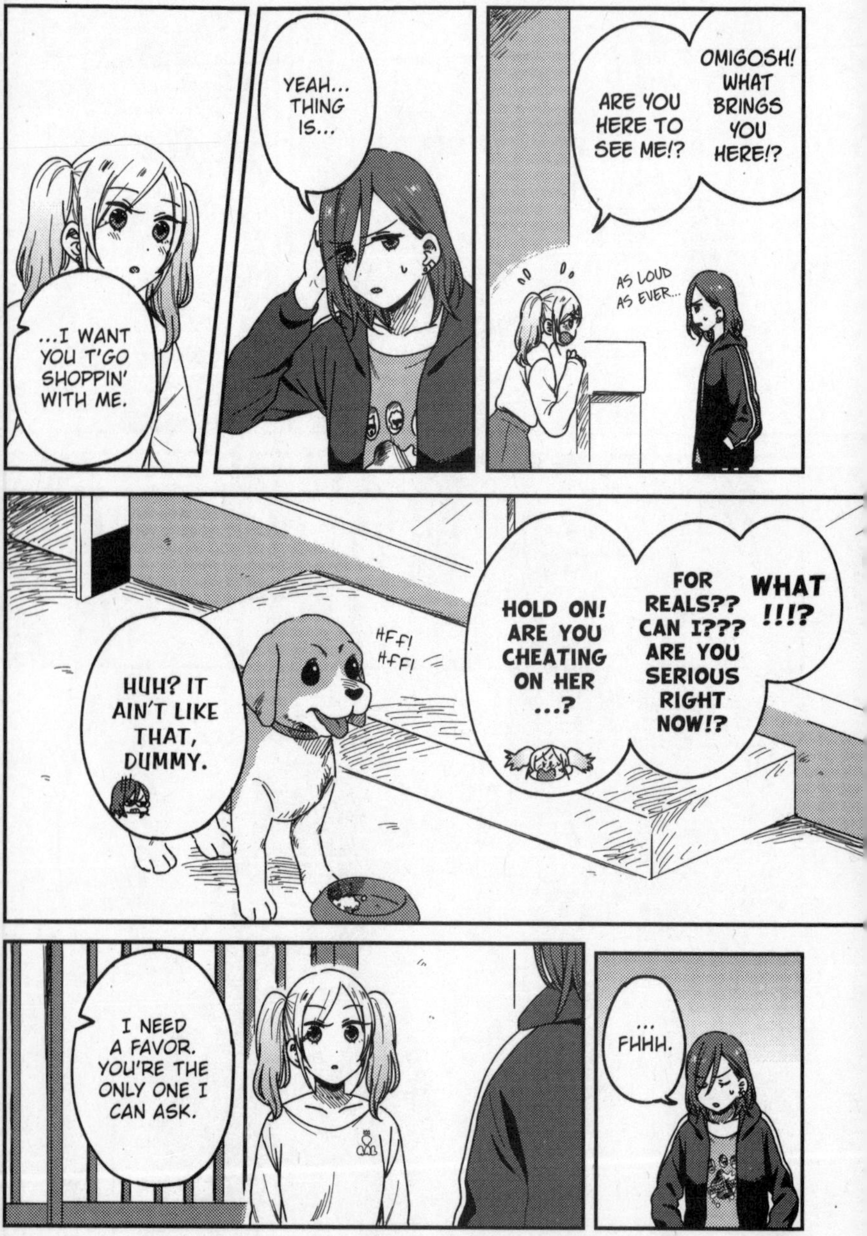
OMIGOSH! WHAT BRINGS YOU HERE!?
ARE YOU HERE TO SEE ME!?
AS LOUD AS EVER...
YEAH... THING IS...
...I WANT YOU T'GO SHOPPIN' WITH ME.
WHAT !!!?
FOR REALS?? CAN I??? ARE YOU SERIOUS RIGHT NOW!?
HOLD ON! ARE YOU CHEATING ON HER ...?
HFF! HFF!
HUH? IT AIN'T LIKE THAT, DUMMY.
... FHHH.
I NEED A FAVOR. YOU'RE THE ONLY ONE I CAN ASK.

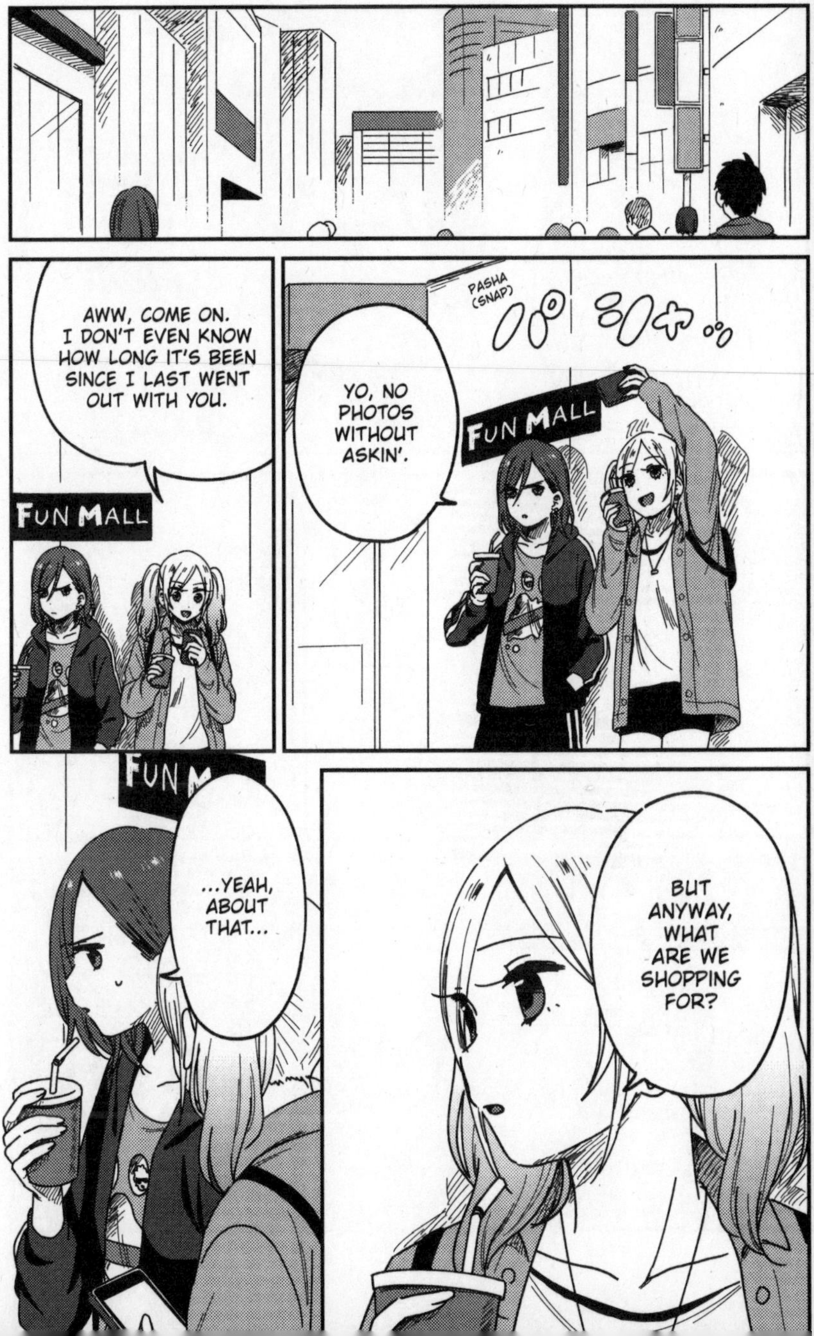
PASHA (SNAP)
FUN MALL
YO, NO PHOTOS WITHOUT ASKIN'.
AWW, COME ON. I DON'T EVEN KNOW HOW LONG IT'S BEEN SINCE I LAST WENT OUT WITH YOU.
FUN MALL
BUT ANYWAY, WHAT ARE WE SHOPPING FOR?
...YEAH, ABOUT THAT...

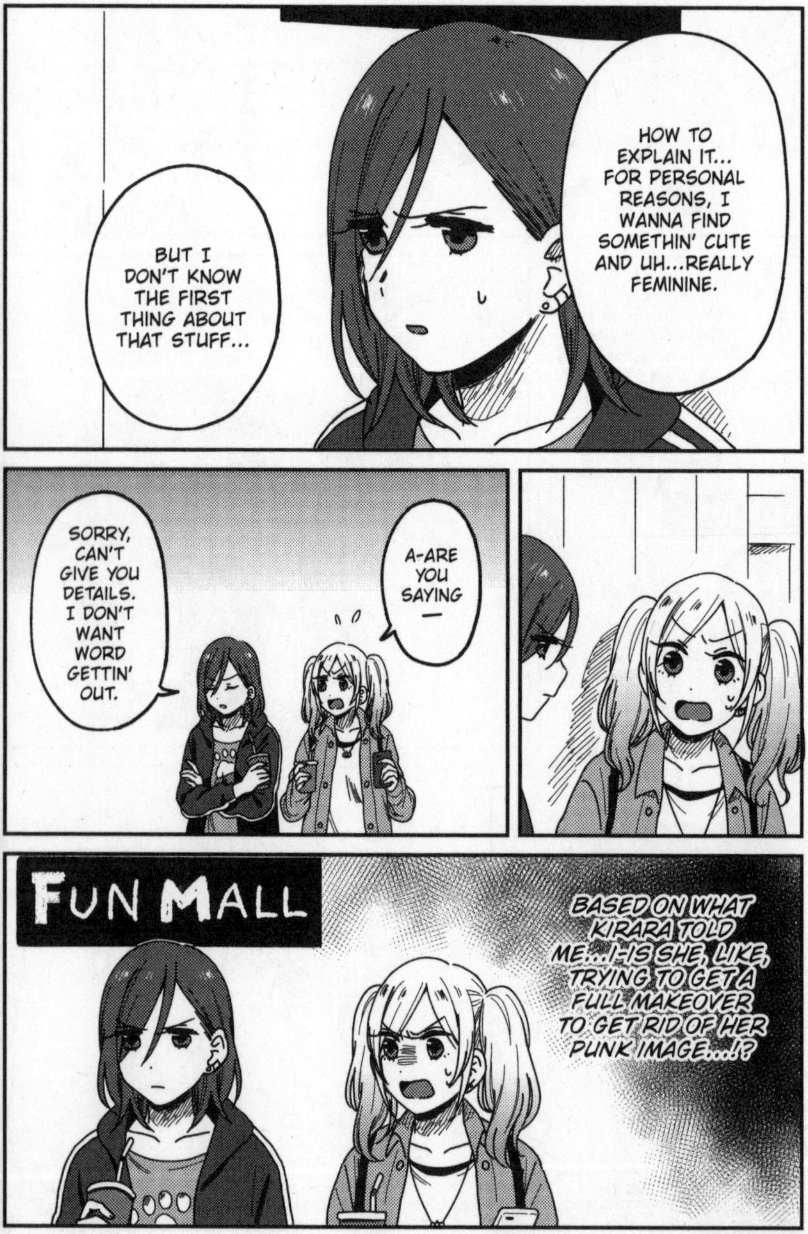
HOW TO EXPLAIN IT... FOR PERSONAL REASONS, I WANNA FIND SOMETHIN' CUTE AND UH...REALLY FEMININE.
BUT I DON'T KNOW THE FIRST THING ABOUT THAT STUFF...
A-ARE YOU SAYING—
SORRY, CAN'T GIVE YOU DETAILS. I DON'T WANT WORD GETTIN' OUT.
FUN MALL
BASED ON WHAT KIRARA TOLD ME...I-IS SHE, LIKE, TRYING TO GET A FULL MAKEOVER TO GET RID OF HER PUNK IMAGE...!?

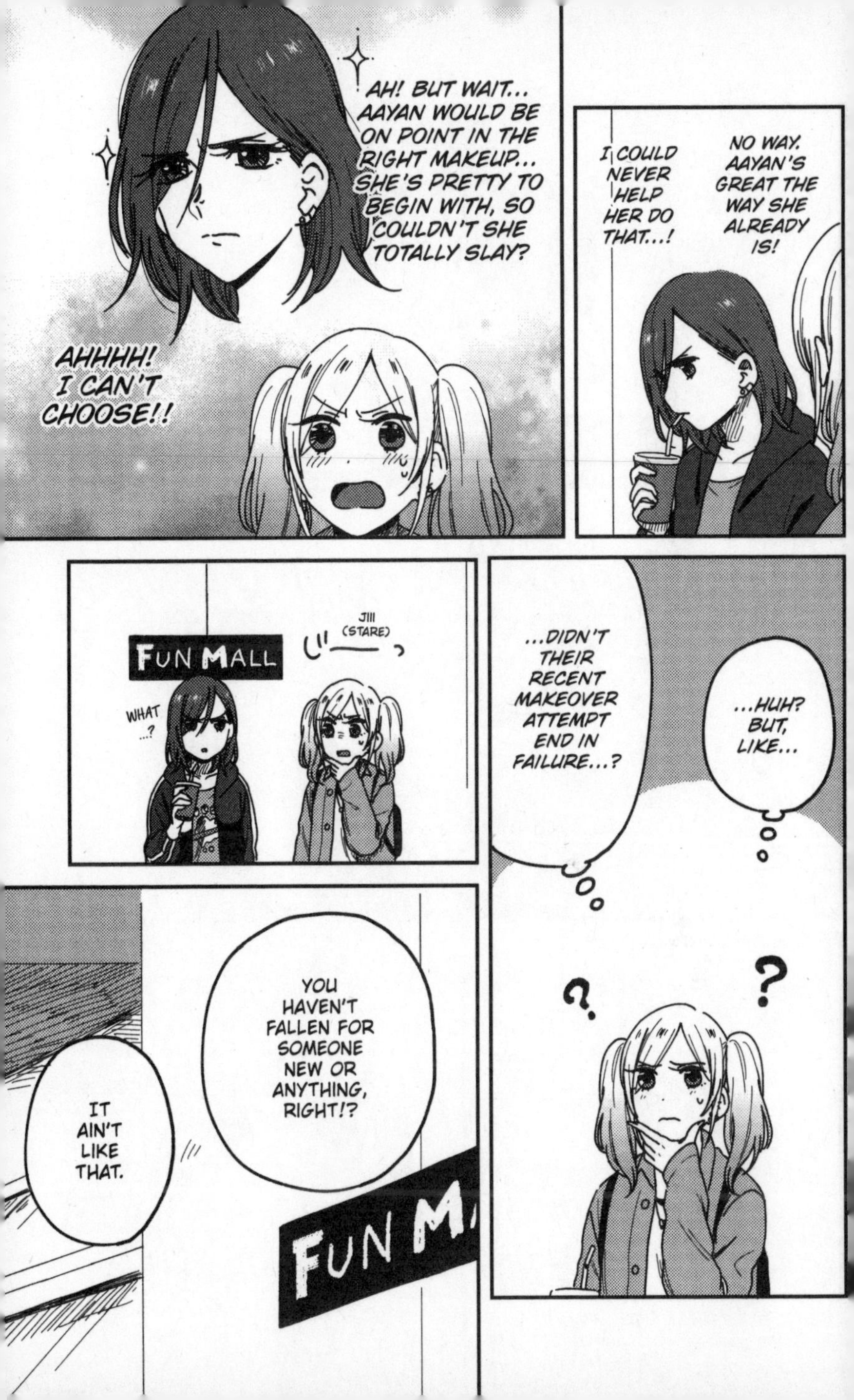
NO WAY. AAYAN'S GREAT THE WAY SHE ALREADY IS!
I COULD NEVER HELP HER DO THAT...!
AH! BUT WAIT... AAYAN WOULD BE ON POINT IN THE RIGHT MAKEUP... SHE'S PRETTY TO BEGIN WITH, SO COULDN'T SHE TOTALLY SLAY?
AHHHH! I CAN'T CHOOSE!!
...HUH? BUT, LIKE...
...DIDN'T THEIR RECENT MAKEOVER ATTEMPT END IN FAILURE...?
JIII (STARE)
FUN MALL
WHAT ...?
YOU HAVEN'T FALLEN FOR SOMEONE NEW OR ANYTHING, RIGHT!?
IT AIN'T LIKE THAT.
FUN M

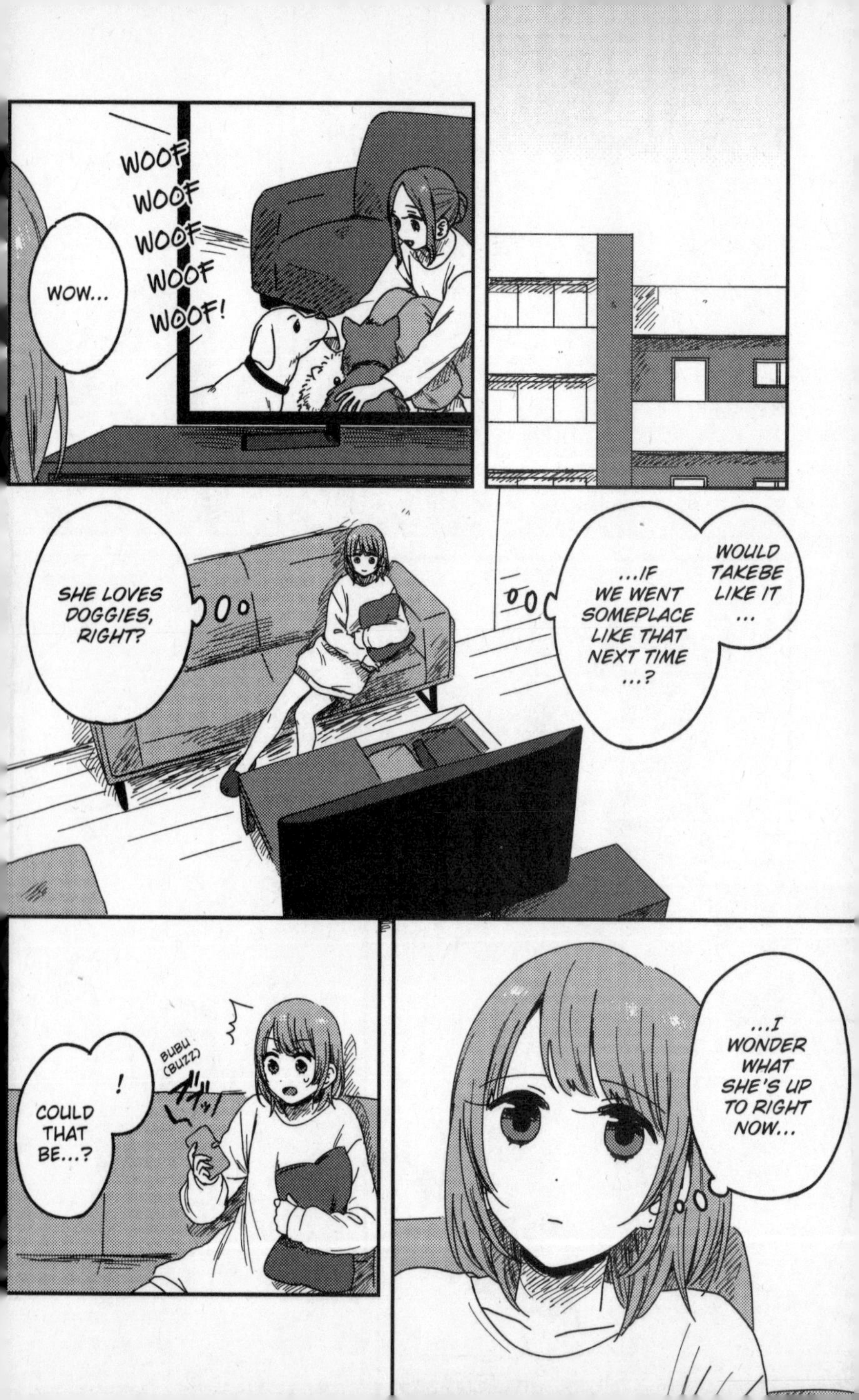
WOOF
WOOF
WOOF
WOOF
WOOF!
WOW...
WOULD TAKEBE LIKE IT ...
...IF WE WENT SOMEPLACE LIKE THAT NEXT TIME ...?
SHE LOVES DOGGIES, RIGHT?
...I WONDER WHAT SHE'S UP TO RIGHT NOW...
BUBU (BUZZ)
!
COULD THAT BE...?

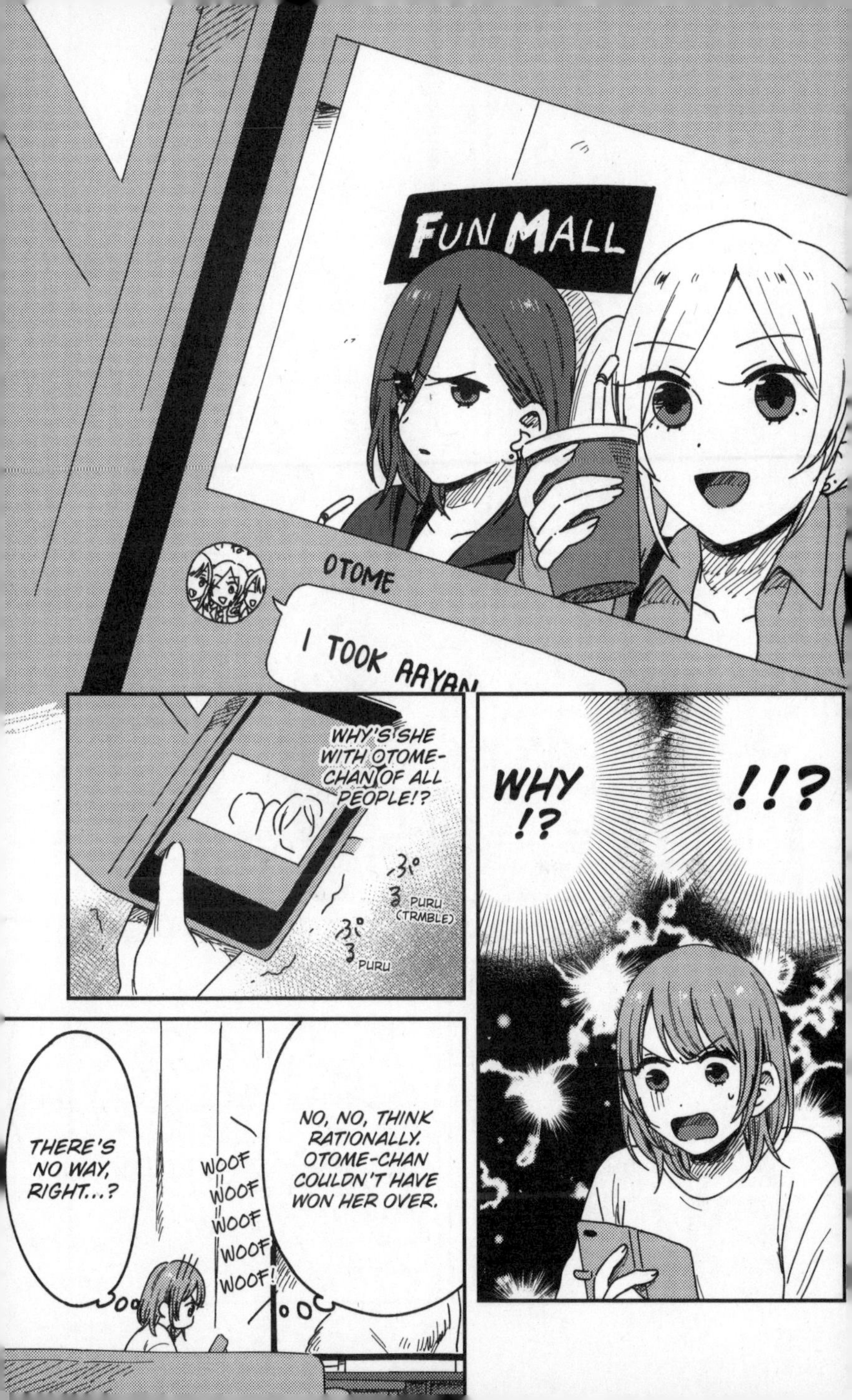
FUN MALL
OTOME
I TOOK AAYAN
WHY !? !!?
WHY'S SHE WITH OTOME-CHAN OF ALL PEOPLE!?
ぷる PURU (TRMBLE)
ぷる PURU
NO, NO, THINK RATIONALLY. OTOME-CHAN COULDN'T HAVE WON HER OVER.
WOOF WOOF WOOF WOOF WOOF!
THERE'S NO WAY, RIGHT...?

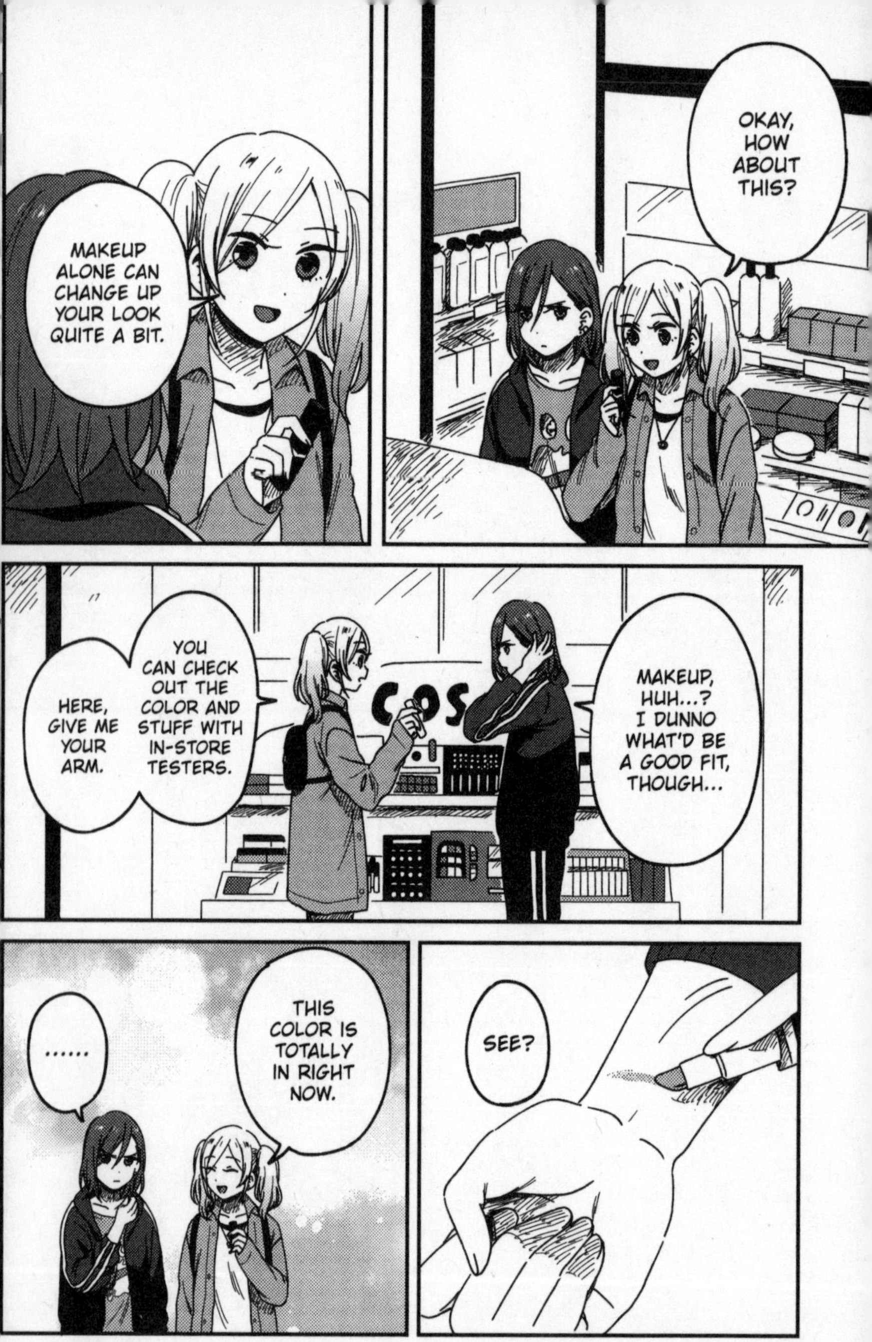
OKAY, HOW ABOUT THIS?
MAKEUP ALONE CAN CHANGE UP YOUR LOOK QUITE A BIT.
MAKEUP, HUH...? I DUNNO WHAT'D BE A GOOD FIT, THOUGH...
YOU CAN CHECK OUT THE COLOR AND STUFF WITH IN-STORE TESTERS.
HERE, GIVE ME YOUR ARM.
SEE?
THIS COLOR IS TOTALLY IN RIGHT NOW.
......

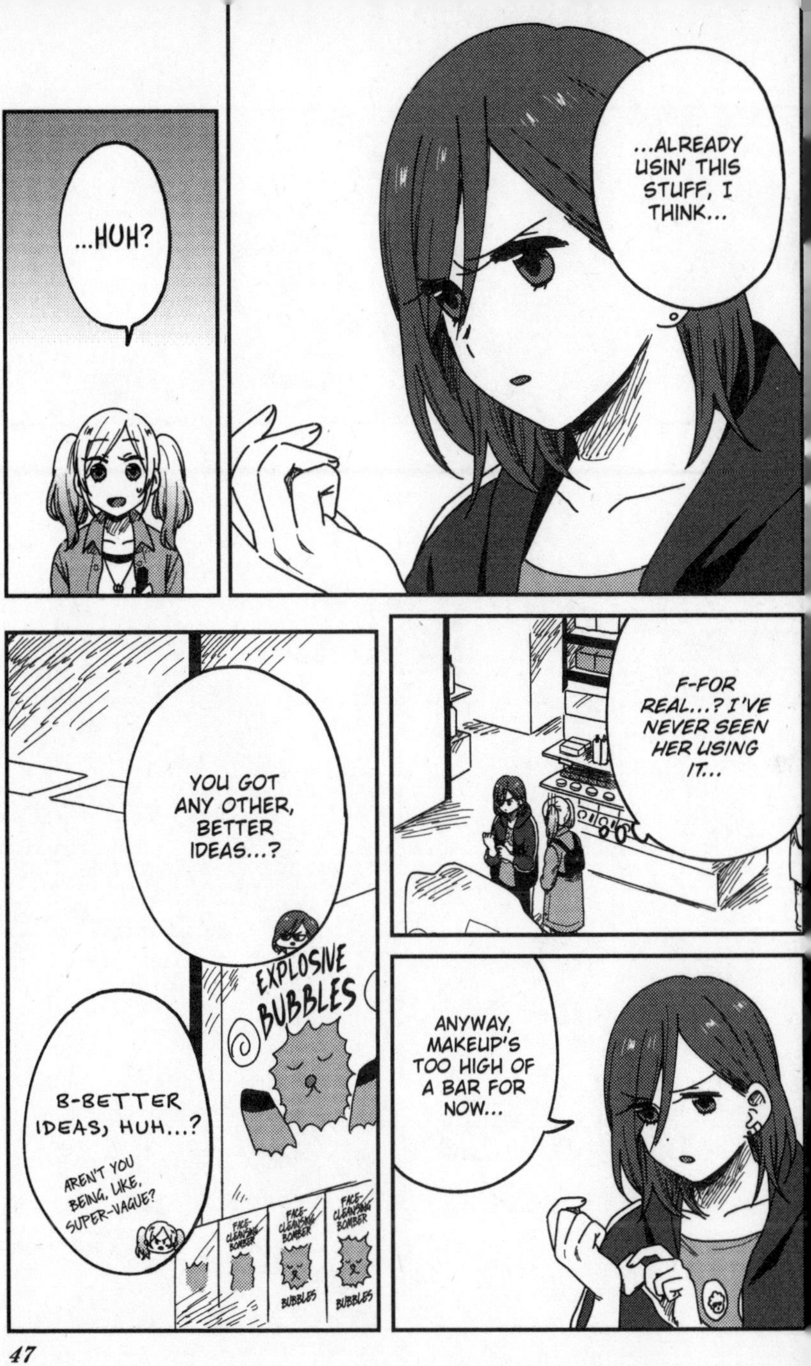
...ALREADY USIN' THIS STUFF, I THINK...
...HUH?
F-FOR REAL...? I'VE NEVER SEEN HER USING IT...
ANYWAY, MAKEUP'S TOO HIGH OF A BAR FOR NOW...
YOU GOT ANY OTHER, BETTER IDEAS...?
EXPLOSIVE BUBBLES
B-BETTER IDEAS, HUH...?
AREN'T YOU BEING, LIKE, SUPER-VAGUE?
FACE-CLEANSING BOMBER
FACE-CLEANSING BOMBER
BUBBLES
FACE-CLEANSING BOMBER
BUBBLES

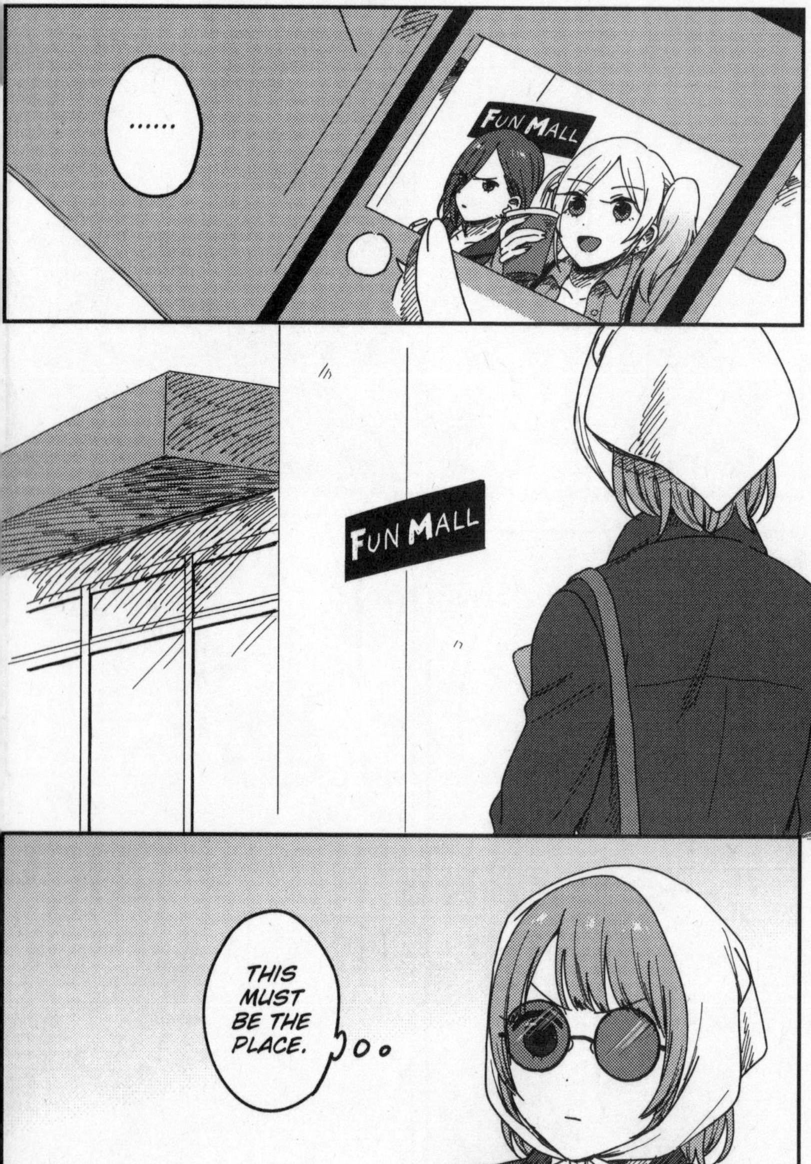
FUN MALL
......
FUN MALL
THIS MUST BE THE PLACE.

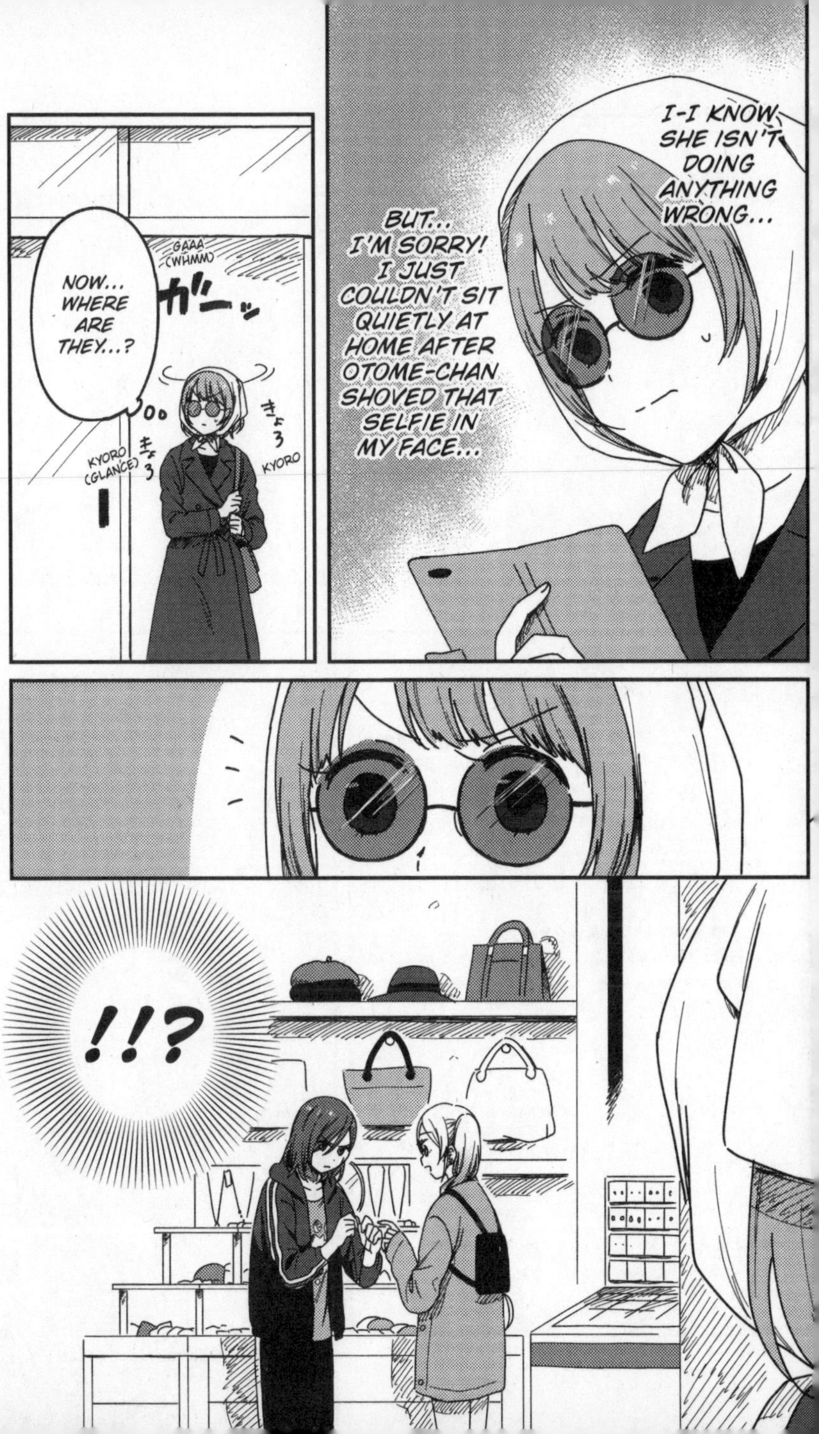
I-I KNOW SHE ISN'T DOING ANYTHING WRONG...
BUT... I'M SORRY! I JUST COULDN'T SIT QUIETLY AT HOME AFTER OTOME-CHAN SHOVED THAT SELFIE IN MY FACE...
ガーッ
GAAA (WHMM)
NOW... WHERE ARE THEY...?
きょろ
KYORO
きょろ
KYORO (GLANCE)
!!?

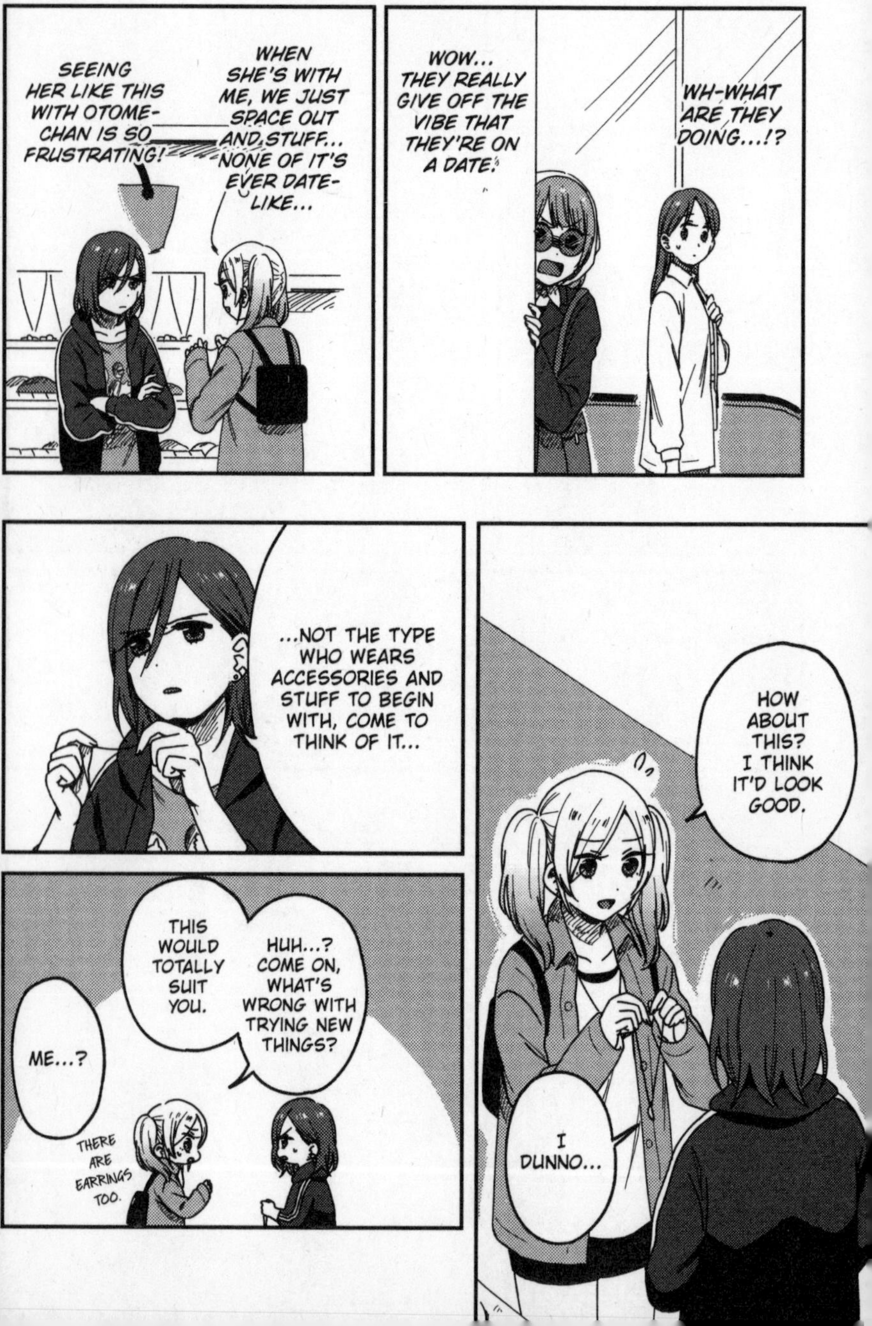
WH-WHAT ARE THEY DOING...!?
WOW... THEY REALLY GIVE OFF THE VIBE THAT THEY'RE ON A DATE.
WHEN SHE'S WITH ME, WE JUST SPACE OUT AND STUFF... NONE OF IT'S EVER DATE-LIKE...
SEEING HER LIKE THIS WITH OTOME-CHAN IS SO FRUSTRATING!
HOW ABOUT THIS? I THINK IT'D LOOK GOOD.
I DUNNO...
...NOT THE TYPE WHO WEARS ACCESSORIES AND STUFF TO BEGIN WITH, COME TO THINK OF IT...
HUH...? COME ON, WHAT'S WRONG WITH TRYING NEW THINGS?
THIS WOULD TOTALLY SUIT YOU.
ME...?
THERE ARE EARRINGS TOO.

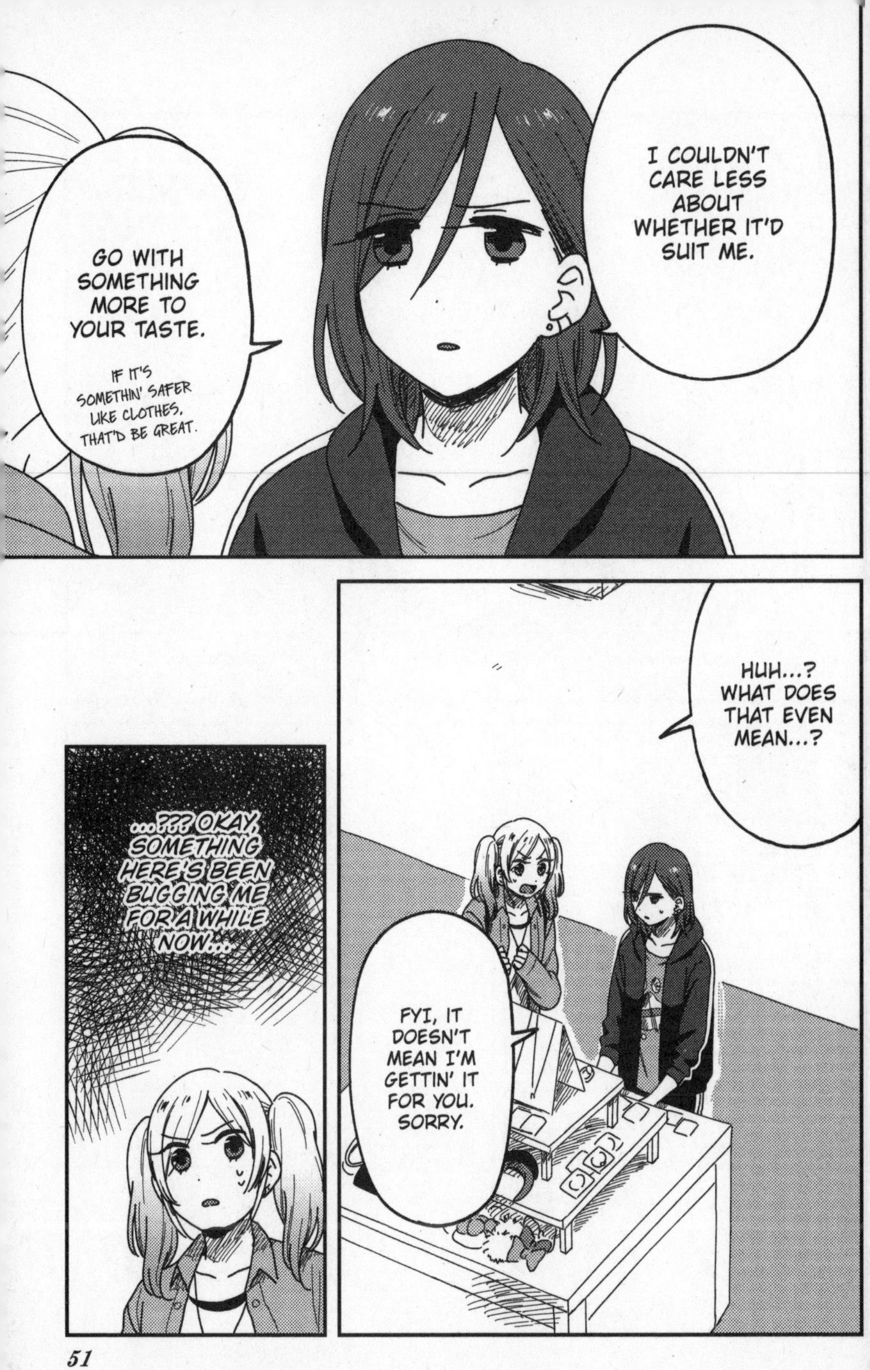
I COULDN'T CARE LESS ABOUT WHETHER IT'D SUIT ME.
GO WITH SOMETHING MORE TO YOUR TASTE.
IF IT'S SOMETHIN' SAFER LIKE CLOTHES, THAT'D BE GREAT.
HUH...? WHAT DOES THAT EVEN MEAN...?
FYI, IT DOESN'T MEAN I'M GETTIN' IT FOR YOU. SORRY.
...??? OKAY, SOMETHING HERE'S BEEN BUGGING ME FOR A WHILE NOW...

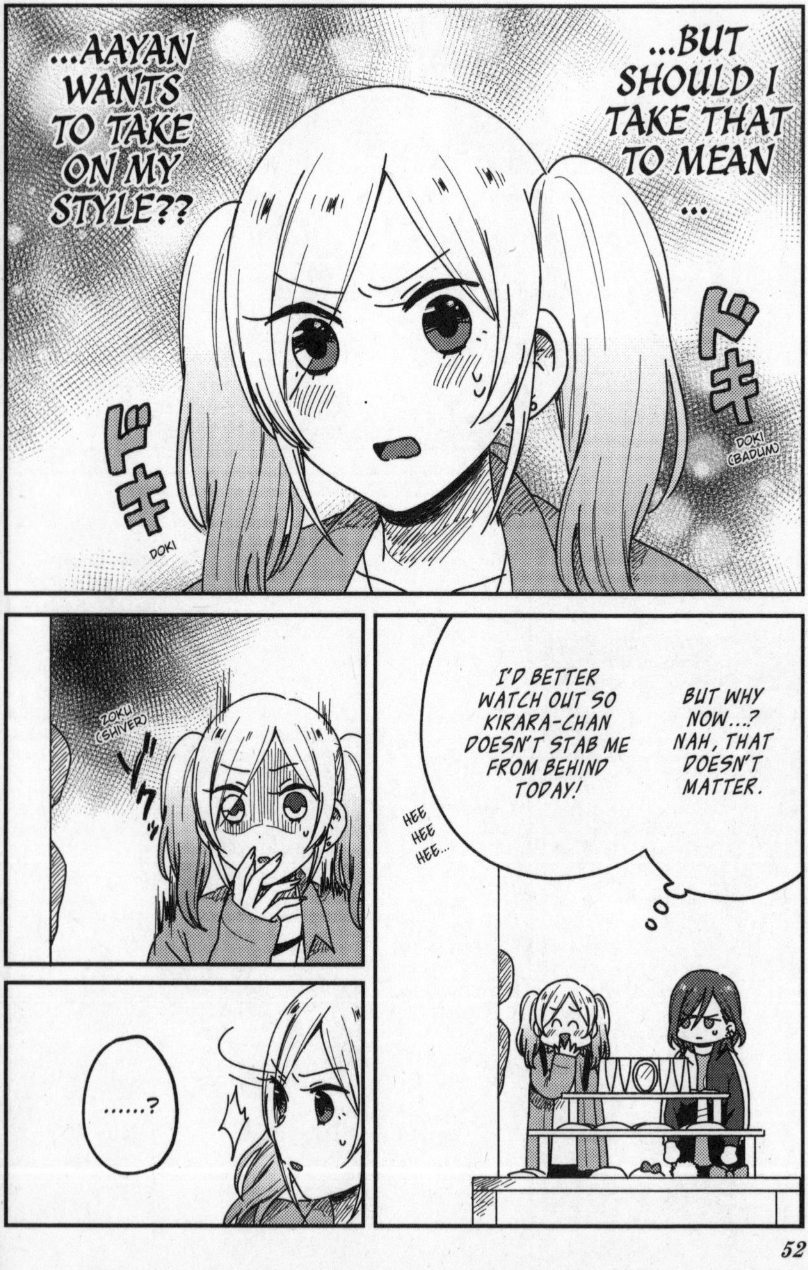
...BUT SHOULD I TAKE THAT TO MEAN ...
...AAYAN WANTS TO TAKE ON MY STYLE??
ドキ
DOKI (BADUM)
ドキ
DOKI
BUT WHY NOW...? NAH, THAT DOESN'T MATTER.
I'D BETTER WATCH OUT SO KIRARA-CHAN DOESN'T STAB ME FROM BEHIND TODAY!
HEE HEE HEE...
ゾクッ
ZOKU (SHIVER)
......?

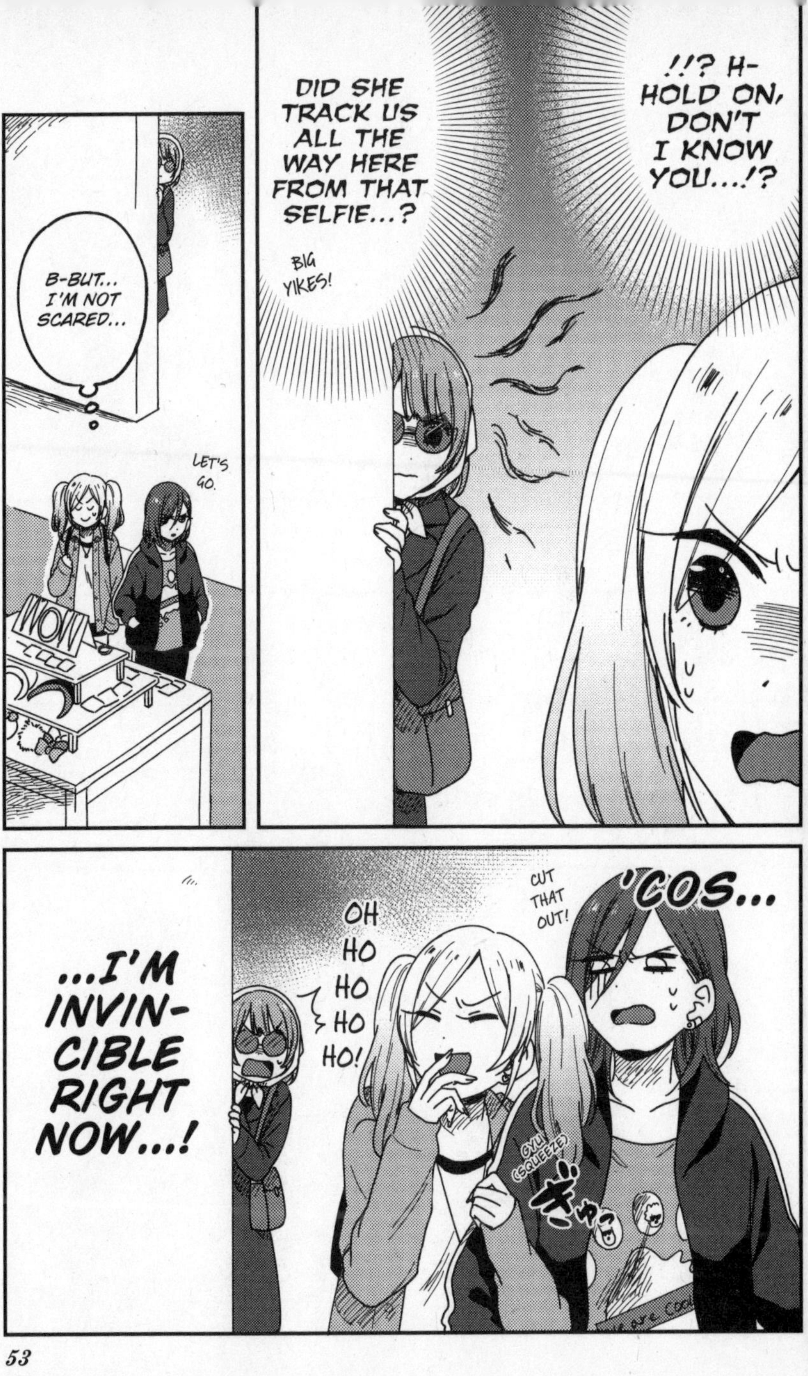
!!? H-HOLD ON, DON'T I KNOW YOU...!?
DID SHE TRACK US ALL THE WAY HERE FROM THAT SELFIE...?
BIG YIKES!
B-BUT... I'M NOT SCARED...
LET'S GO.
'COS...
CUT THAT OUT!
OH HO HO HO HO!
GYU (SQUEEZE)
...I'M INVINCIBLE RIGHT NOW...!

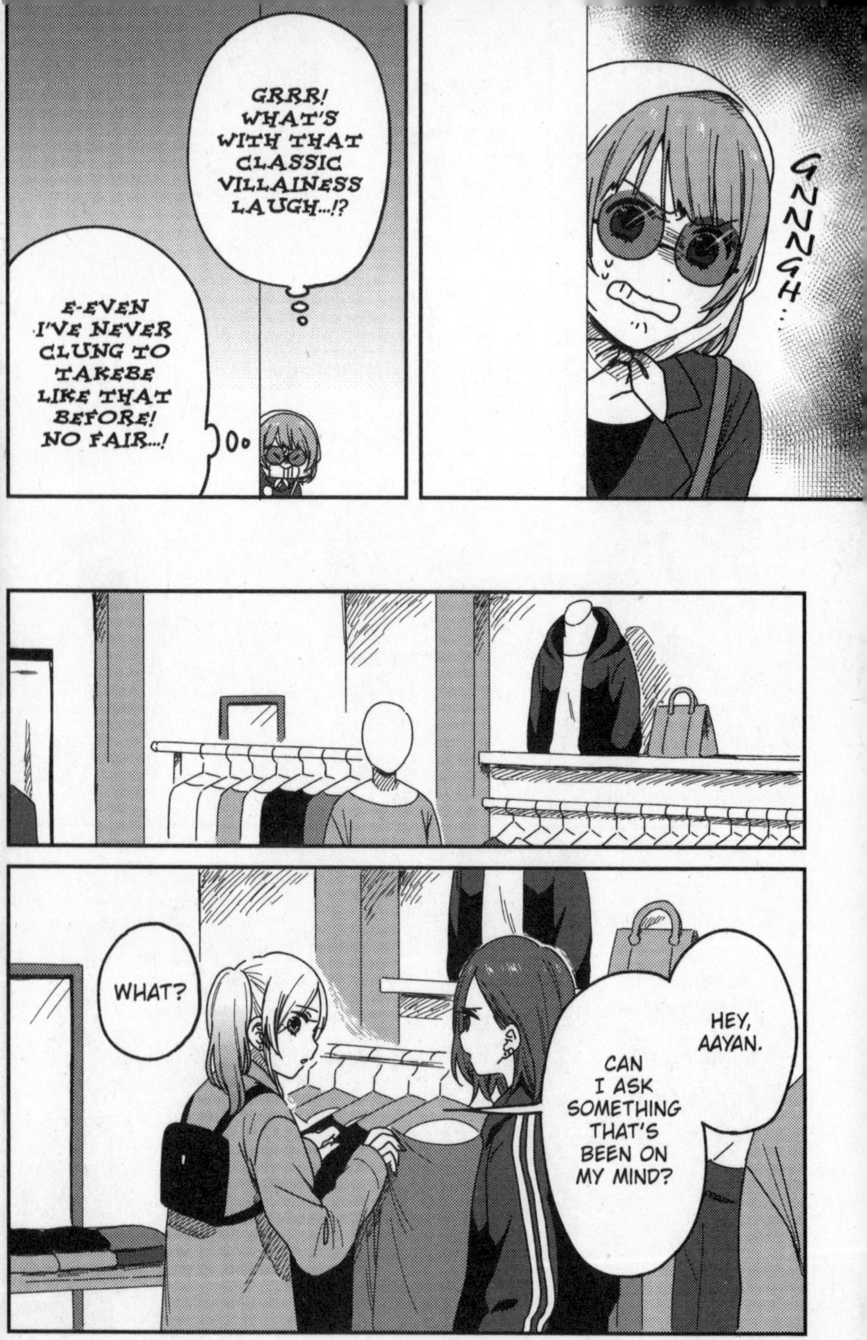
GNNNGH...
GRRR! WHAT'S WITH THAT CLASSIC VILLAINESS LAUGH...!?
E-EVEN I'VE NEVER CLUNG TO TAKEBE LIKE THAT BEFORE! NO FAIR...!
HEY, AAYAN.
CAN I ASK SOMETHING THAT'S BEEN ON MY MIND?
WHAT?

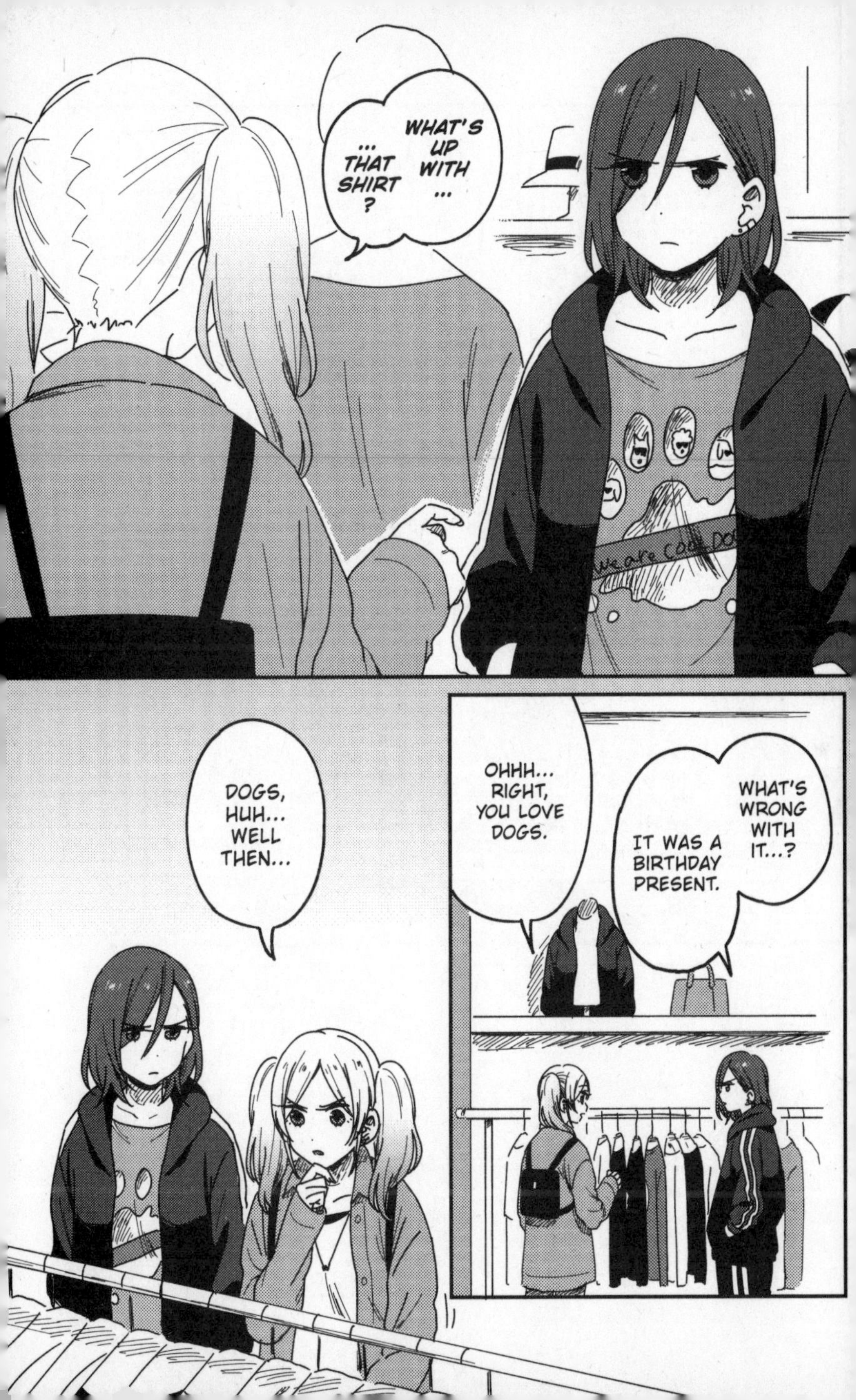
WHAT'S UP WITH ...
... THAT SHIRT ?
WHAT'S WRONG WITH IT...?
IT WAS A BIRTHDAY PRESENT.
OHHH... RIGHT, YOU LOVE DOGS.
DOGS, HUH... WELL THEN...

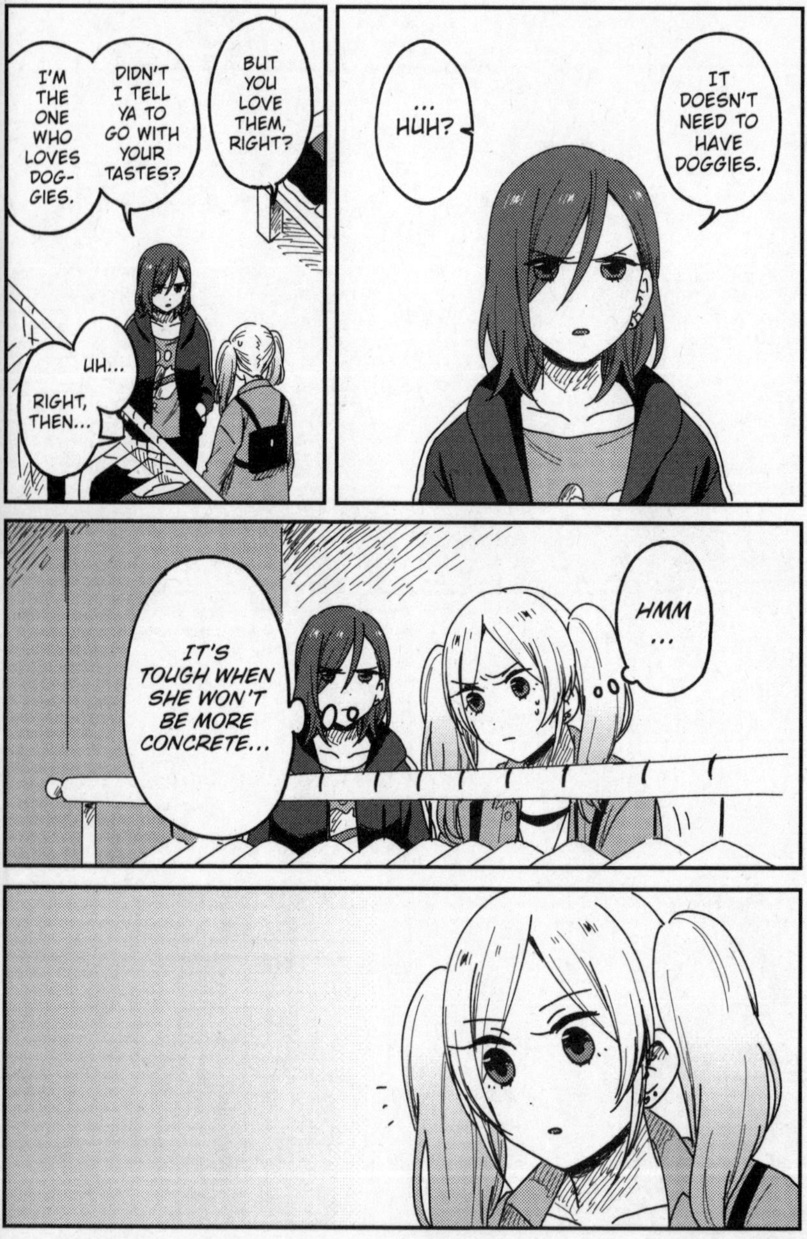
IT DOESN'T NEED TO HAVE DOGGIES.
... HUH?
BUT YOU LOVE THEM, RIGHT?
DIDN'T I TELL YA TO GO WITH YOUR TASTES?
I'M THE ONE WHO LOVES DOG-GIES.
UH... RIGHT, THEN...
HMM ...
IT'S TOUGH WHEN SHE WON'T BE MORE CONCRETE...

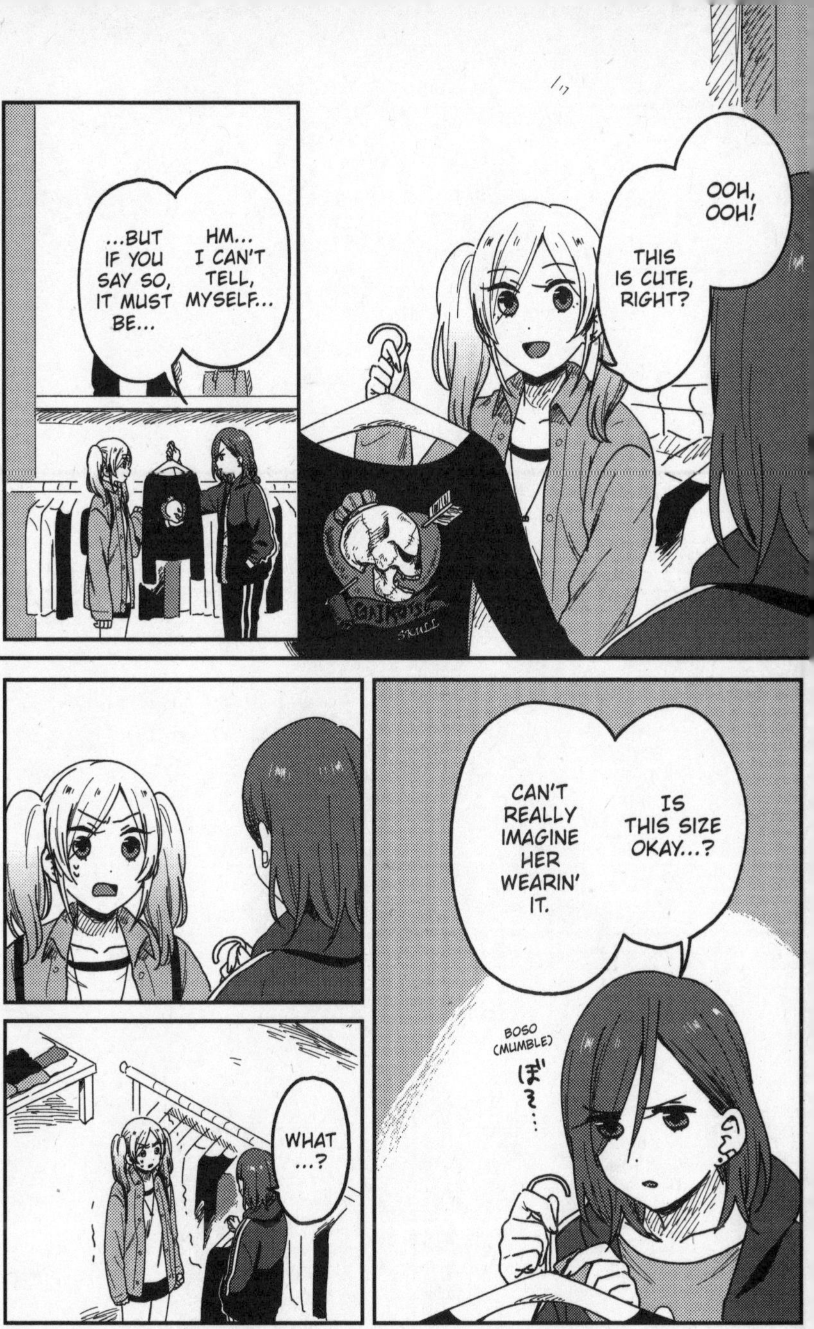
OOH, OOH!
THIS IS CUTE, RIGHT?
SKULL
HM... I CAN'T TELL, MYSELF...
...BUT IF YOU SAY SO, IT MUST BE...
IS THIS SIZE OKAY...?
CAN'T REALLY IMAGINE HER WEARIN' IT.
BOSO (MUMBLE)
ぼそ…
WHAT...?

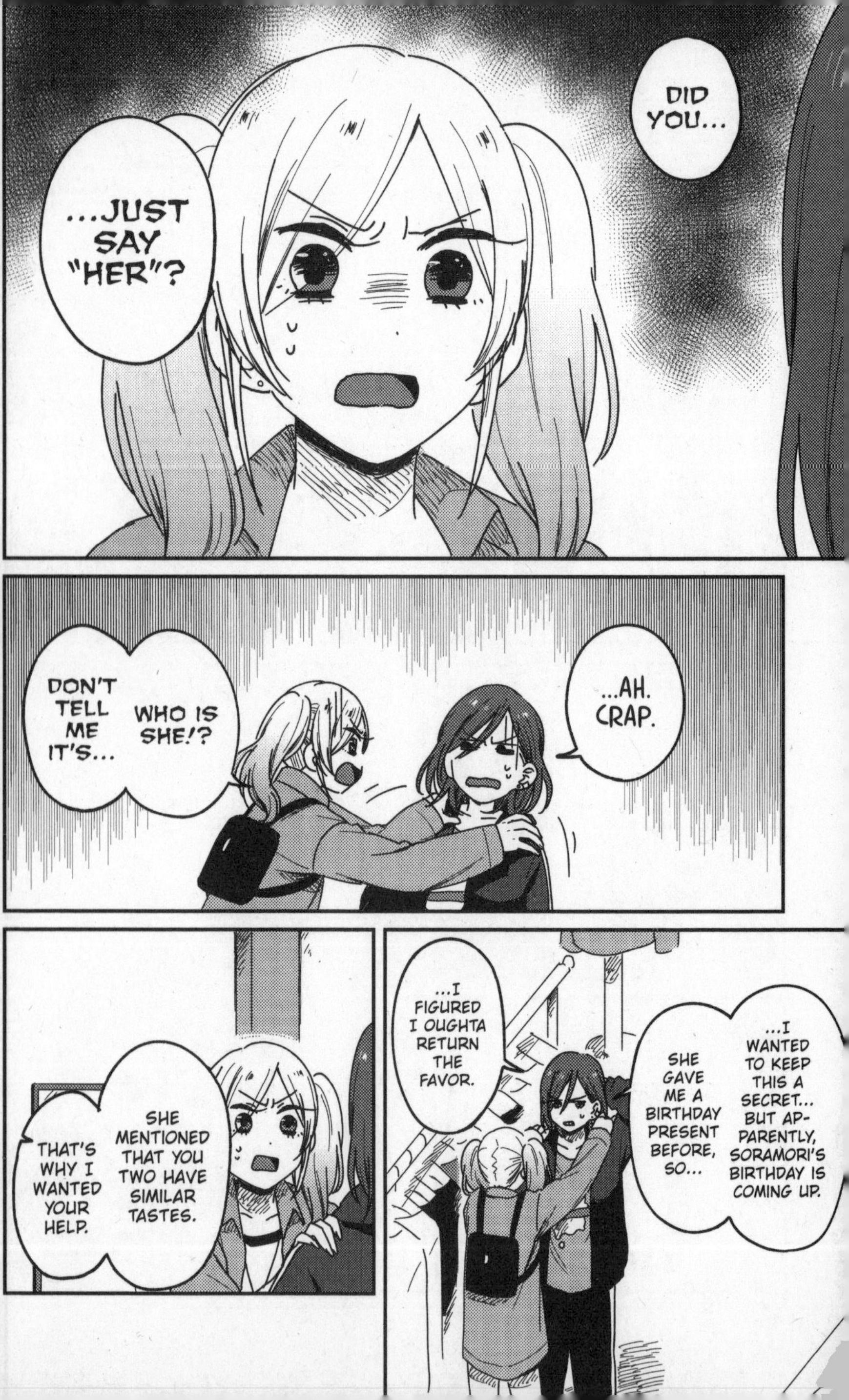
DID YOU...
...JUST SAY "HER"?
...AH. CRAP.
WHO IS SHE!?
DON'T TELL ME IT'S...
...I WANTED TO KEEP THIS A SECRET... BUT AP-PARENTLY, SORAMORI'S BIRTHDAY IS COMING UP.
SHE GAVE ME A BIRTHDAY PRESENT BEFORE, SO...
...I FIGURED I OUGHTA RETURN THE FAVOR.
SHE MENTIONED THAT YOU TWO HAVE SIMILAR TASTES.
THAT'S WHY I WANTED YOUR HELP.

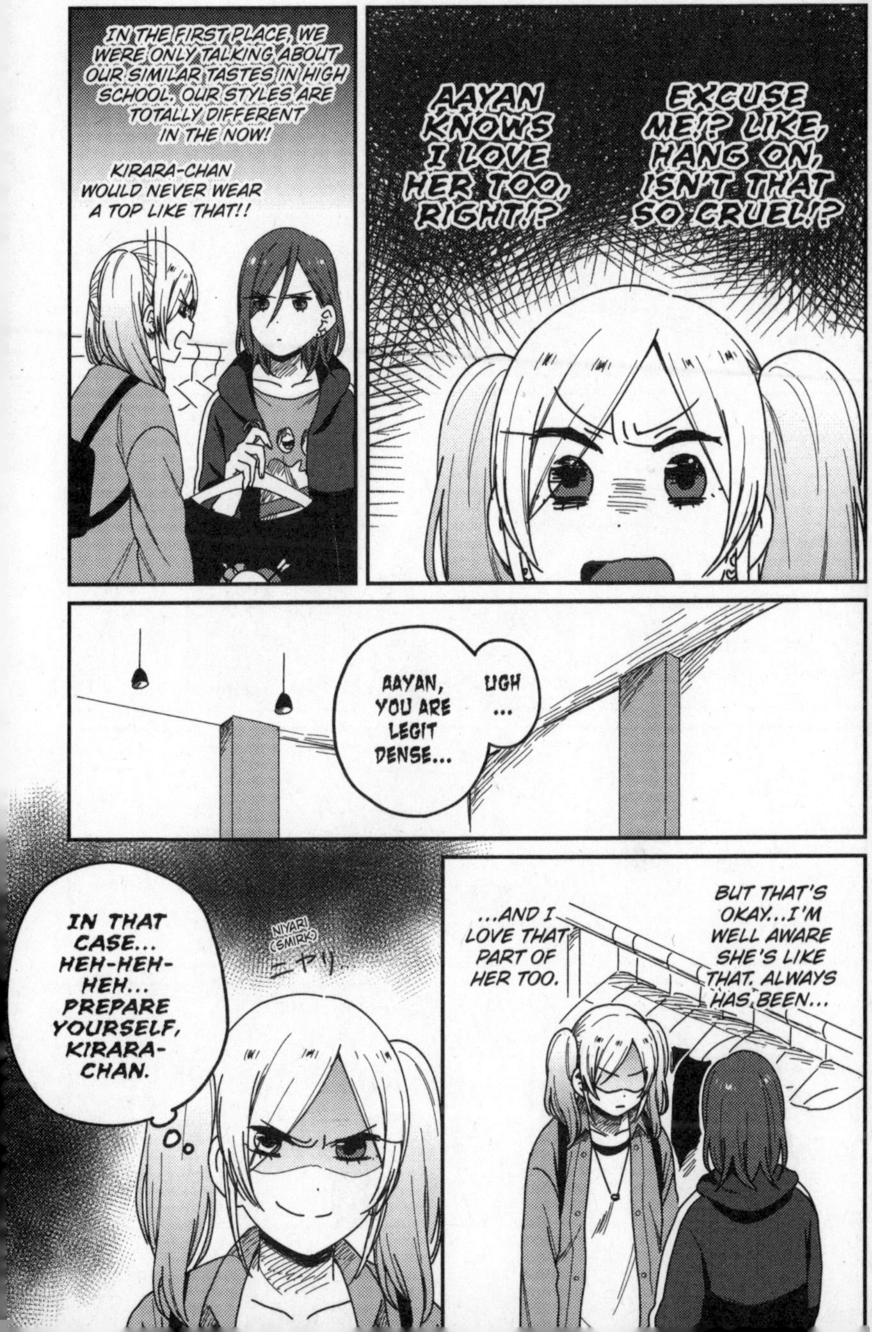
EXCUSE ME!? LIKE, HANG ON, ISN'T THAT SO CRUEL!?
AAYAN KNOWS I LOVE HER TOO, RIGHT!?
IN THE FIRST PLACE, WE WERE ONLY TALKING ABOUT OUR SIMILAR TASTES IN HIGH SCHOOL. OUR STYLES ARE TOTALLY DIFFERENT IN THE NOW!
KIRARA-CHAN WOULD NEVER WEAR A TOP LIKE THAT!!
UGH...
AAYAN, YOU ARE LEGIT DENSE...
BUT THAT'S OKAY...I'M WELL AWARE SHE'S LIKE THAT. ALWAYS HAS BEEN...
...AND I LOVE THAT PART OF HER TOO.
IN THAT CASE... HEH-HEH-HEH... PREPARE YOURSELF, KIRARA-CHAN.
NIYARI (SMIRK)
ニヤリ

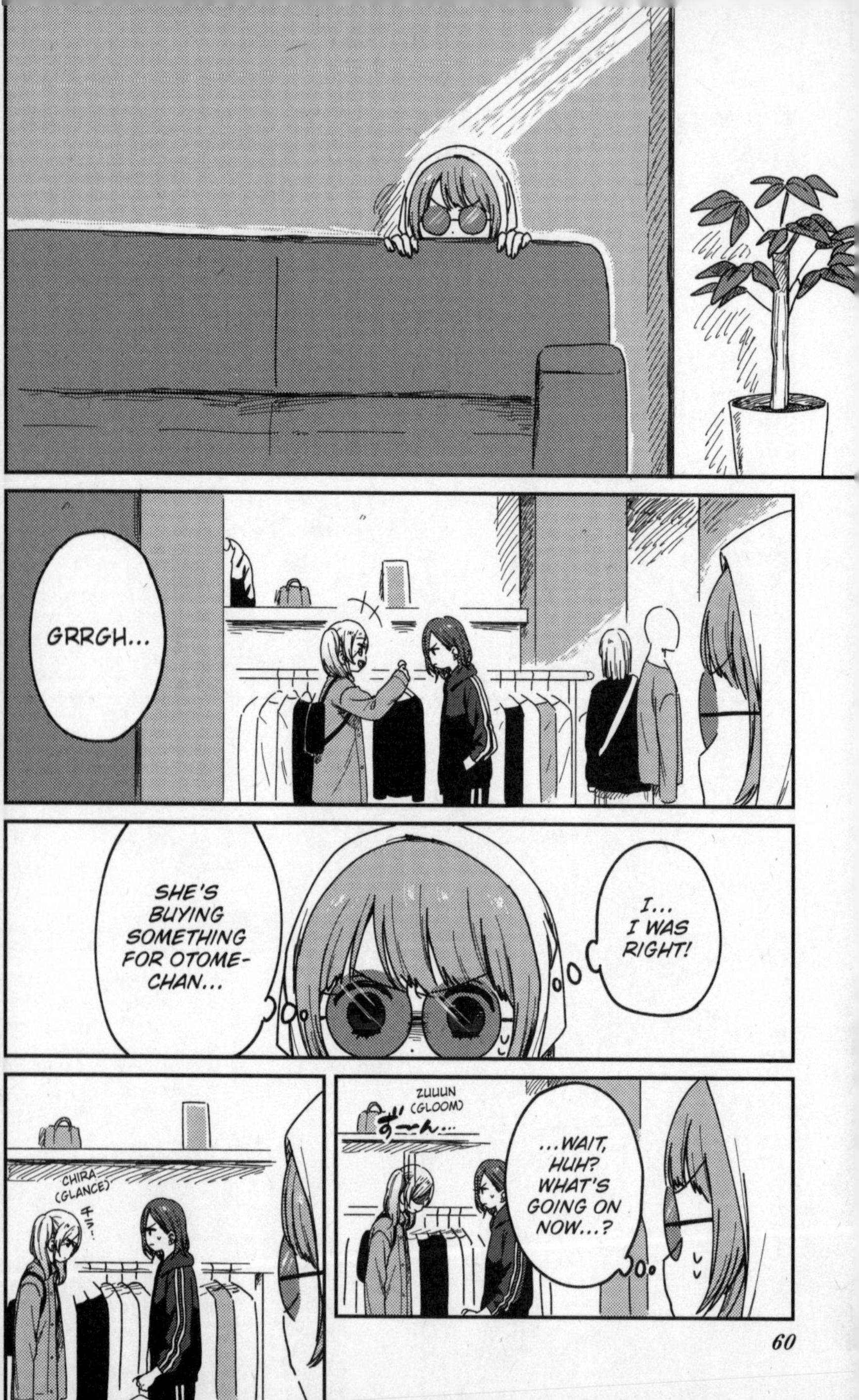
GRRGH...
I... I WAS RIGHT!
SHE'S BUYING SOMETHING FOR OTOME-CHAN...
ZUUUN (GLOOM)
ず〜ん...
...WAIT, HUH? WHAT'S GOING ON NOW...?
CHIRA (GLANCE)
チラ

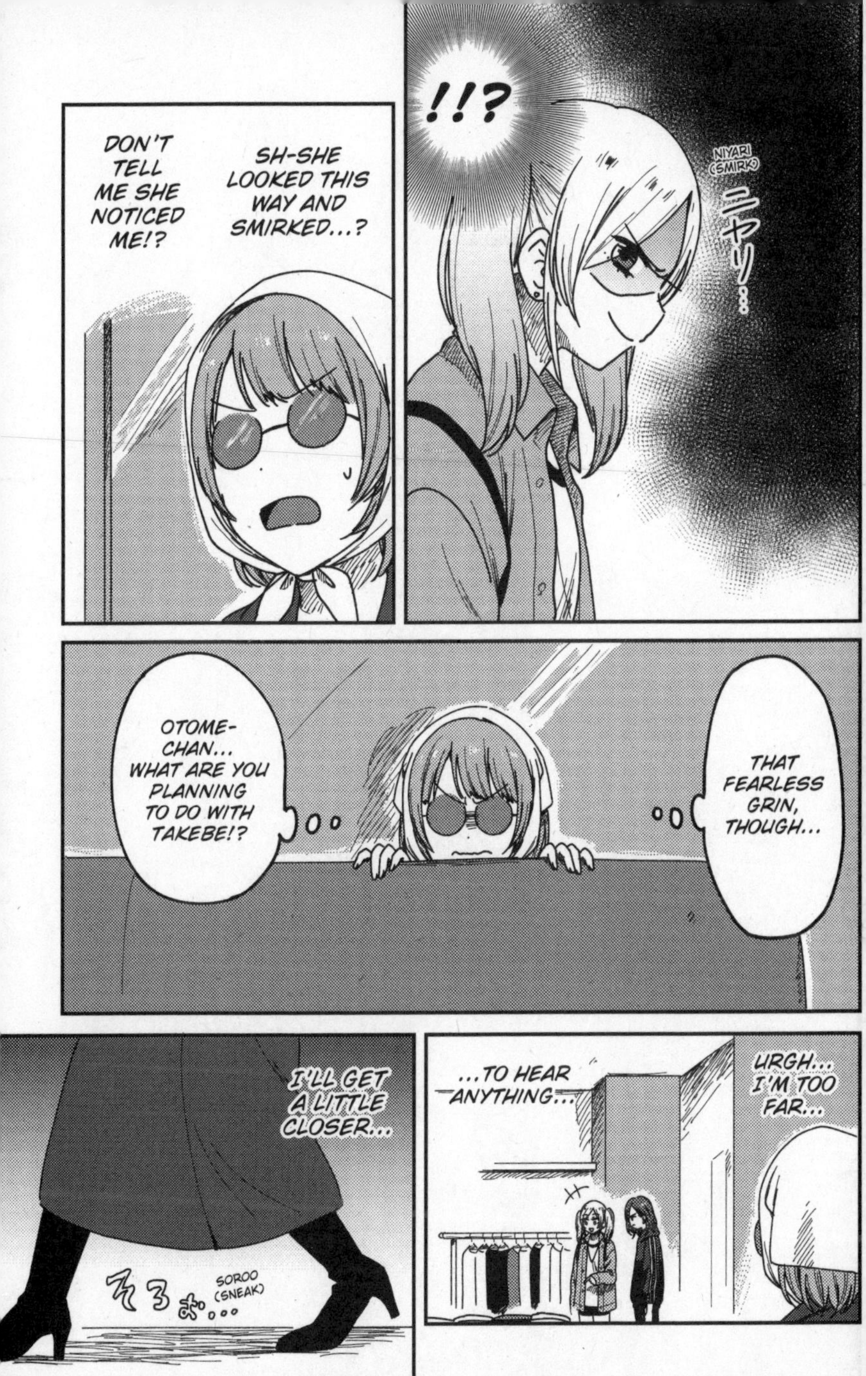
!!?
ニヤリ…
NIYARI (SMIRK)
SH-SHE LOOKED THIS WAY AND SMIRKED...?
DON'T TELL ME SHE NOTICED ME!?
THAT FEARLESS GRIN, THOUGH...
OTOME-CHAN... WHAT ARE YOU PLANNING TO DO WITH TAKEBE!?
URGH... I'M TOO FAR...
...TO HEAR ANYTHING...
I'LL GET A LITTLE CLOSER...
そろぉ…
SOROO (SNEAK)

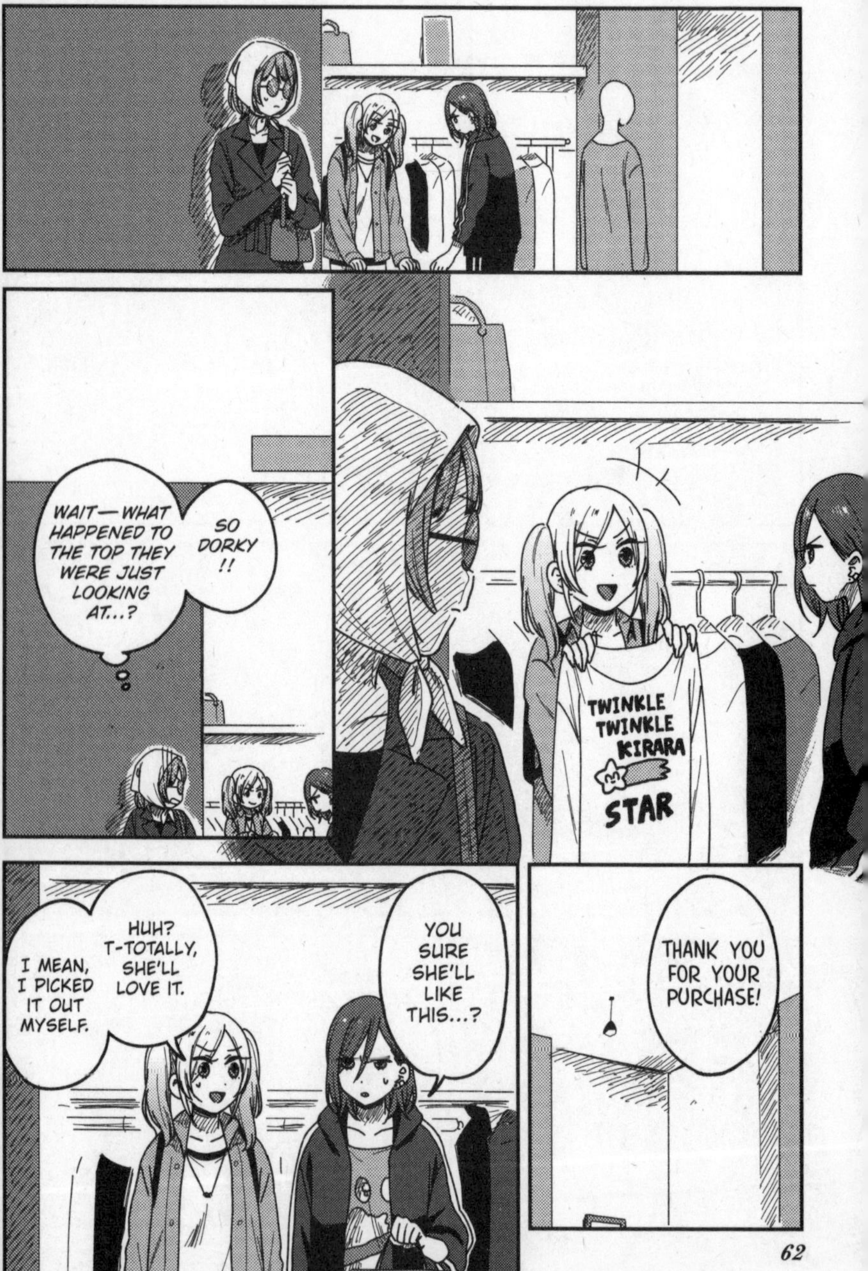
TWINKLE TWINKLE KIRARA STAR
SO DORKY !!
WAIT—WHAT HAPPENED TO THE TOP THEY WERE JUST LOOKING AT...?
THANK YOU FOR YOUR PURCHASE!
YOU SURE SHE'LL LIKE THIS...?
HUH? T-TOTALLY, SHE'LL LOVE IT.
I MEAN, I PICKED IT OUT MYSELF.

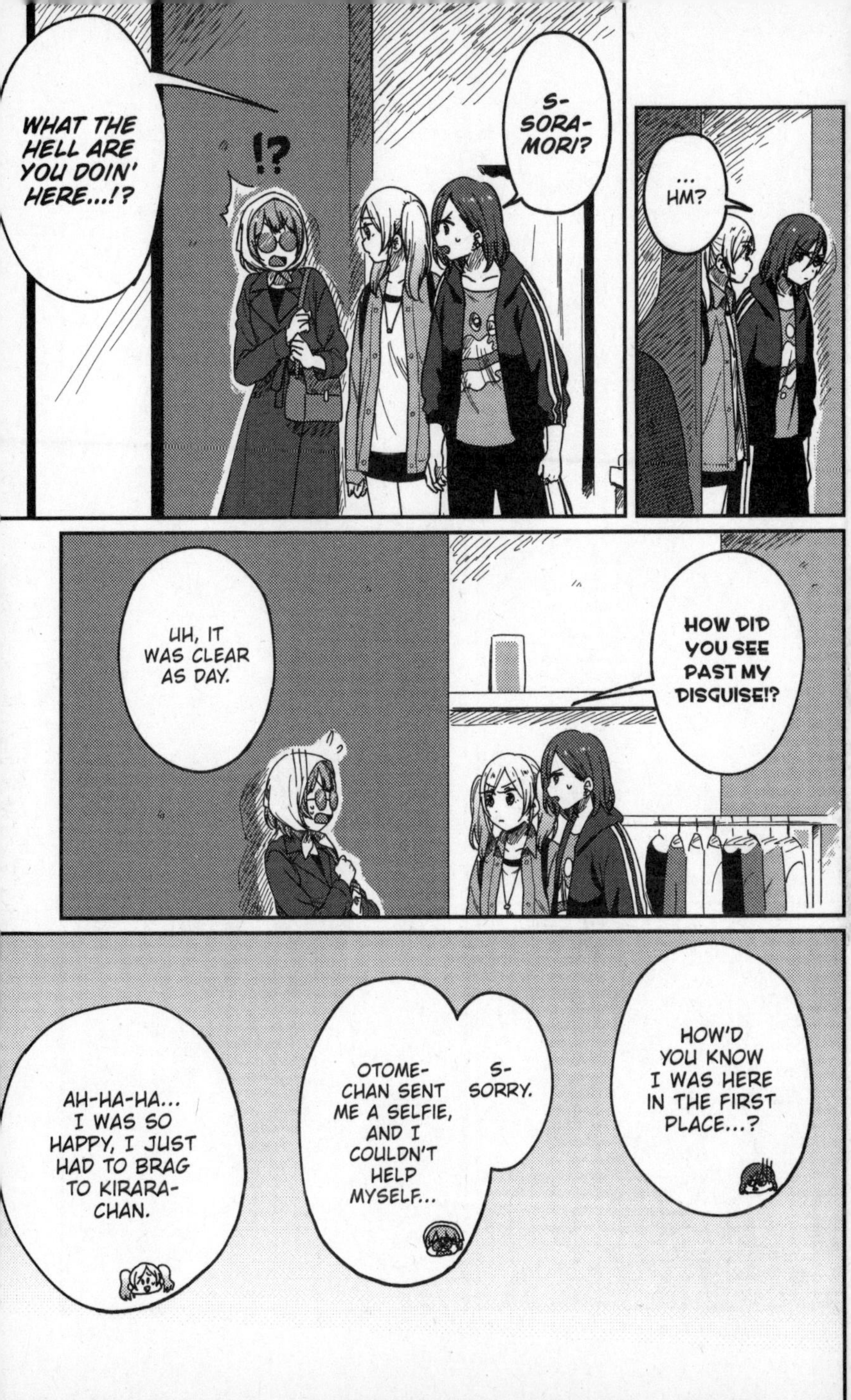

... HM?
S- SORA-MORI?
!?
WHAT THE HELL ARE YOU DOIN' HERE...!?
HOW DID YOU SEE PAST MY DISGUISE!?
UH, IT WAS CLEAR AS DAY.
HOW'D YOU KNOW I WAS HERE IN THE FIRST PLACE...?
S- SORRY.
OTOME-CHAN SENT ME A SELFIE, AND I COULDN'T HELP MYSELF...
AH-HA-HA... I WAS SO HAPPY, I JUST HAD TO BRAG TO KIRARA-CHAN.

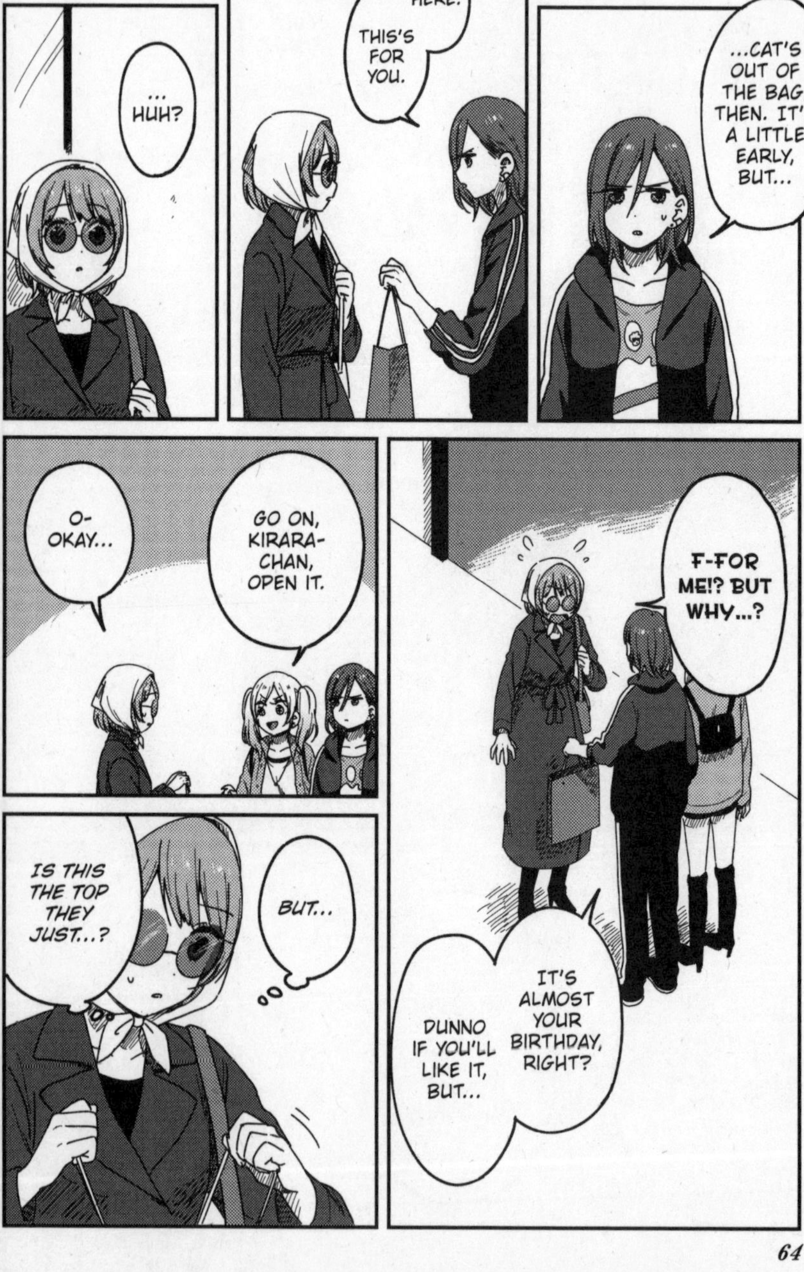
...CAT'S OUT OF THE BAG, THEN. IT'S A LITTLE EARLY, BUT...
HERE.
THIS'S FOR YOU.
... HUH?
F-FOR ME!? BUT WHY...?
IT'S ALMOST YOUR BIRTHDAY, RIGHT?
DUNNO IF YOU'LL LIKE IT, BUT...
GO ON, KIRARA-CHAN, OPEN IT.
O-OKAY...
BUT...
IS THIS THE TOP THEY JUST...?

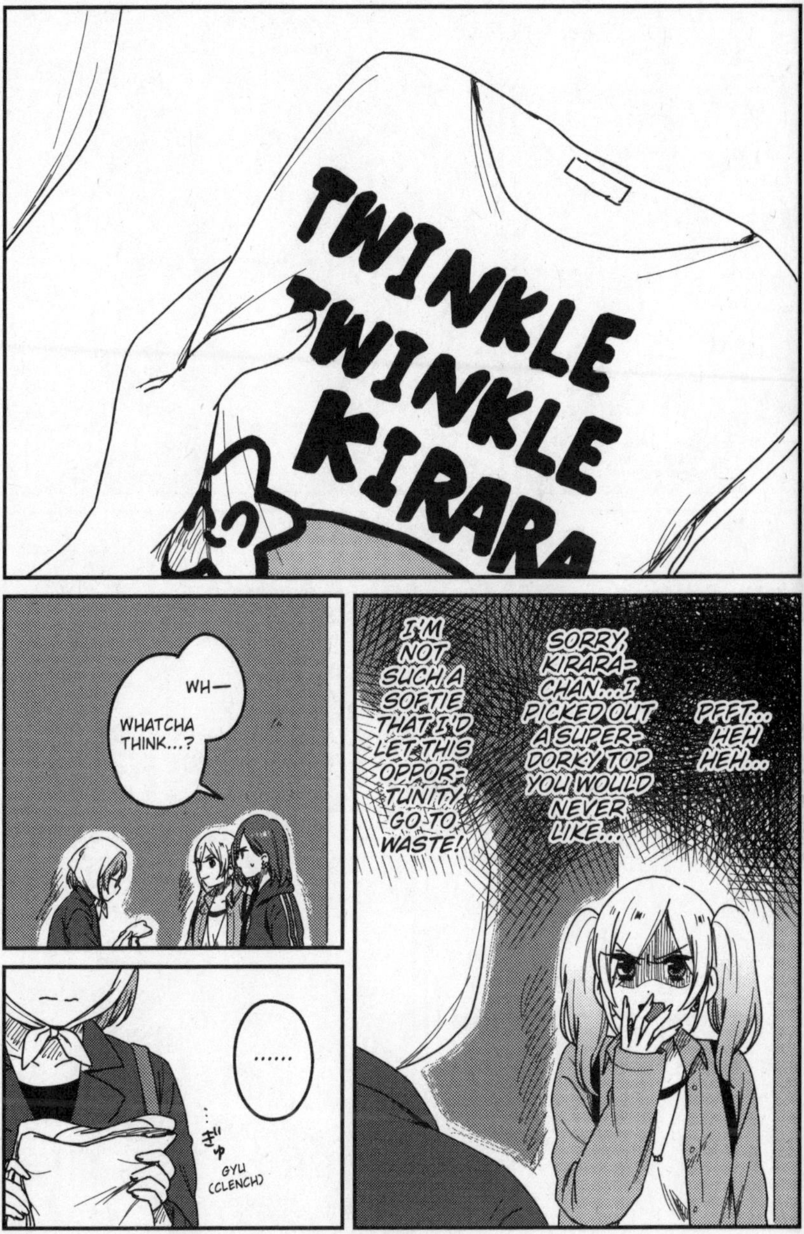
TWINKLE TWINKLE KIRARA
PFFT... HEH HEH...
SORRY, KIRARA-CHAN...I PICKED OUT A SUPER-DORKY TOP YOU WOULD NEVER LIKE...
I'M NOT SUCH A SOFTIE THAT I'D LET THIS OPPORTUNITY GO TO WASTE!
WH— WHATCHA THINK...?
......
...ぎゅ
GYU (CLENCH)

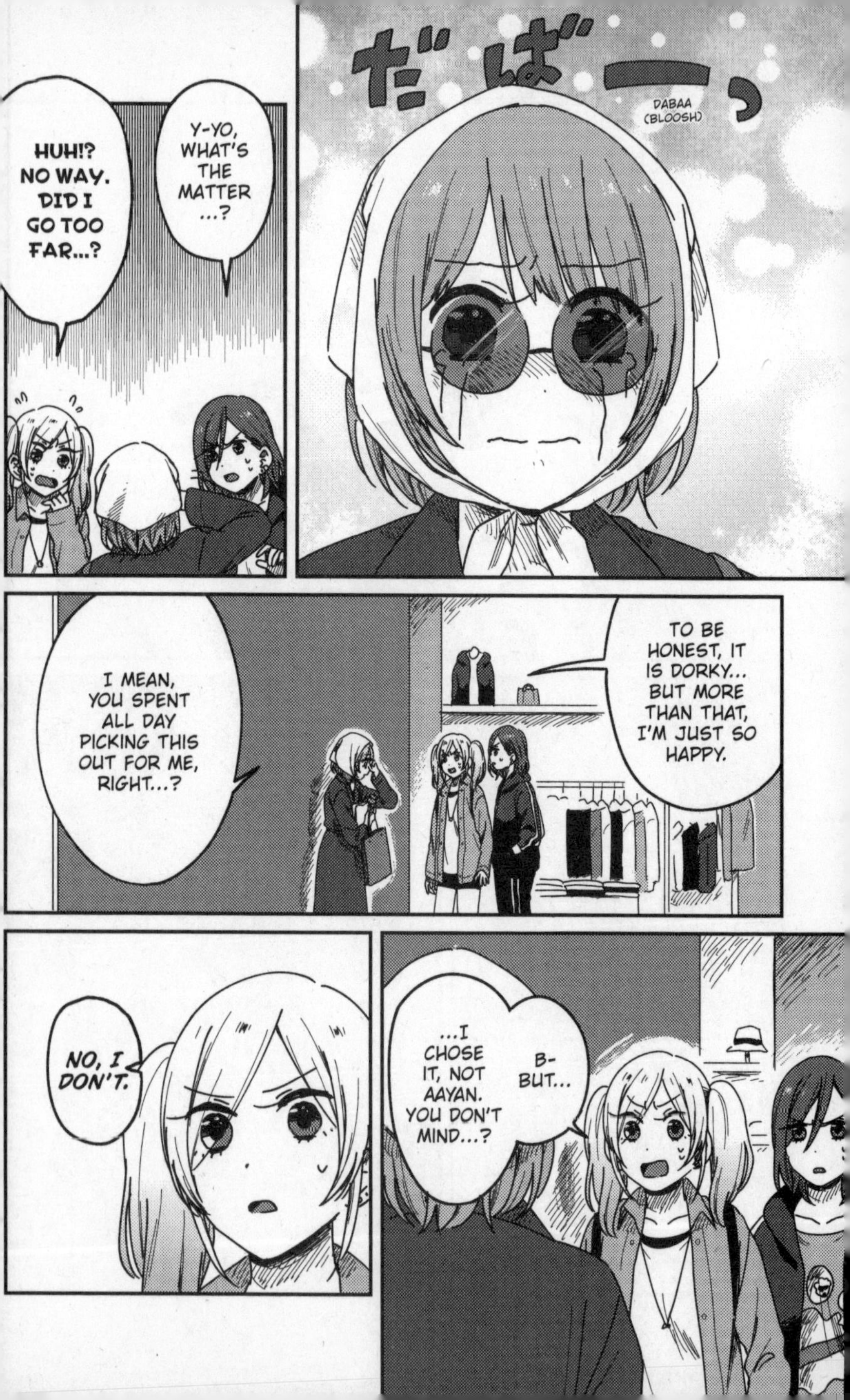
だばーっ
DABAA (BLOOSH)
Y-YO, WHAT'S THE MATTER ...?
HUH!? NO WAY. DID I GO TOO FAR...?
TO BE HONEST, IT IS DORKY... BUT MORE THAN THAT, I'M JUST SO HAPPY.
I MEAN, YOU SPENT ALL DAY PICKING THIS OUT FOR ME, RIGHT...?
B-BUT...
...I CHOSE IT, NOT AAYAN. YOU DON'T MIND...?
NO, I DON'T.

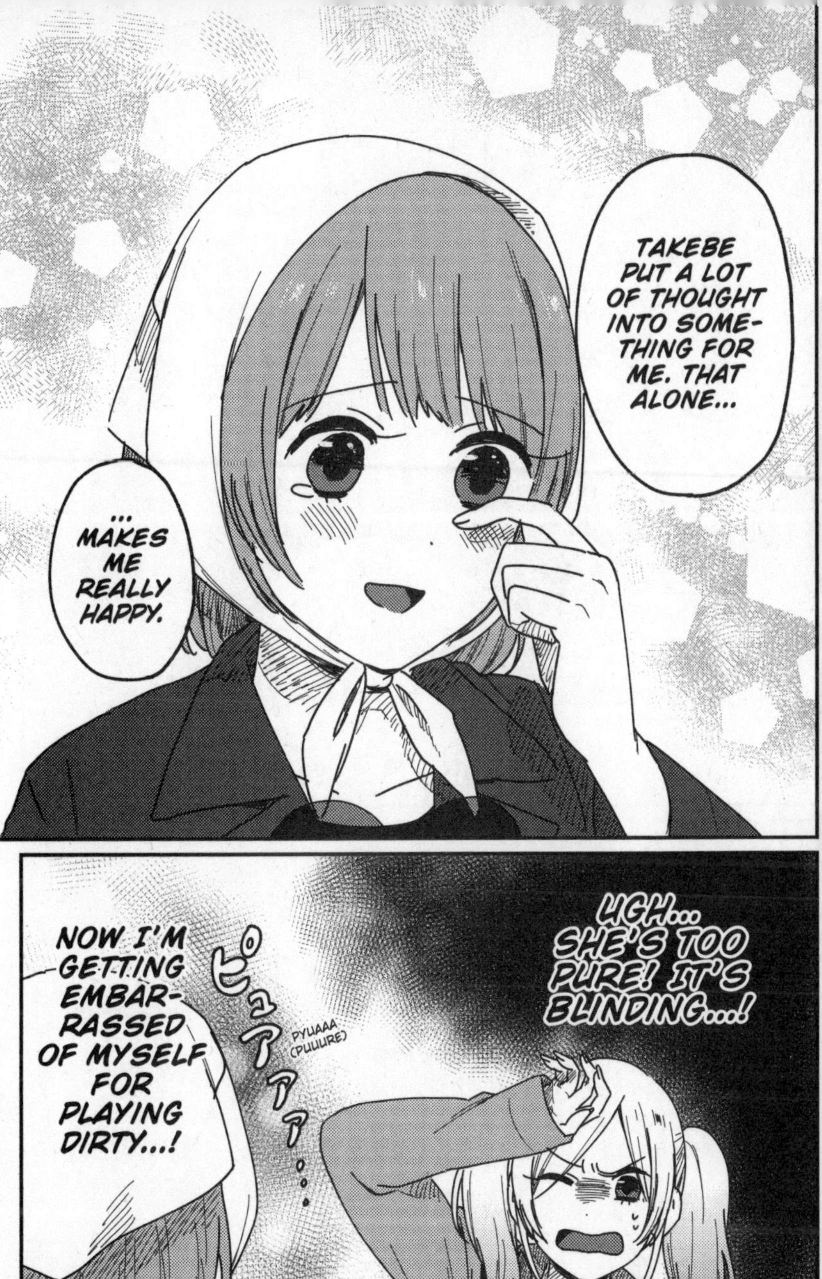
TAKEBE PUT A LOT OF THOUGHT INTO SOME-THING FOR ME. THAT ALONE...
...MAKES ME REALLY HAPPY.
UGH... SHE'S TOO PURE! IT'S BLINDING...!
ピュアァァ...
PYUAAA (PUUURE)
NOW I'M GETTING EMBAR-RASSED OF MYSELF FOR PLAYING DIRTY...!

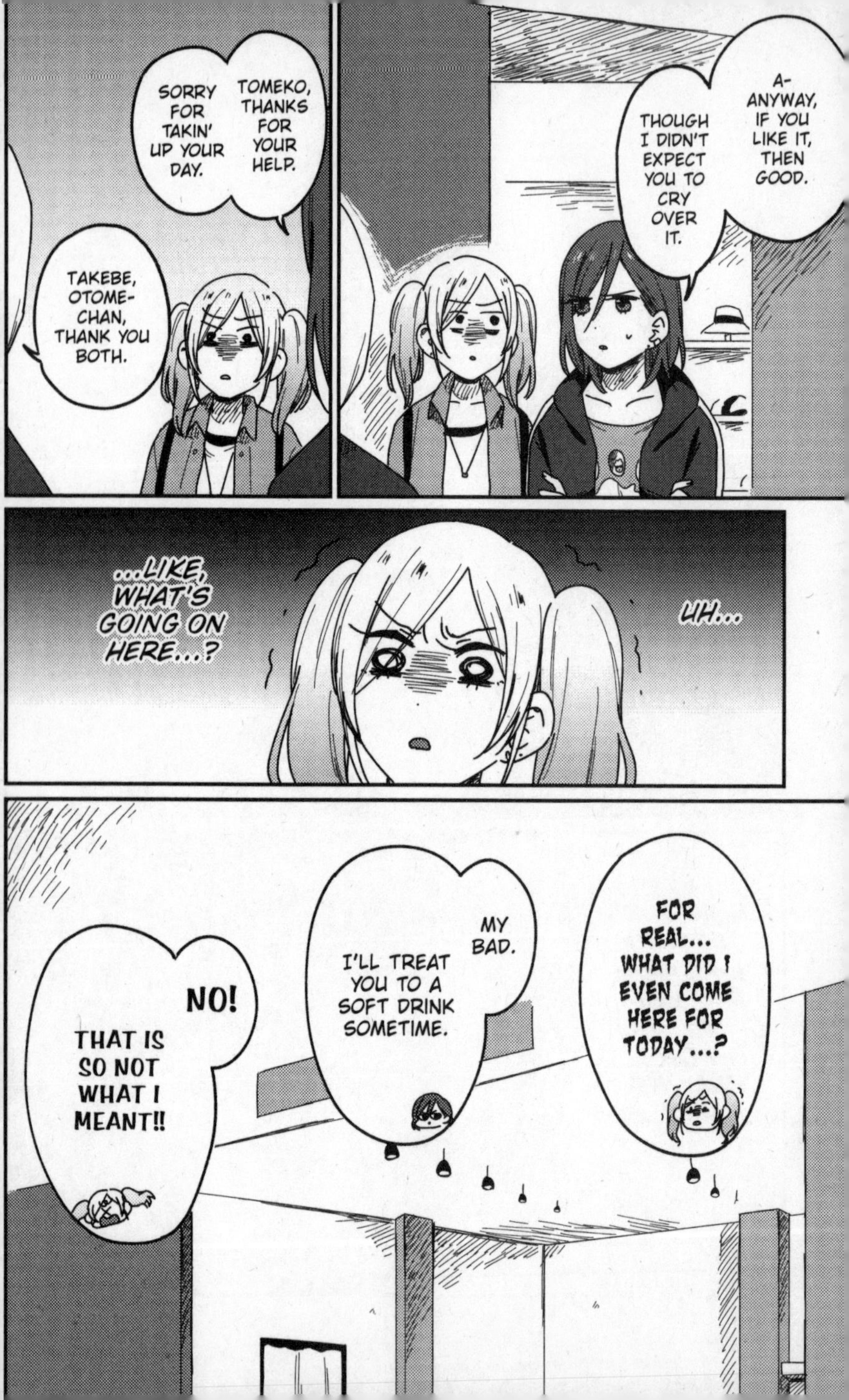
A-ANYWAY, IF YOU LIKE IT, THEN GOOD.
THOUGH I DIDN'T EXPECT YOU TO CRY OVER IT.
TOMEKO, THANKS FOR YOUR HELP.
SORRY FOR TAKIN' UP YOUR DAY.
TAKEBE, OTOME-CHAN, THANK YOU BOTH.
UH...
...LIKE, WHAT'S GOING ON HERE...?
FOR REAL... WHAT DID I EVEN COME HERE FOR TODAY...?
MY BAD.
I'LL TREAT YOU TO A SOFT DRINK SOMETIME.
NO!
THAT IS SO NOT WHAT I MEANT!!

Catch These Hands!

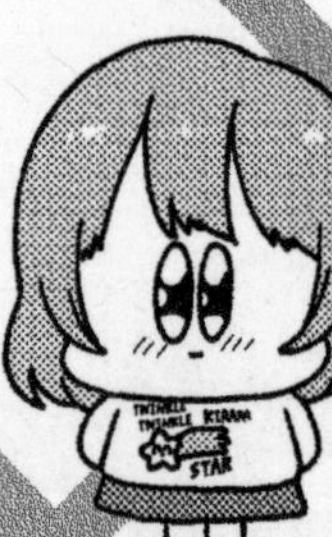
TWINKLE TWINKLE KIRAN STAR

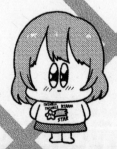

Catch These Hands!

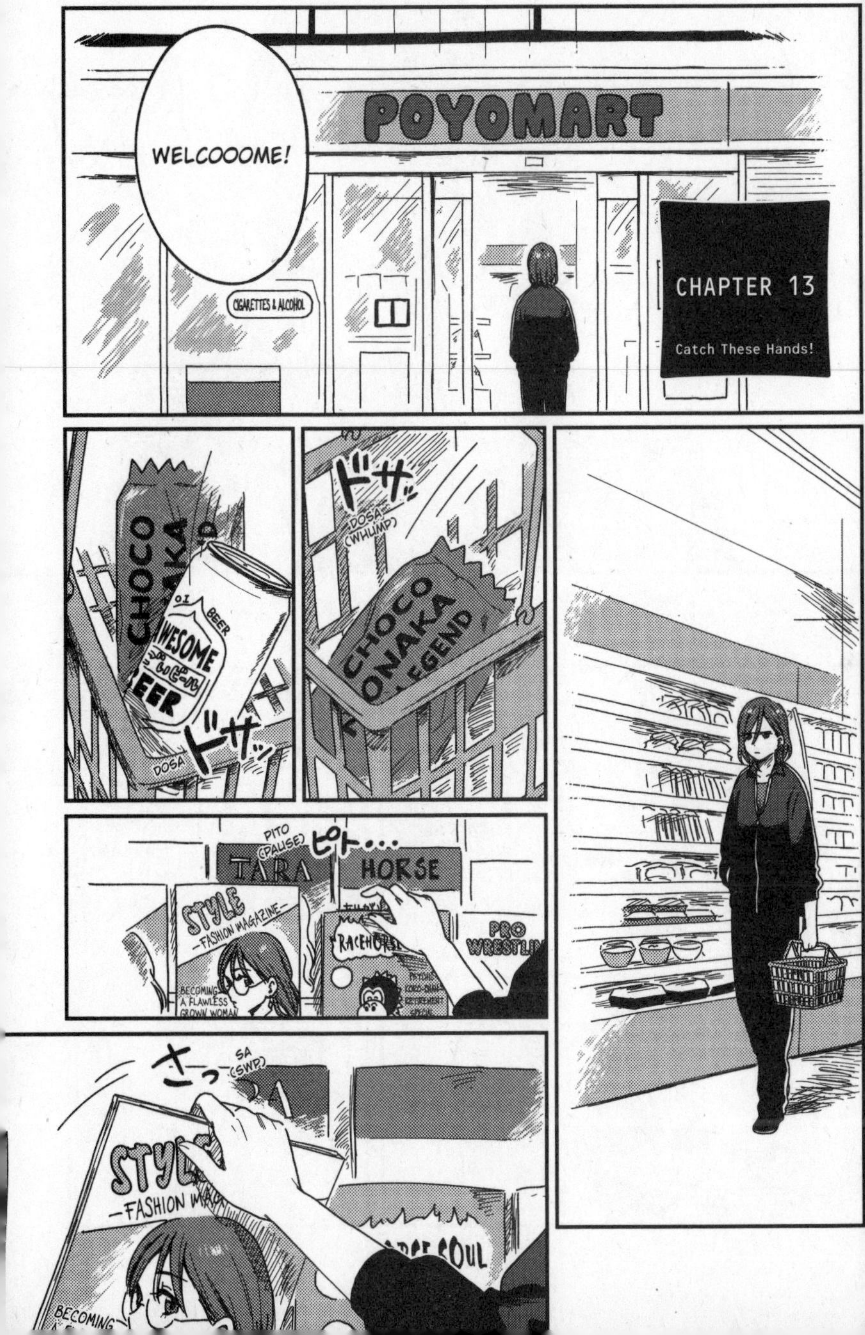
CHAPTER 13
Catch These Hands!
POYOMART
WELCOOOME!
CIGARETTES & ALCOHOL
ドザッ
DOSA (WHUMP)
CHOCO ONAKA LEGEND
CHOCO ONAKA
OI BEER
AWESOME BEER
ドサッ
DOSA
ピト…
PITO (PAUSE)
TARA
HORSE
STYLE
FASHION MAGAZINE
BECOMING A FLAWLESS GROWN WOMAN
RACEHORSE
PRO WRESTLIN
PSYCHIC KOKO-CHAN RETIREMENT SPECIAL
さっ
SA (SWP)
STYL
FASHION MA
BECOMING

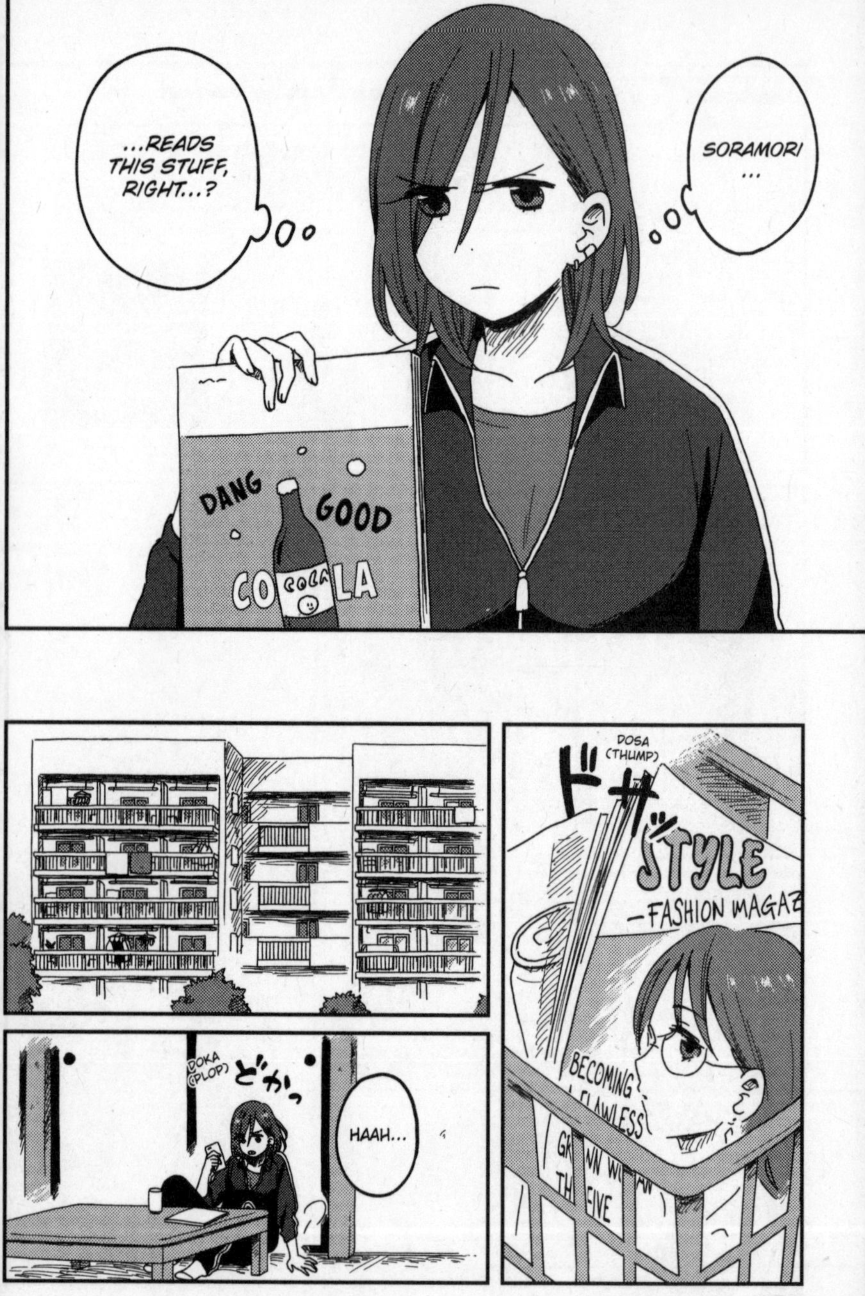
SORAMORI ...
...READS THIS STUFF, RIGHT...?
DANG GOOD
COCOLA
COLA
ドサ
DOSA (THUMP)
STYLE
—FASHION MAGAZ
BECOMING
FLAWLESS
THE FIVE
どかっ
DOKA (PLOP)
HAAH...

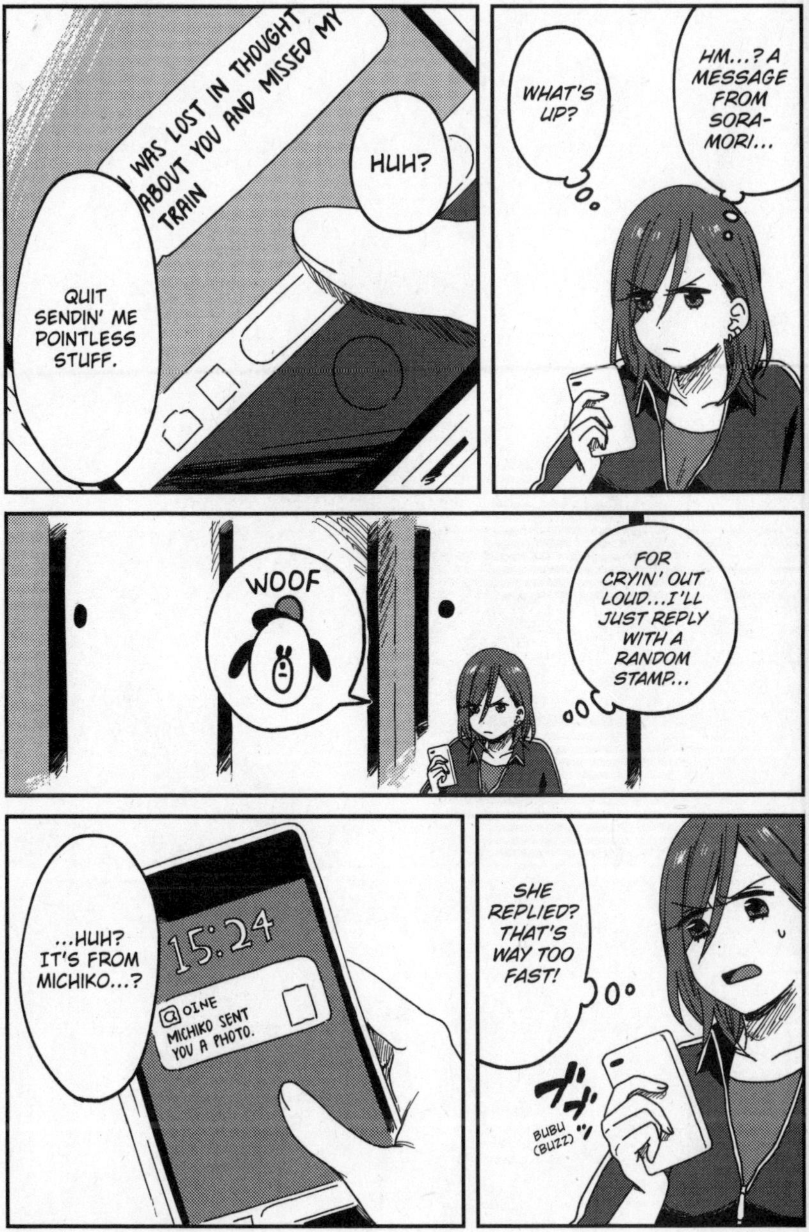

HM...? A MESSAGE FROM SORA-MORI...
WHAT'S UP?
WAS LOST IN THOUGHT ABOUT YOU AND MISSED MY TRAIN
HUH?
QUIT SENDIN' ME POINTLESS STUFF.
FOR CRYIN' OUT LOUD...I'LL JUST REPLY WITH A RANDOM STAMP...
WOOF
SHE REPLIED? THAT'S WAY TOO FAST!
BUBU (BUZZ)
15:24
OINE
MICHIKO SENT YOU A PHOTO.
...HUH? IT'S FROM MICHIKO...?

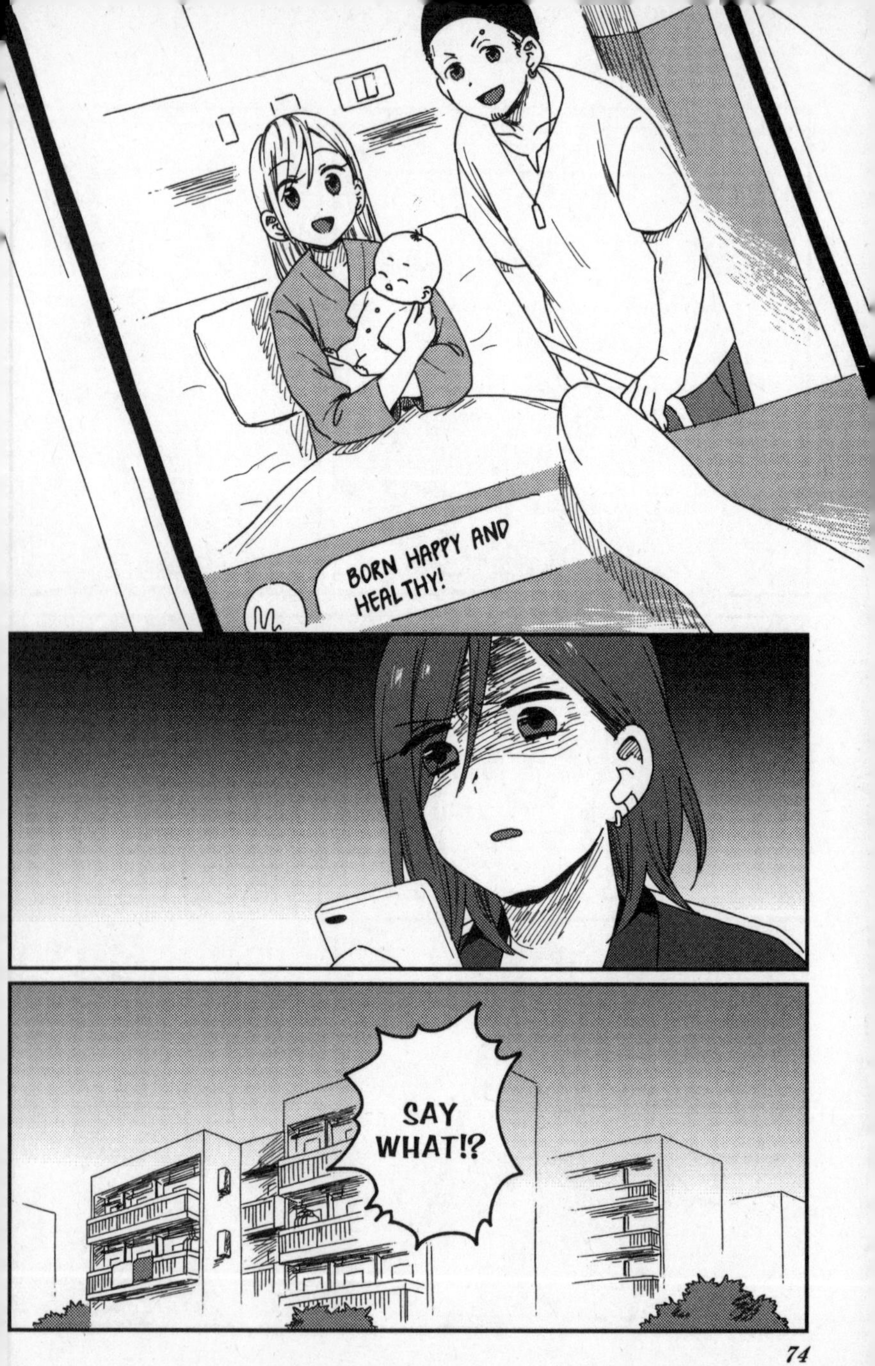
BORN HAPPY AND HEALTHY!
SAY WHAT!?

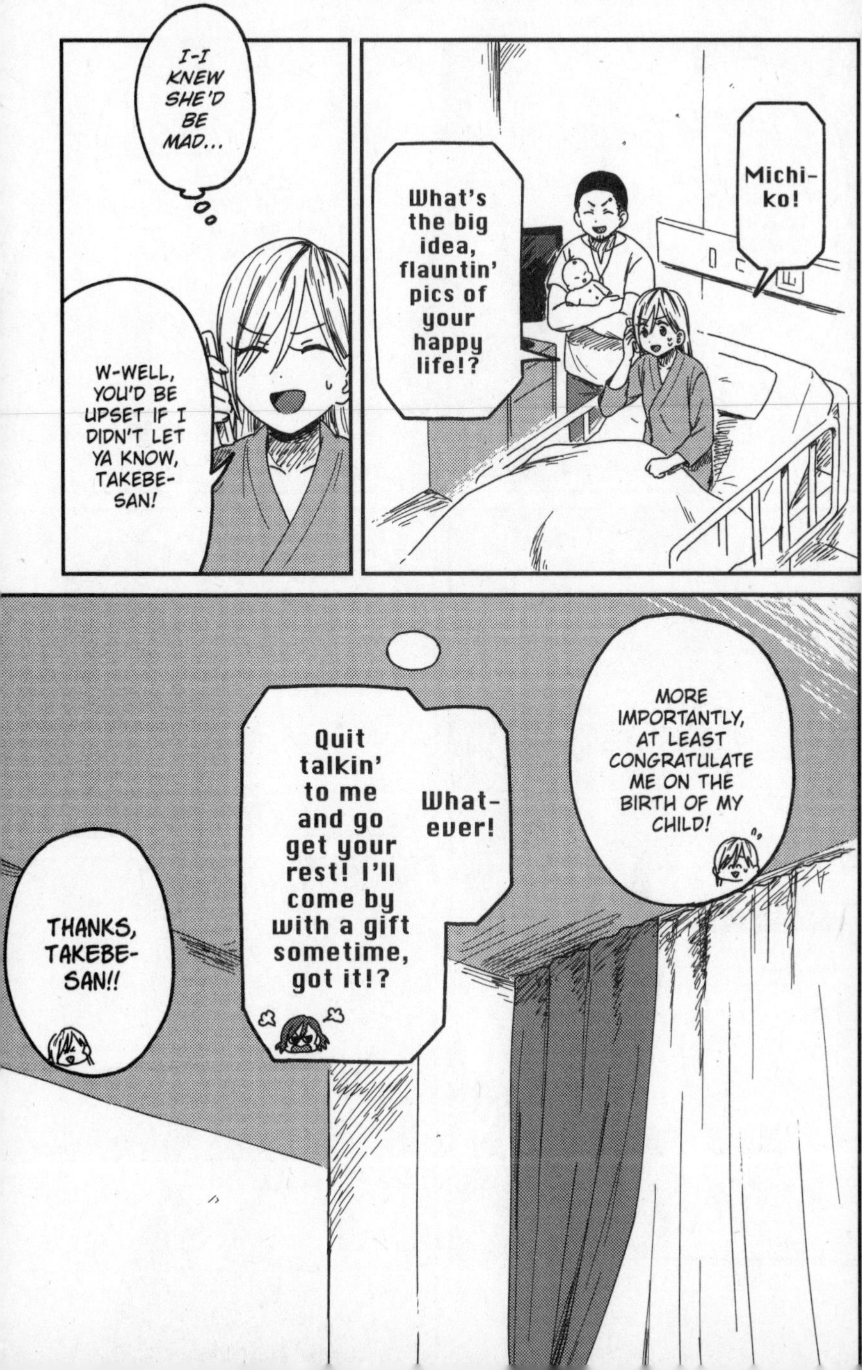
Michi-ko!
What's the big idea, flauntin' pics of your happy life!?
I-I KNEW SHE'D BE MAD...
W-WELL, YOU'D BE UPSET IF I DIDN'T LET YA KNOW, TAKEBE-SAN!
MORE IMPORTANTLY, AT LEAST CONGRATULATE ME ON THE BIRTH OF MY CHILD!
What-ever!
Quit talkin' to me and go get your rest! I'll come by with a gift sometime, got it!?
THANKS, TAKEBE-SAN!!

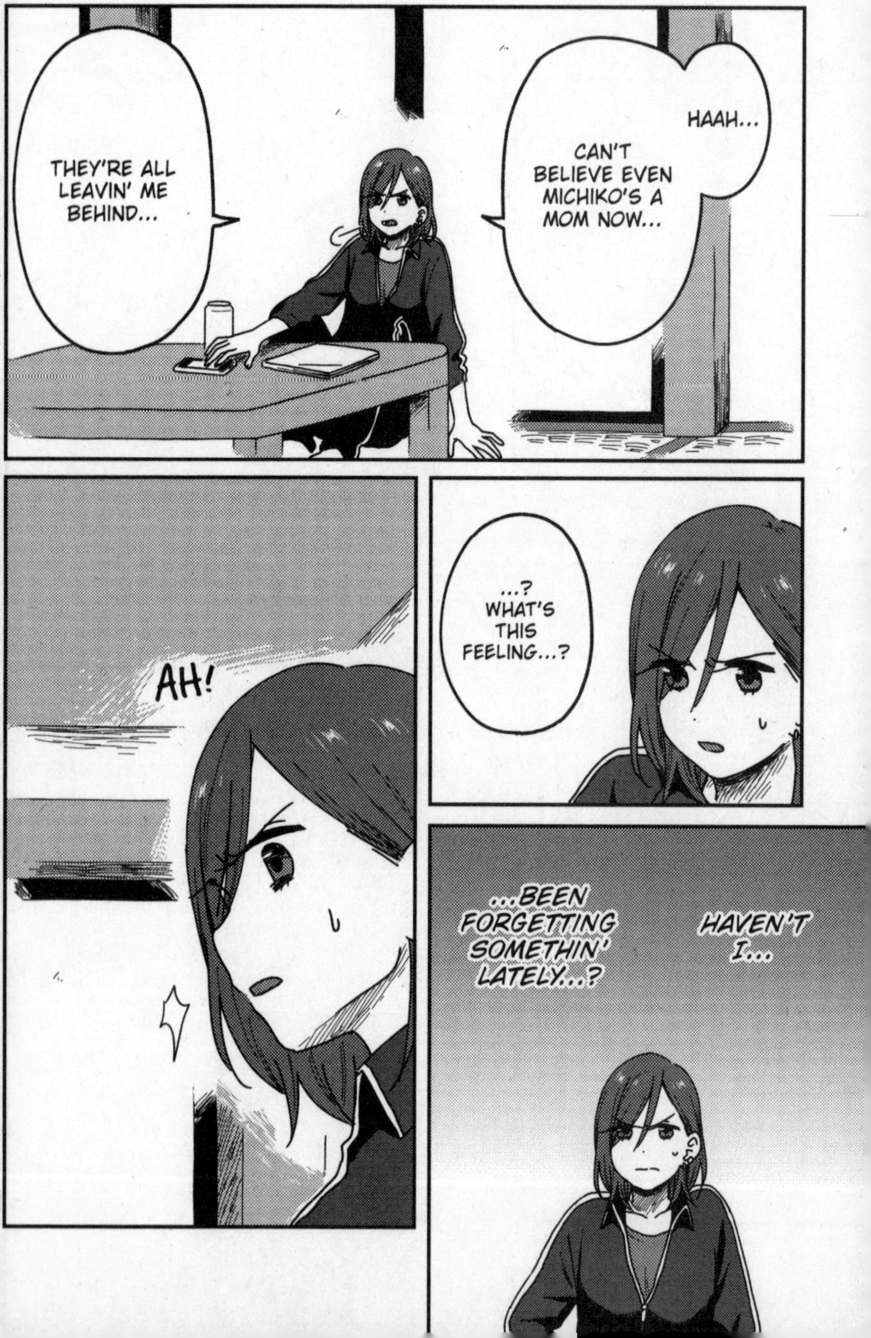
HAAH...
CAN'T BELIEVE EVEN MICHIKO'S A MOM NOW...
THEY'RE ALL LEAVIN' ME BEHIND...
...? WHAT'S THIS FEELING...?
HAVEN'T I...
...BEEN FORGETTING SOMETHIN' LATELY...?
AH!

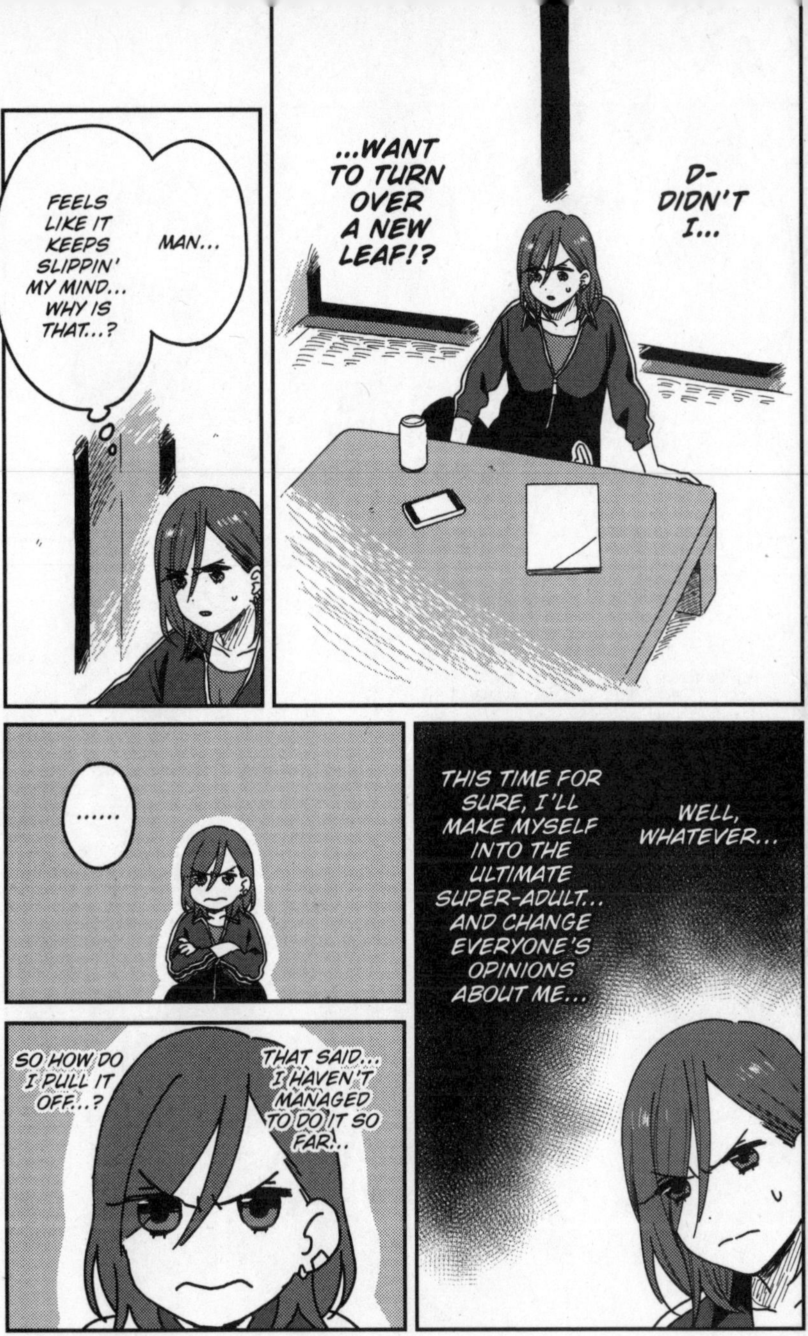
D-DIDN'T I...
...WANT TO TURN OVER A NEW LEAF!?
MAN...
FEELS LIKE IT KEEPS SLIPPIN' MY MIND... WHY IS THAT...?
WELL, WHATEVER...
THIS TIME FOR SURE, I'LL MAKE MYSELF INTO THE ULTIMATE SUPER-ADULT... AND CHANGE EVERYONE'S OPINIONS ABOUT ME...
......
THAT SAID... I HAVEN'T MANAGED TO DO IT SO FAR...
SO HOW DO I PULL IT OFF...?

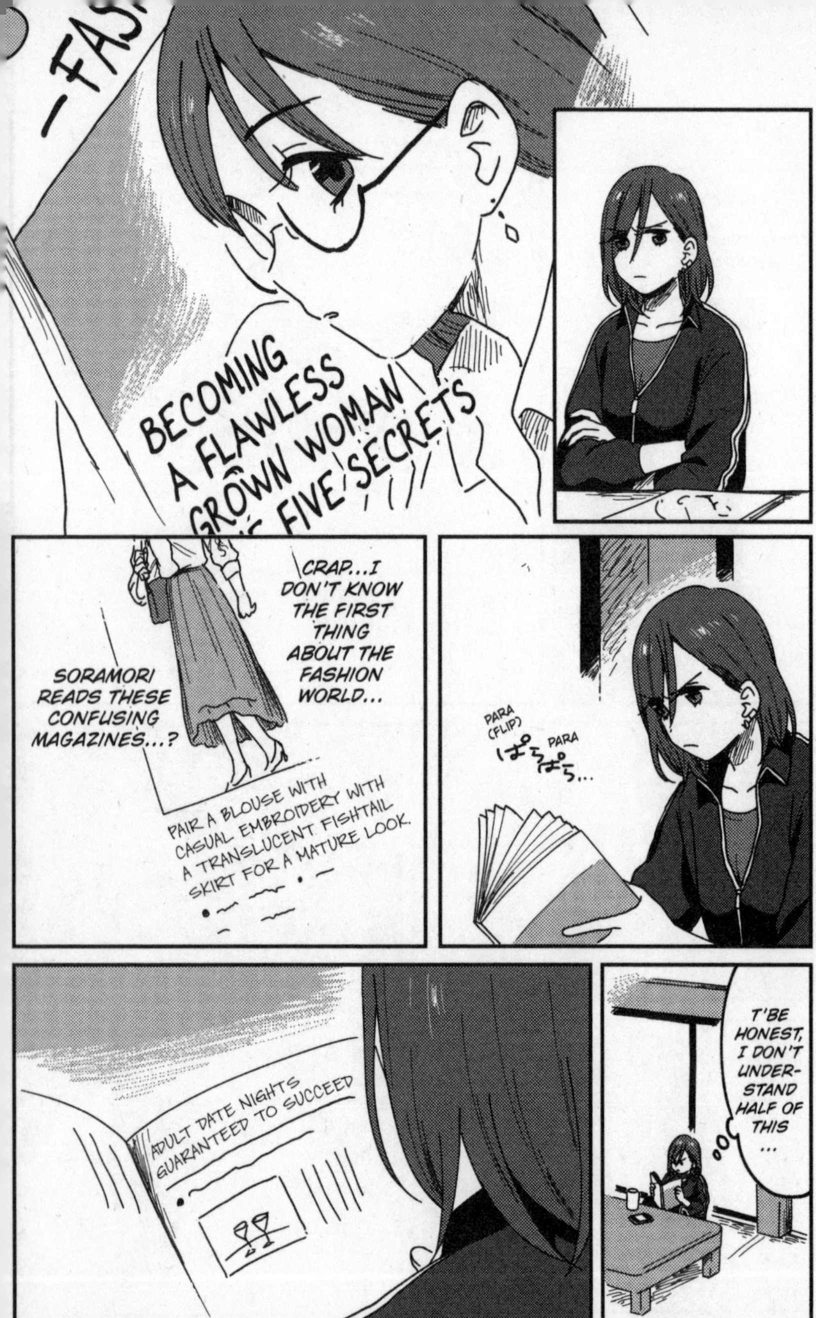

—FAS
BECOMING A FLAWLESS GROWN WOMAN
FIVE SECRETS
PARA (FLIP) ぱらぱら… PARA
CRAP…I DON'T KNOW THE FIRST THING ABOUT THE FASHION WORLD…
SORAMORI READS THESE CONFUSING MAGAZINES…?
PAIR A BLOUSE WITH CASUAL EMBROIDERY WITH A TRANSLUCENT FISHTAIL SKIRT FOR A MATURE LOOK.
T'BE HONEST, I DON'T UNDER-STAND HALF OF THIS…
ADULT DATE NIGHTS GUARANTEED TO SUCCEED

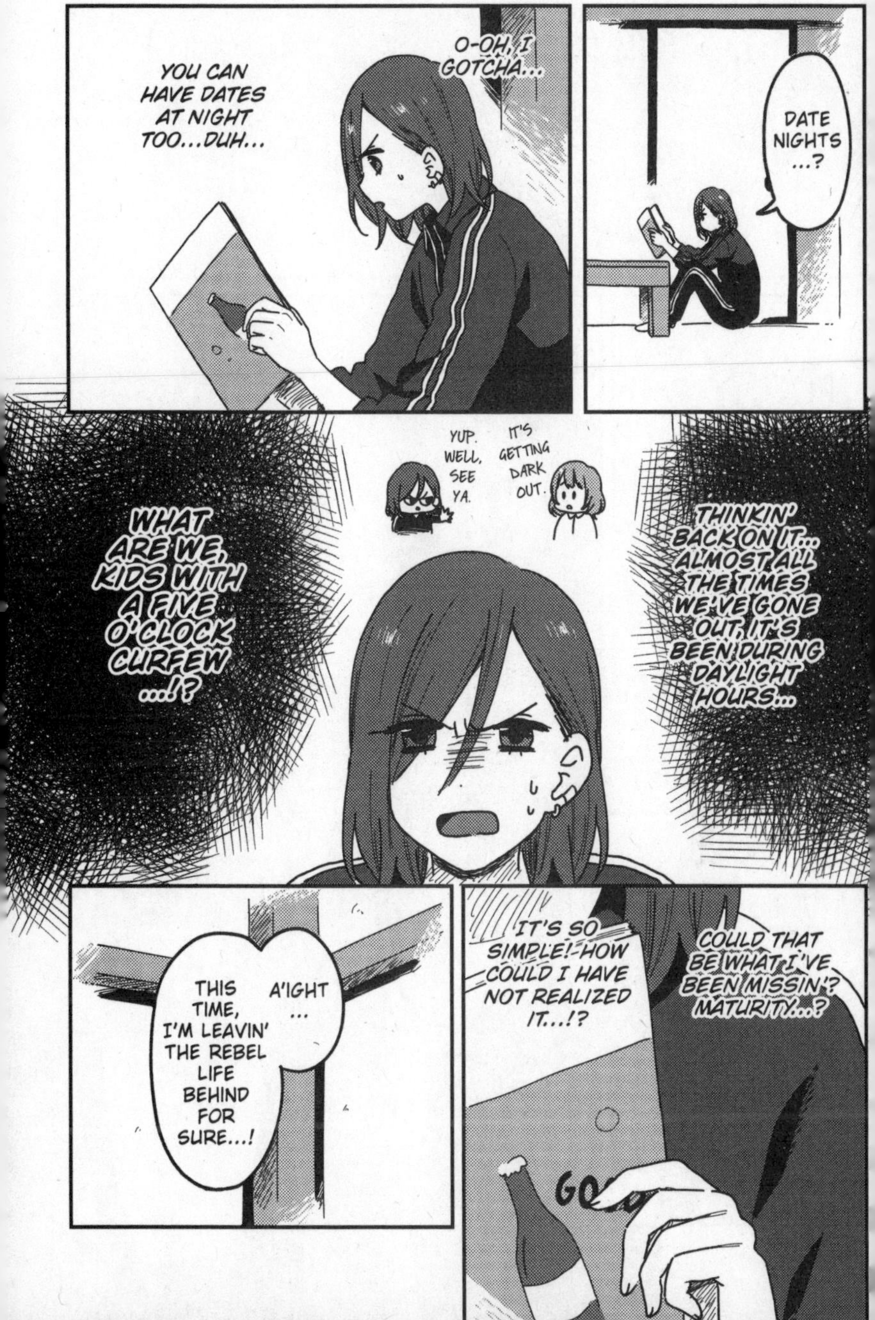
DATE NIGHTS ...?
O-OH, I GOTCHA...
YOU CAN HAVE DATES AT NIGHT TOO...DUH...
THINKIN' BACK ON IT... ALMOST ALL THE TIMES WE'VE GONE OUT, IT'S BEEN DURING DAYLIGHT HOURS...
IT'S GETTING DARK OUT.
YUP. WELL, SEE YA.
WHAT ARE WE, KIDS WITH A FIVE O'CLOCK CURFEW ...!?
COULD THAT BE WHAT I'VE BEEN MISSIN'? MATURITY...?
IT'S SO SIMPLE! HOW COULD I HAVE NOT REALIZED IT...!?
A'IGHT ...
THIS TIME, I'M LEAVIN' THE REBEL LIFE BEHIND FOR SURE...!

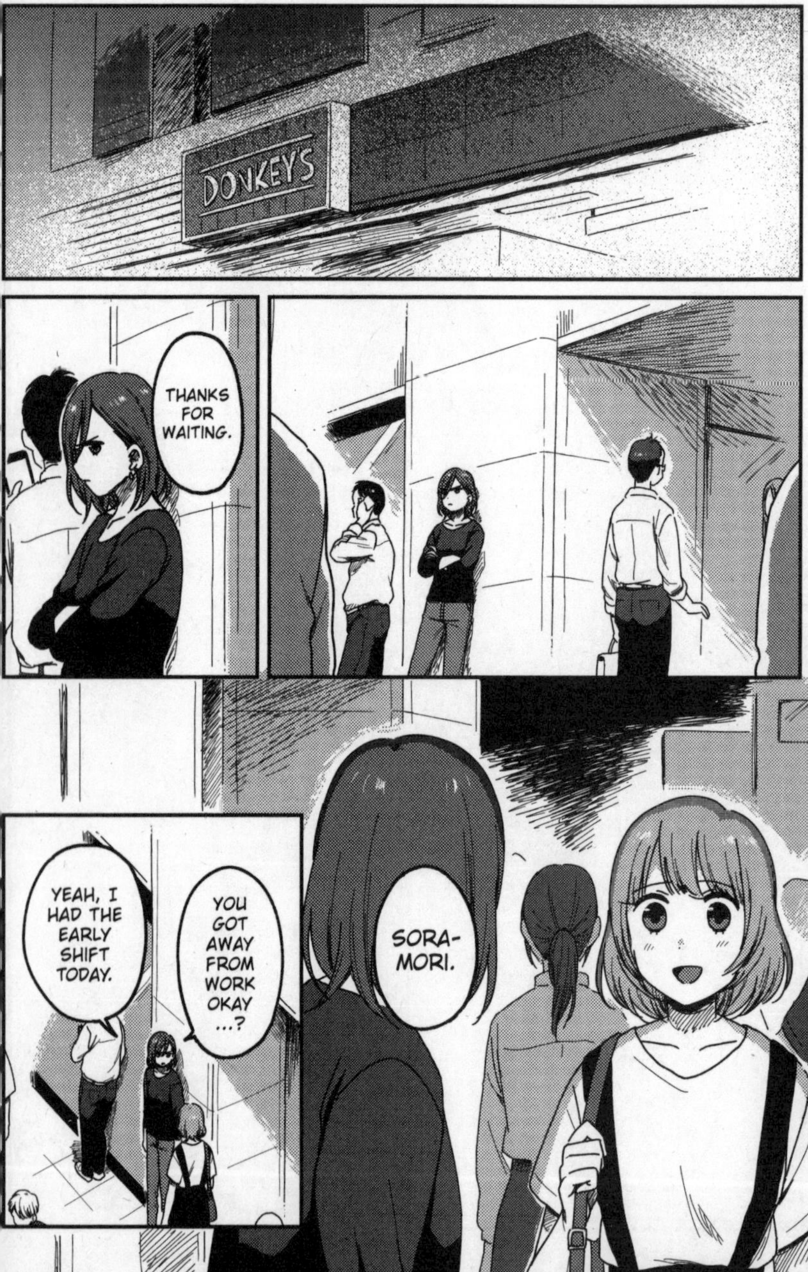
DONKEY'S
THANKS FOR WAITING.
SORA-MORI.
YOU GOT AWAY FROM WORK OKAY ...?
YEAH, I HAD THE EARLY SHIFT TODAY.

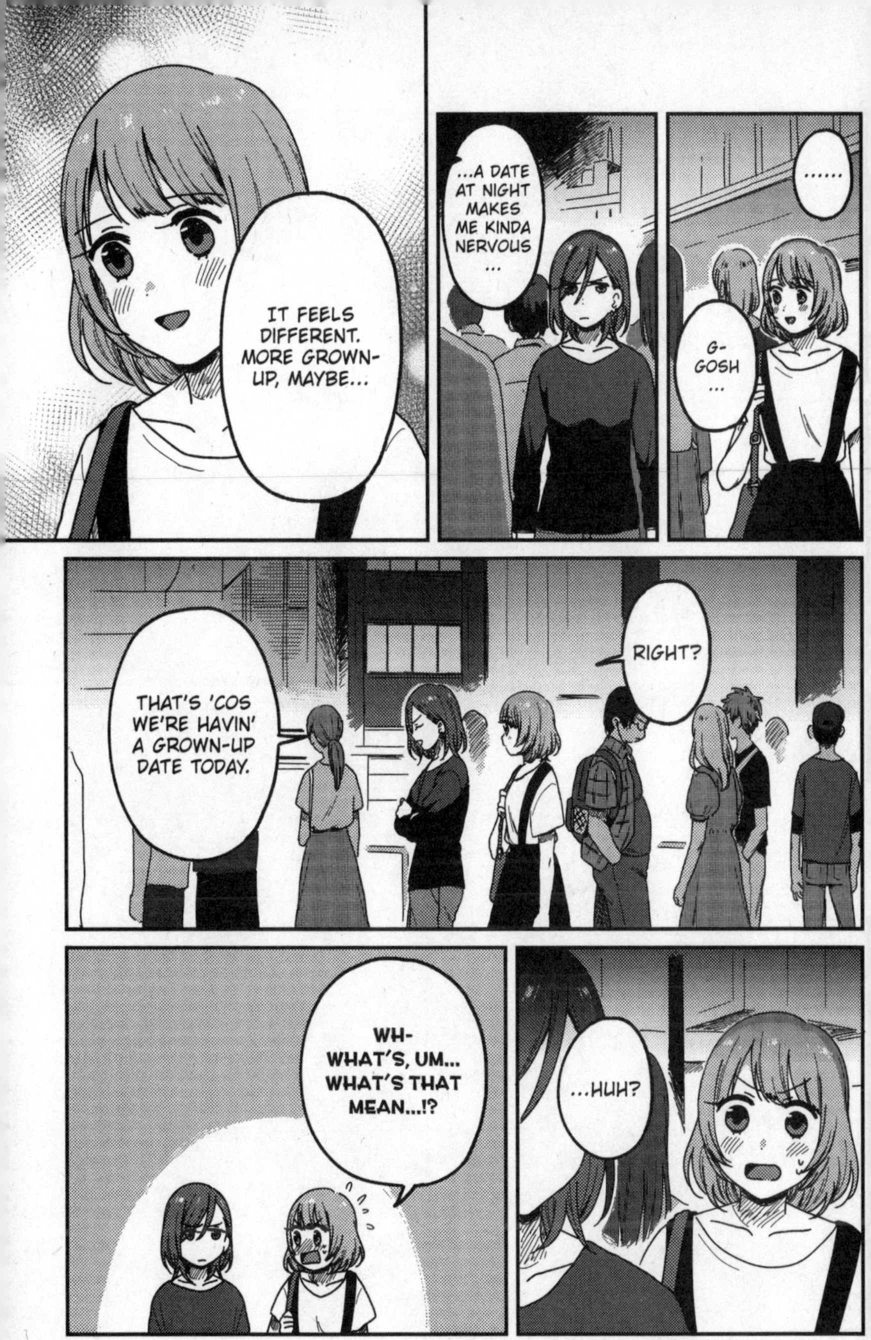
......
G-GOSH ...
...A DATE AT NIGHT MAKES ME KINDA NERVOUS ...
IT FEELS DIFFERENT. MORE GROWN-UP, MAYBE...
RIGHT?
THAT'S 'COS WE'RE HAVIN' A GROWN-UP DATE TODAY.
...HUH?
WH- WHAT'S, UM... WHAT'S THAT MEAN...!?

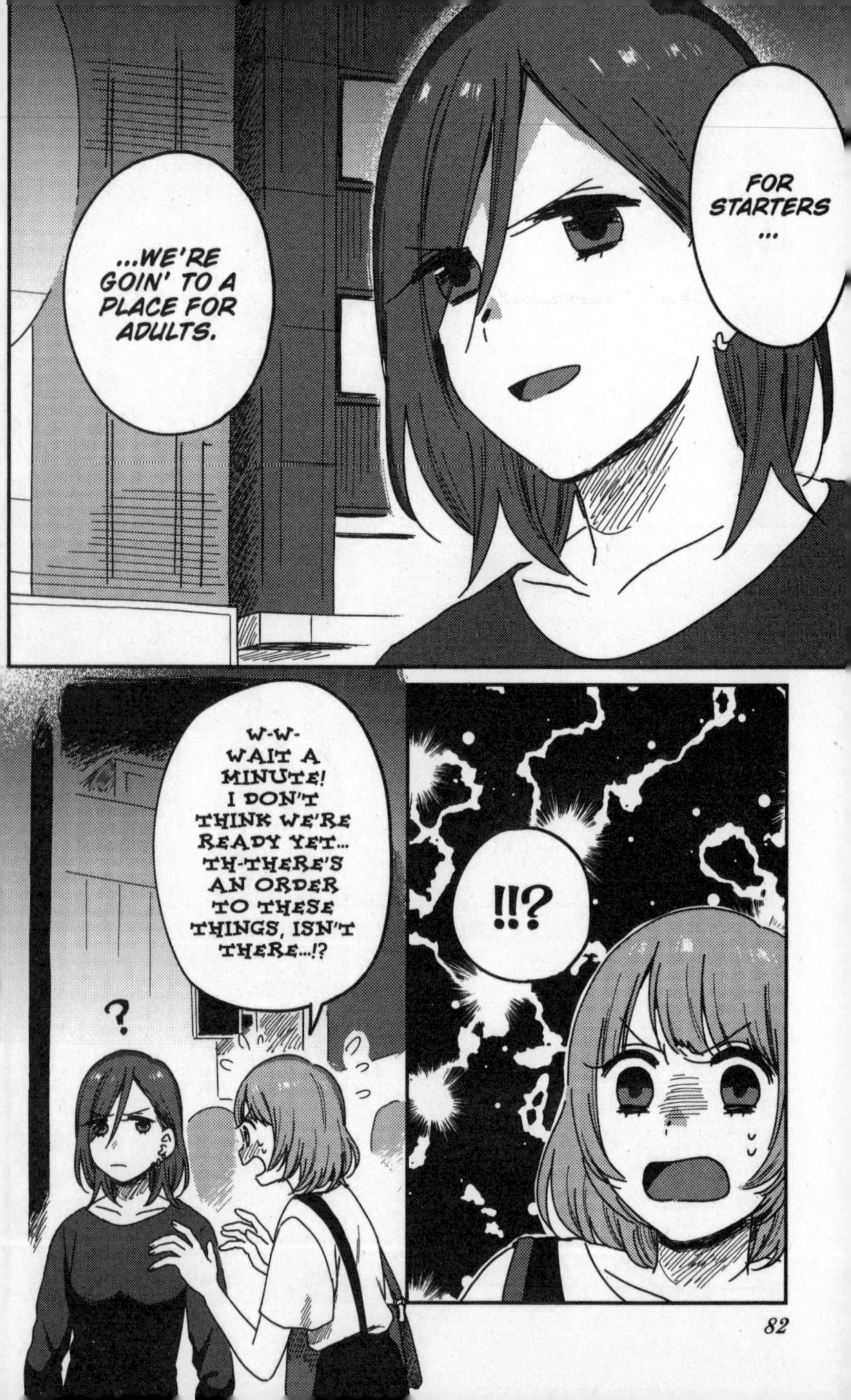
FOR STARTERS ...
...WE'RE GOIN' TO A PLACE FOR ADULTS.
!!?
W-W-WAIT A MINUTE! I DON'T THINK WE'RE READY YET... TH-THERE'S AN ORDER TO THESE THINGS, ISN'T THERE...!?
?

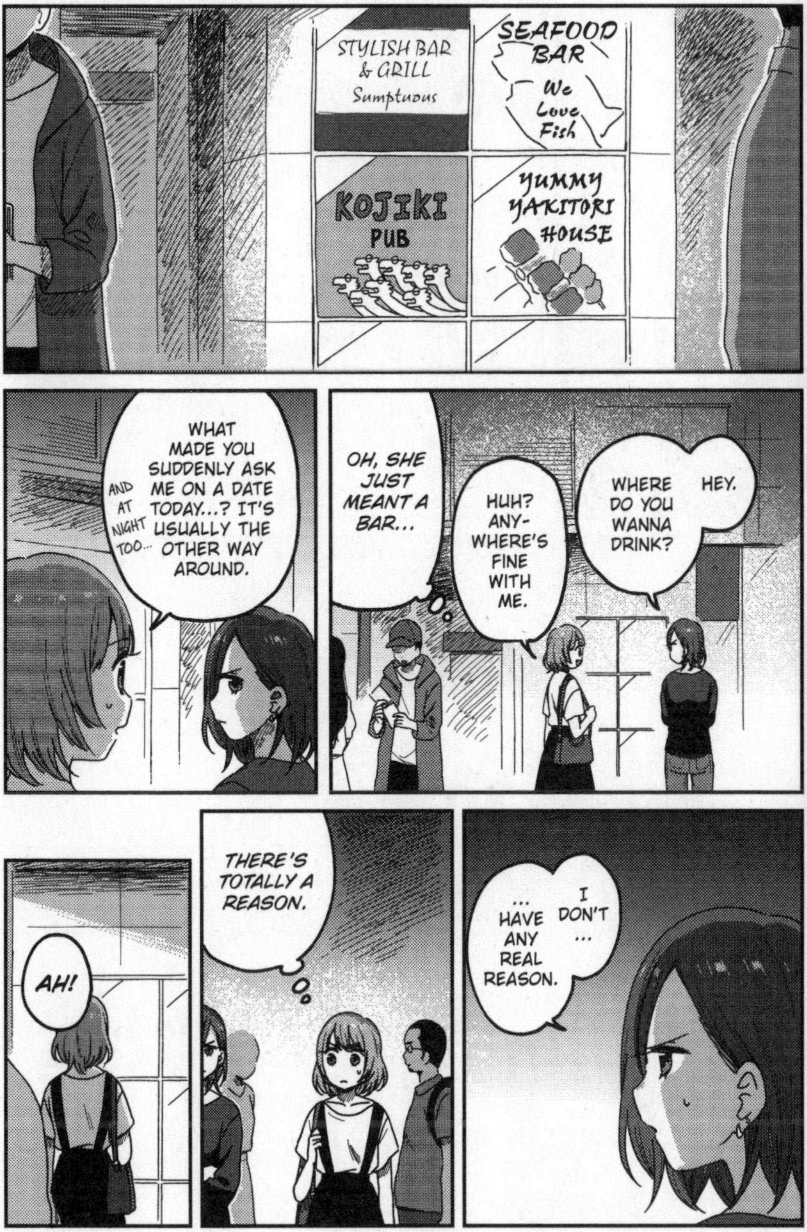
SEAFOOD BAR We Love Fish
STYLISH BAR & GRILL Sumptuous
YUMMY YAKITORI HOUSE
KOJIKI PUB
HEY.
WHERE DO YOU WANNA DRINK?
HUH? ANY-WHERE'S FINE WITH ME.
OH, SHE JUST MEANT A BAR...
WHAT MADE YOU SUDDENLY ASK ME ON A DATE TODAY...? IT'S USUALLY THE OTHER WAY AROUND.
AND AT NIGHT TOO...
I DON'T ...
... HAVE ANY REAL REASON.
THERE'S TOTALLY A REASON.
AH!

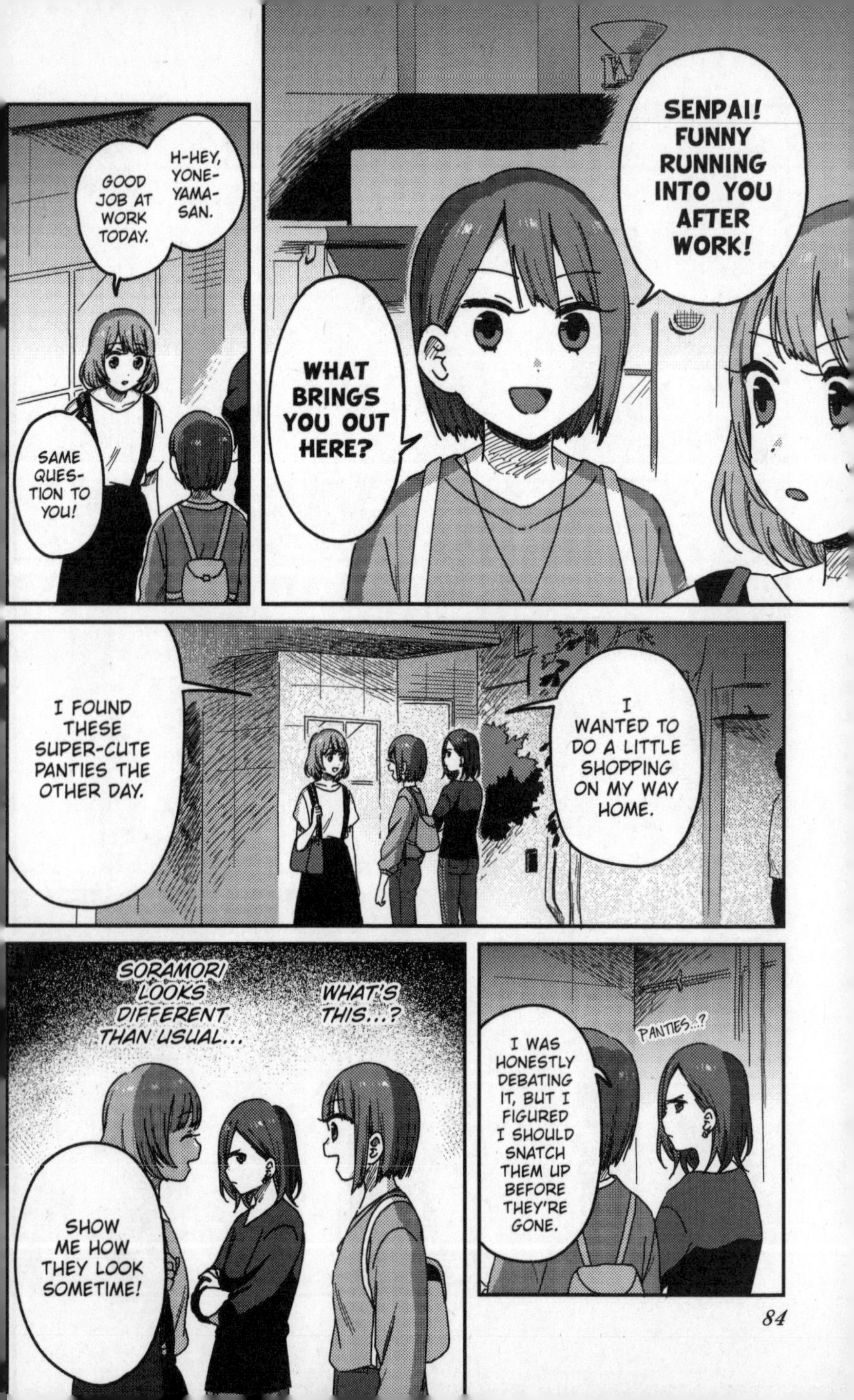
SENPAI! FUNNY RUNNING INTO YOU AFTER WORK!
WHAT BRINGS YOU OUT HERE?
H-HEY, YONE-YAMA-SAN.
GOOD JOB AT WORK TODAY.
SAME QUESTION TO YOU!
I WANTED TO DO A LITTLE SHOPPING ON MY WAY HOME.
I FOUND THESE SUPER-CUTE PANTIES THE OTHER DAY.
I WAS HONESTLY DEBATING IT, BUT I FIGURED I SHOULD SNATCH THEM UP BEFORE THEY'RE GONE.
PANTIES...?
WHAT'S THIS...?
SORAMORI LOOKS DIFFERENT THAN USUAL...
SHOW ME HOW THEY LOOK SOMETIME!

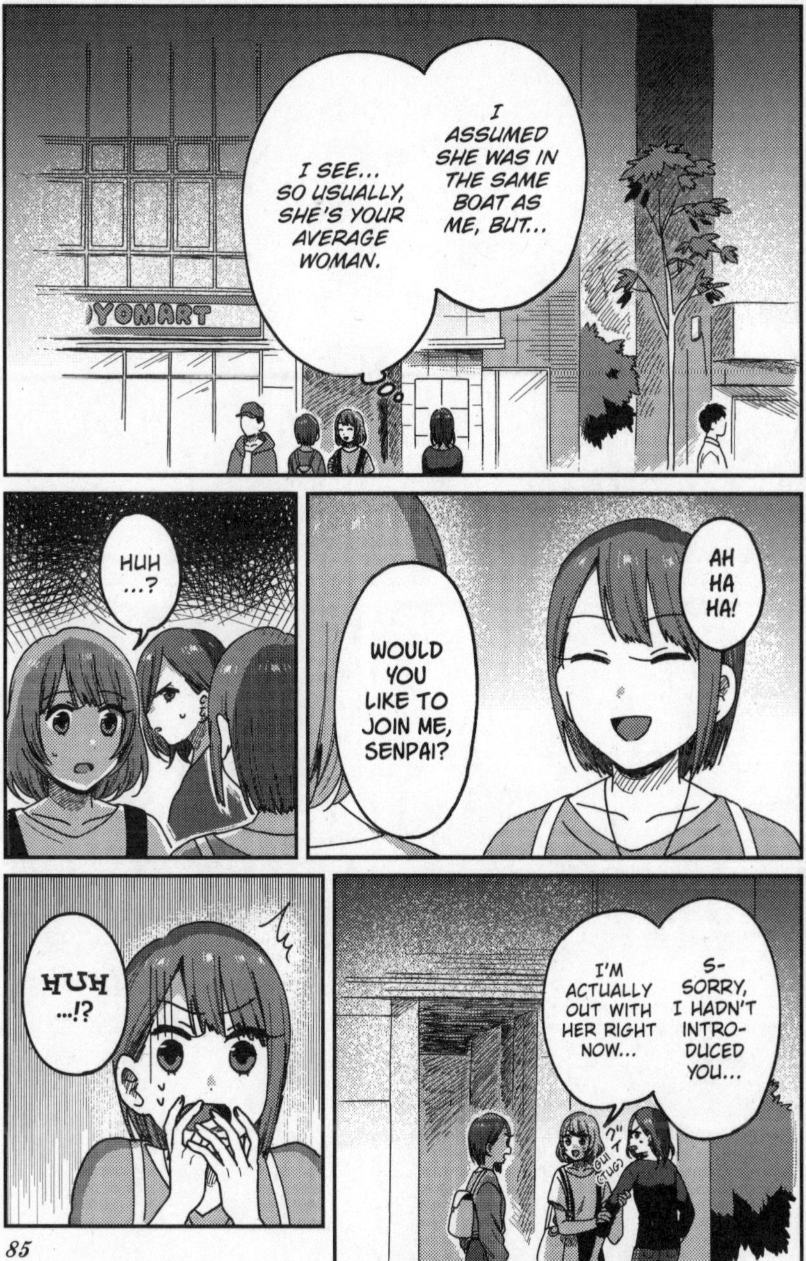

YOMART
I ASSUMED SHE WAS IN THE SAME BOAT AS ME, BUT...
I SEE... SO USUALLY, SHE'S YOUR AVERAGE WOMAN.
AH HA HA!
WOULD YOU LIKE TO JOIN ME, SENPAI?
HUH...?
S-SORRY, I HADN'T INTRODUCED YOU...
I'M ACTUALLY OUT WITH HER RIGHT NOW...
GUI (TUG)
HUH...!?

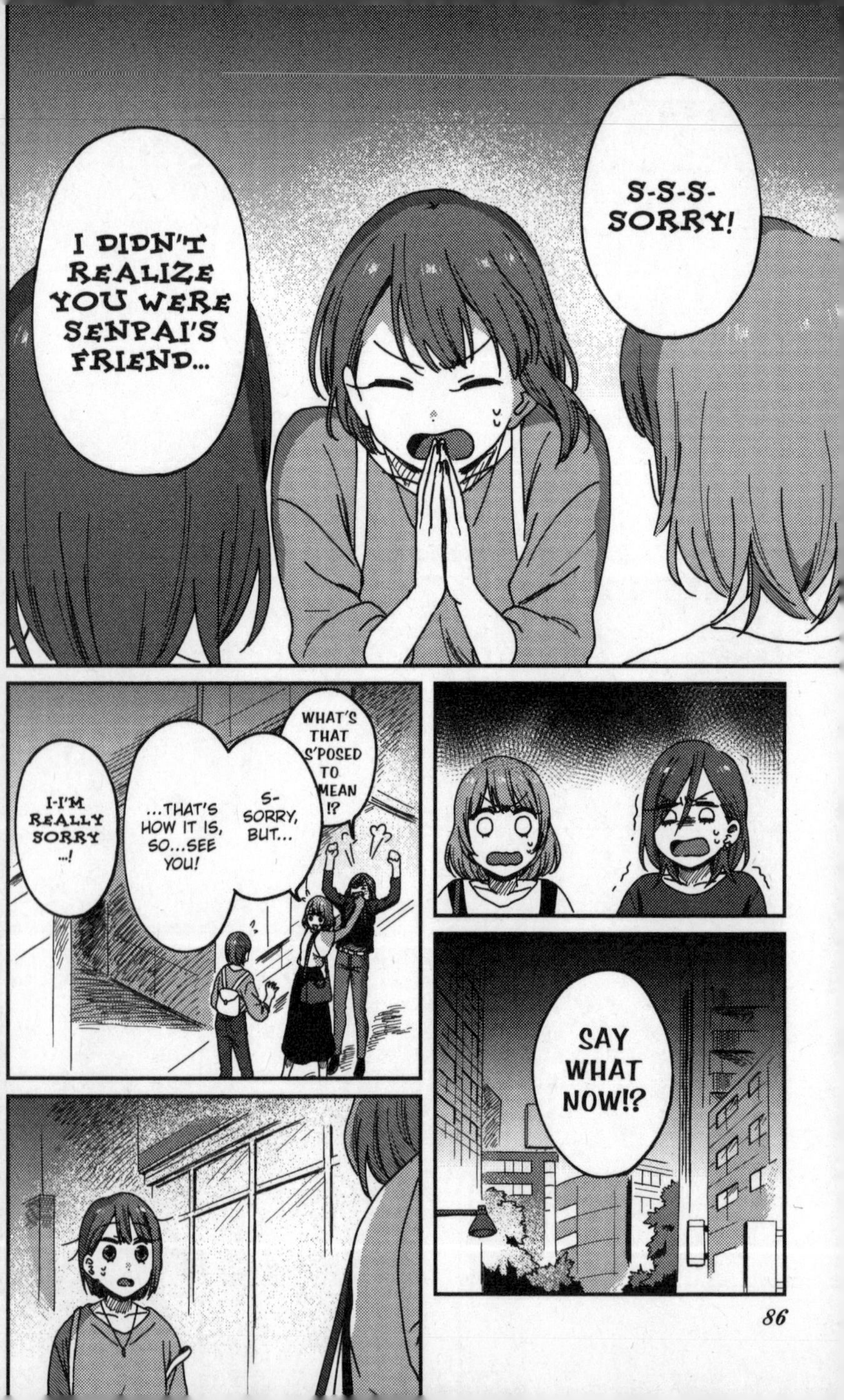

S-S-S-SORRY!
I DIDN'T REALIZE YOU WERE SENPAI'S FRIEND...
WHAT'S THAT S'POSED TO MEAN!?
S-SORRY, BUT...
...THAT'S HOW IT IS, SO...SEE YOU!
I-I'M REALLY SORRY...!
SAY WHAT NOW!?

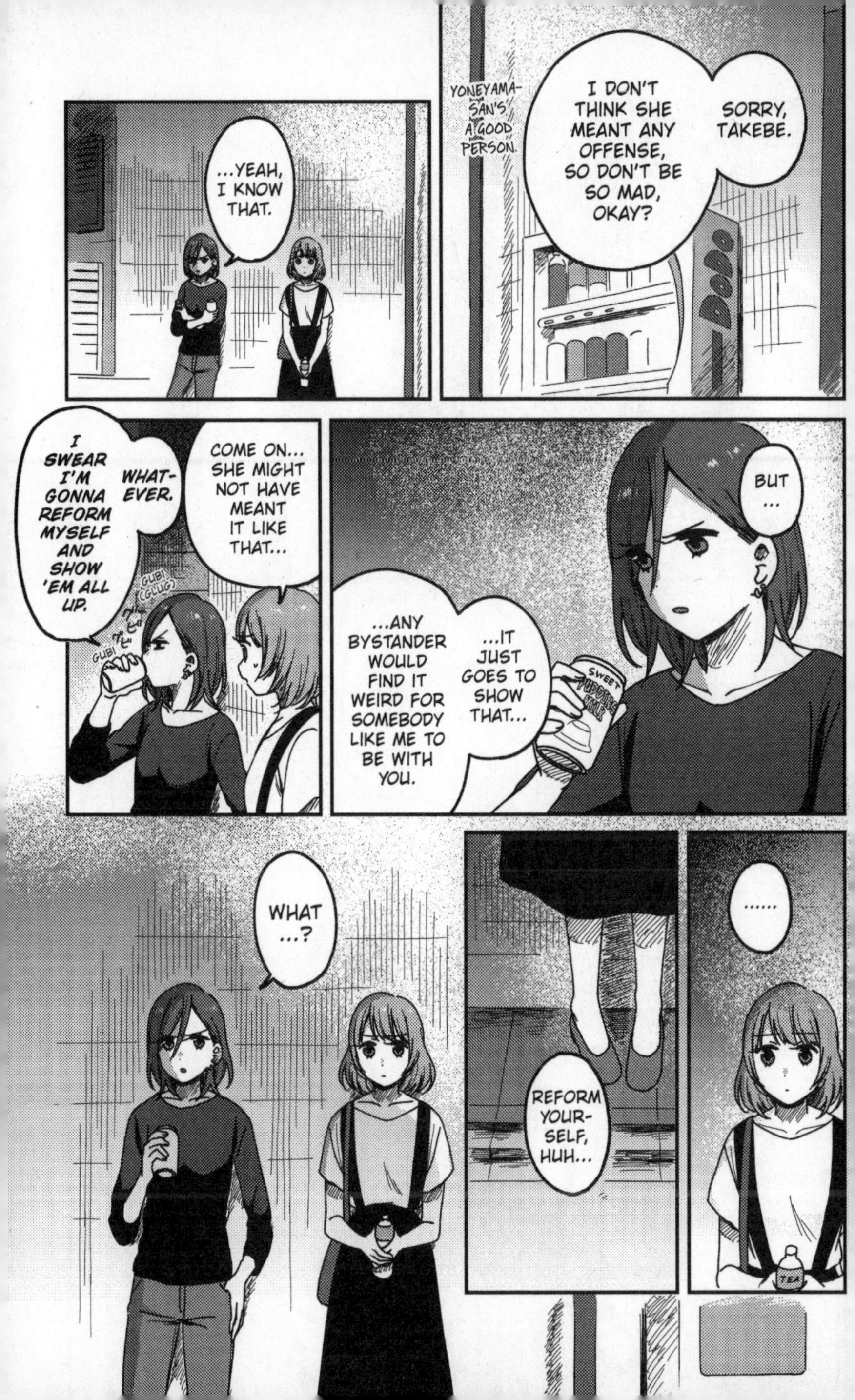
SORRY, TAKEBE.
I DON'T THINK SHE MEANT ANY OFFENSE, SO DON'T BE SO MAD, OKAY?
YONEYAMA-SAN'S A GOOD PERSON.
...YEAH, I KNOW THAT.
BUT ...
SWEET PUDDING MILK
...IT JUST GOES TO SHOW THAT...
...ANY BYSTANDER WOULD FIND IT WEIRD FOR SOMEBODY LIKE ME TO BE WITH YOU.
COME ON... SHE MIGHT NOT HAVE MEANT IT LIKE THAT...
WHAT-EVER.
GUBI (GLUG)
GUBI
I SWEAR I'M GONNA REFORM MYSELF AND SHOW 'EM ALL UP.
......
TEA
REFORM YOUR-SELF, HUH...
WHAT ...?

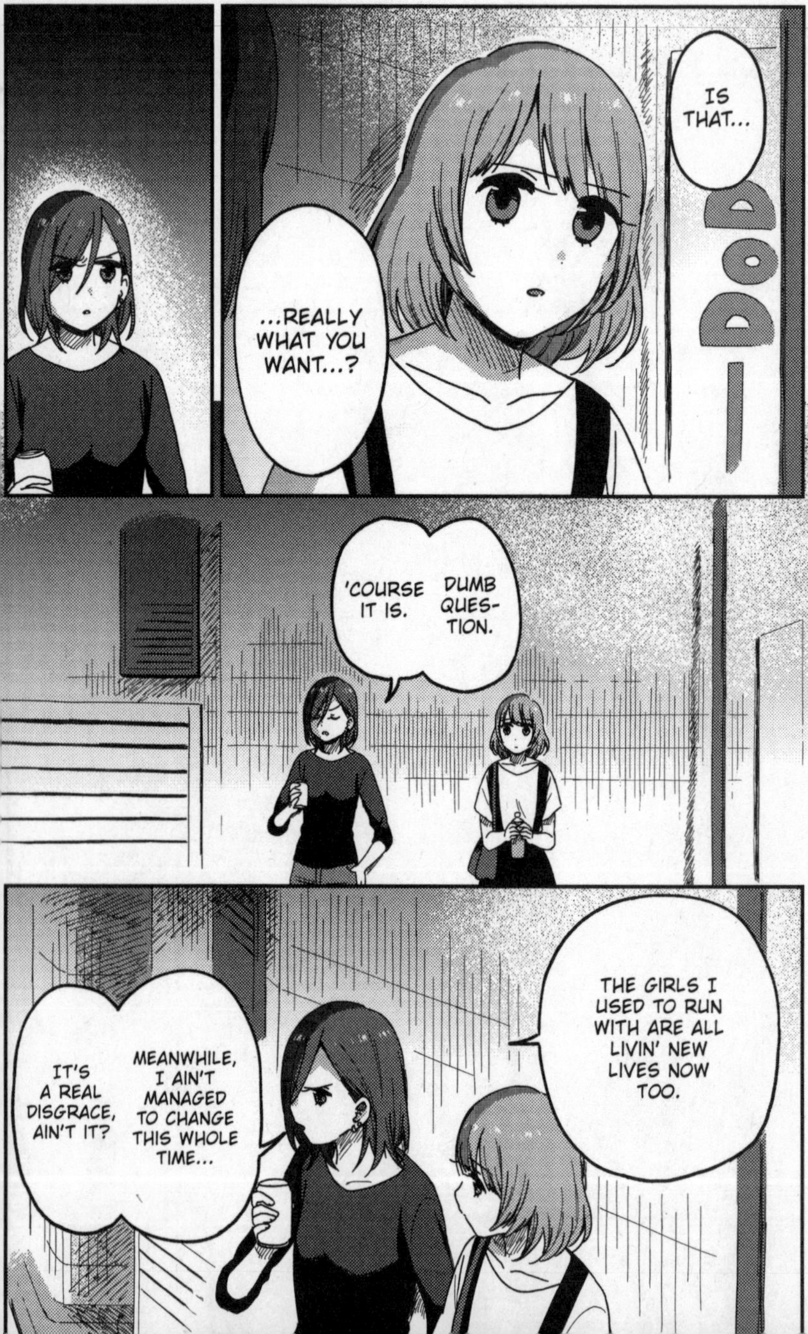
IS THAT...
...REALLY WHAT YOU WANT...?
'COURSE IT IS. DUMB QUES-TION.
THE GIRLS I USED TO RUN WITH ARE ALL LIVIN' NEW LIVES NOW TOO.
MEANWHILE, I AIN'T MANAGED TO CHANGE THIS WHOLE TIME...
IT'S A REAL DISGRACE, AIN'T IT?

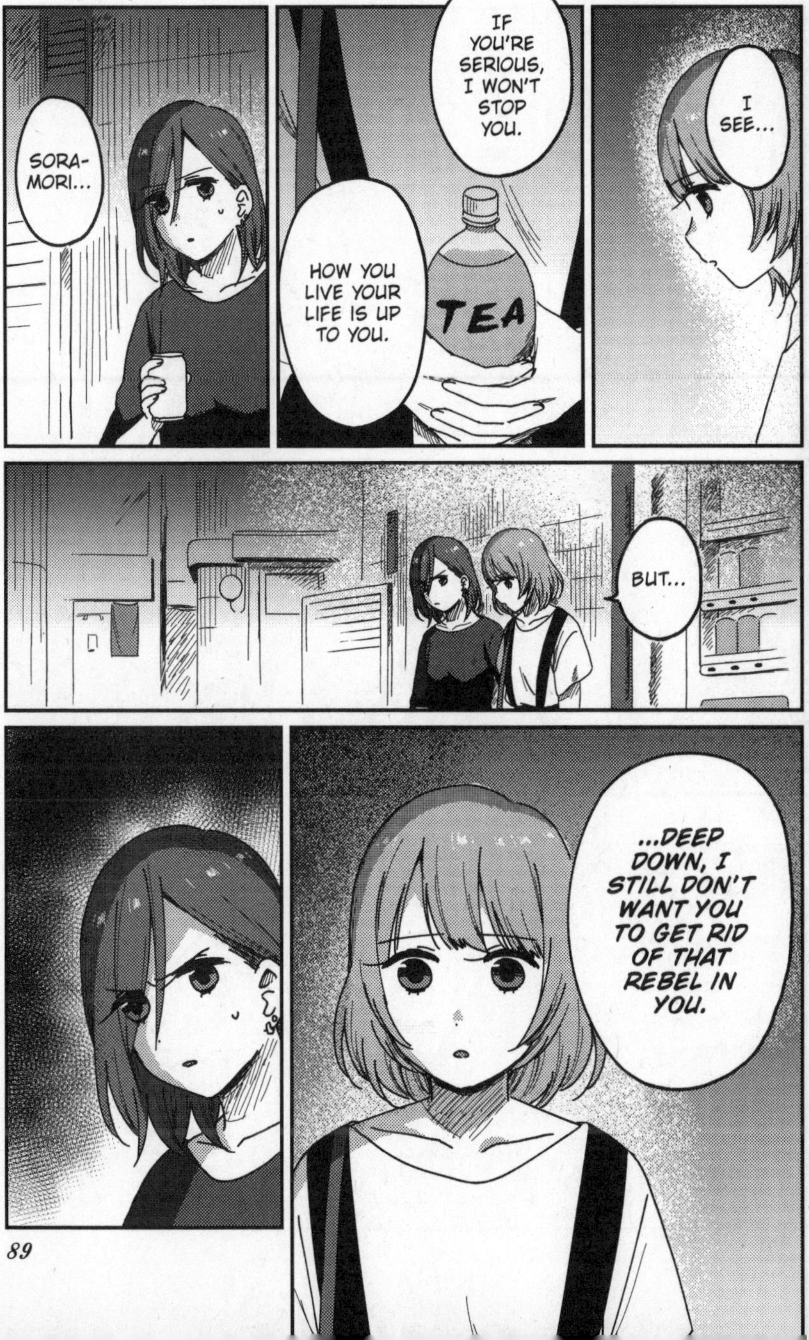
I SEE...
IF YOU'RE SERIOUS, I WON'T STOP YOU.
HOW YOU LIVE YOUR LIFE IS UP TO YOU.
TEA
SORA-MORI...
BUT...
...DEEP DOWN, I STILL DON'T WANT YOU TO GET RID OF THAT REBEL IN YOU.

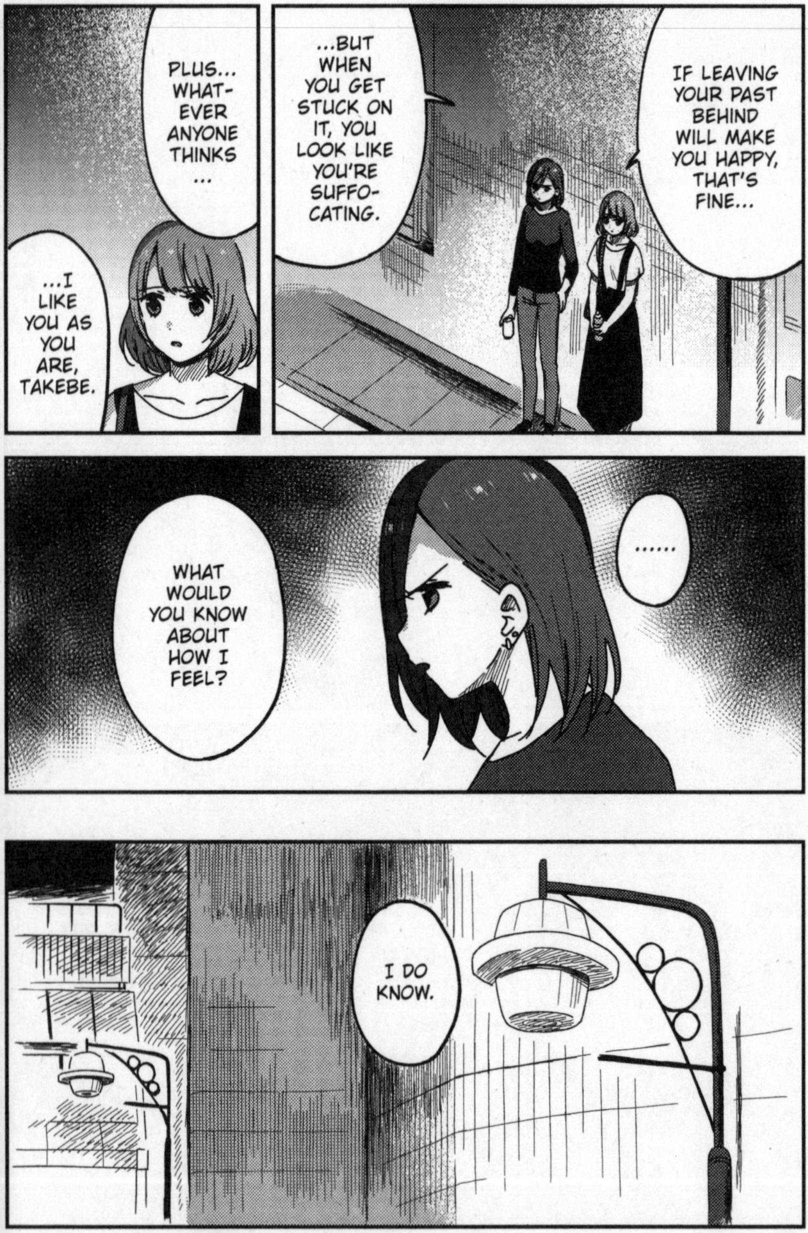
IF LEAVING YOUR PAST BEHIND WILL MAKE YOU HAPPY, THAT'S FINE...
...BUT WHEN YOU GET STUCK ON IT, YOU LOOK LIKE YOU'RE SUFFOCATING.
PLUS... WHAT-EVER ANYONE THINKS...
...I LIKE YOU AS YOU ARE, TAKEBE.
......
WHAT WOULD YOU KNOW ABOUT HOW I FEEL?
I DO KNOW.

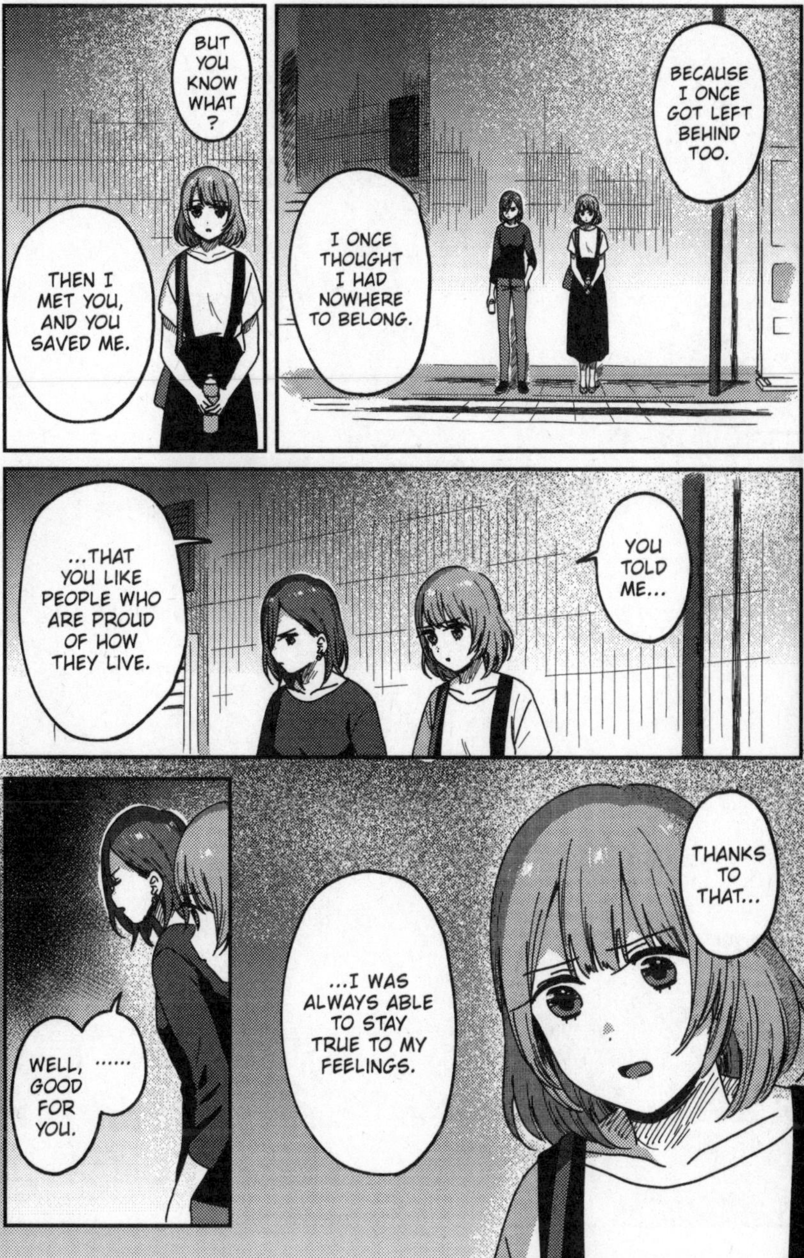
BECAUSE I ONCE GOT LEFT BEHIND TOO.
I ONCE THOUGHT I HAD NOWHERE TO BELONG.
BUT YOU KNOW WHAT?
THEN I MET YOU, AND YOU SAVED ME.
YOU TOLD ME...
...THAT YOU LIKE PEOPLE WHO ARE PROUD OF HOW THEY LIVE.
THANKS TO THAT...
...I WAS ALWAYS ABLE TO STAY TRUE TO MY FEELINGS.
......
WELL, GOOD FOR YOU.

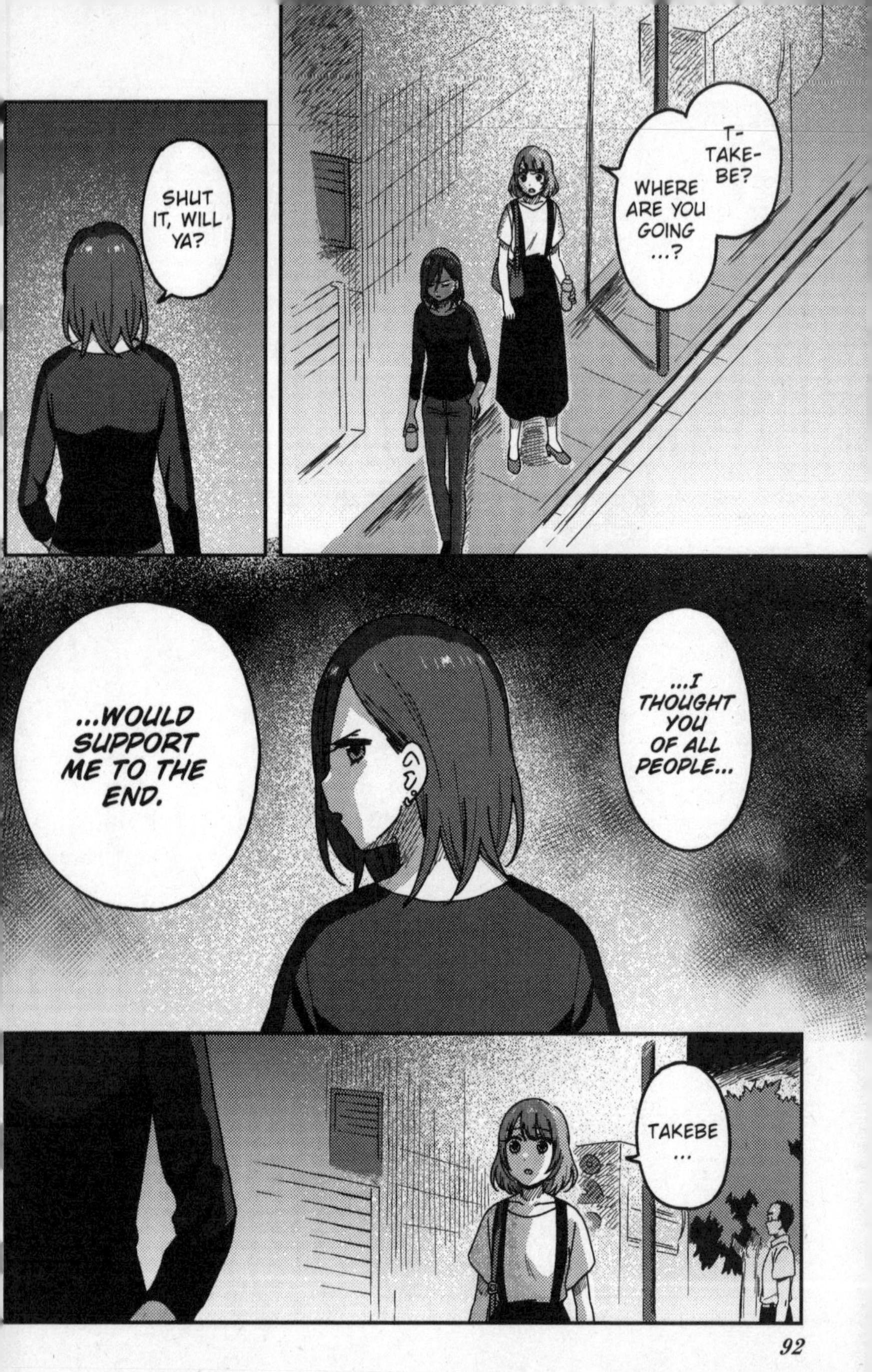
T-TAKE-BE? WHERE ARE YOU GOING ...?
SHUT IT, WILL YA?
...I THOUGHT YOU OF ALL PEOPLE...
...WOULD SUPPORT ME TO THE END.
TAKEBE ...

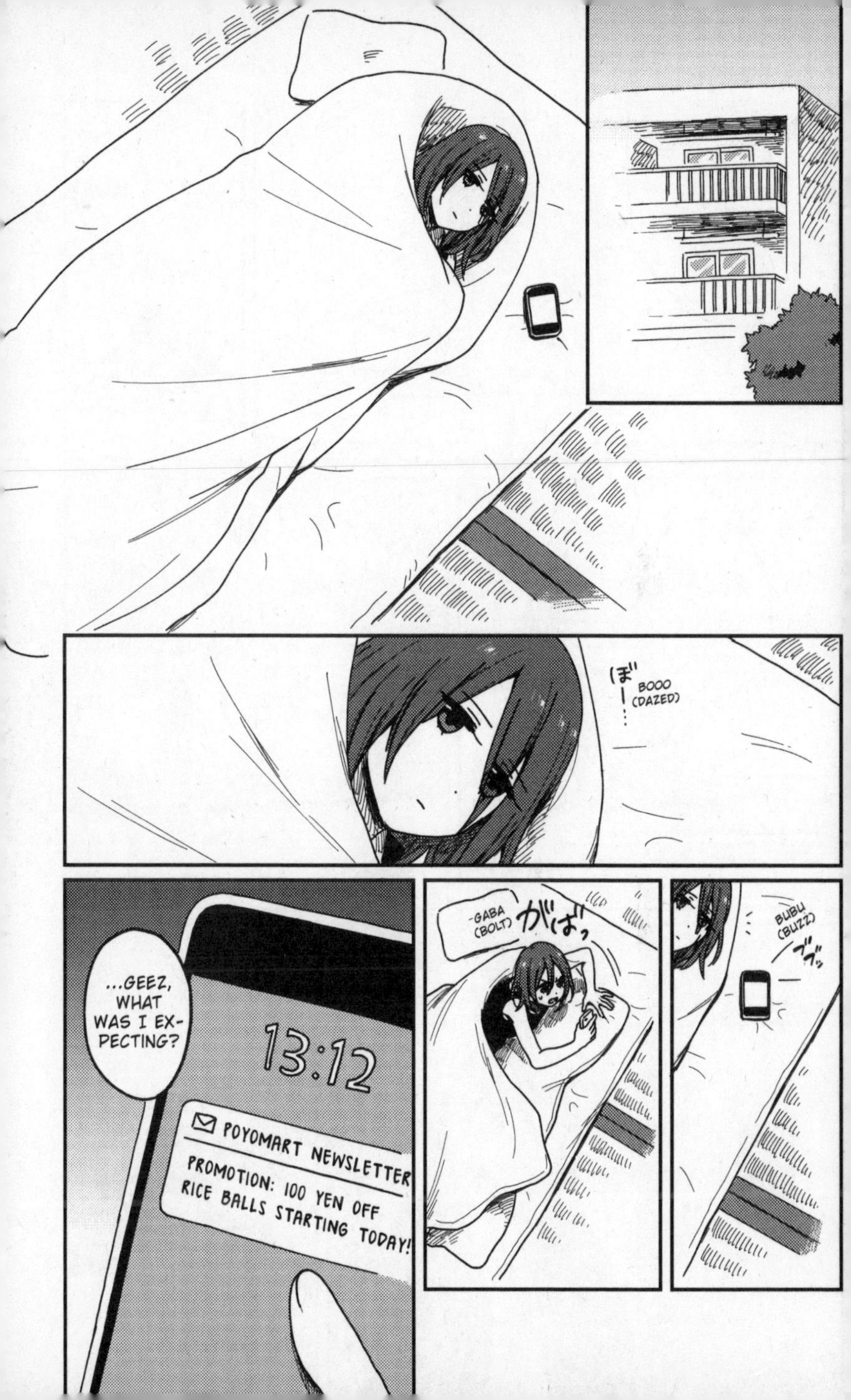
ぼー…
BOOO (DAZED)
BUBU (BUZZ)
ブブッ
がばっ
GABA (BOLT)
...GEEZ, WHAT WAS I EXPECTING?
13:12
POYOMART NEWSLETTER
PROMOTION: 100 YEN OFF RICE BALLS STARTING TODAY!

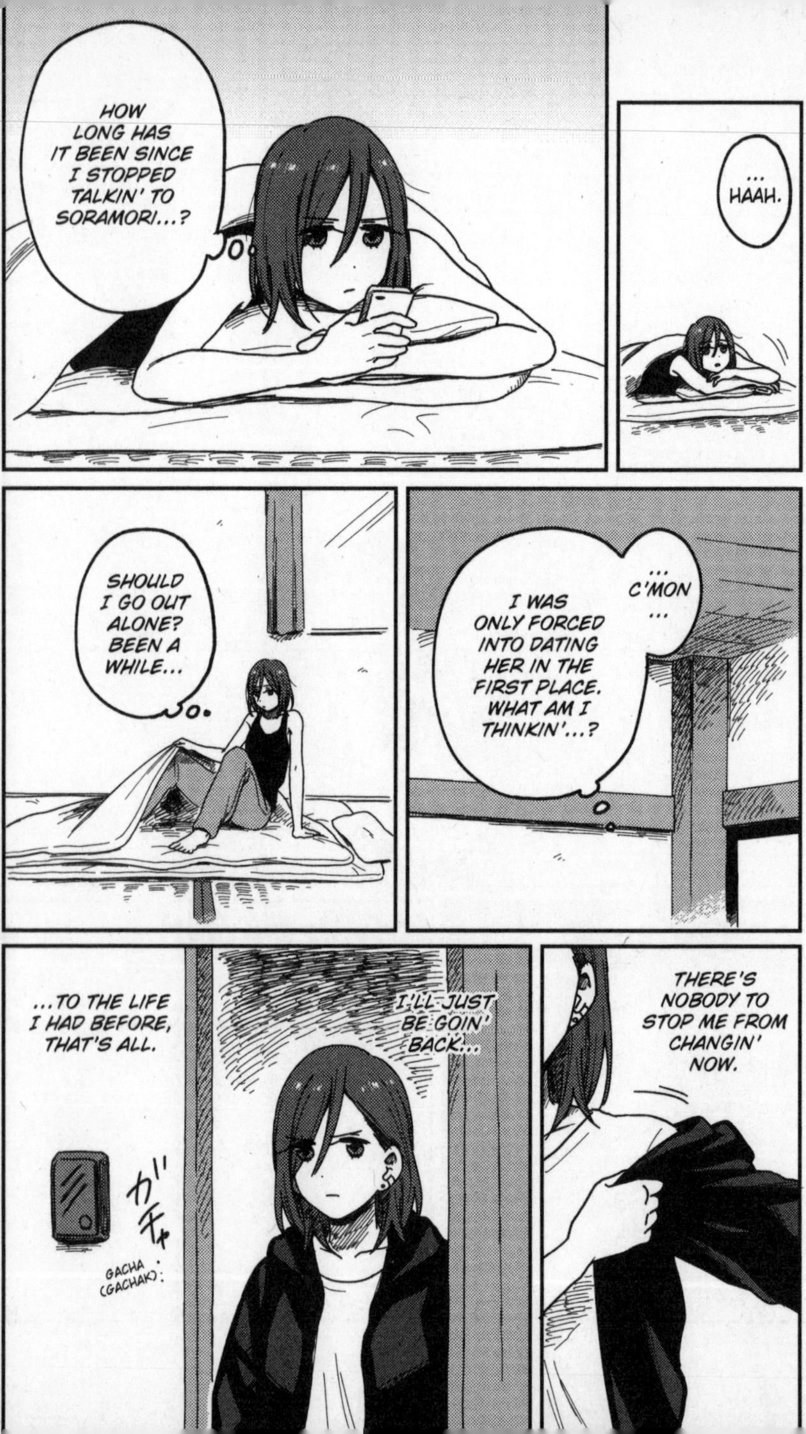
...HAAH.
HOW LONG HAS IT BEEN SINCE I STOPPED TALKIN' TO SORAMORI...?
...C'MON...
I WAS ONLY FORCED INTO DATING HER IN THE FIRST PLACE. WHAT AM I THINKIN'...?
SHOULD I GO OUT ALONE? BEEN A WHILE...
THERE'S NOBODY TO STOP ME FROM CHANGIN' NOW.
I'LL JUST BE GOIN' BACK...
...TO THE LIFE I HAD BEFORE, THAT'S ALL.
ガチャ
GACHA (GACHAK)

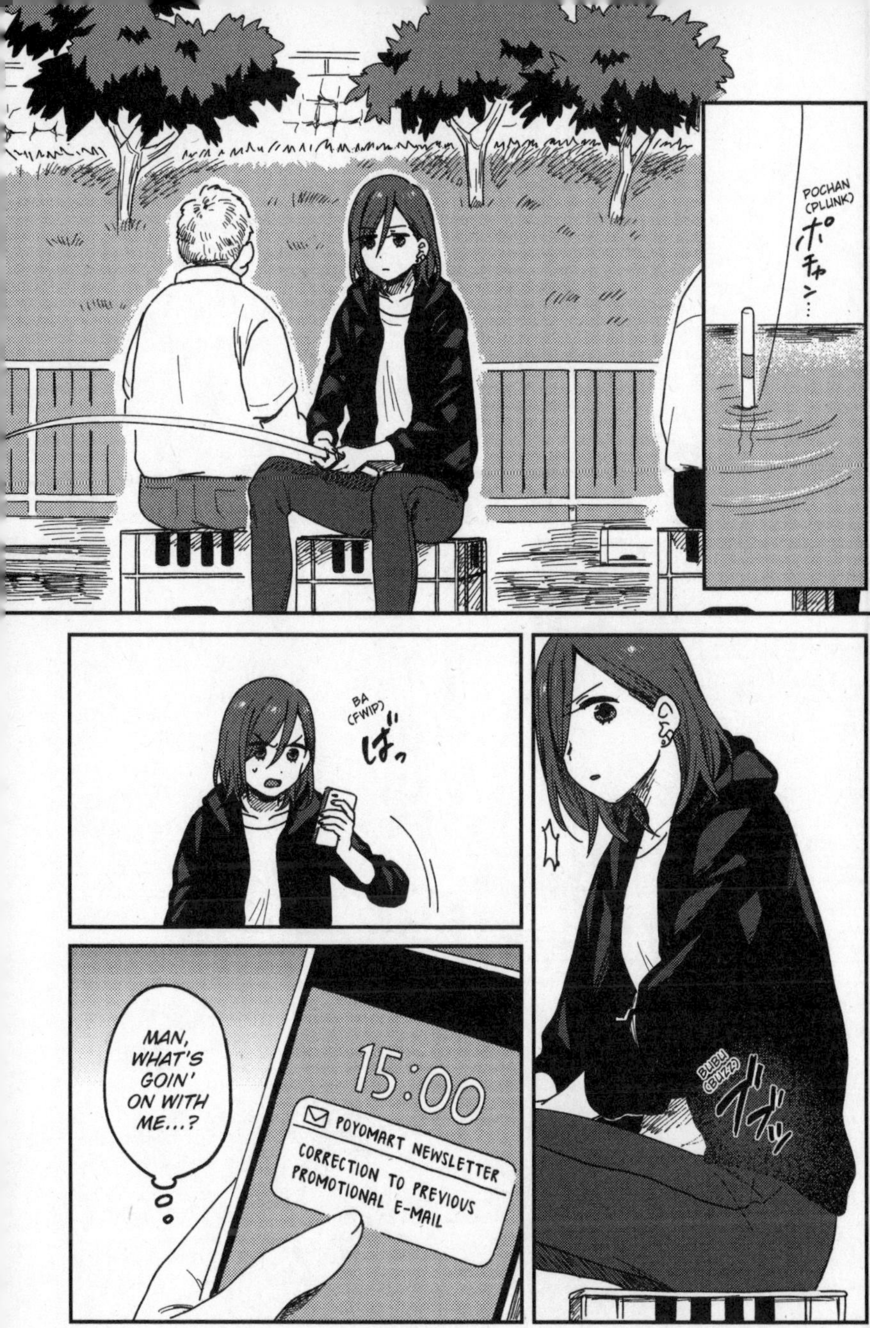
POCHAN (PLUNK)
ポチャン…
BUBU (BUZZ)
ブブッ
BA (FWIP)
ばっ
15:00
POYOMART NEWSLETTER
CORRECTION TO PREVIOUS PROMOTIONAL E-MAIL
MAN, WHAT'S GOIN' ON WITH ME...?

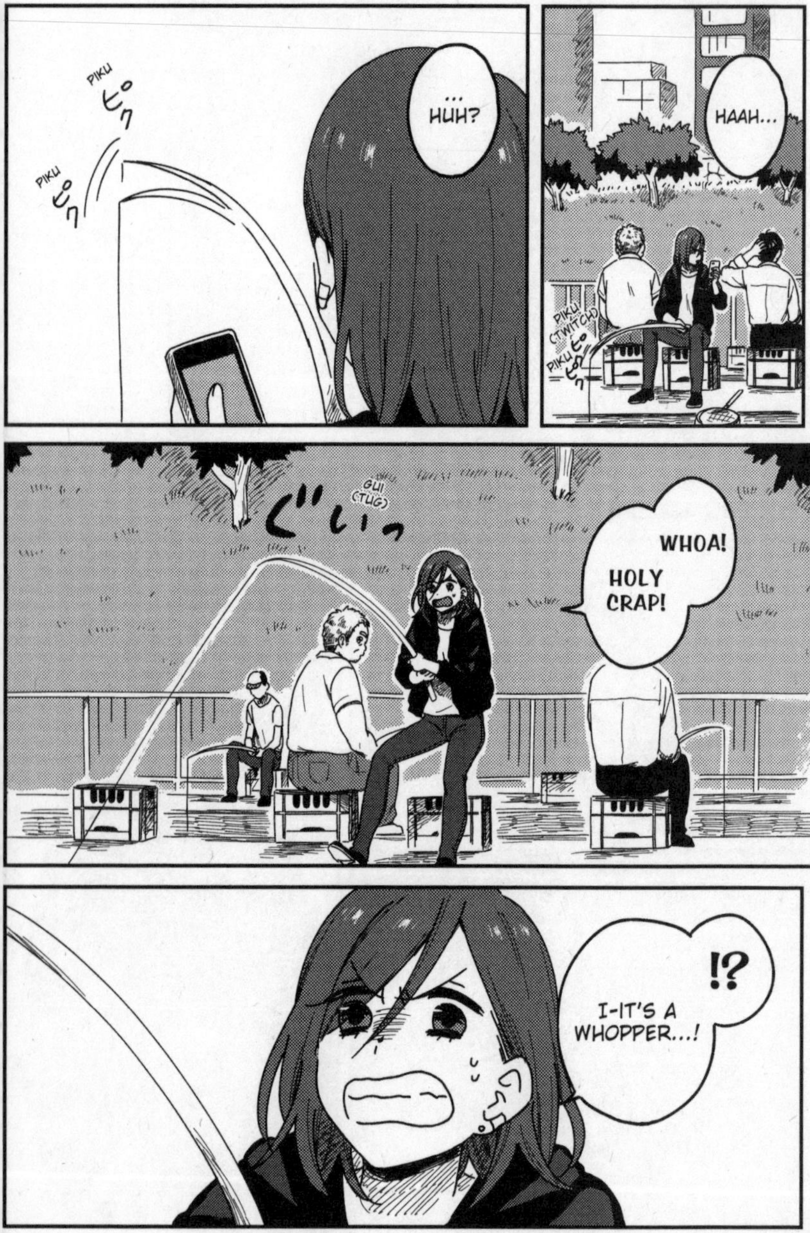
HAAH...
PIKU (TWITCH)
ピク
PIKU
ピク
... HUH?
PIKU
ピク
PIKU
ピク
GUI (TUG)
ぐいっ
WHOA!
HOLY CRAP!
!?
I-IT'S A WHOPPER...!

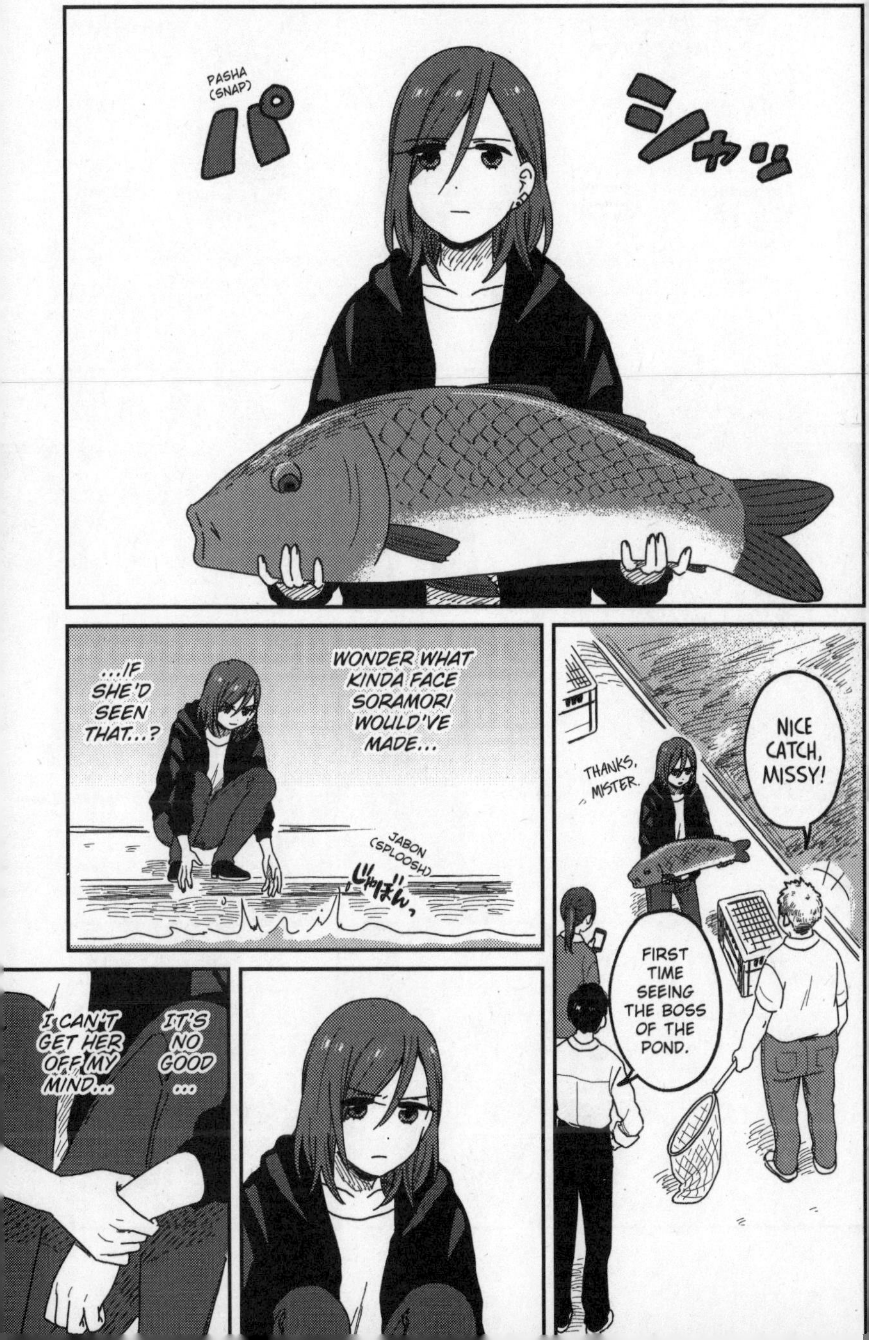
PASHA (SNAP)
パシャッ
NICE CATCH, MISSY!
THANKS, MISTER.
FIRST TIME SEEING THE BOSS OF THE POND.
WONDER WHAT KINDA FACE SORAMORI WOULD'VE MADE...
...IF SHE'D SEEN THAT...?
JABON (SPLOOSH)
じゃぼんっ
IT'S NO GOOD...
I CAN'T GET HER OFF MY MIND...

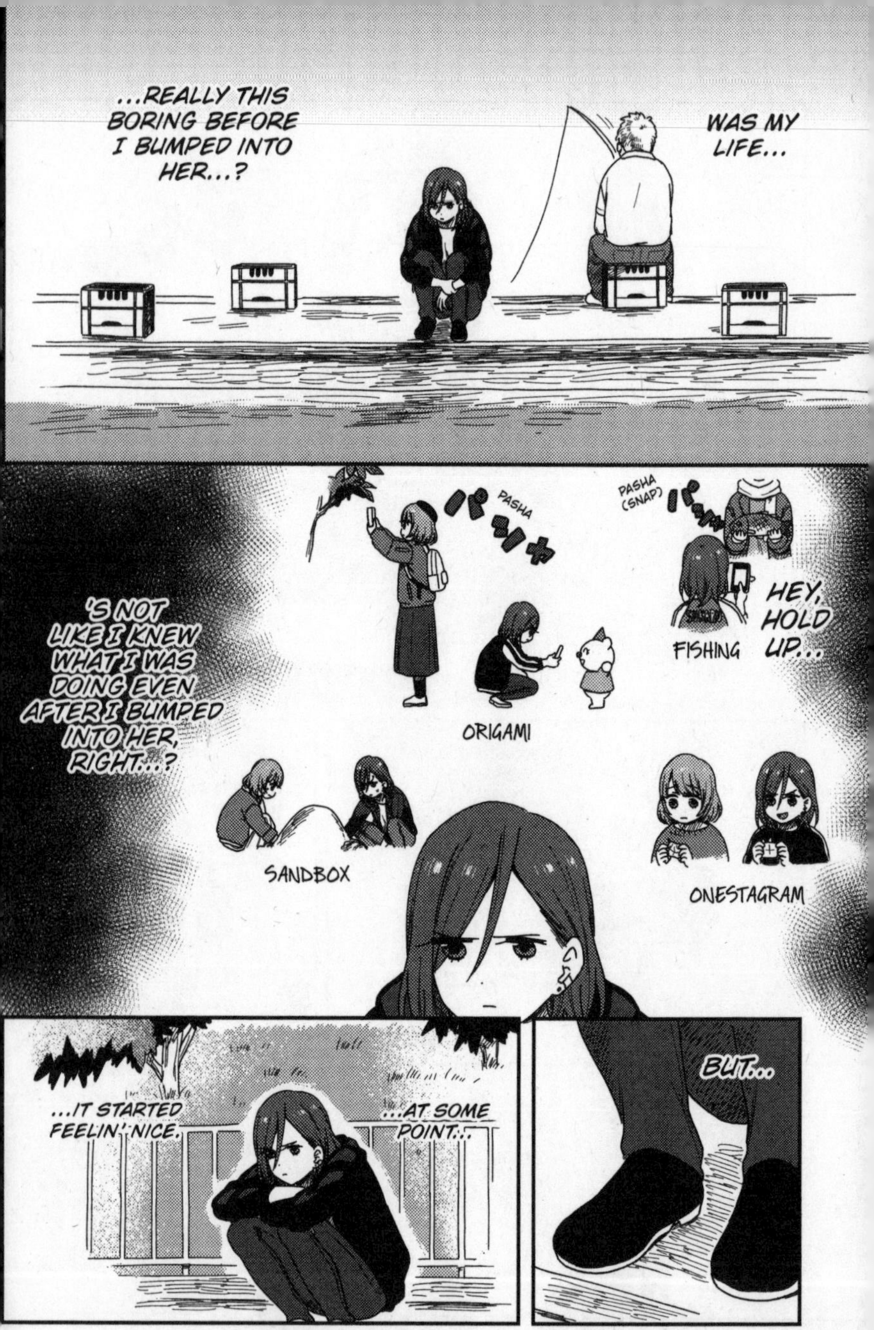
WAS MY LIFE...
...REALLY THIS BORING BEFORE I BUMPED INTO HER...?
PASHA (SNAP)
パシャ
HEY, HOLD UP...
FISHING
PASHA
パシャ
ORIGAMI
'S NOT LIKE I KNEW WHAT I WAS DOING EVEN AFTER I BUMPED INTO HER, RIGHT...?
ONESTAGRAM
SANDBOX
BUT...
...AT SOME POINT...
...IT STARTED FEELIN' NICE.

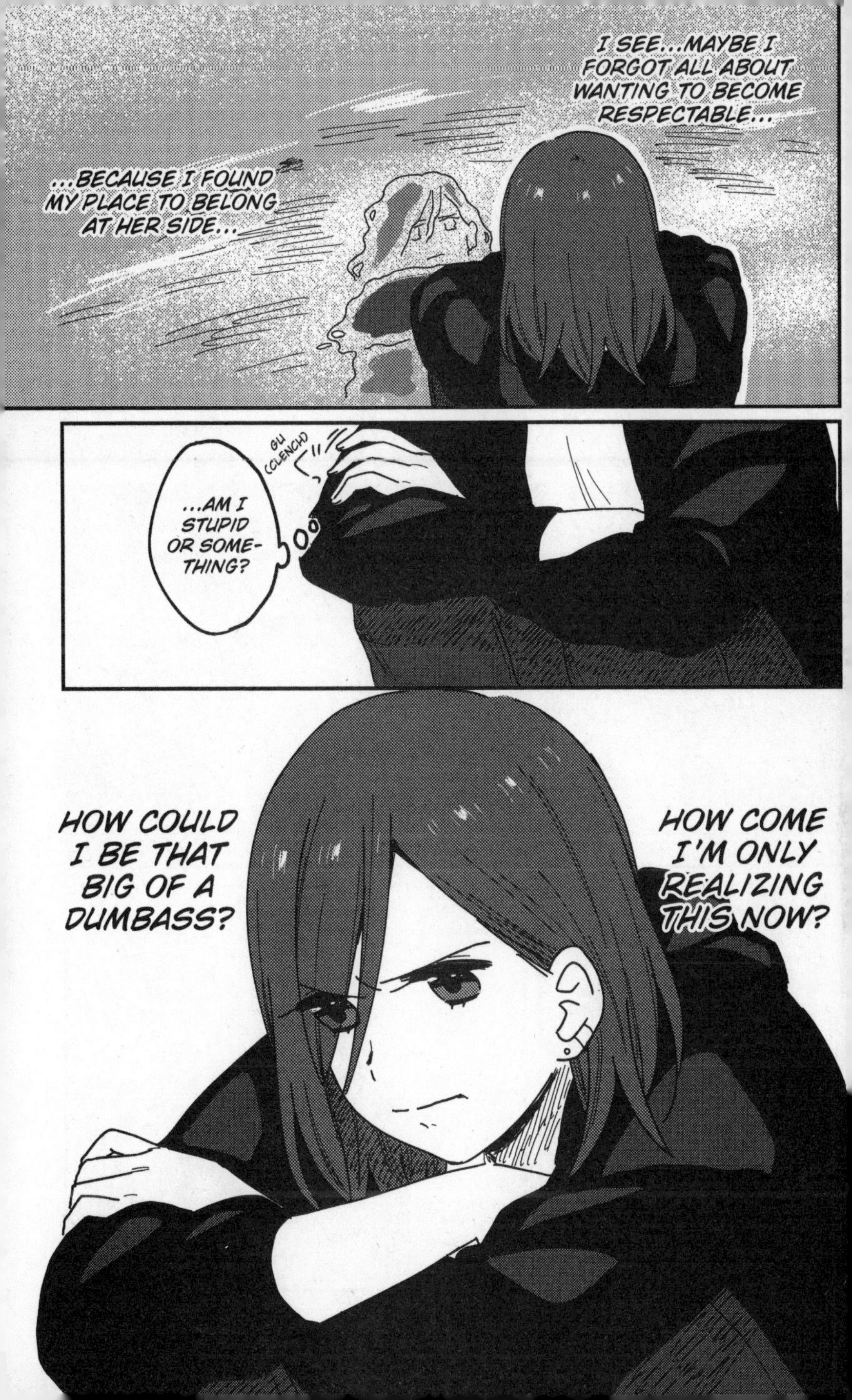
I SEE...MAYBE I FORGOT ALL ABOUT WANTING TO BECOME RESPECTABLE...
...BECAUSE I FOUND MY PLACE TO BELONG AT HER SIDE...
GU (CLENCH)
...AM I STUPID OR SOME-THING?
HOW COME I'M ONLY REALIZING THIS NOW?
HOW COULD I BE THAT BIG OF A DUMBASS?

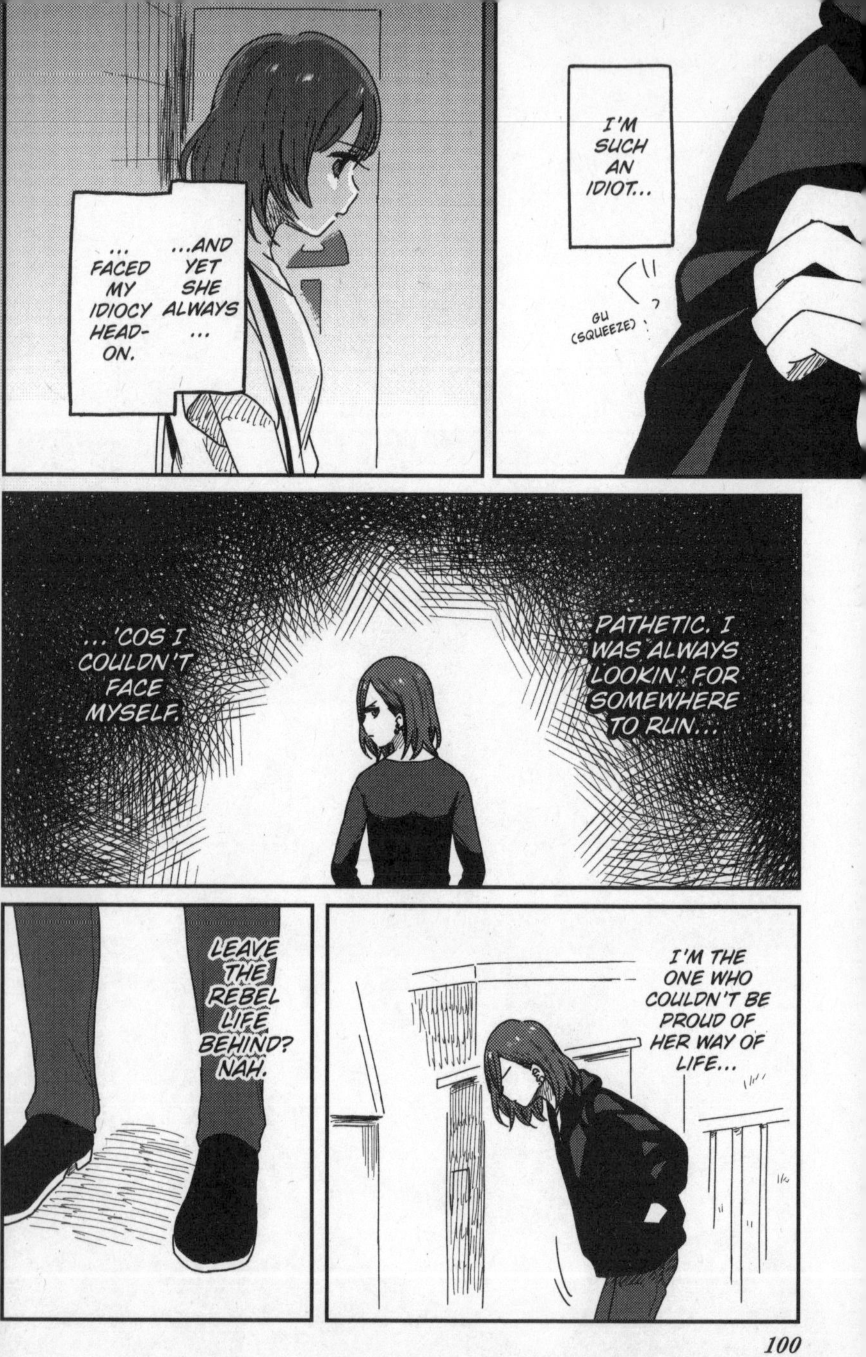
I'M SUCH AN IDIOT...
GU (SQUEEZE)
...AND YET SHE ALWAYS...
...FACED MY IDIOCY HEAD-ON.
PATHETIC. I WAS ALWAYS LOOKIN' FOR SOMEWHERE TO RUN...
...'COS I COULDN'T FACE MYSELF.
I'M THE ONE WHO COULDN'T BE PROUD OF HER WAY OF LIFE...
LEAVE THE REBEL LIFE BEHIND? NAH.

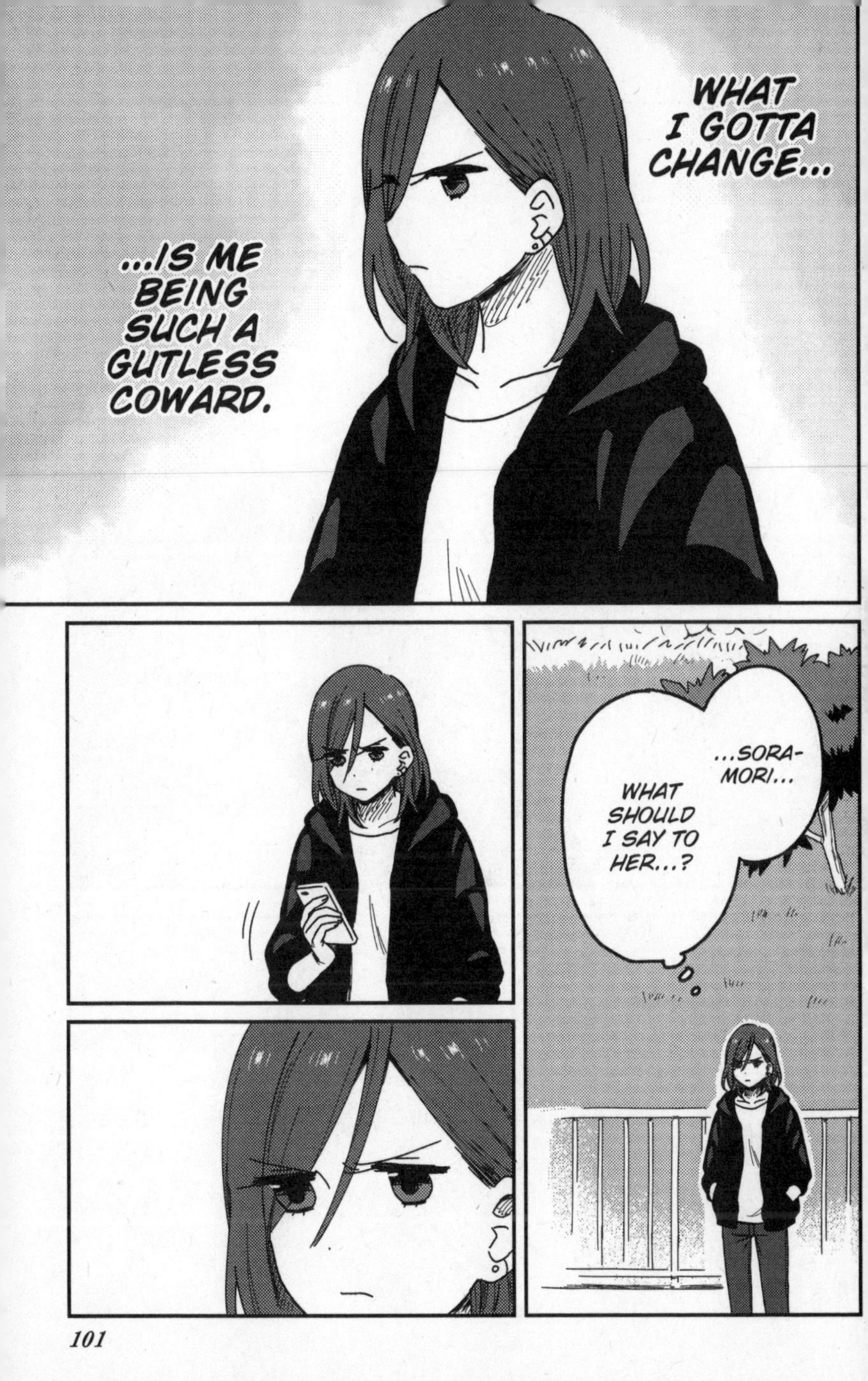
WHAT I GOTTA CHANGE...
...IS ME BEING SUCH A GUTLESS COWARD.
...SORA-MORI...
WHAT SHOULD I SAY TO HER...?

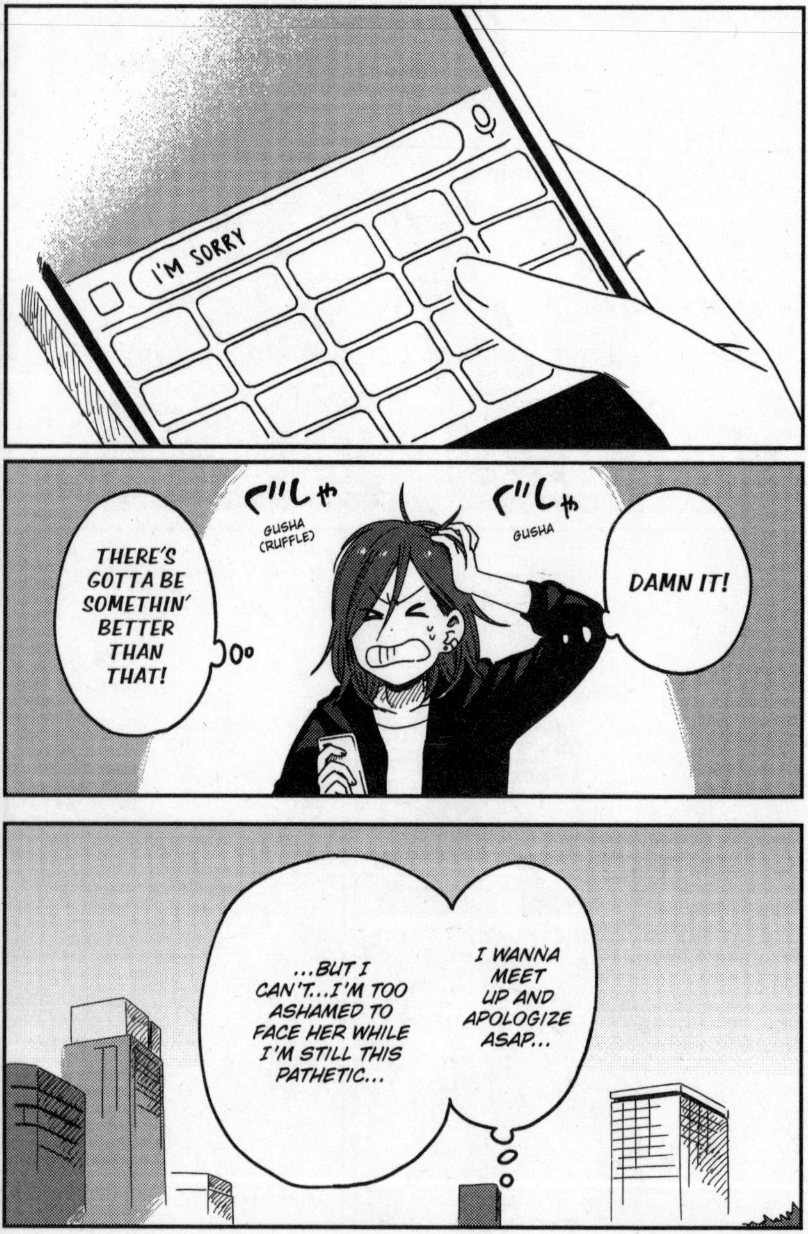
I'M SORRY
DAMN IT!
ぐしゃ
GUSHA
ぐしゃ
GUSHA (RUFFLE)
THERE'S GOTTA BE SOMETHIN' BETTER THAN THAT!
I WANNA MEET UP AND APOLOGIZE ASAP...
...BUT I CAN'T...I'M TOO ASHAMED TO FACE HER WHILE I'M STILL THIS PATHETIC...

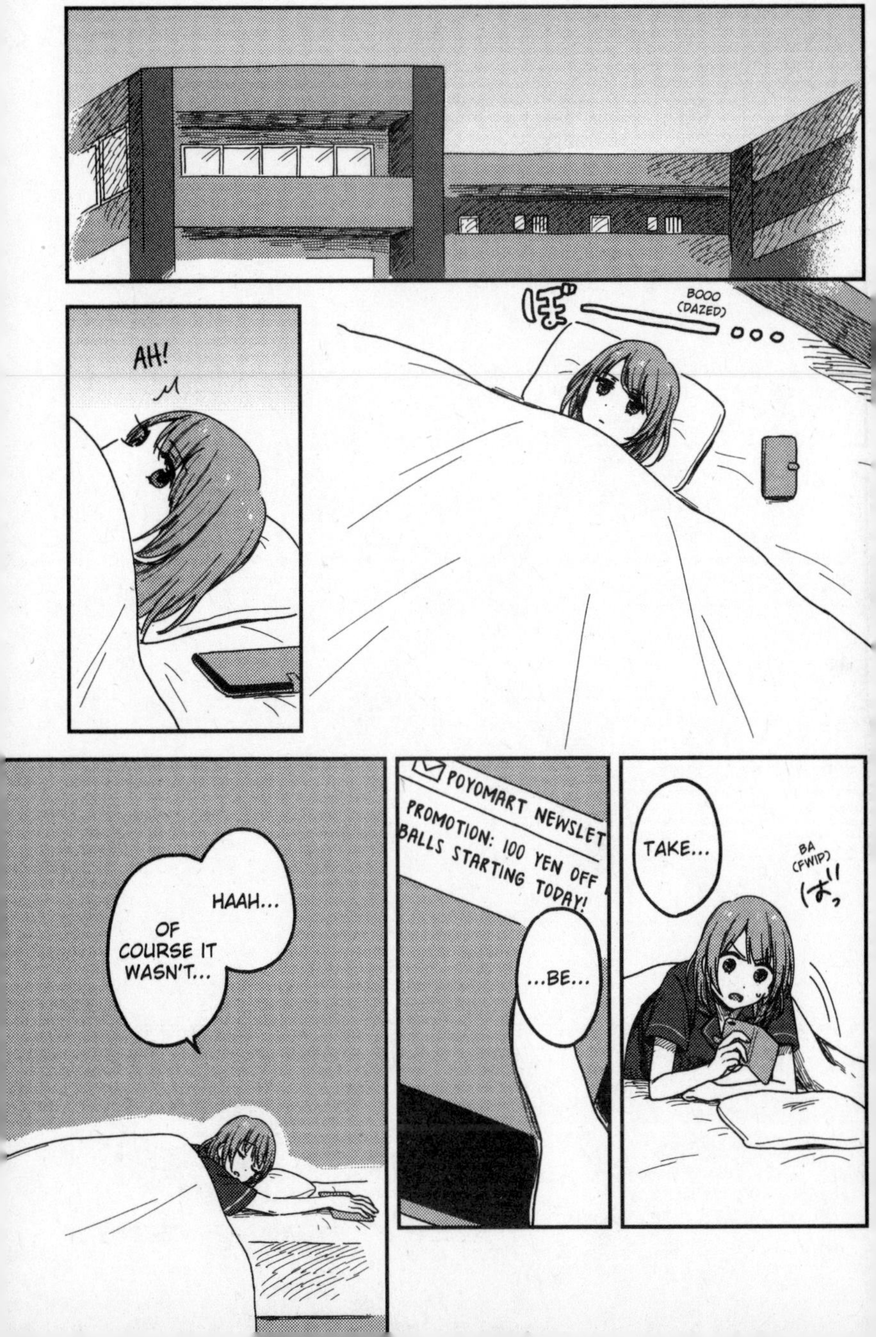
ぼ
BOOO (DAZED)
AH!
TAKE...
BA (FWIP)
ばっ
POYOMART NEWSLET
PROMOTION: 100 YEN OFF
BALLS STARTING TODAY!
...BE...
HAAH...
OF COURSE IT WASN'T...

Catch These Hands!

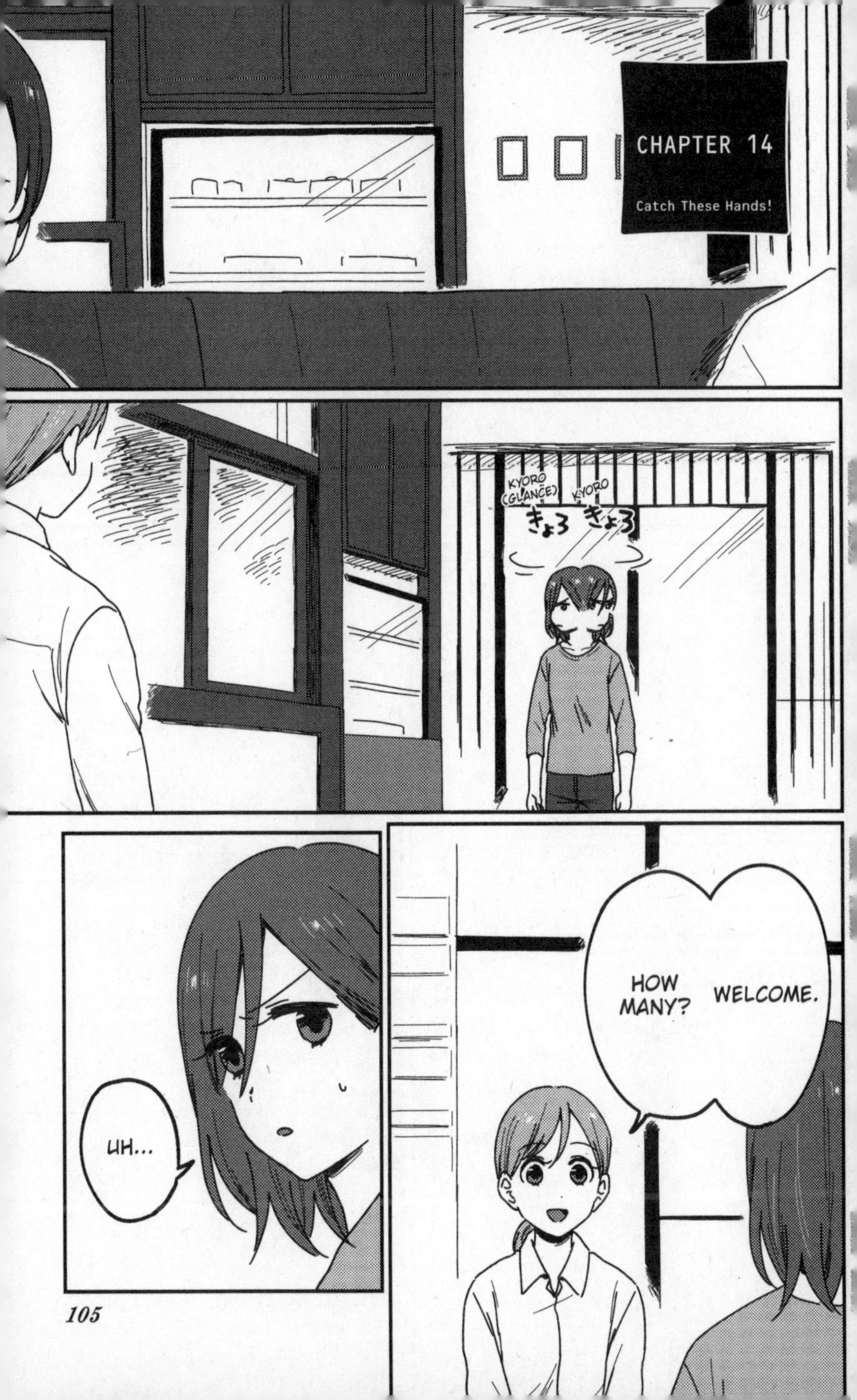
CHAPTER 14
Catch These Hands!
KYORO きょろ
KYORO (GLANCE) きょろ
WELCOME. HOW MANY?
UH...

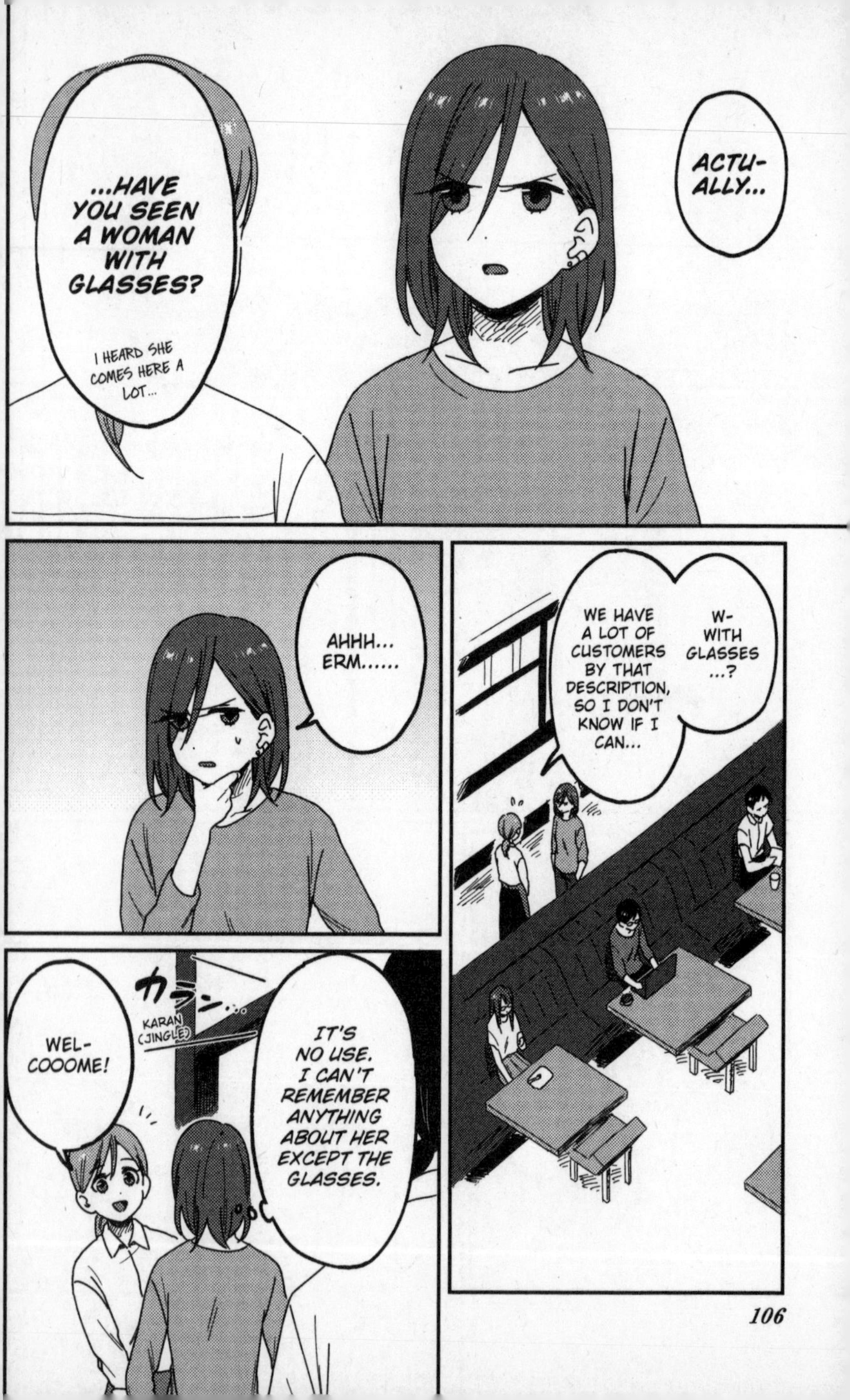
ACTU-ALLY...
...HAVE YOU SEEN A WOMAN WITH GLASSES?
I HEARD SHE COMES HERE A LOT...
W-WITH GLASSES ...?
WE HAVE A LOT OF CUSTOMERS BY THAT DESCRIPTION, SO I DON'T KNOW IF I CAN...
AHHH... ERM......
IT'S NO USE. I CAN'T REMEMBER ANYTHING ABOUT HER EXCEPT THE GLASSES.
カラン
KARAN (JINGLE)
WEL-COOOME!

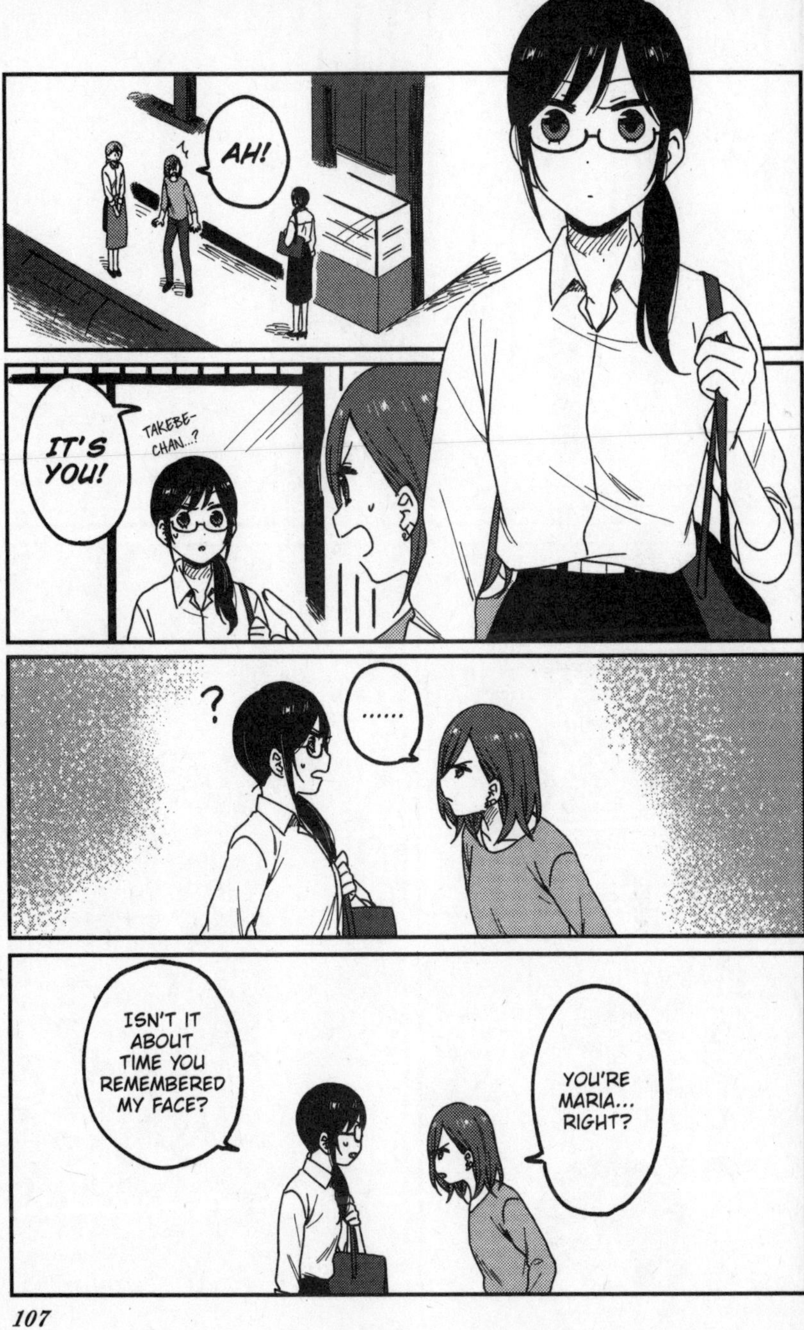
AH!
TAKEBE-CHAN...?
IT'S YOU!
......
?
YOU'RE MARIA... RIGHT?
ISN'T IT ABOUT TIME YOU REMEMBERED MY FACE?

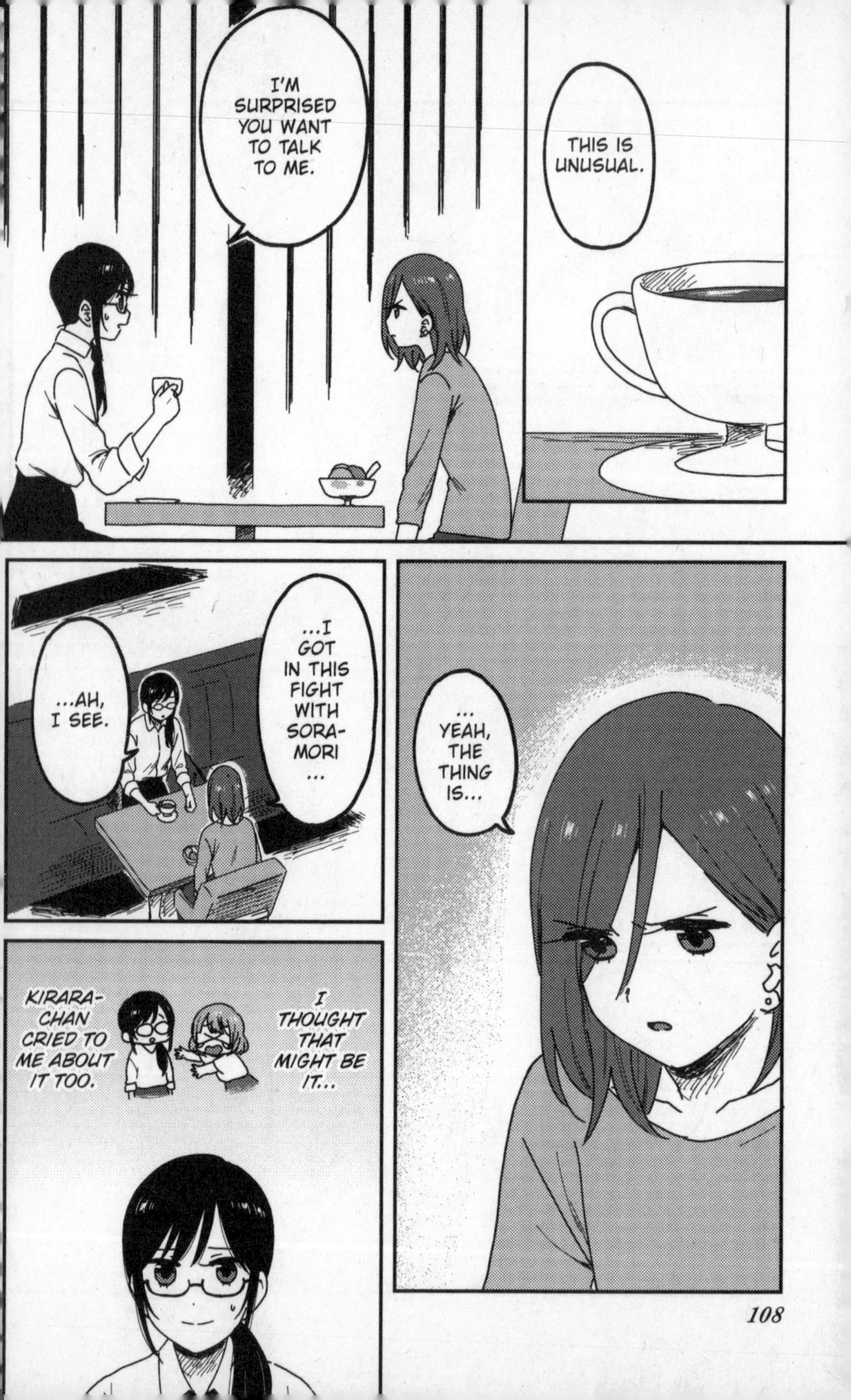
THIS IS UNUSUAL.
I'M SURPRISED YOU WANT TO TALK TO ME.
...YEAH, THE THING IS...
...I GOT IN THIS FIGHT WITH SORA-MORI...
...AH, I SEE.
I THOUGHT THAT MIGHT BE IT...
KIRARA-CHAN CRIED TO ME ABOUT IT TOO.

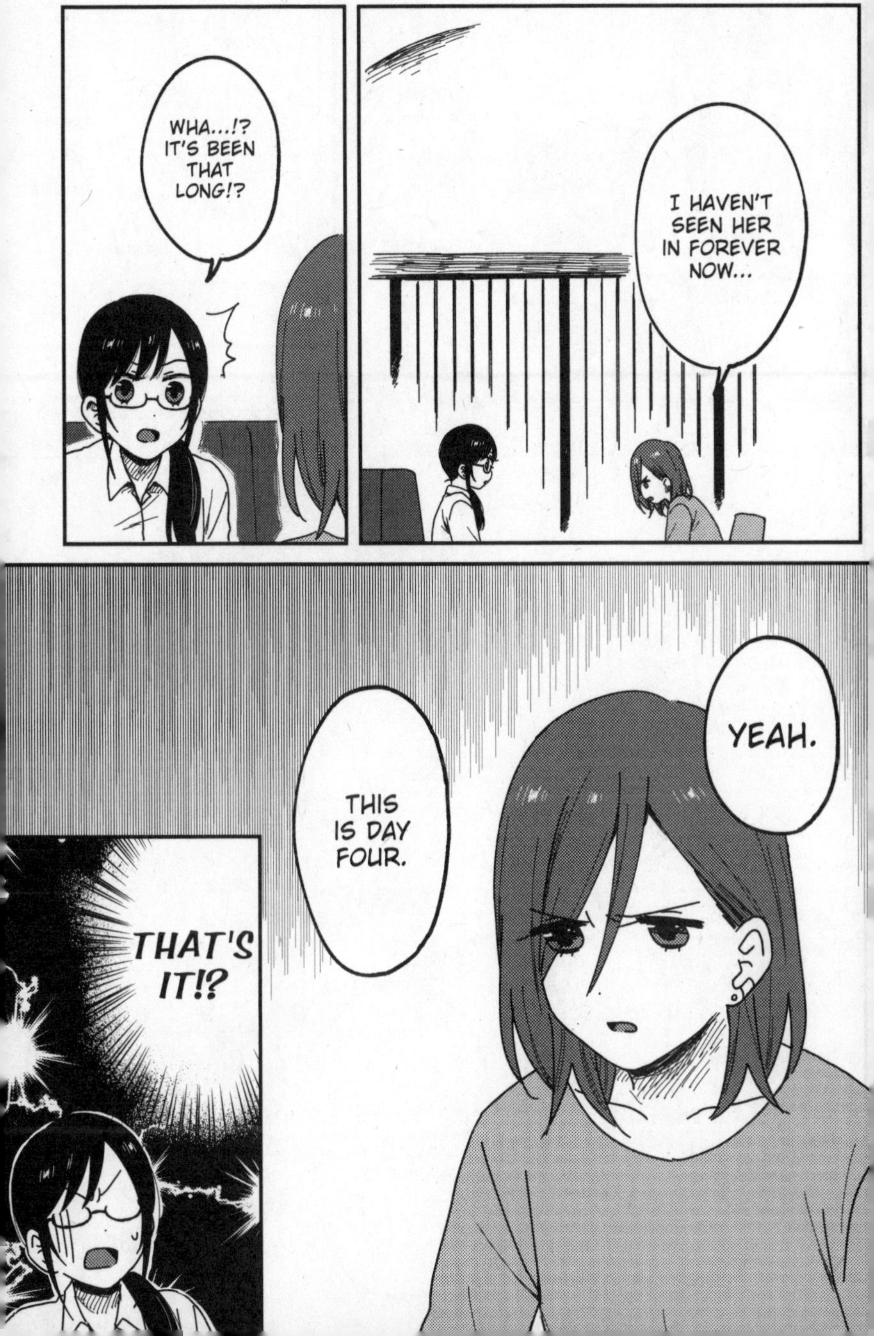
I HAVEN'T SEEN HER IN FOREVER NOW...
WHA...!? IT'S BEEN THAT LONG!?
YEAH.
THIS IS DAY FOUR.
THAT'S IT!?

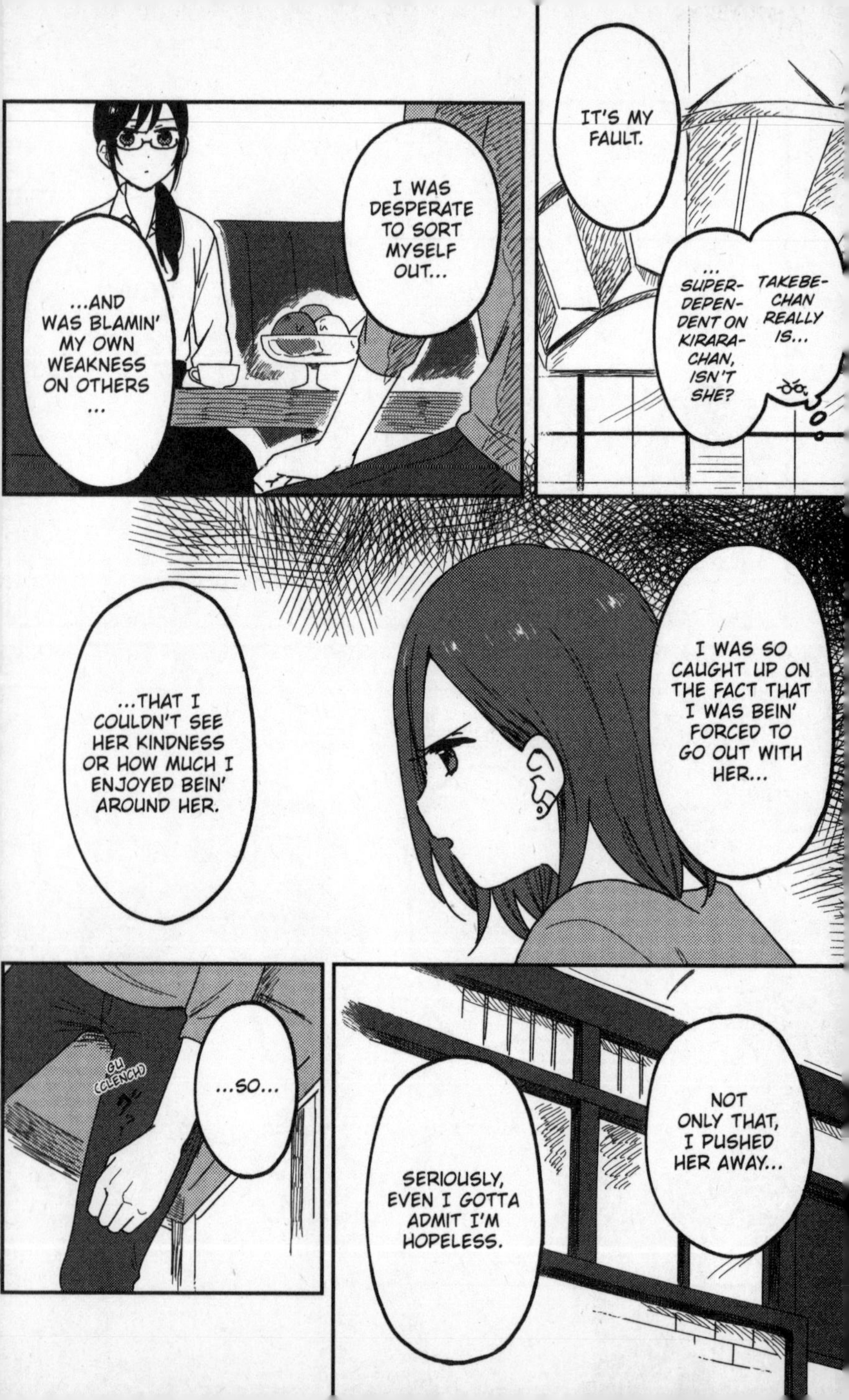
IT'S MY FAULT.
TAKEBE-CHAN REALLY IS...
...SUPER-DEPENDENT ON KIRARA-CHAN, ISN'T SHE?
I WAS DESPERATE TO SORT MYSELF OUT...
...AND WAS BLAMIN' MY OWN WEAKNESS ON OTHERS...
I WAS SO CAUGHT UP ON THE FACT THAT I WAS BEIN' FORCED TO GO OUT WITH HER...
...THAT I COULDN'T SEE HER KINDNESS OR HOW MUCH I ENJOYED BEIN' AROUND HER.
NOT ONLY THAT, I PUSHED HER AWAY...
SERIOUSLY, EVEN I GOTTA ADMIT I'M HOPELESS.
...SO...
GU (CLENCH)

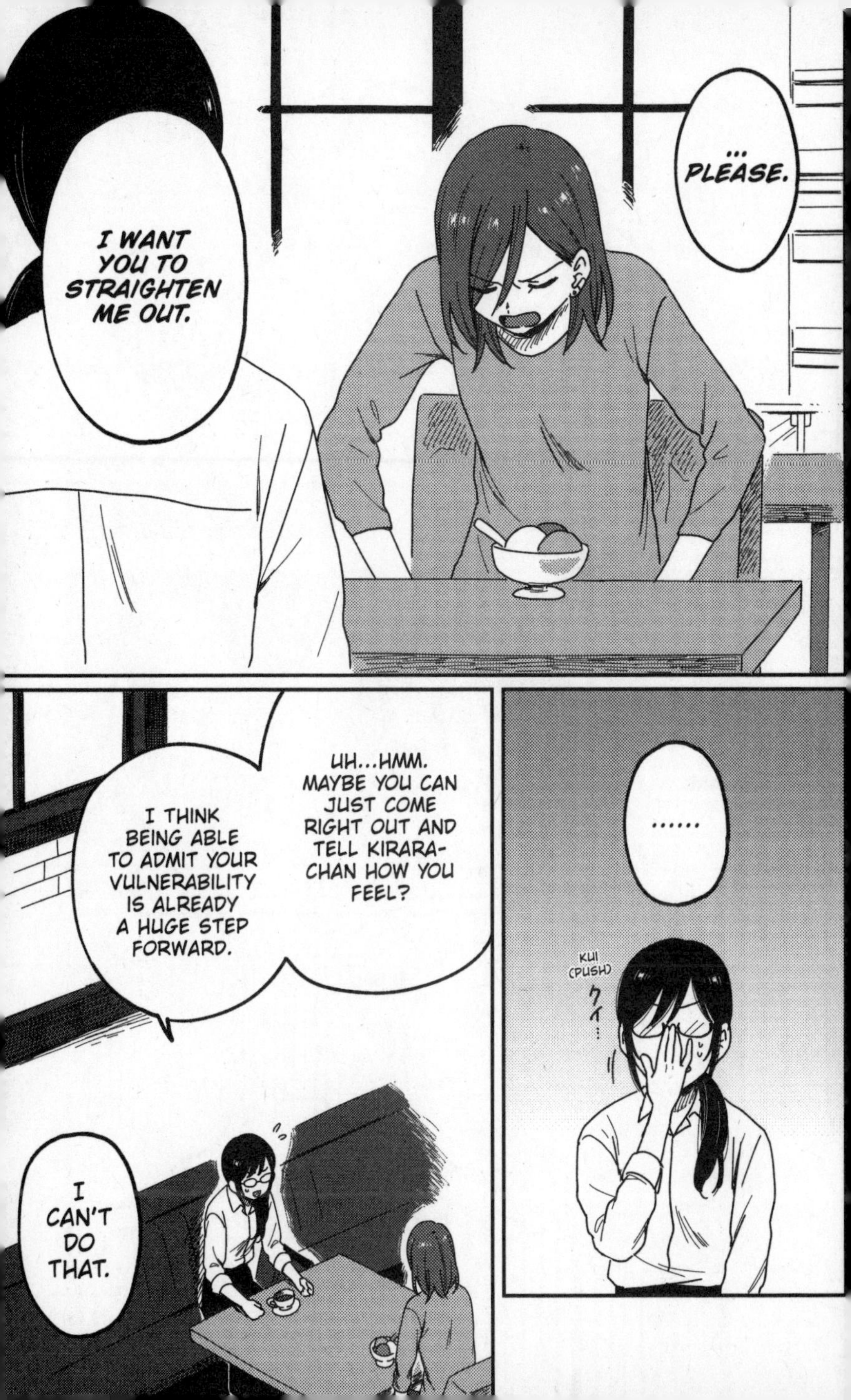

...PLEASE.
I WANT YOU TO STRAIGHTEN ME OUT.
......
KUI (PUSH)
クイ…
UH...HMM. MAYBE YOU CAN JUST COME RIGHT OUT AND TELL KIRARA-CHAN HOW YOU FEEL?
I THINK BEING ABLE TO ADMIT YOUR VULNERABILITY IS ALREADY A HUGE STEP FORWARD.
I CAN'T DO THAT.

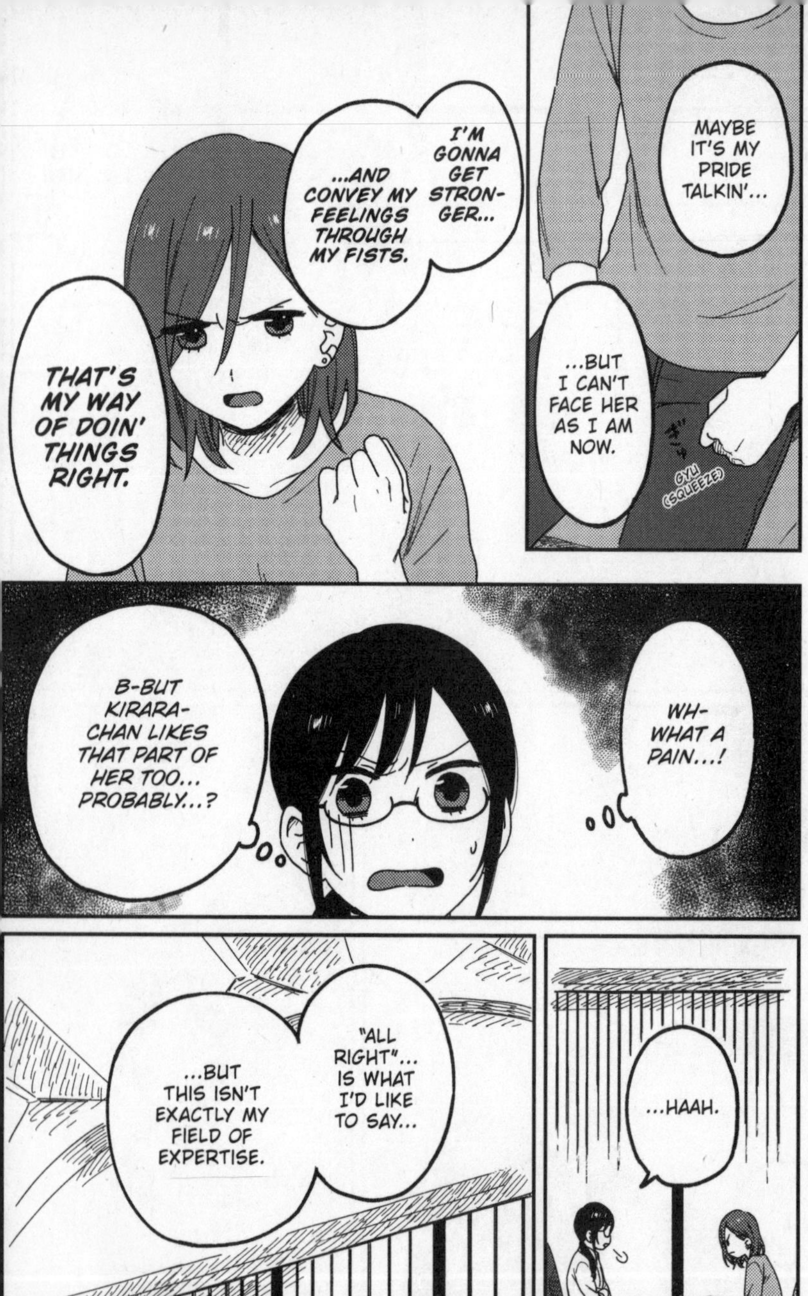
MAYBE IT'S MY PRIDE TALKIN'...
...BUT I CAN'T FACE HER AS I AM NOW.
GYU (SQUEEZE)
I'M GONNA GET STRONGER...
...AND CONVEY MY FEELINGS THROUGH MY FISTS.
THAT'S MY WAY OF DOIN' THINGS RIGHT.
WH-WHAT A PAIN...!
B-BUT KIRARA-CHAN LIKES THAT PART OF HER TOO... PROBABLY...?
...HAAH.
"ALL RIGHT"... IS WHAT I'D LIKE TO SAY...
...BUT THIS ISN'T EXACTLY MY FIELD OF EXPERTISE.

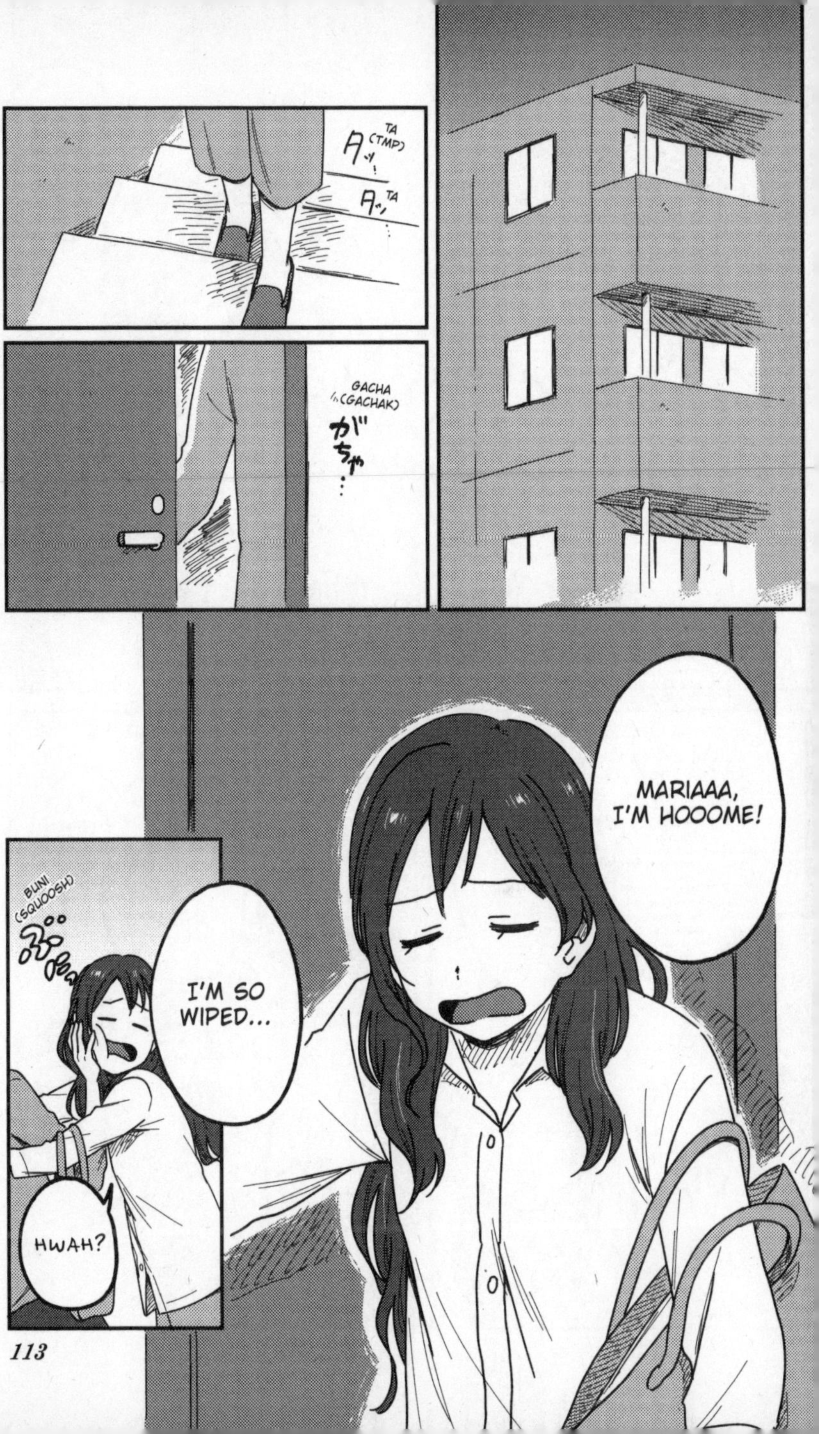
TA (TMP)
TA
GACHA (GACHAK)
MARIAAA, I'M HOOOME!
I'M SO WIPED...
BUNI (SQUOOSH)
HWAH?

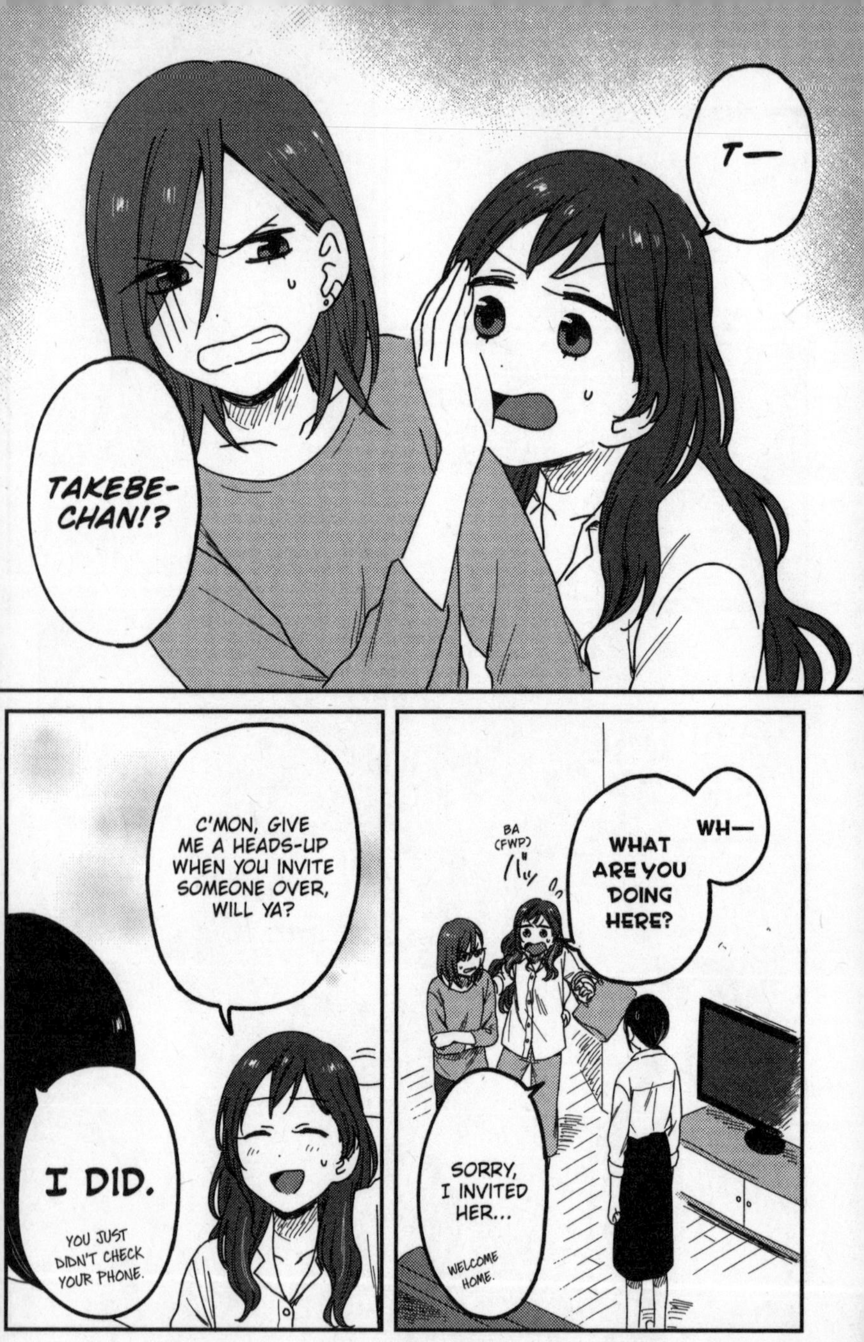
T—
TAKEBE-CHAN!?
WH— WHAT ARE YOU DOING HERE?
BA (FWP)
SORRY, I INVITED HER...
WELCOME HOME.
C'MON, GIVE ME A HEADS-UP WHEN YOU INVITE SOMEONE OVER, WILL YA?
I DID.
YOU JUST DIDN'T CHECK YOUR PHONE.

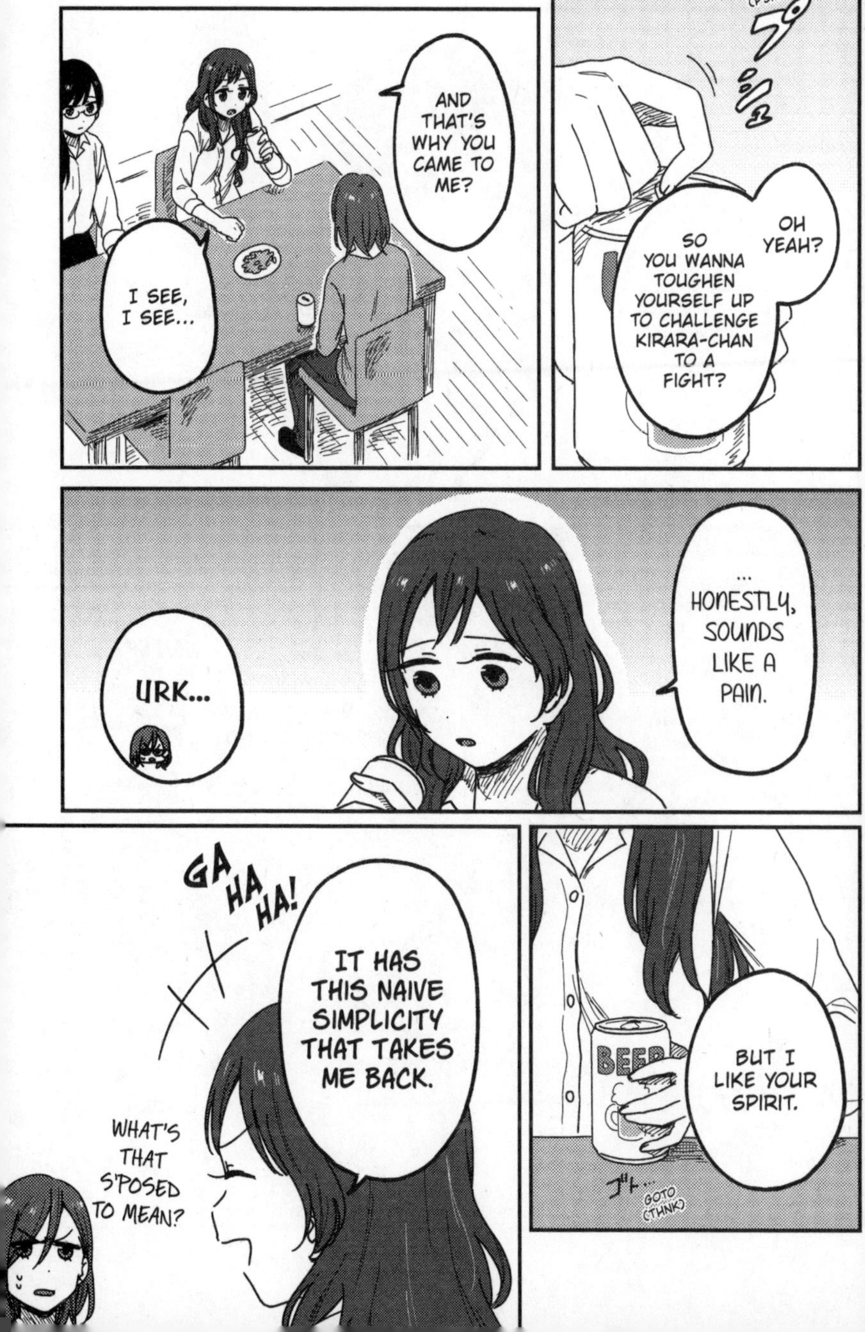
PUSHU (PSK)
OH YEAH?
SO YOU WANNA TOUGHEN YOURSELF UP TO CHALLENGE KIRARA-CHAN TO A FIGHT?
AND THAT'S WHY YOU CAME TO ME?
I SEE, I SEE...
... HONESTLY, SOUNDS LIKE A PAIN.
URK...
BUT I LIKE YOUR SPIRIT.
GOTO (THNK)
GA HA HA!
IT HAS THIS NAIVE SIMPLICITY THAT TAKES ME BACK.
WHAT'S THAT S'POSED TO MEAN?

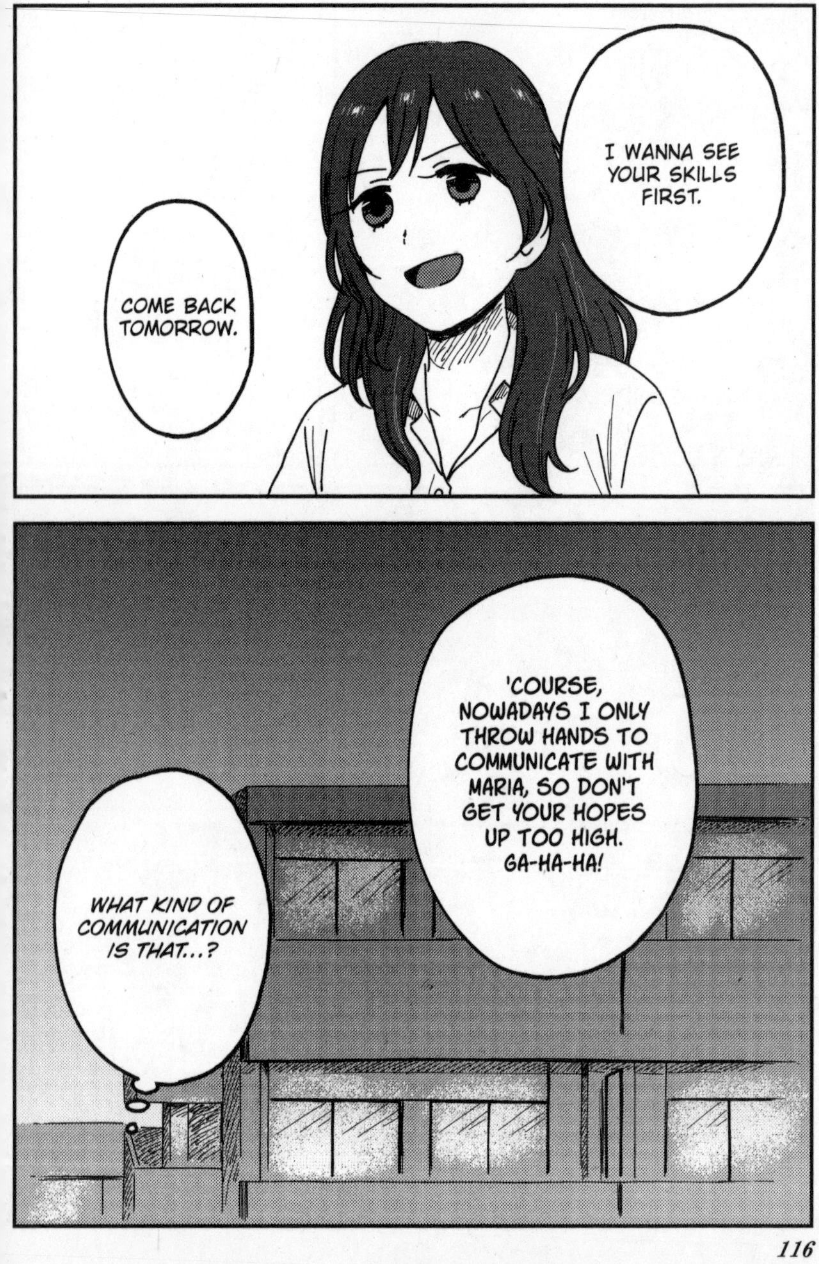
I WANNA SEE YOUR SKILLS FIRST.
COME BACK TOMORROW.
'COURSE, NOWADAYS I ONLY THROW HANDS TO COMMUNICATE WITH MARIA, SO DON'T GET YOUR HOPES UP TOO HIGH. GA-HA-HA!
WHAT KIND OF COMMUNICATION IS THAT...?

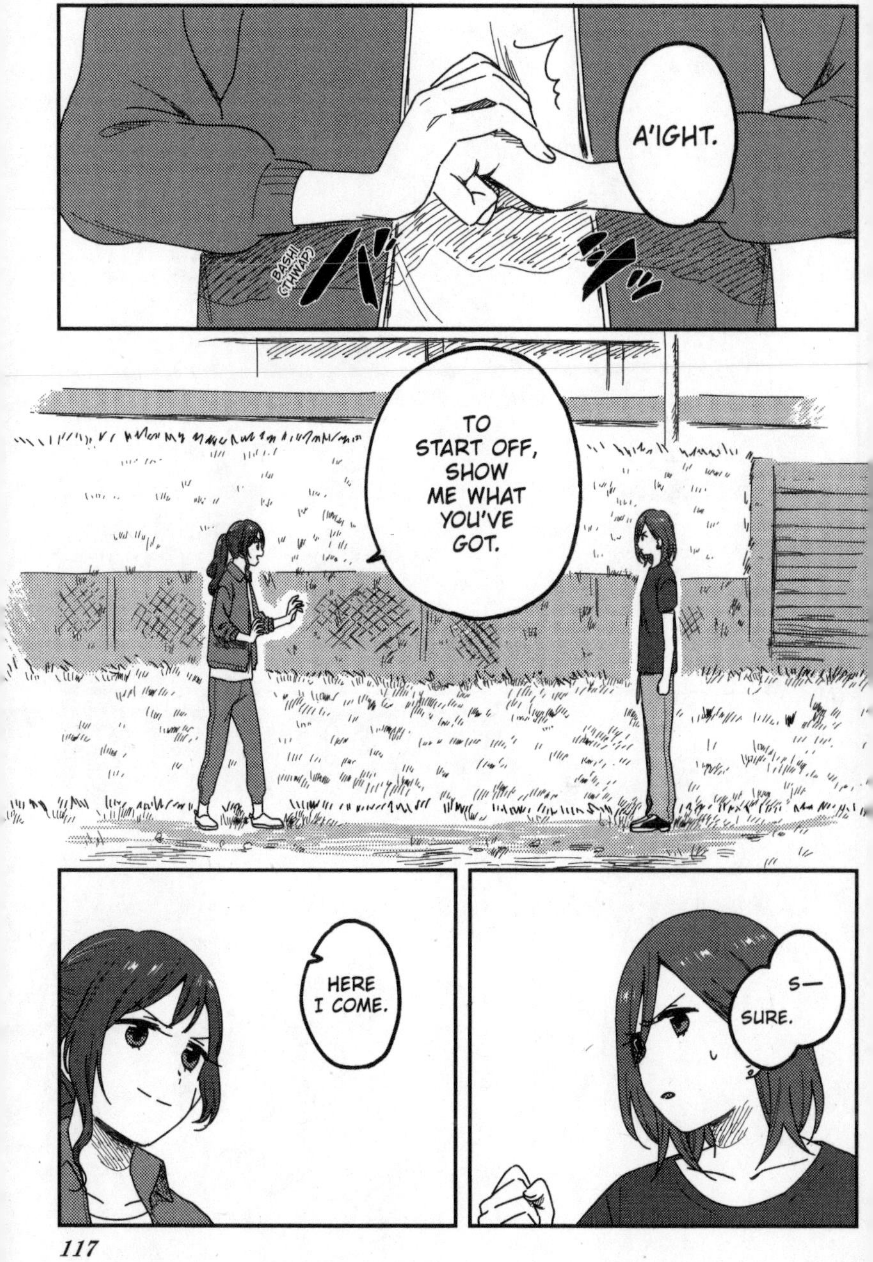
A'IGHT.
BASHI (THWAP)
TO START OFF, SHOW ME WHAT YOU'VE GOT.
S— SURE.
HERE I COME.

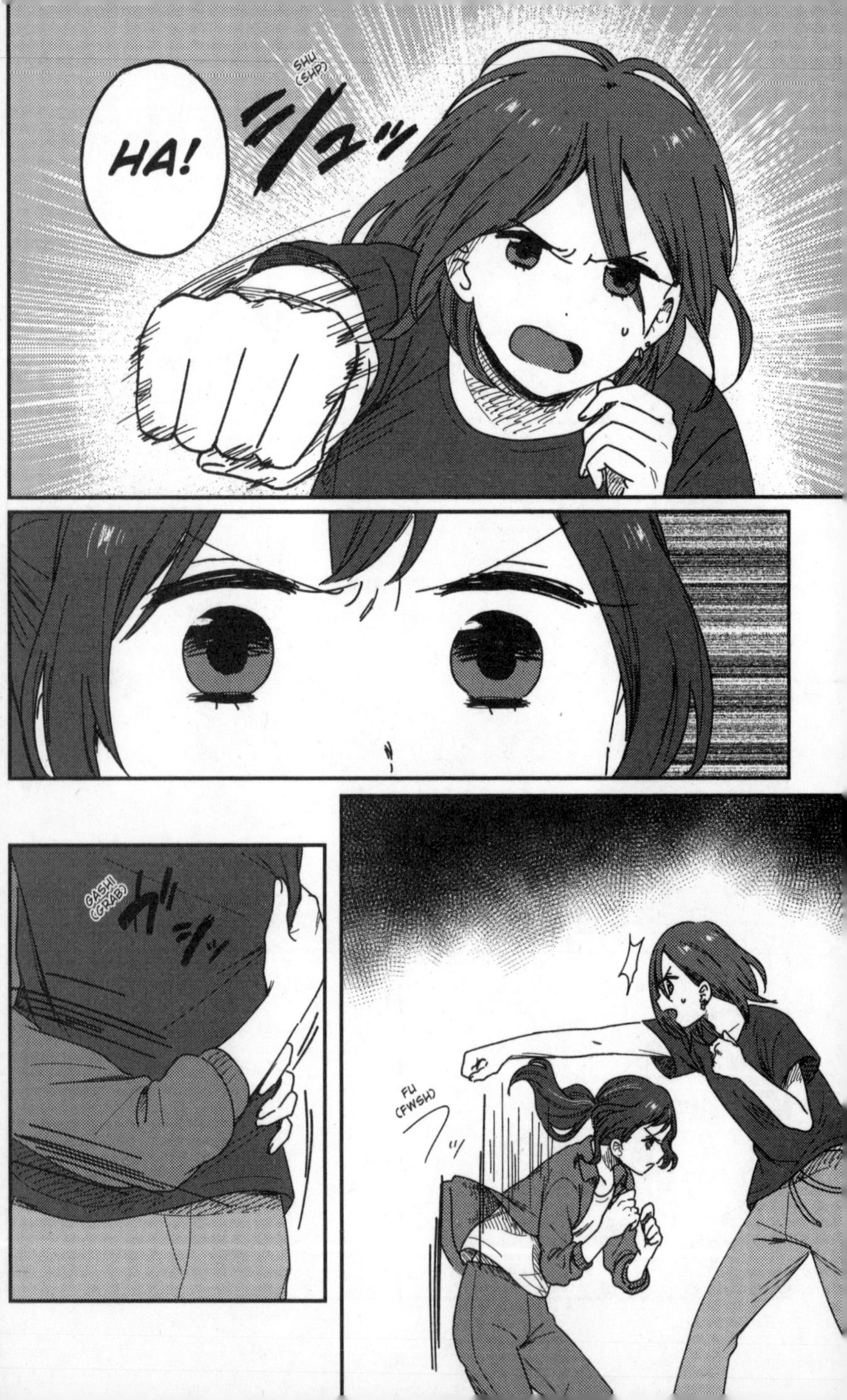
HA!
SHU (SHP)
GASH! (GRAB)
FU (FWSH)

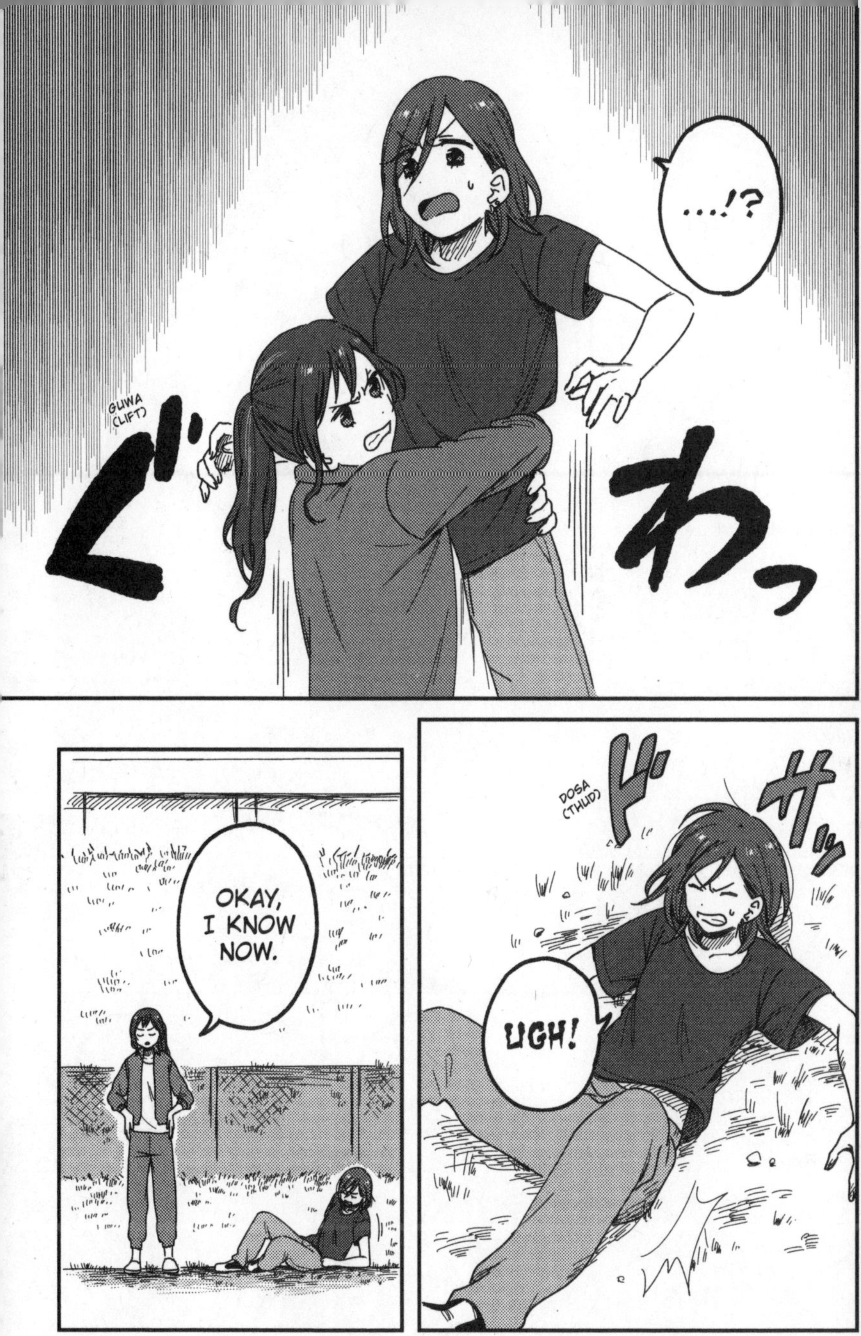
...!?
GUWA (LIFT)
ぐわっ
ドサッ
DOSA (THUD)
UGH!
OKAY, I KNOW NOW.

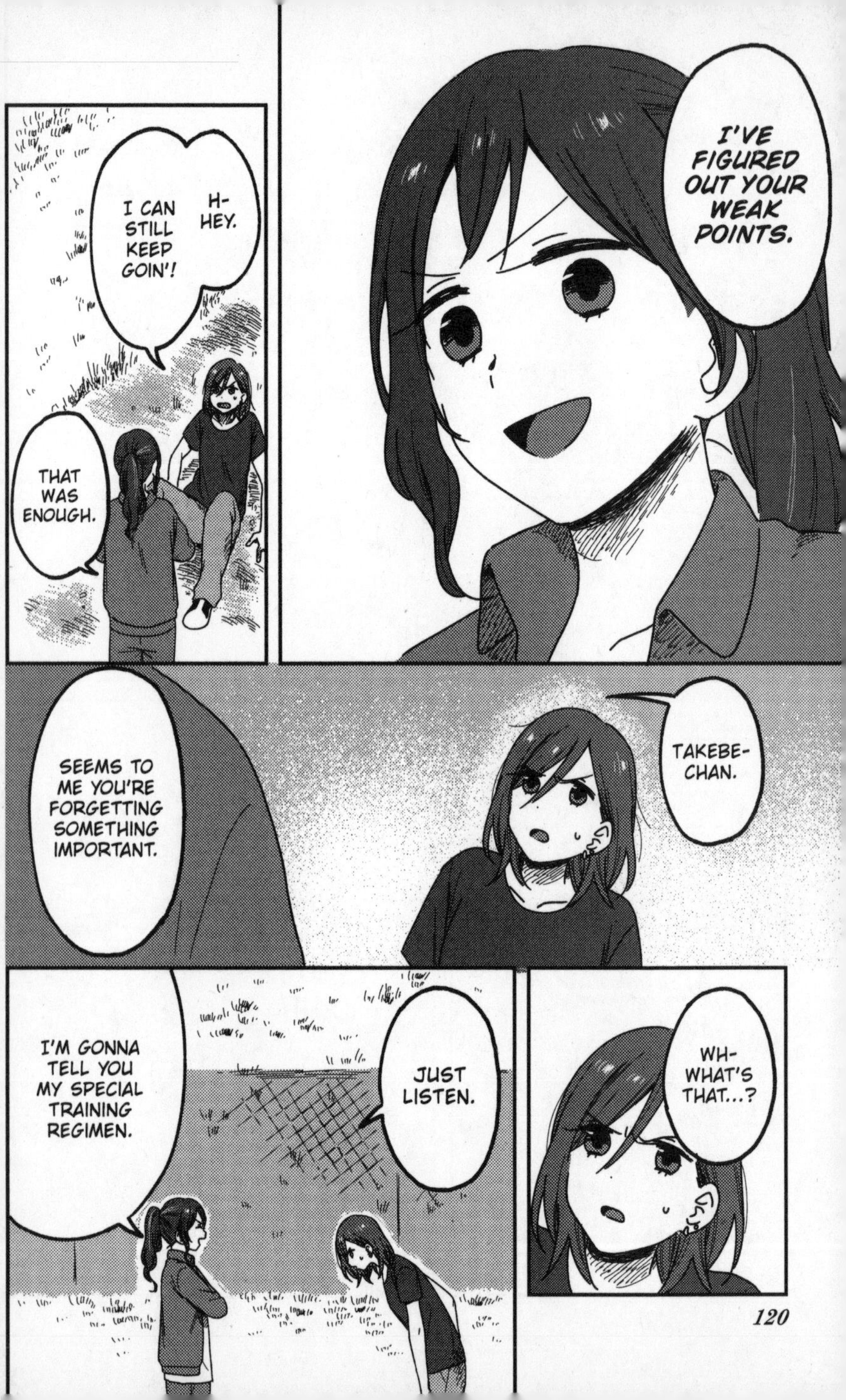
I'VE FIGURED OUT YOUR WEAK POINTS.
H- HEY. I CAN STILL KEEP GOIN'!
THAT WAS ENOUGH.
TAKEBE-CHAN.
SEEMS TO ME YOU'RE FORGETTING SOMETHING IMPORTANT.
WH- WHAT'S THAT...?
JUST LISTEN.
I'M GONNA TELL YOU MY SPECIAL TRAINING REGIMEN.

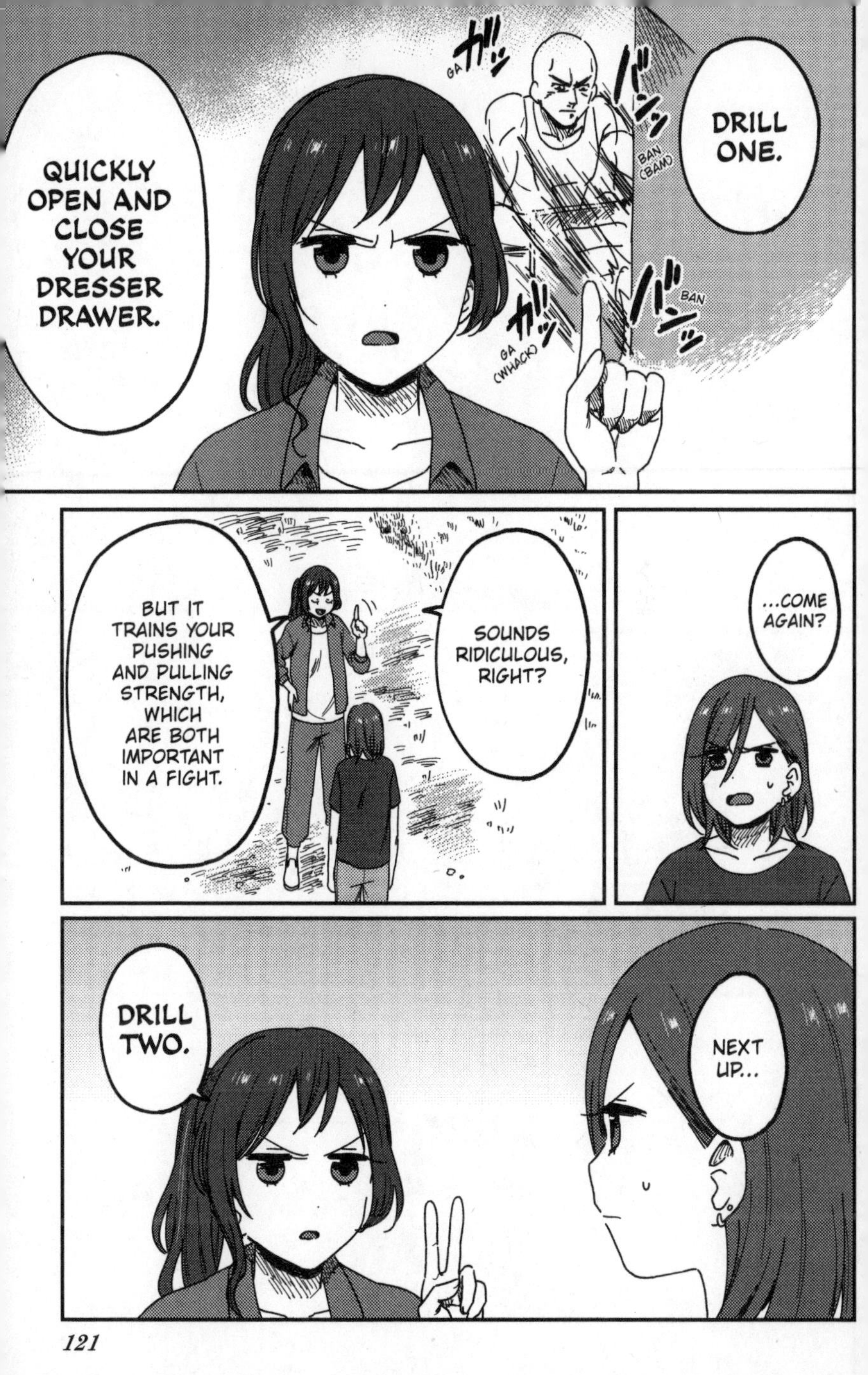
DRILL ONE.
BAN (BAM)
GA
BAN
GA (WHACK)
QUICKLY OPEN AND CLOSE YOUR DRESSER DRAWER.
...COME AGAIN?
SOUNDS RIDICULOUS, RIGHT?
BUT IT TRAINS YOUR PUSHING AND PULLING STRENGTH, WHICH ARE BOTH IMPORTANT IN A FIGHT.
NEXT UP...
DRILL TWO.

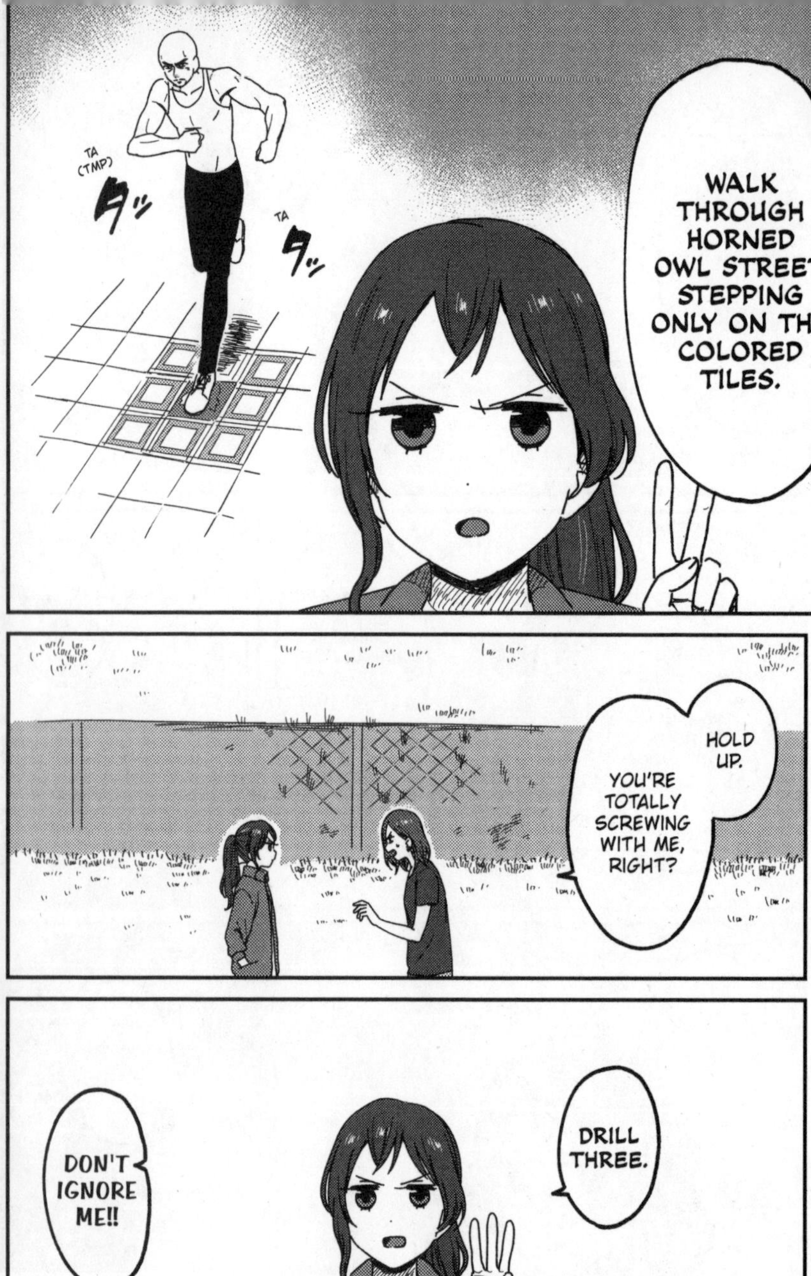
WALK THROUGH HORNED OWL STREET, STEPPING ONLY ON THE COLORED TILES.
TA
タッ
TA (TMP)
タッ
HOLD UP.
YOU'RE TOTALLY SCREWING WITH ME, RIGHT?
DRILL THREE.
DON'T IGNORE ME!!

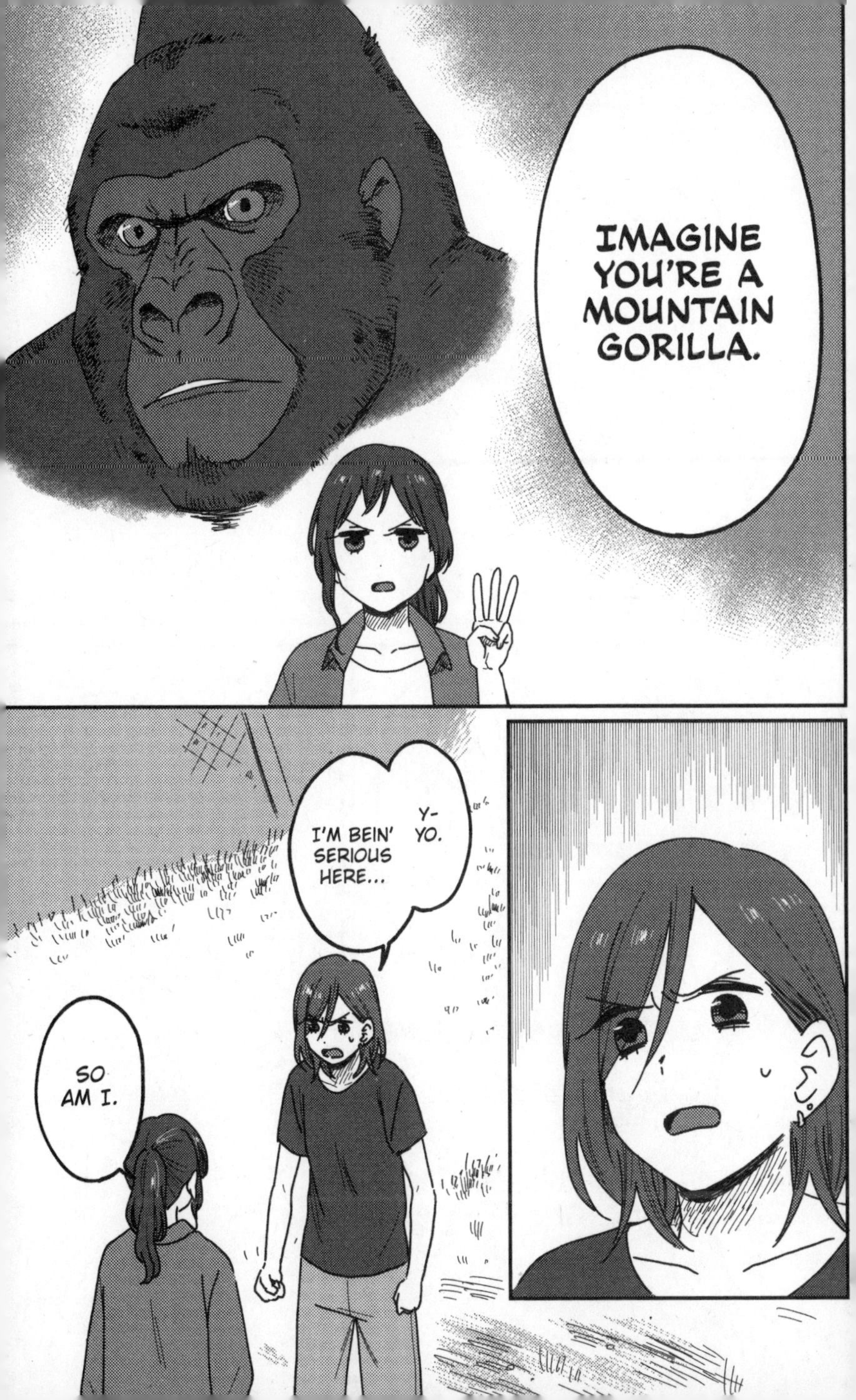
IMAGINE YOU'RE A MOUNTAIN GORILLA.
Y-YO.
I'M BEIN' SERIOUS HERE...
SO AM I.

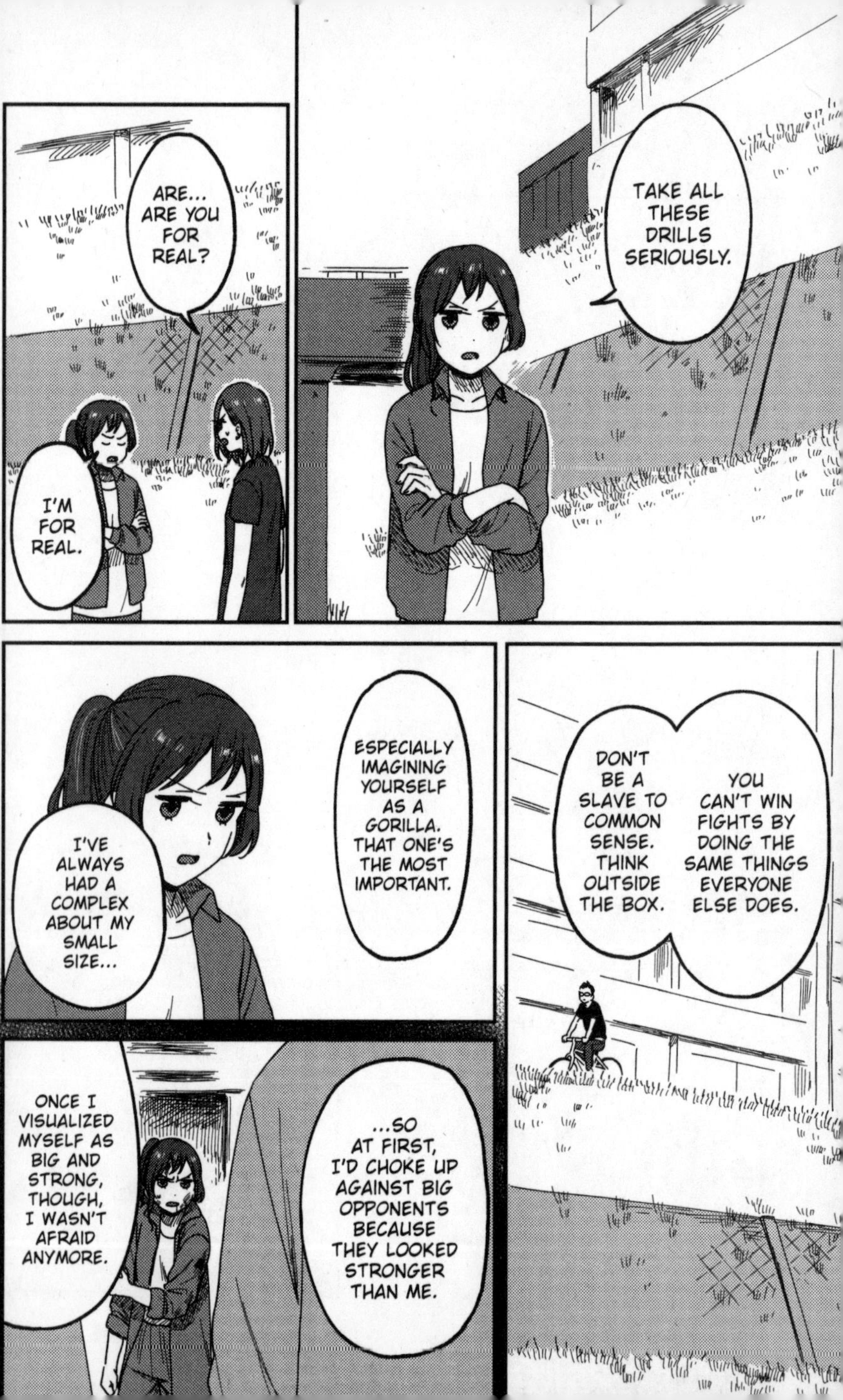
TAKE ALL THESE DRILLS SERIOUSLY.
ARE... ARE YOU FOR REAL?
I'M FOR REAL.
YOU CAN'T WIN FIGHTS BY DOING THE SAME THINGS EVERYONE ELSE DOES.
DON'T BE A SLAVE TO COMMON SENSE. THINK OUTSIDE THE BOX.
ESPECIALLY IMAGINING YOURSELF AS A GORILLA. THAT ONE'S THE MOST IMPORTANT.
I'VE ALWAYS HAD A COMPLEX ABOUT MY SMALL SIZE...
...SO AT FIRST, I'D CHOKE UP AGAINST BIG OPPONENTS BECAUSE THEY LOOKED STRONGER THAN ME.
ONCE I VISUALIZED MYSELF AS BIG AND STRONG, THOUGH, I WASN'T AFRAID ANYMORE.

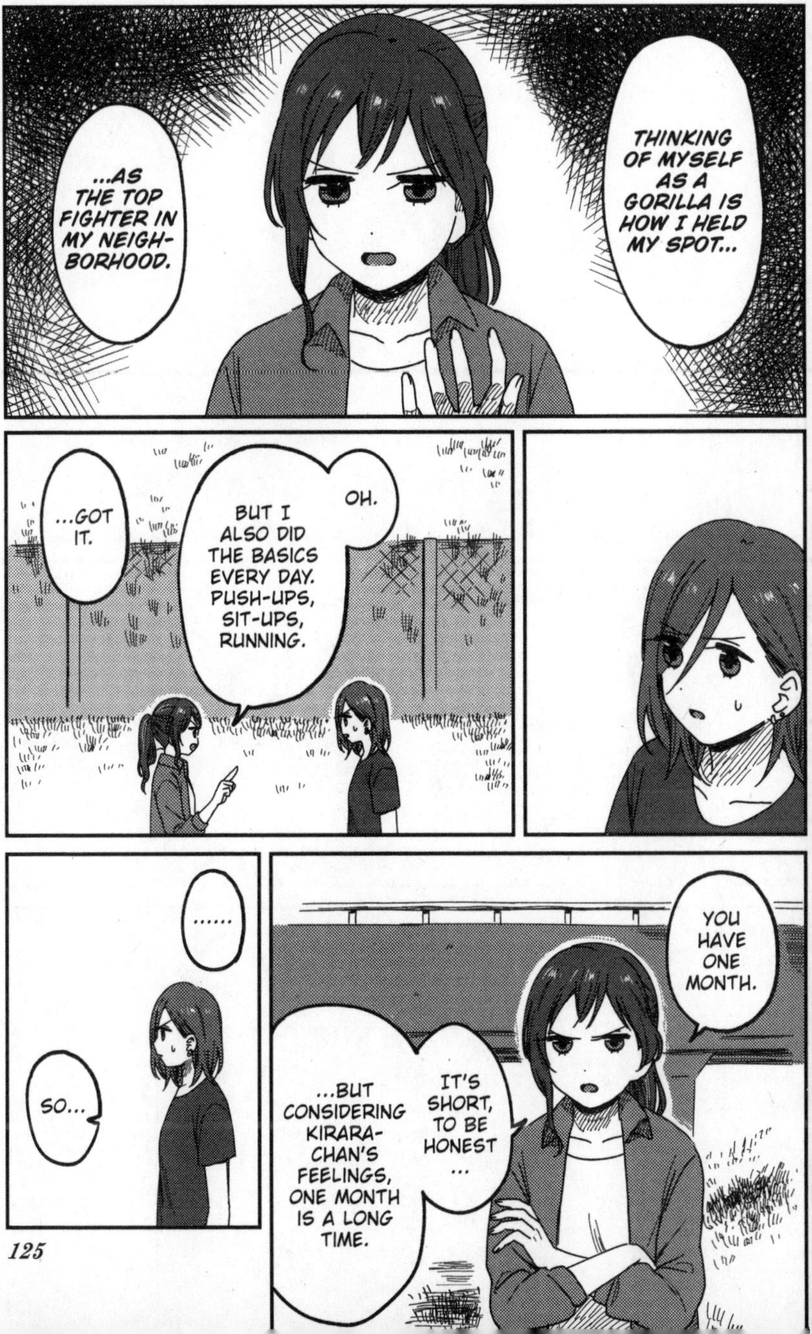
THINKING OF MYSELF AS A GORILLA IS HOW I HELD MY SPOT...
...AS THE TOP FIGHTER IN MY NEIGH-BORHOOD.
OH.
BUT I ALSO DID THE BASICS EVERY DAY. PUSH-UPS, SIT-UPS, RUNNING.
...GOT IT.
YOU HAVE ONE MONTH.
IT'S SHORT, TO BE HONEST...
...BUT CONSIDERING KIRARA-CHAN'S FEELINGS, ONE MONTH IS A LONG TIME.
......
SO...

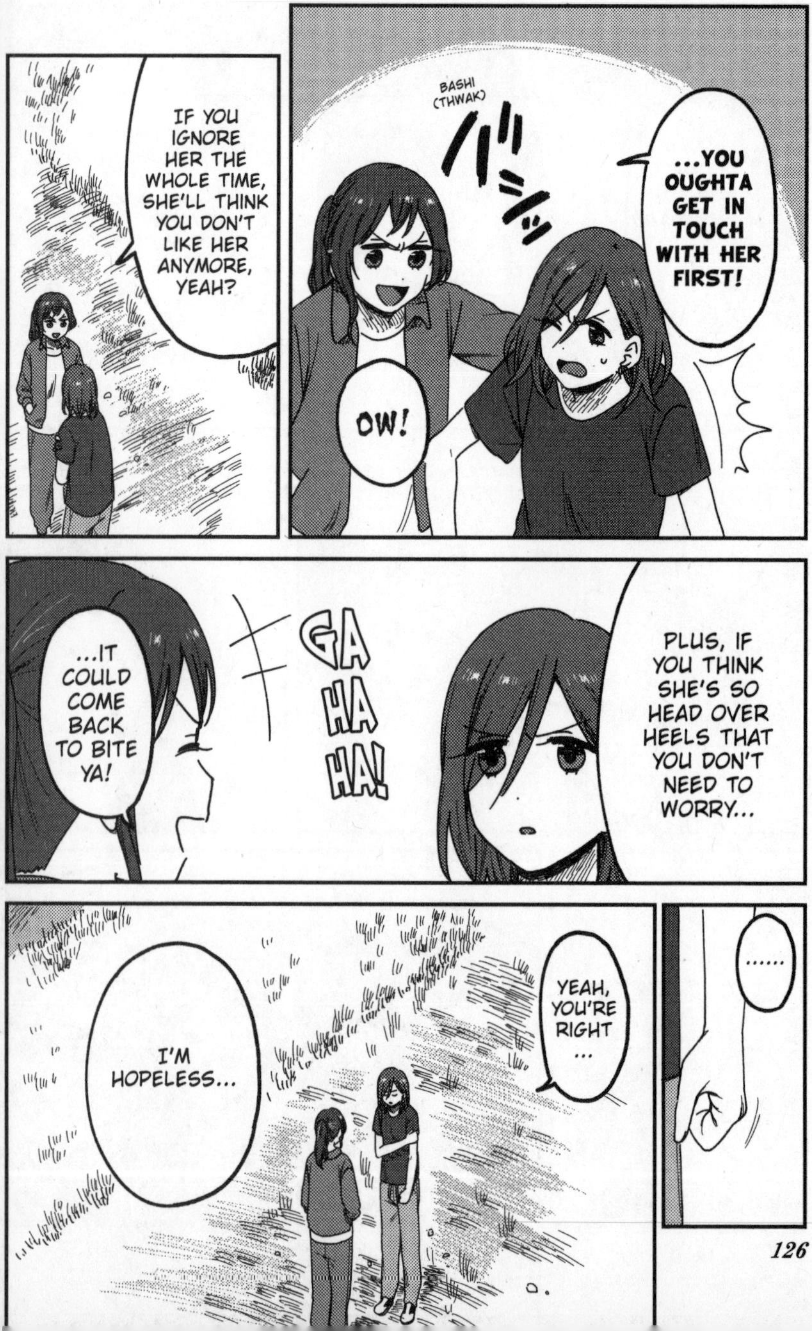
BASHI (THWAK)
...YOU OUGHTA GET IN TOUCH WITH HER FIRST!
OW!
IF YOU IGNORE HER THE WHOLE TIME, SHE'LL THINK YOU DON'T LIKE HER ANYMORE, YEAH?
PLUS, IF YOU THINK SHE'S SO HEAD OVER HEELS THAT YOU DON'T NEED TO WORRY...
GA HA HA!
...IT COULD COME BACK TO BITE YA!
......
YEAH, YOU'RE RIGHT...
I'M HOPELESS...

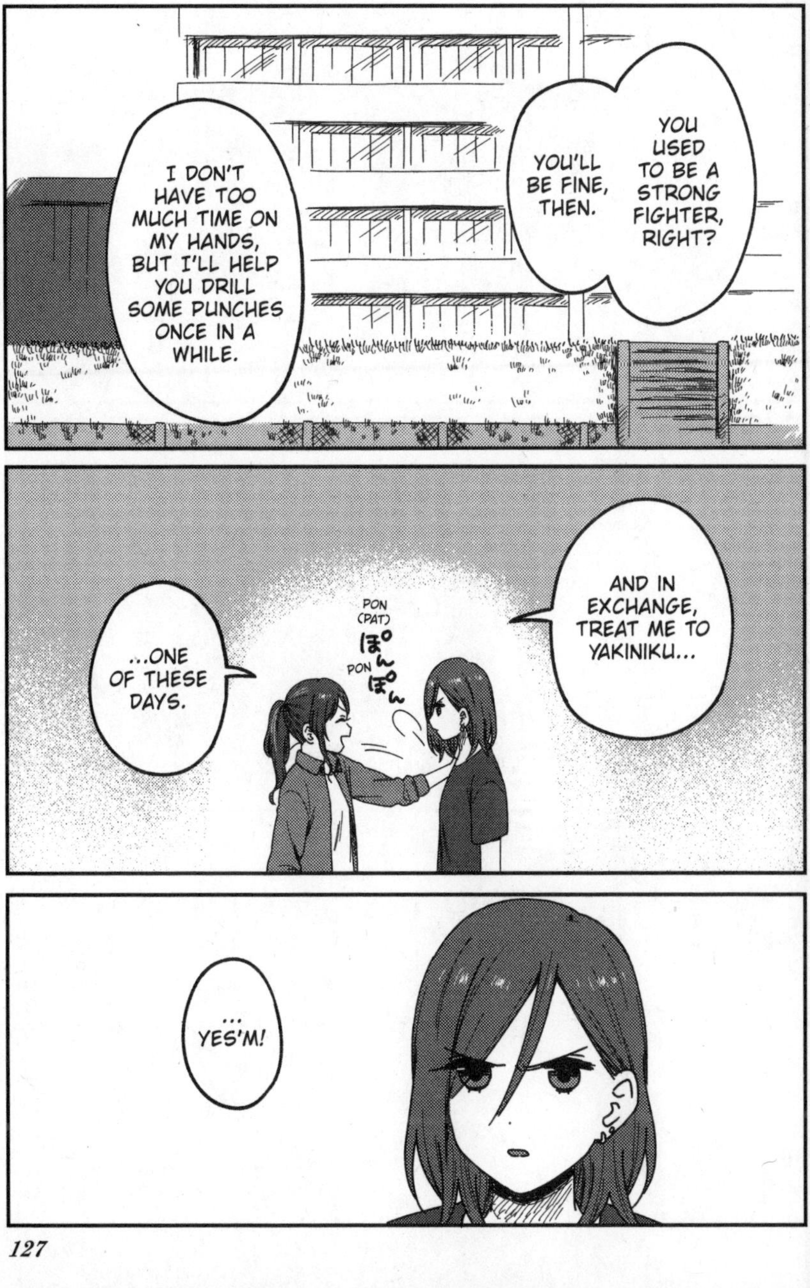
YOU USED TO BE A STRONG FIGHTER, RIGHT?
YOU'LL BE FINE, THEN.
I DON'T HAVE TOO MUCH TIME ON MY HANDS, BUT I'LL HELP YOU DRILL SOME PUNCHES ONCE IN A WHILE.
AND IN EXCHANGE, TREAT ME TO YAKINIKU...
PON (PAT)
ぽん
PON
ぽん
...ONE OF THESE DAYS.
...YES'M!

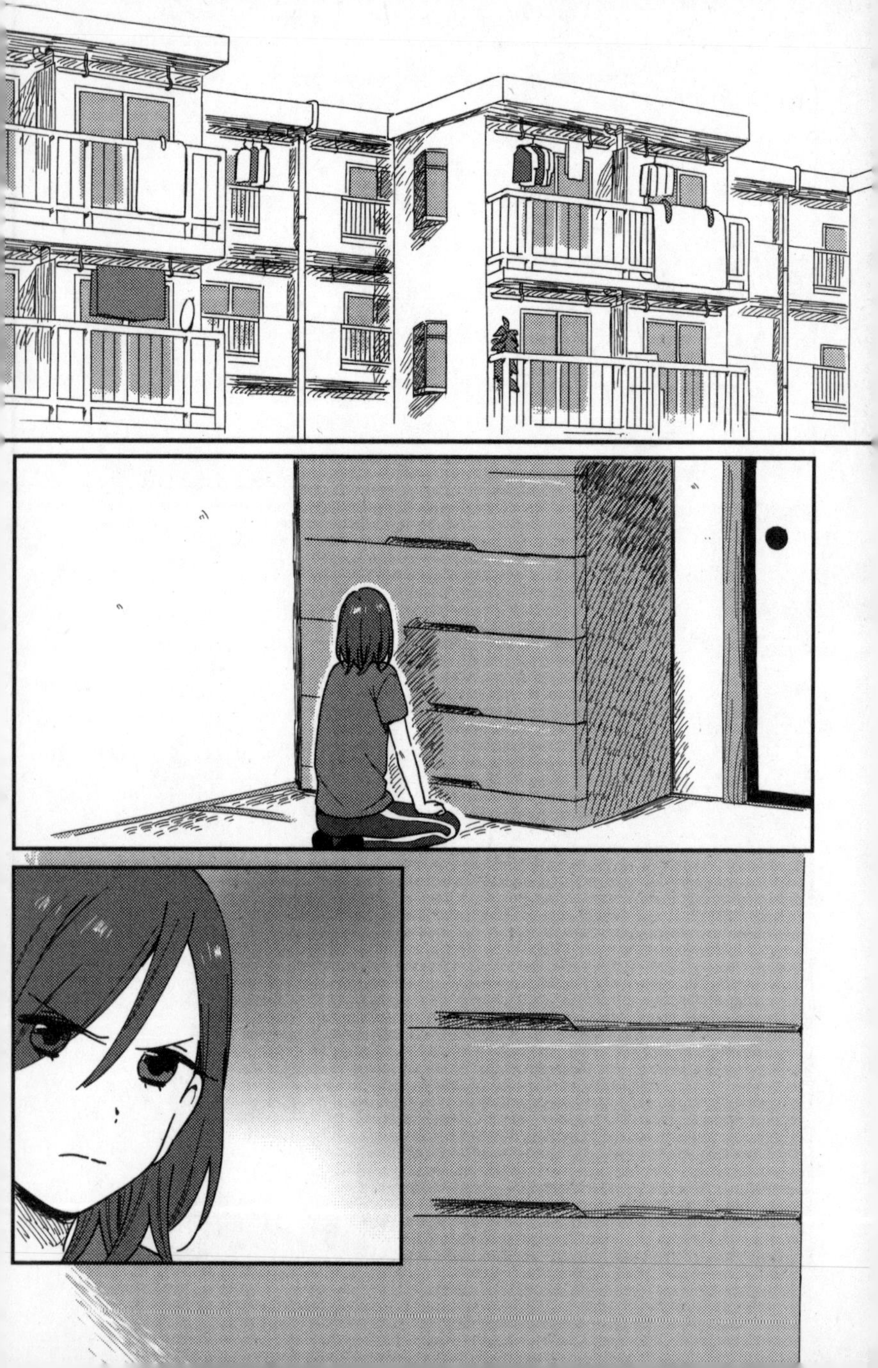

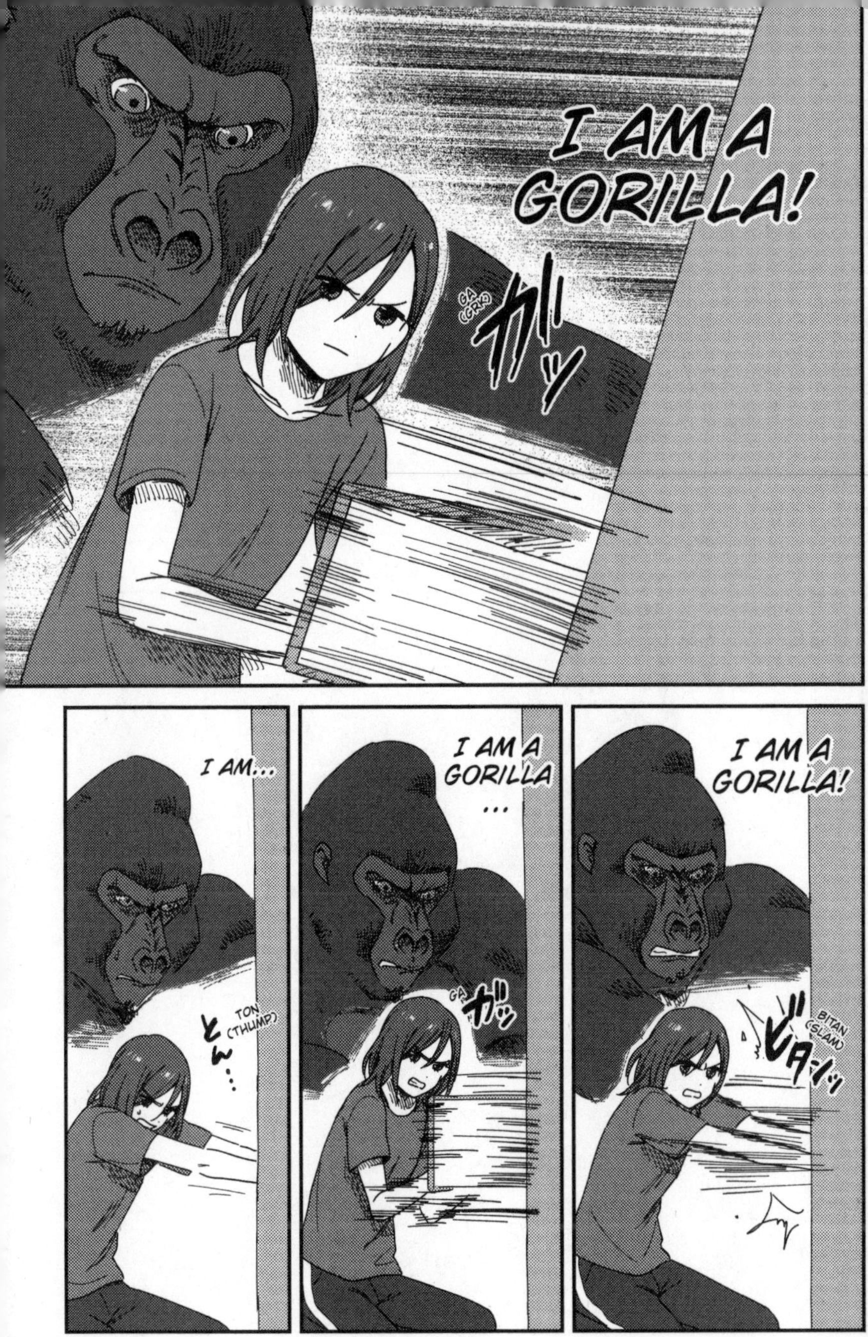
I AM A GORILLA!
GA (GRIP)
I AM A GORILLA!
BITAN (SLAM)
I AM A GORILLA ...
GA
I AM...
TON (THUMP)

IT'S TOUGHER THAN I THOUGHT...

THE DRAWER'S WEIGHT IS REALLY TAKIN' A TOLL ON ME...

DAMN IT....!

FOR A GORILLA, THIS SHOULD BE A PIECE OF CAKE...

DAN (WHAM)

...NO.

MAYBE I STILL...

...HAVEN'T COMPLETELY EMBODIED THE GORILLA...

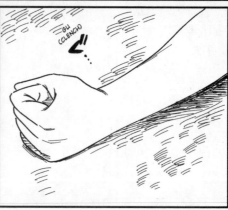

GU (CLENCH)

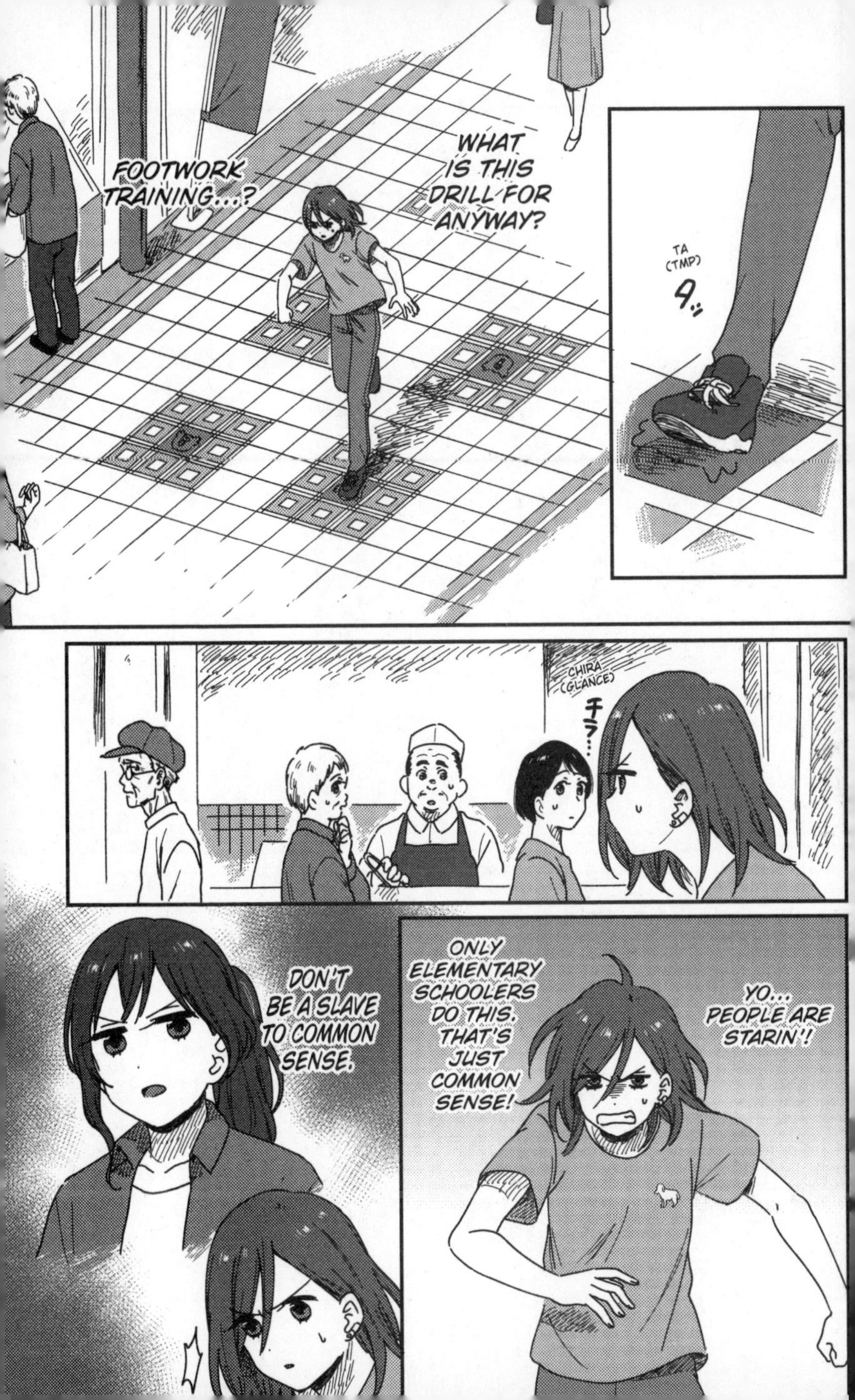
WHAT IS THIS DRILL FOR ANYWAY?
FOOTWORK TRAINING...?
TA (TMP)
タ
CHIRA (GLANCE)
チラ…
YO... PEOPLE ARE STARIN'!
ONLY ELEMENTARY SCHOOLERS DO THIS. THAT'S JUST COMMON SENSE!
DON'T BE A SLAVE TO COMMON SENSE.

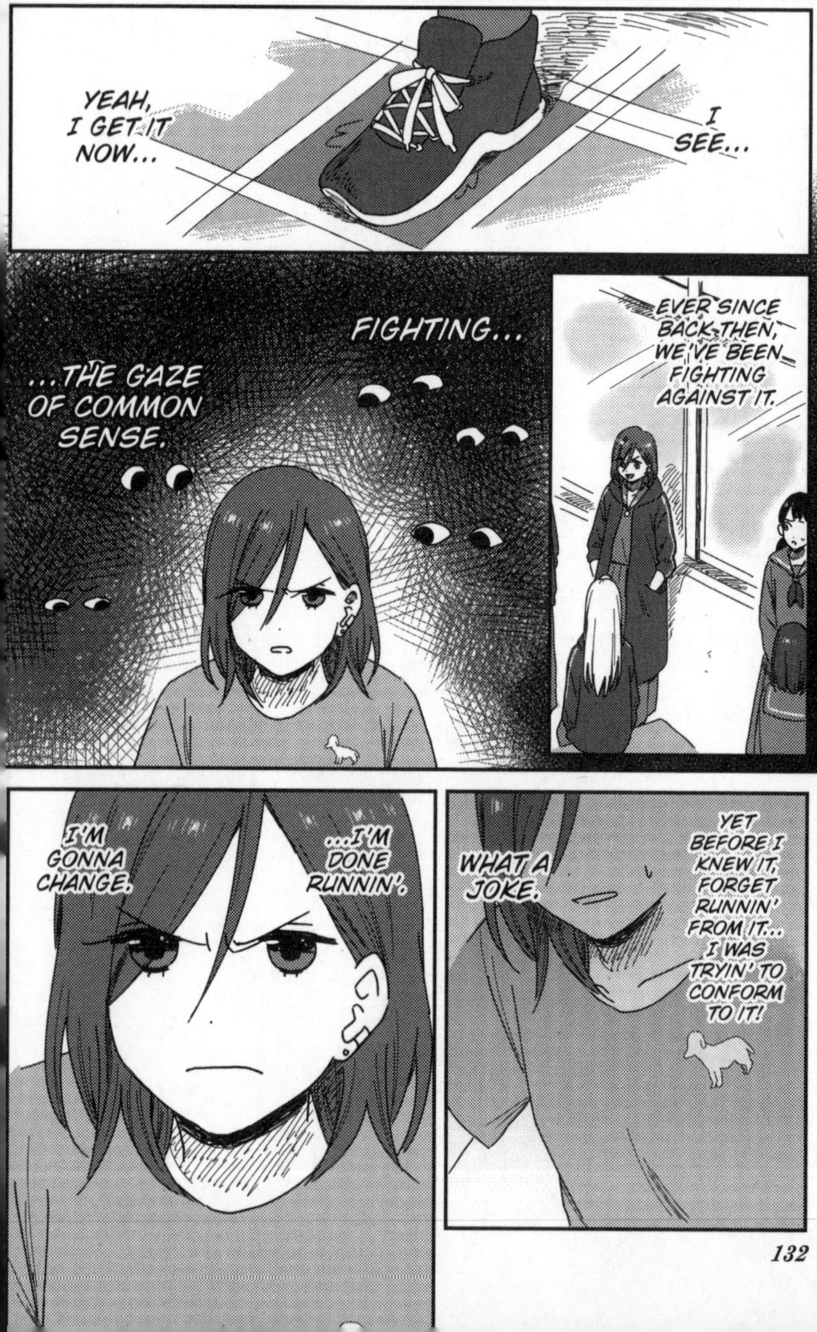
I SEE...
YEAH, I GET IT NOW...
EVER SINCE BACK THEN, WE'VE BEEN FIGHTING AGAINST IT.
FIGHTING...
...THE GAZE OF COMMON SENSE.
YET BEFORE I KNEW IT, FORGET RUNNIN' FROM IT... I WAS TRYIN' TO CONFORM TO IT!
WHAT A JOKE.
...I'M DONE RUNNIN'.
I'M GONNA CHANGE.

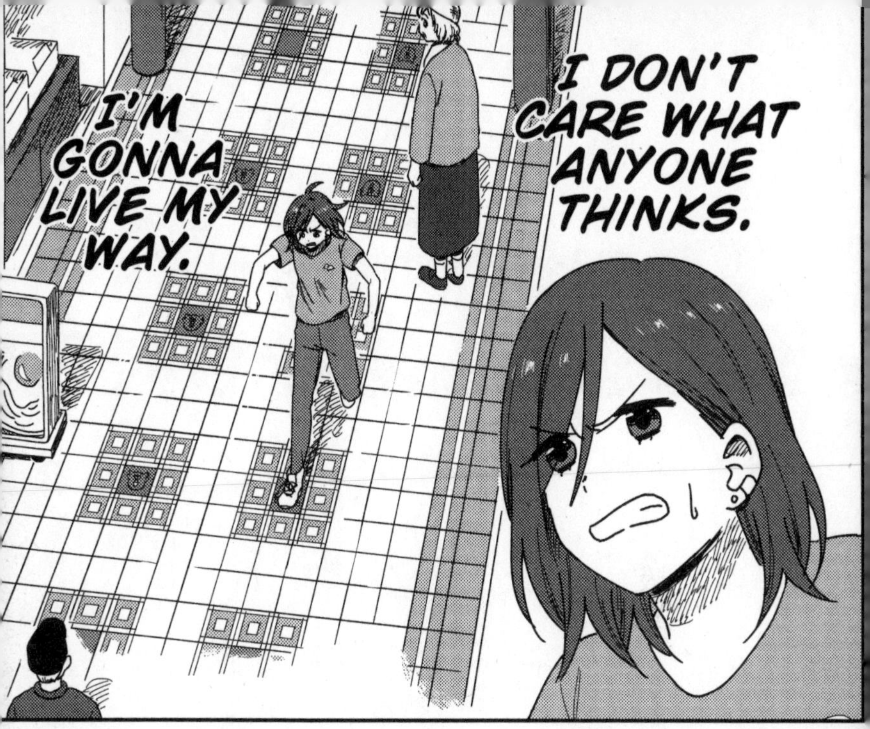
I DON'T CARE WHAT ANYONE THINKS.
I'M GONNA LIVE MY WAY.

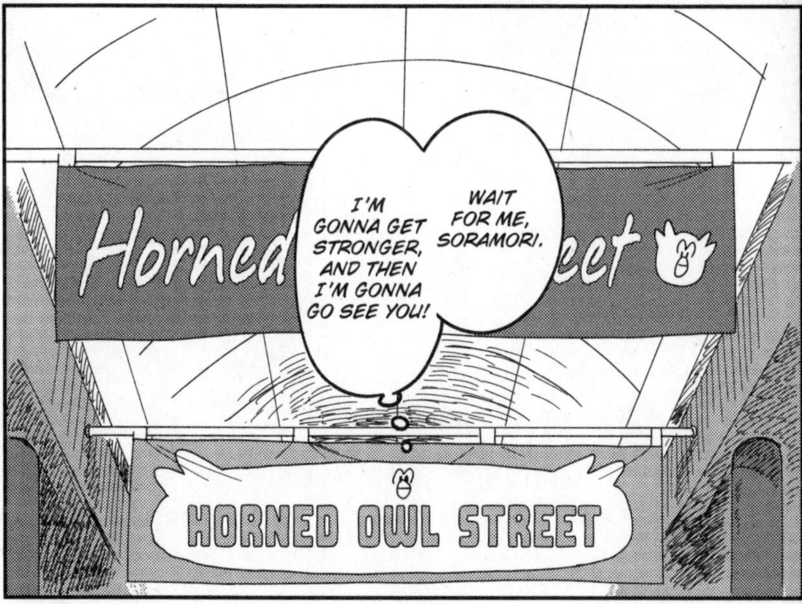
WAIT FOR ME, SORAMORI.
I'M GONNA GET STRONGER, AND THEN I'M GONNA GO SEE YOU!
HORNED OWL STREET

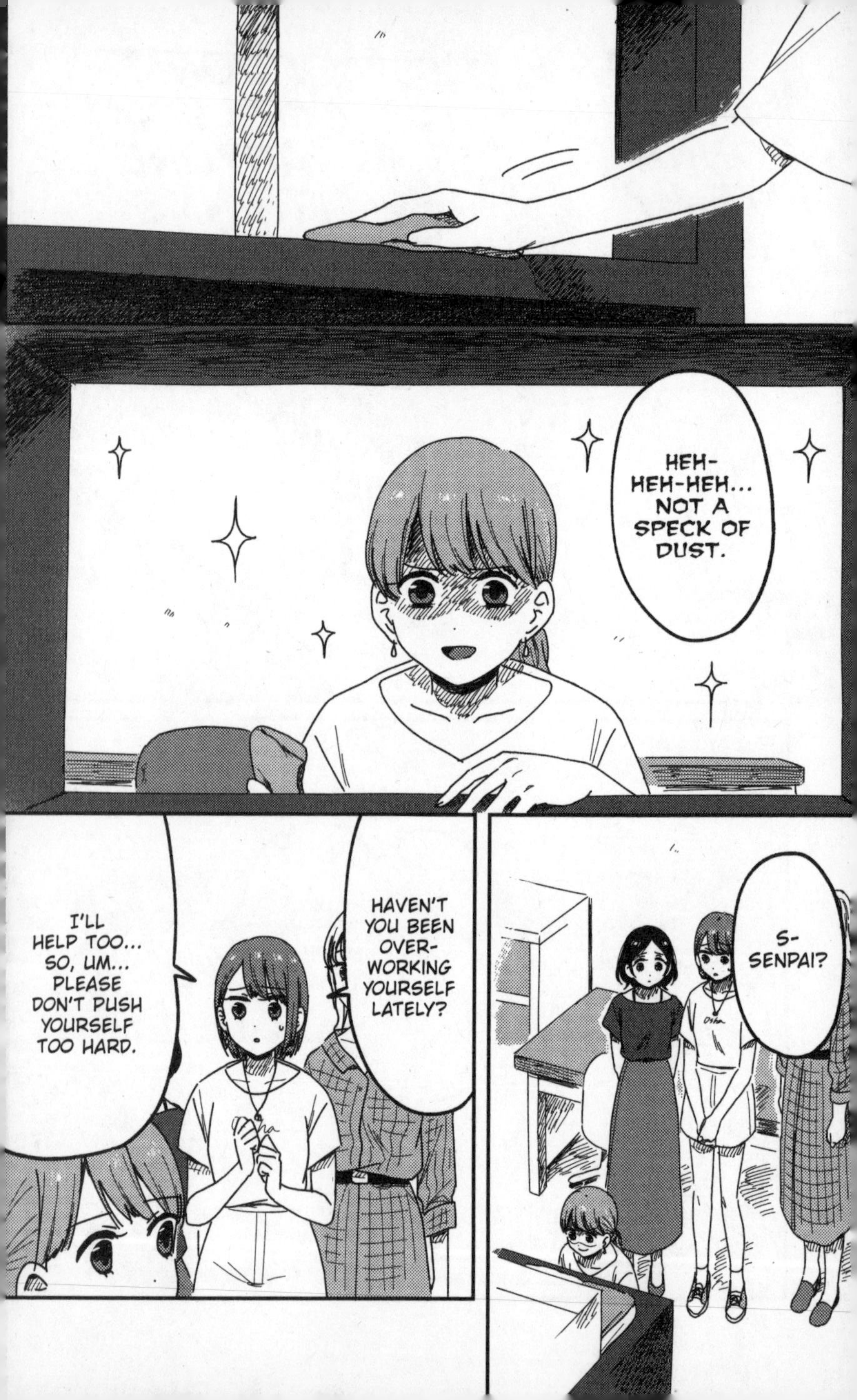
HEH-HEH-HEH... NOT A SPECK OF DUST.
S-SENPAI?
HAVEN'T YOU BEEN OVER-WORKING YOURSELF LATELY?
I'LL HELP TOO... SO, UM... PLEASE DON'T PUSH YOURSELF TOO HARD.

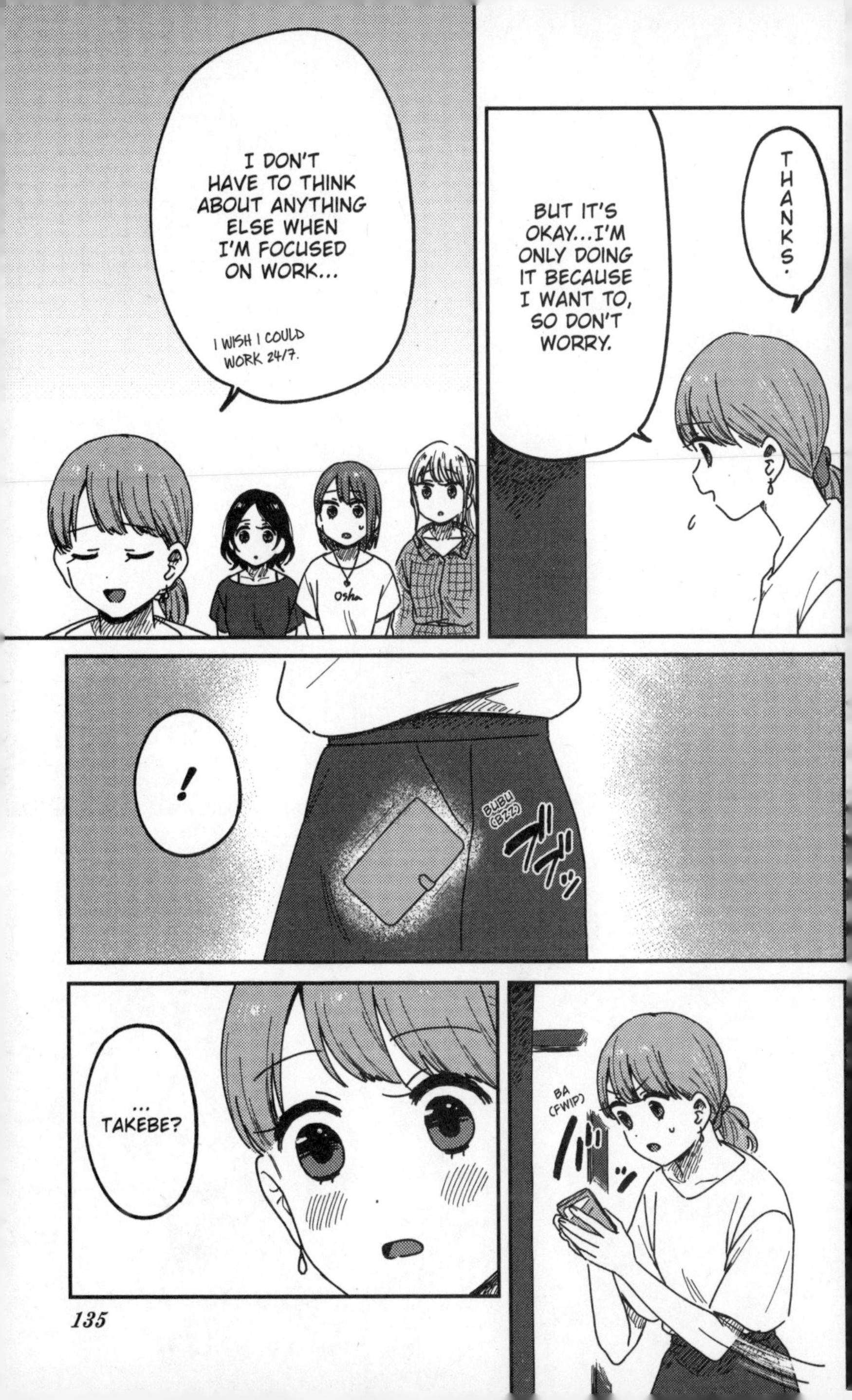
THANKS.
BUT IT'S OKAY...I'M ONLY DOING IT BECAUSE I WANT TO, SO DON'T WORRY.
I DON'T HAVE TO THINK ABOUT ANYTHING ELSE WHEN I'M FOCUSED ON WORK...
I WISH I COULD WORK 24/7.
!
BUBU (BZZZ)
BA (FWIP)
... TAKEBE?

Catch These Hands!

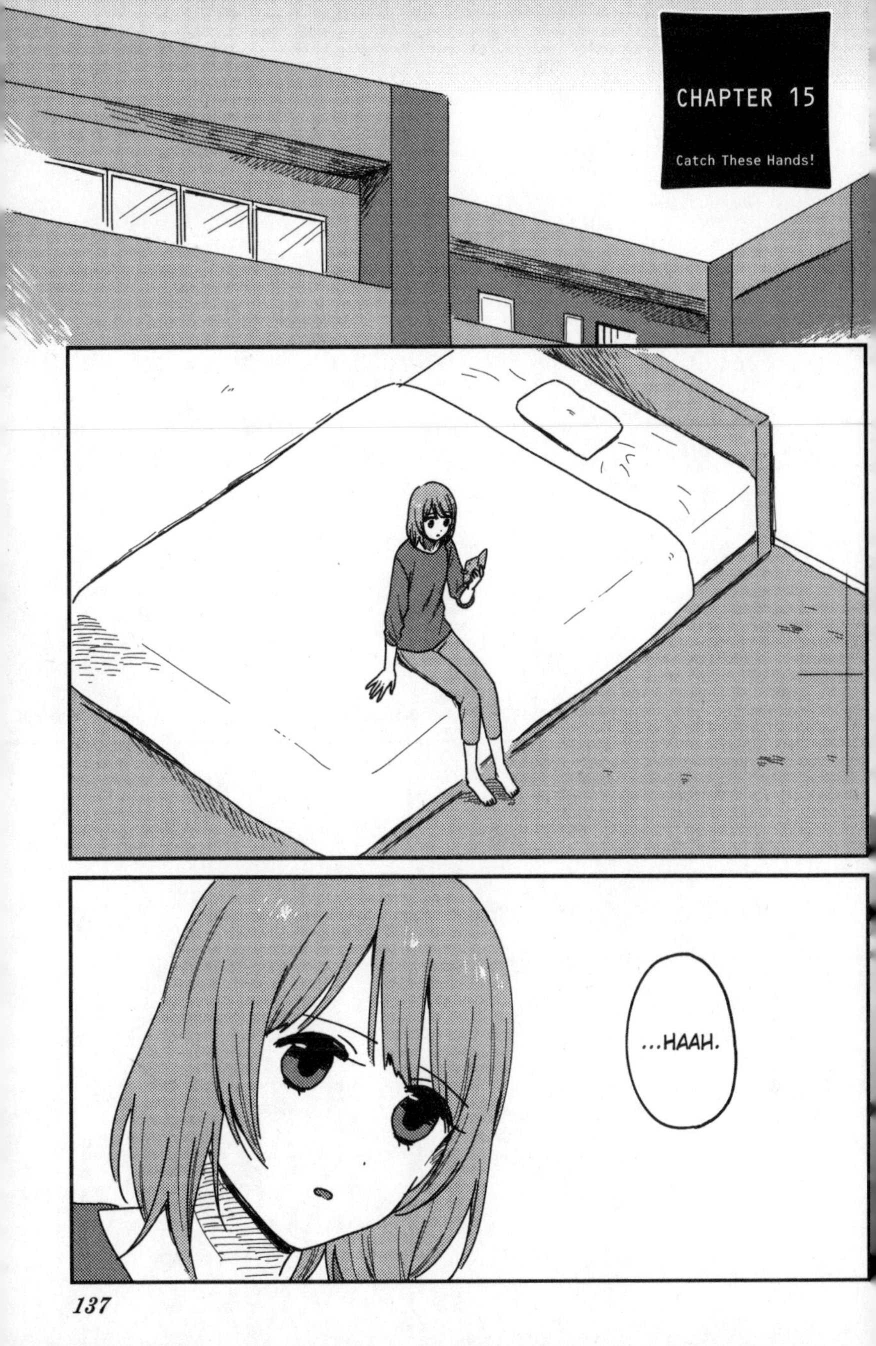
CHAPTER 15
Catch These Hands!
...HAAH.

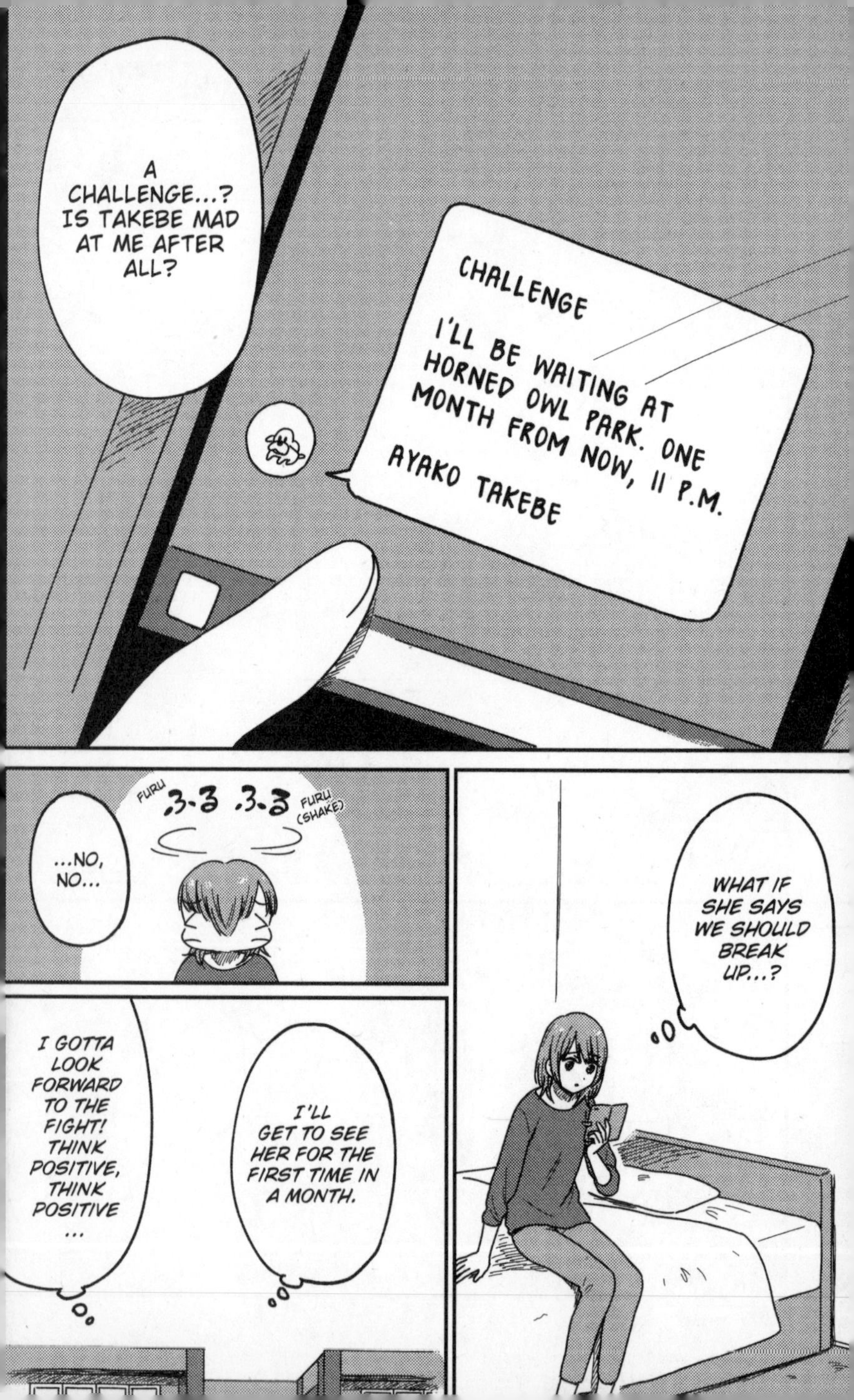
CHALLENGE
I'LL BE WAITING AT HORNED OWL PARK. ONE MONTH FROM NOW, 11 P.M.
AYAKO TAKEBE
A CHALLENGE...? IS TAKEBE MAD AT ME AFTER ALL?
WHAT IF SHE SAYS WE SHOULD BREAK UP...?
ふる ふる
FURU FURU (SHAKE)
...NO, NO...
I'LL GET TO SEE HER FOR THE FIRST TIME IN A MONTH.
I GOTTA LOOK FORWARD TO THE FIGHT! THINK POSITIVE, THINK POSITIVE...

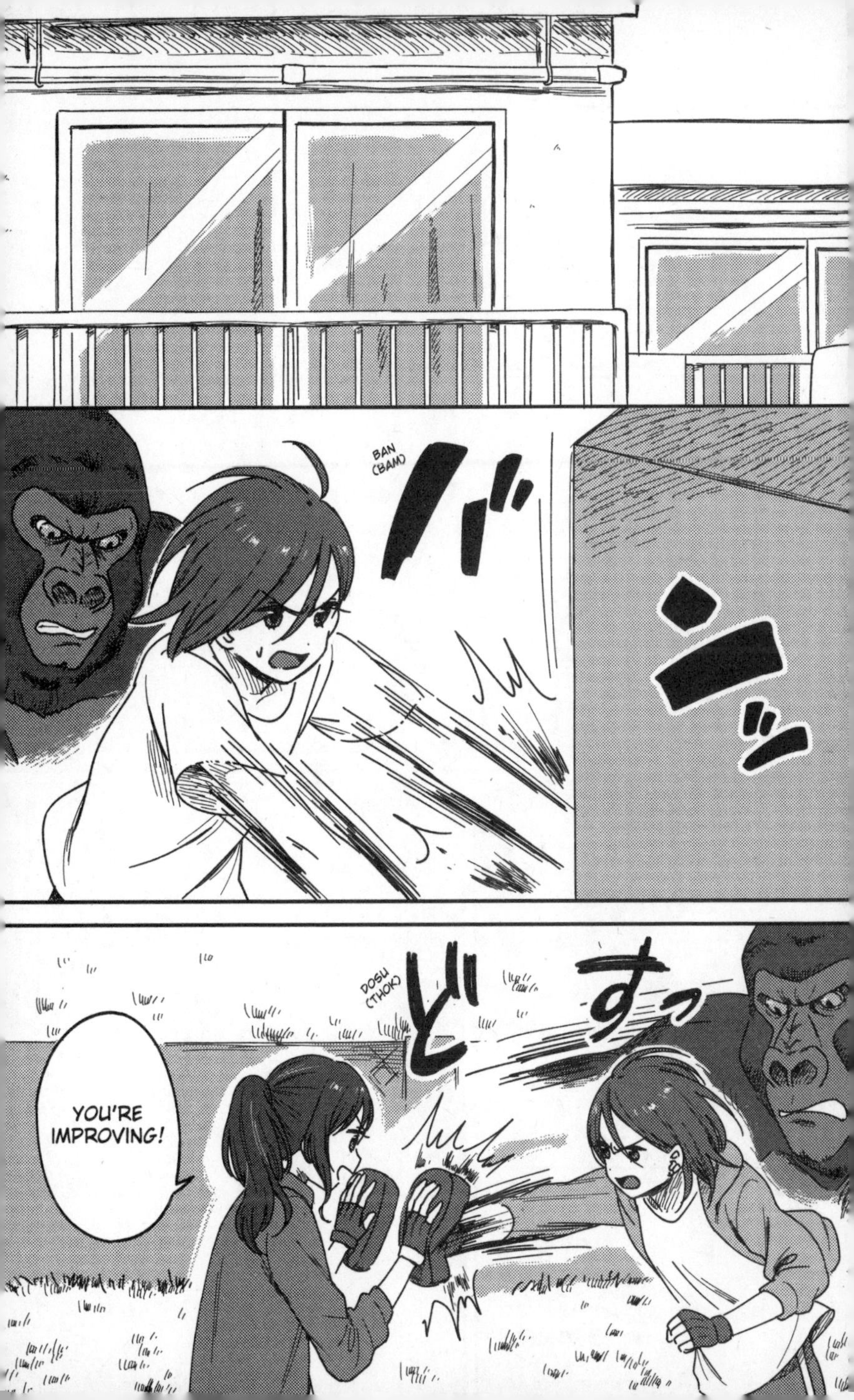

BAN (BAM)
バンッ
DOSU (THOK)
どすっ
YOU'RE IMPROVING!

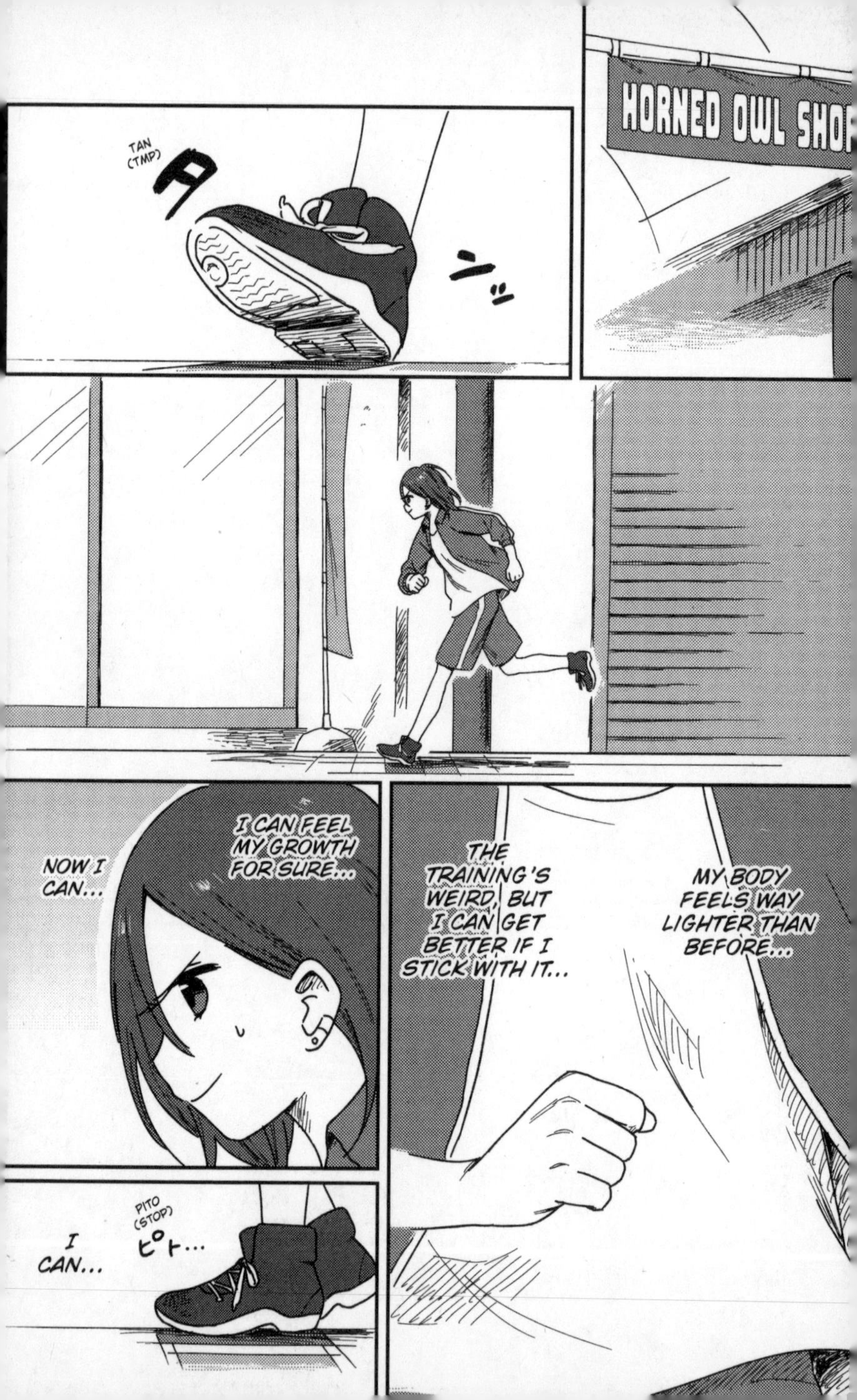
HORNED OWL SHOP
TAN (TMP)
タンッ
MY BODY FEELS WAY LIGHTER THAN BEFORE...
THE TRAINING'S WEIRD, BUT I CAN GET BETTER IF I STICK WITH IT...
I CAN FEEL MY GROWTH FOR SURE...
NOW I CAN...
PITO (STOP)
ピト...
I CAN...

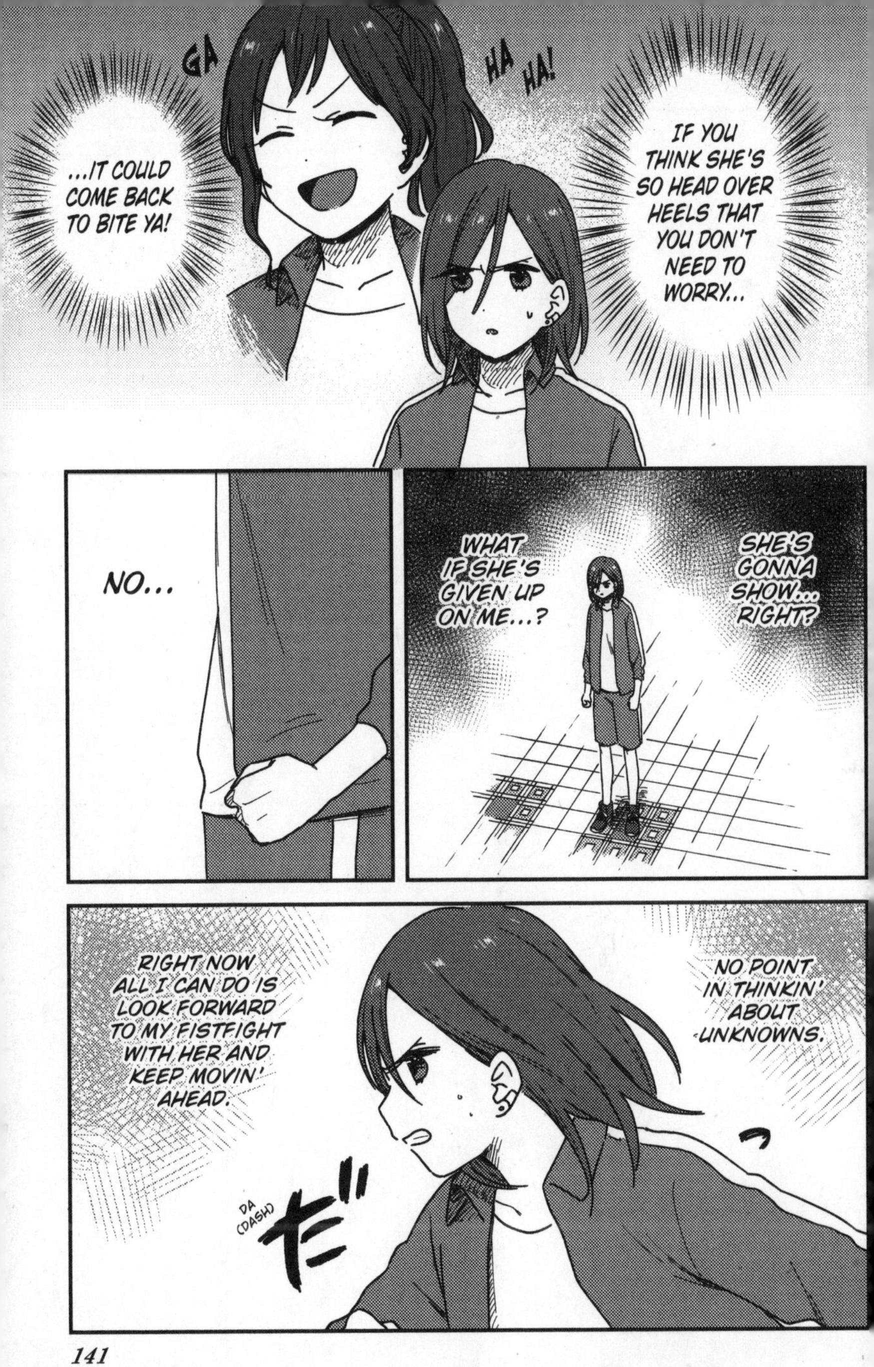
GA HA HA!
IF YOU THINK SHE'S SO HEAD OVER HEELS THAT YOU DON'T NEED TO WORRY...
...IT COULD COME BACK TO BITE YA!
SHE'S GONNA SHOW... RIGHT?
WHAT IF SHE'S GIVEN UP ON ME...?
NO...
NO POINT IN THINKIN' ABOUT UNKNOWNS.
RIGHT NOW ALL I CAN DO IS LOOK FORWARD TO MY FISTFIGHT WITH HER AND KEEP MOVIN' AHEAD.
DA (DASH)

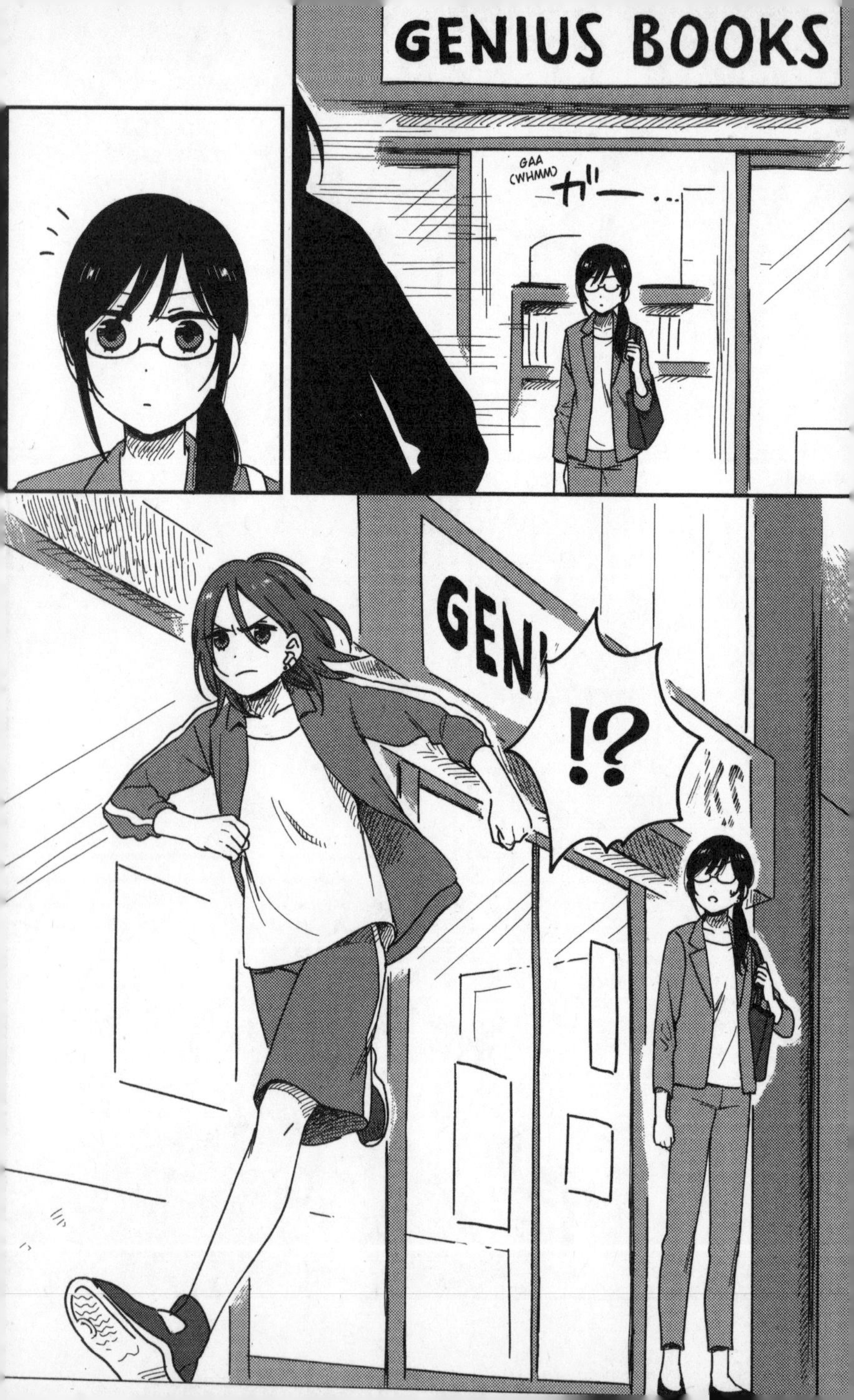
GENIUS BOOKS
GAA (WHMM)
ガー…
GEN
!?

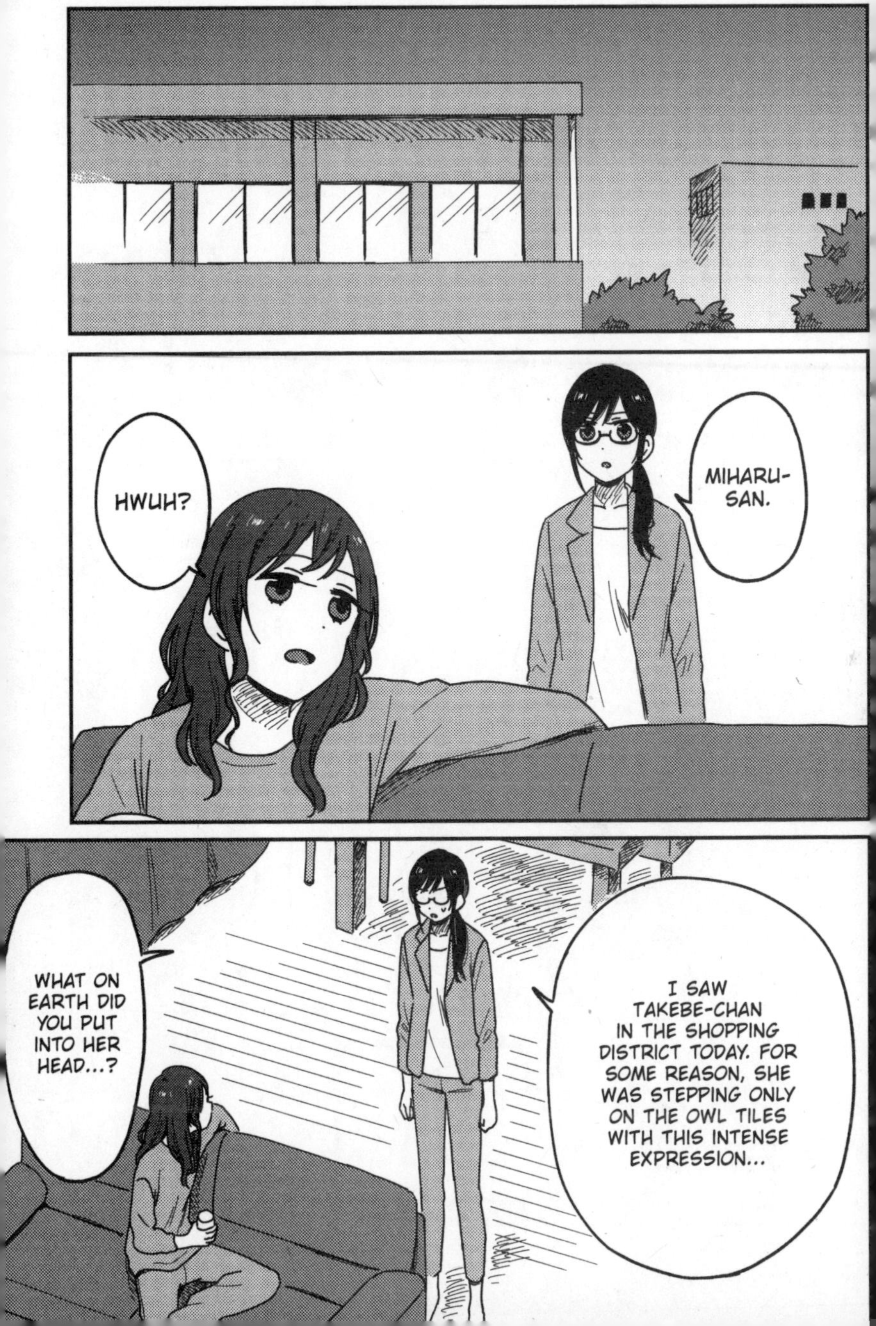
MIHARU-SAN.
HWUH?
I SAW TAKEBE-CHAN IN THE SHOPPING DISTRICT TODAY. FOR SOME REASON, SHE WAS STEPPING ONLY ON THE OWL TILES WITH THIS INTENSE EXPRESSION...
WHAT ON EARTH DID YOU PUT INTO HER HEAD...?

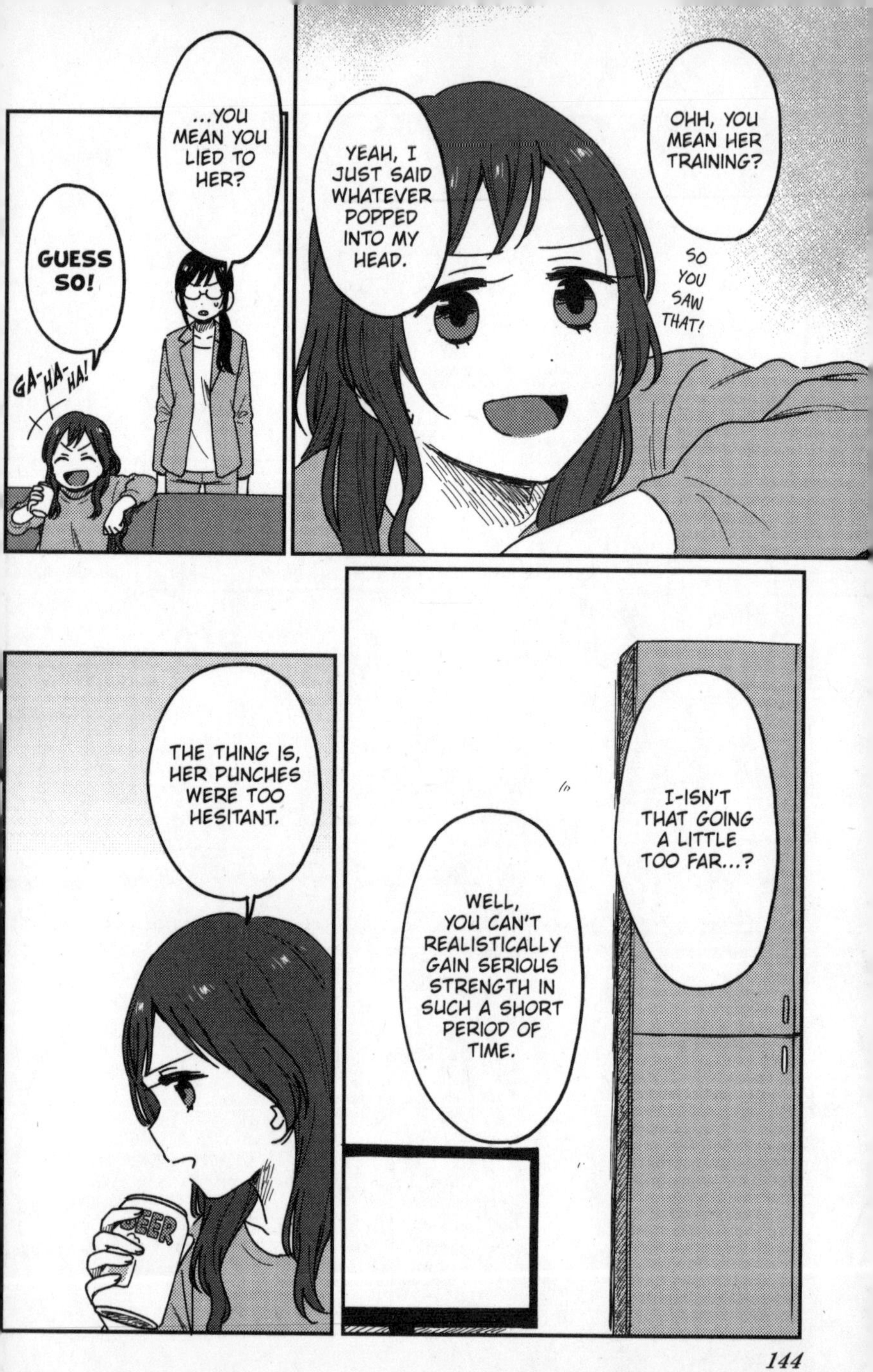
OHH, YOU MEAN HER TRAINING?
SO YOU SAW THAT!
YEAH, I JUST SAID WHATEVER POPPED INTO MY HEAD.
...YOU MEAN YOU LIED TO HER?
GUESS SO!
GA-HA-HA!
I-ISN'T THAT GOING A LITTLE TOO FAR...?
WELL, YOU CAN'T REALISTICALLY GAIN SERIOUS STRENGTH IN SUCH A SHORT PERIOD OF TIME.
THE THING IS, HER PUNCHES WERE TOO HESITANT.

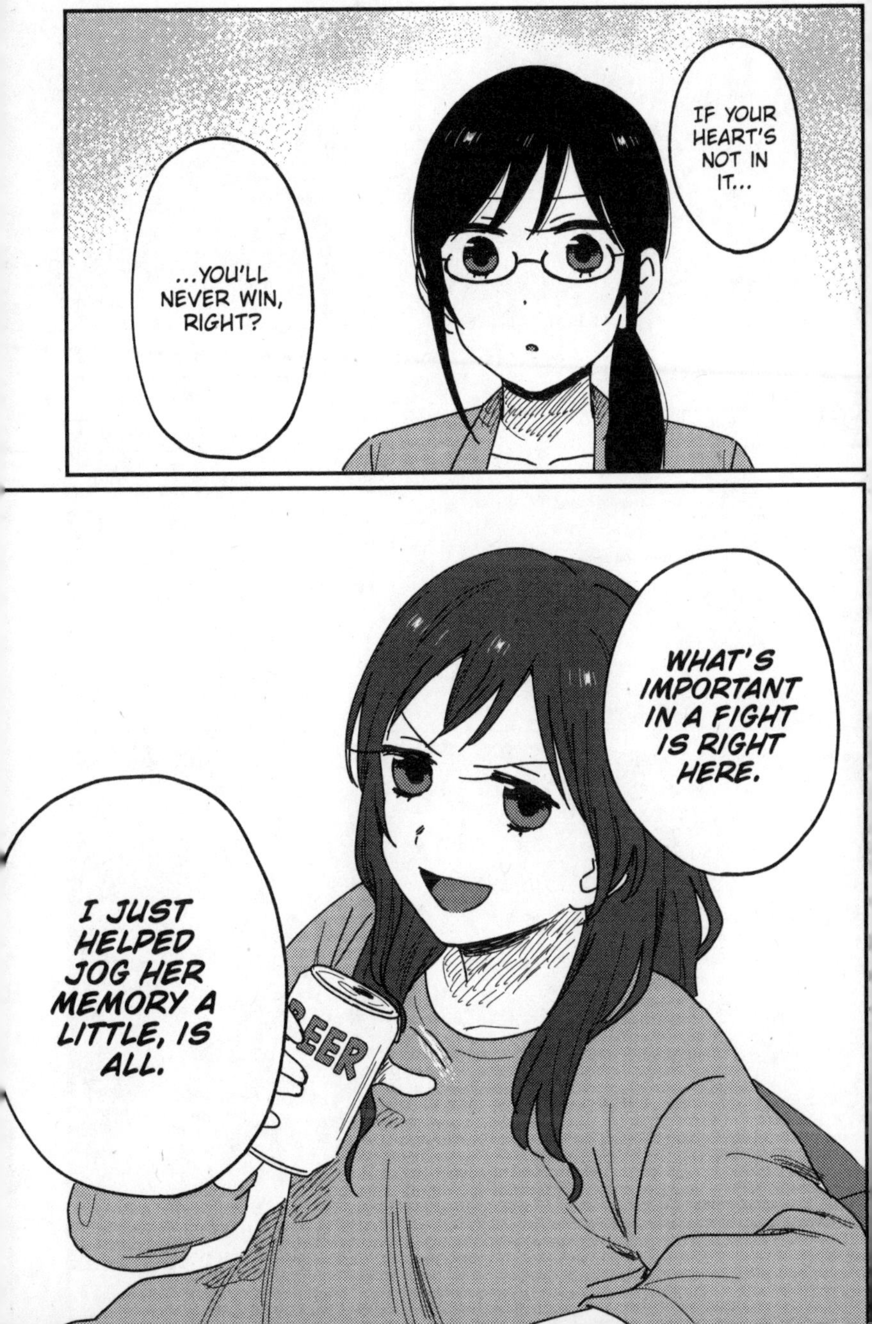
IF YOUR HEART'S NOT IN IT...
...YOU'LL NEVER WIN, RIGHT?
WHAT'S IMPORTANT IN A FIGHT IS RIGHT HERE.
I JUST HELPED JOG HER MEMORY A LITTLE, IS ALL.

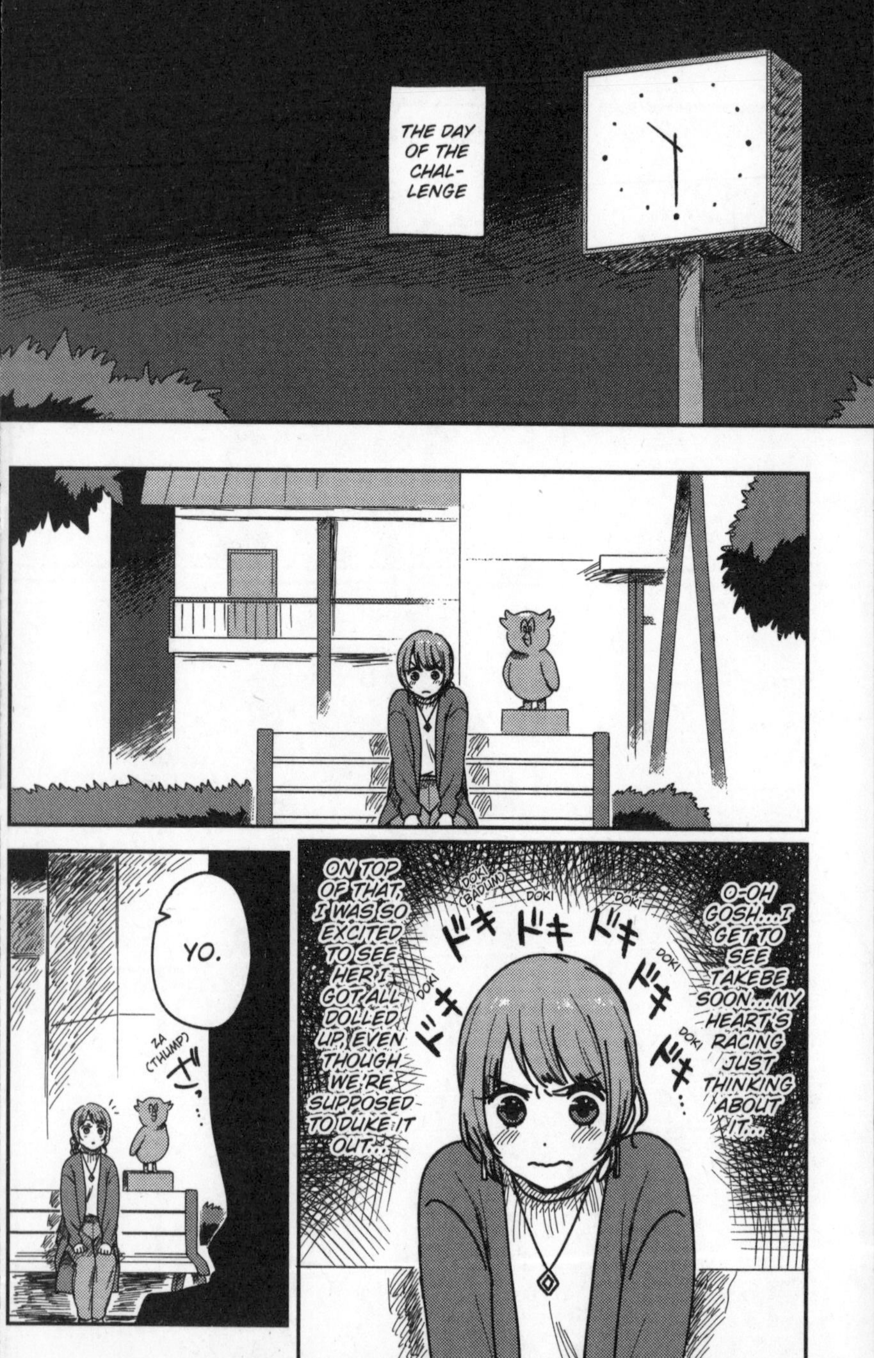
THE DAY OF THE CHAL-LENGE
O-OH GOSH... I GET TO SEE TAKEBE SOON... MY HEART'S RACING JUST THINKING ABOUT IT...
DOKI (BADUMP) DOKI DOKI DOKI DOKI DOKI
ドキ ドキ ドキ ドキ ドキ ドキ...
ON TOP OF THAT, I WAS SO EXCITED TO SEE HER I GOT ALL DOLLED UP, EVEN THOUGH WE'RE SUPPOSED TO DUKE IT OUT...
YO.
ZA (THUMP)
ザッ...

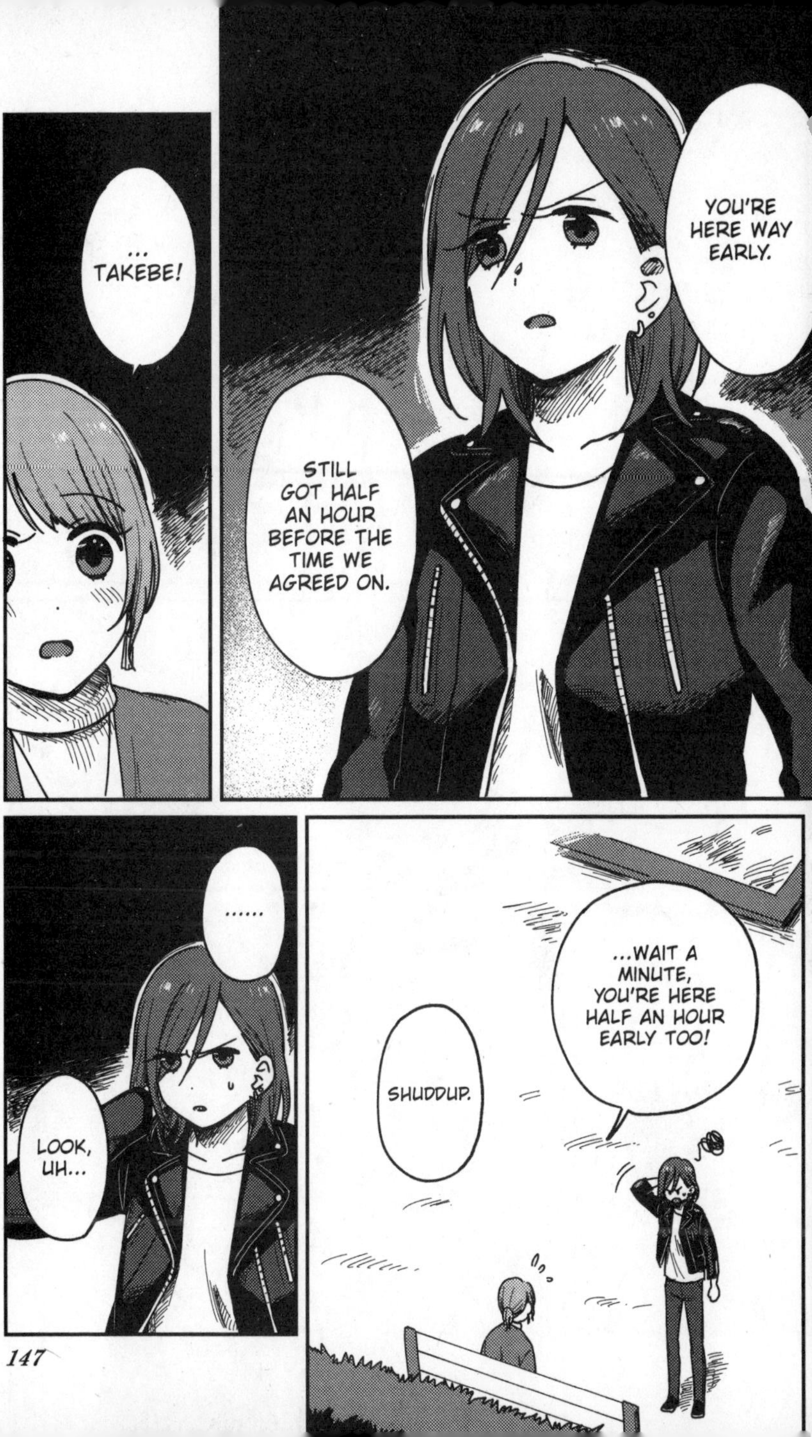
YOU'RE HERE WAY EARLY.
STILL GOT HALF AN HOUR BEFORE THE TIME WE AGREED ON.
... TAKEBE!
...WAIT A MINUTE, YOU'RE HERE HALF AN HOUR EARLY TOO!
SHUDDUP.
......
LOOK, UH...

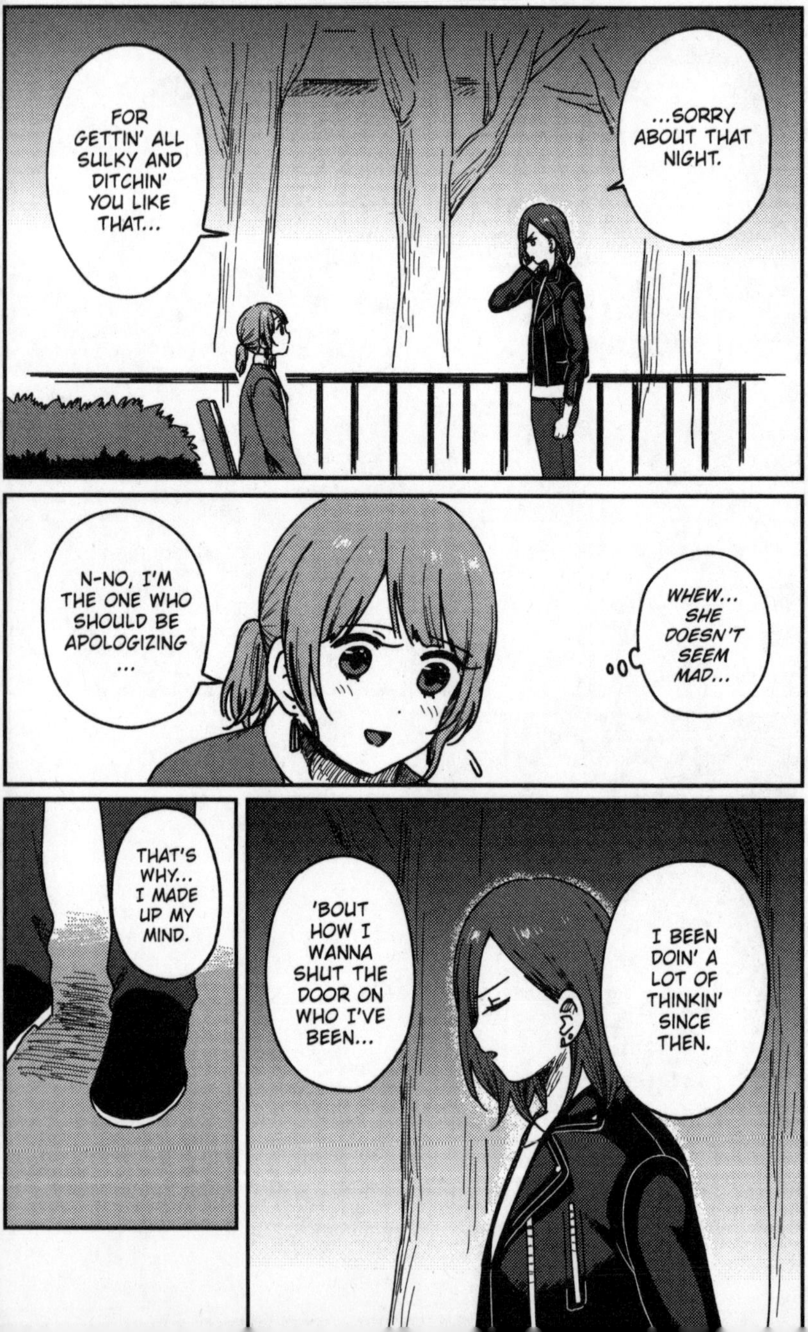
...SORRY ABOUT THAT NIGHT.
FOR GETTIN' ALL SULKY AND DITCHIN' YOU LIKE THAT...
N-NO, I'M THE ONE WHO SHOULD BE APOLOGIZING ...
WHEW... SHE DOESN'T SEEM MAD...
I BEEN DOIN' A LOT OF THINKIN' SINCE THEN.
'BOUT HOW I WANNA SHUT THE DOOR ON WHO I'VE BEEN...
THAT'S WHY... I MADE UP MY MIND.

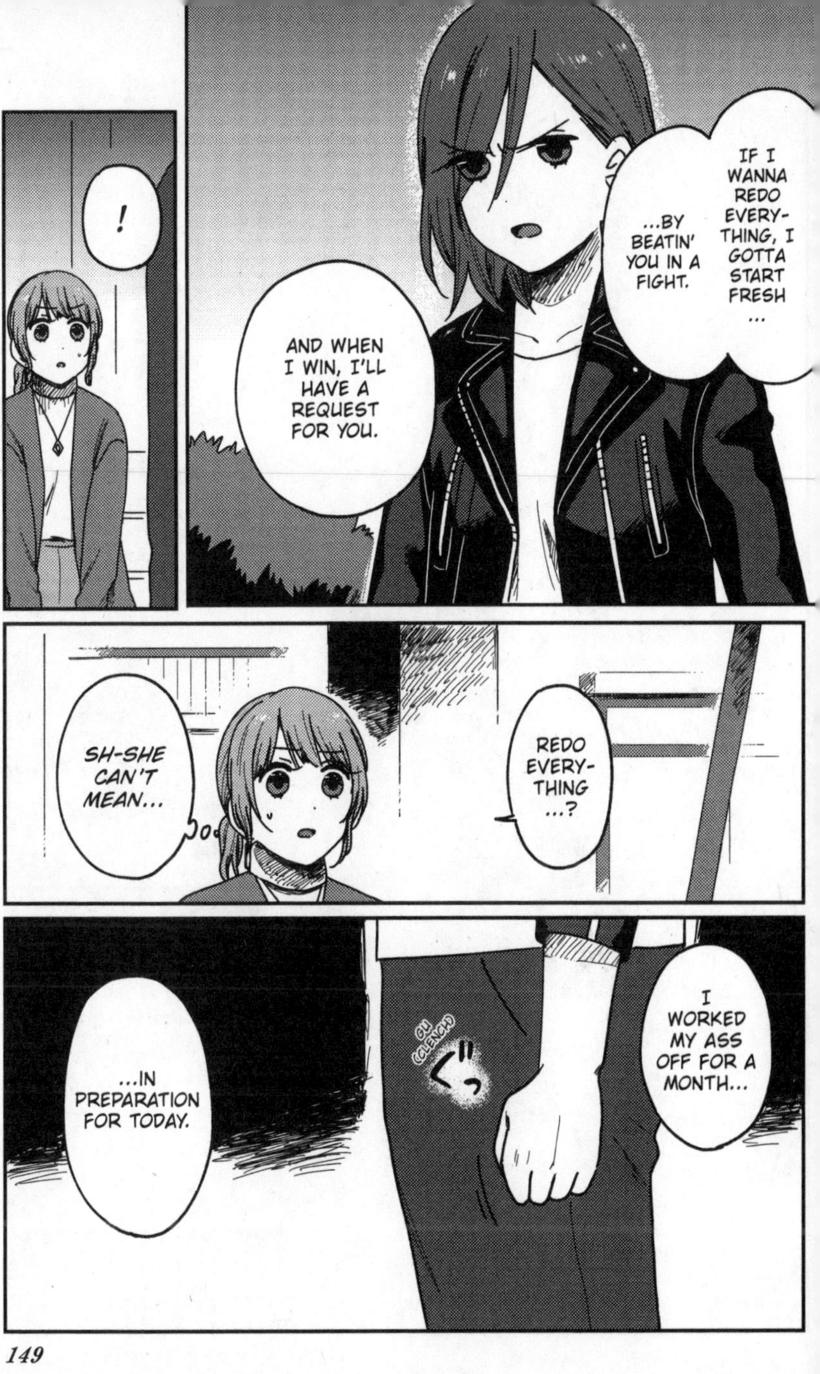
IF I WANNA REDO EVERYTHING, I GOTTA START FRESH...
...BY BEATIN' YOU IN A FIGHT.
AND WHEN I WIN, I'LL HAVE A REQUEST FOR YOU.
!
REDO EVERYTHING...?
SH-SHE CAN'T MEAN...
I WORKED MY ASS OFF FOR A MONTH...
GU (CLENCH)
ぐっ
...IN PREPARATION FOR TODAY.

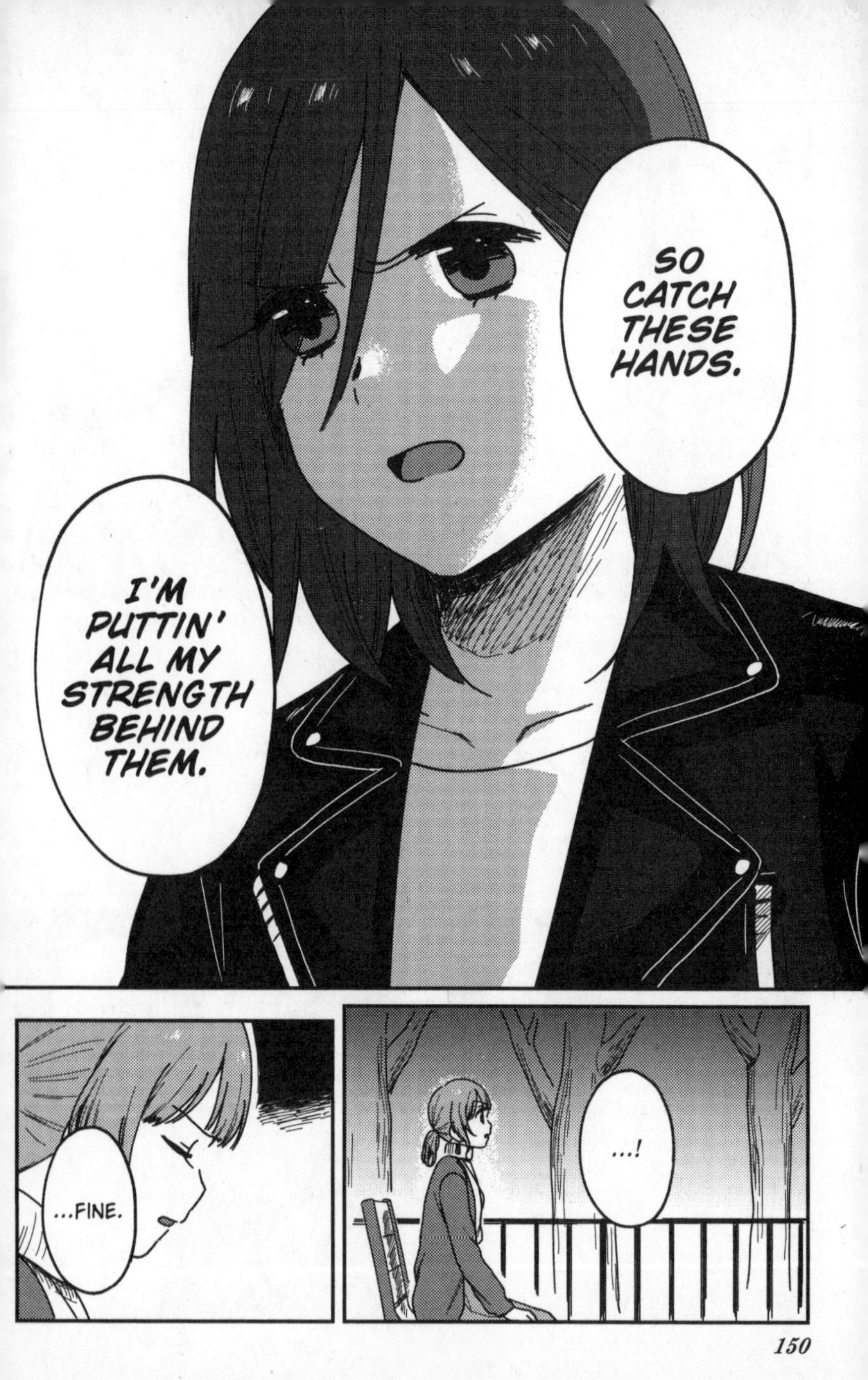
SO CATCH THESE HANDS.
I'M PUTTIN' ALL MY STRENGTH BEHIND THEM.
...!
...FINE.

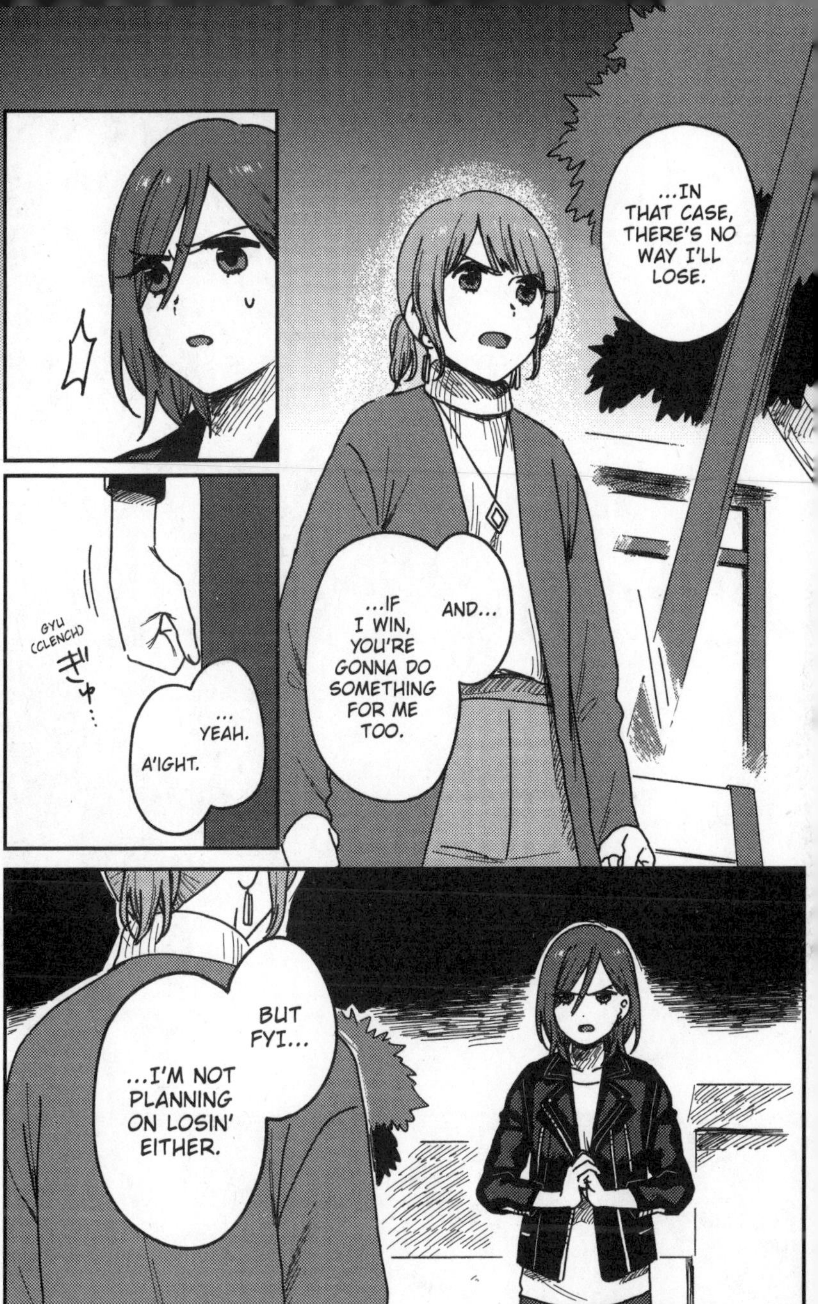
...IN THAT CASE, THERE'S NO WAY I'LL LOSE.
AND...
...IF I WIN, YOU'RE GONNA DO SOMETHING FOR ME TOO.
GYU (CLENCH)
ぎゅ...
...YEAH.
A'IGHT.
BUT FYI...
...I'M NOT PLANNING ON LOSIN' EITHER.

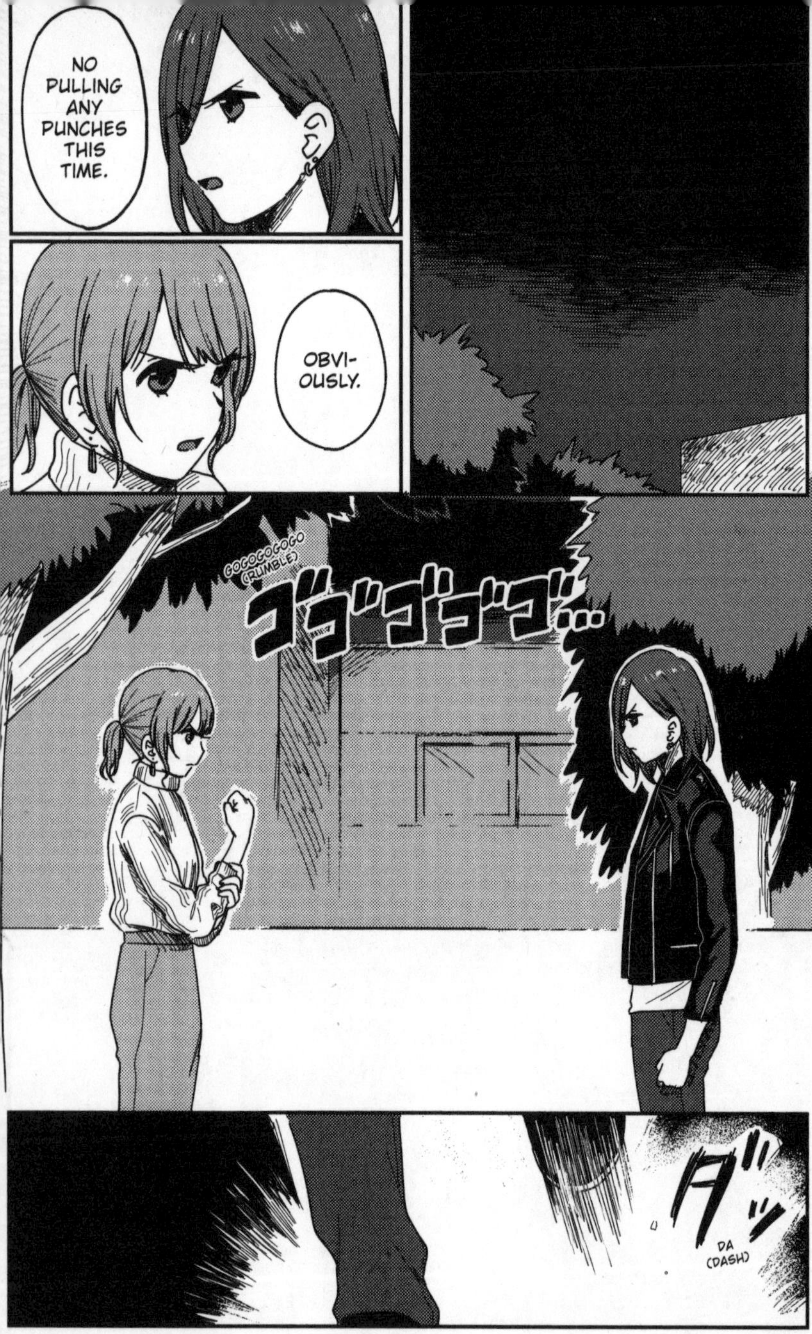
NO PULLING ANY PUNCHES THIS TIME.
OBVI-OUSLY.
GOGOGOGOGO (RUMBLE)
ゴゴゴゴゴ…
ダッ
DA (DASH)

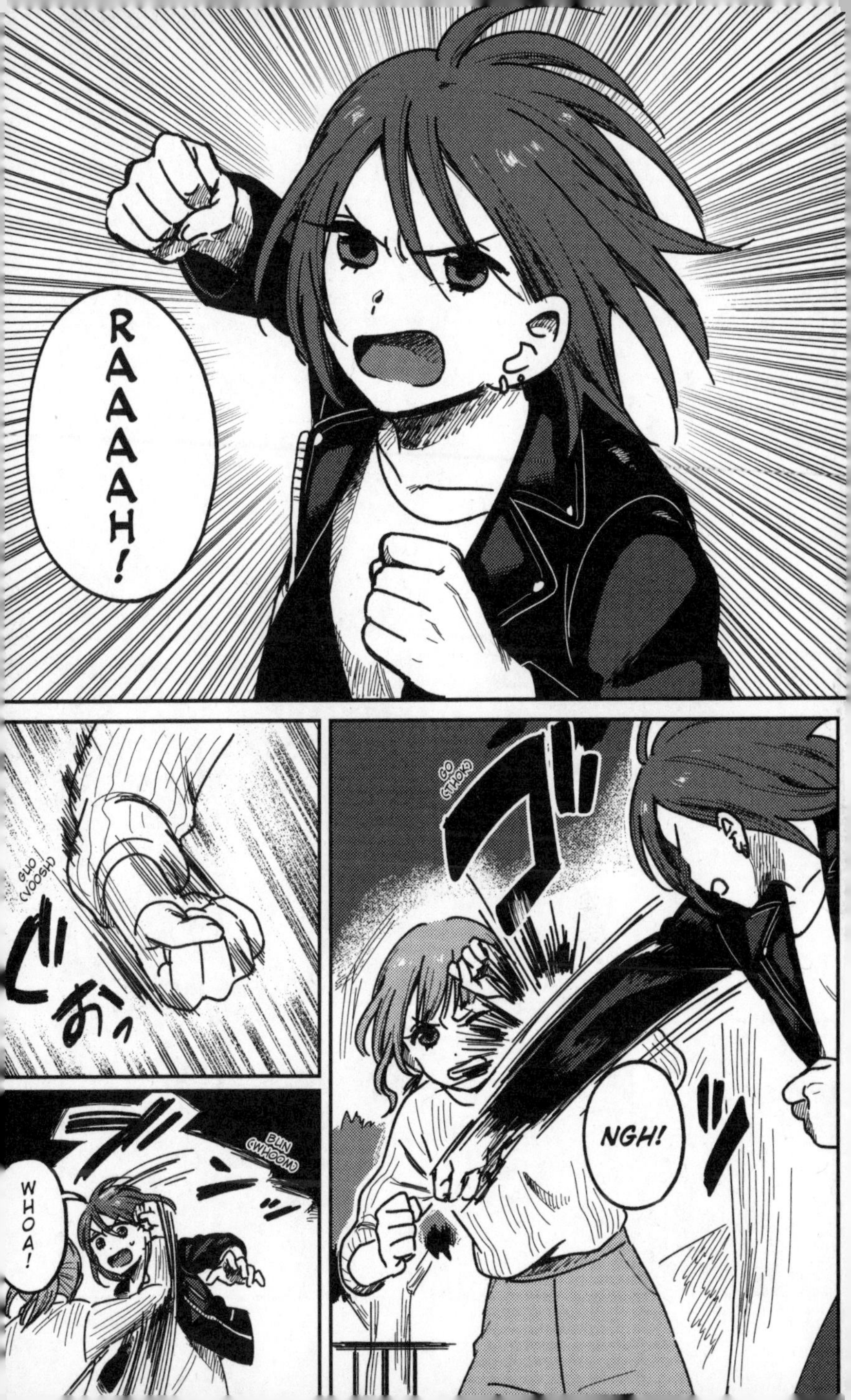
RAAAAAH!
GO (THOK)
NGH!
GUO (WOOSH)
BUN (WHOOM)
WHOA!

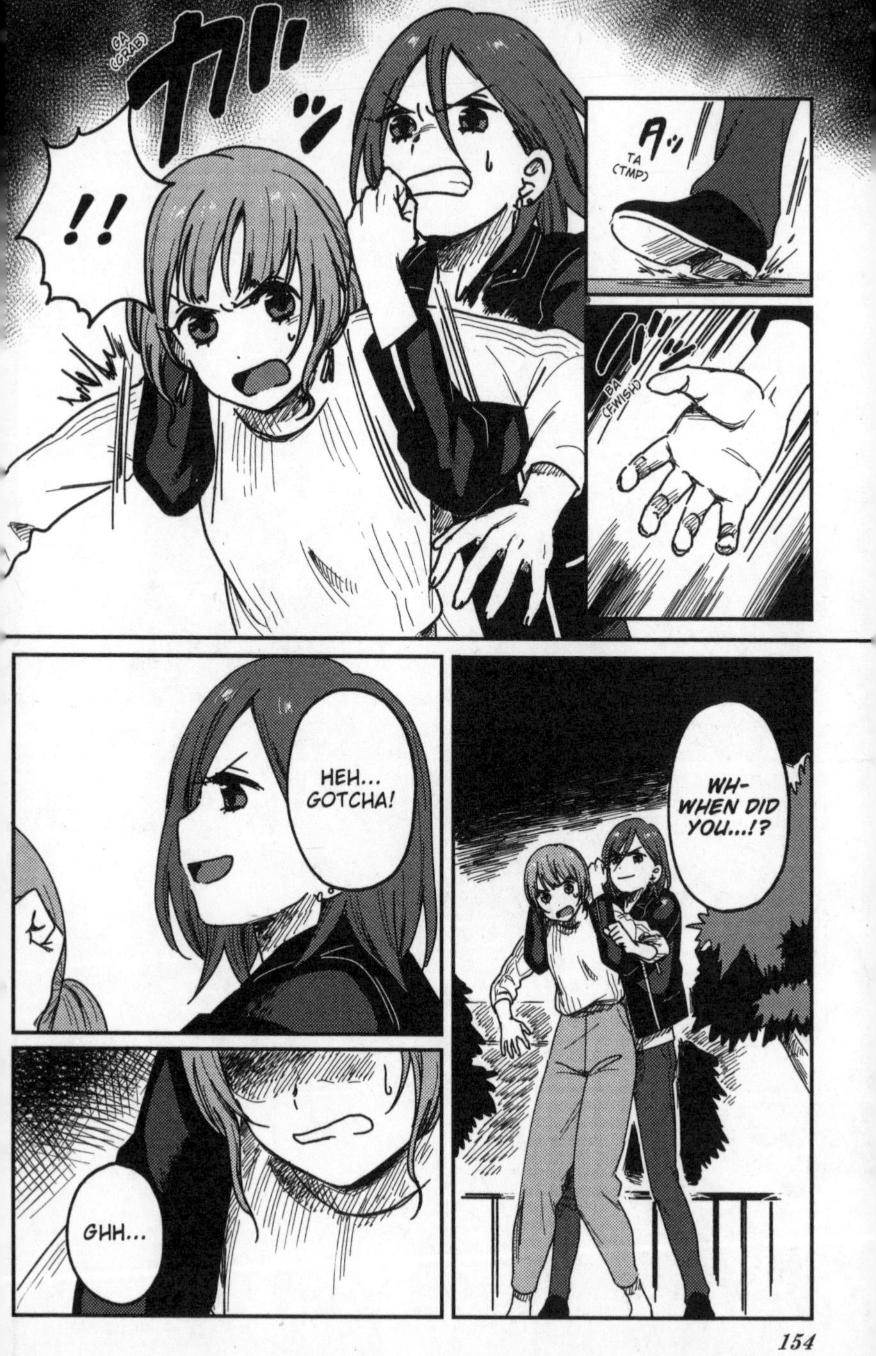
TA (TMP)
BA (FWISH)
GA (GRAB)
!!
WH- WHEN DID YOU...!?
HEH... GOTCHA!
GHH...

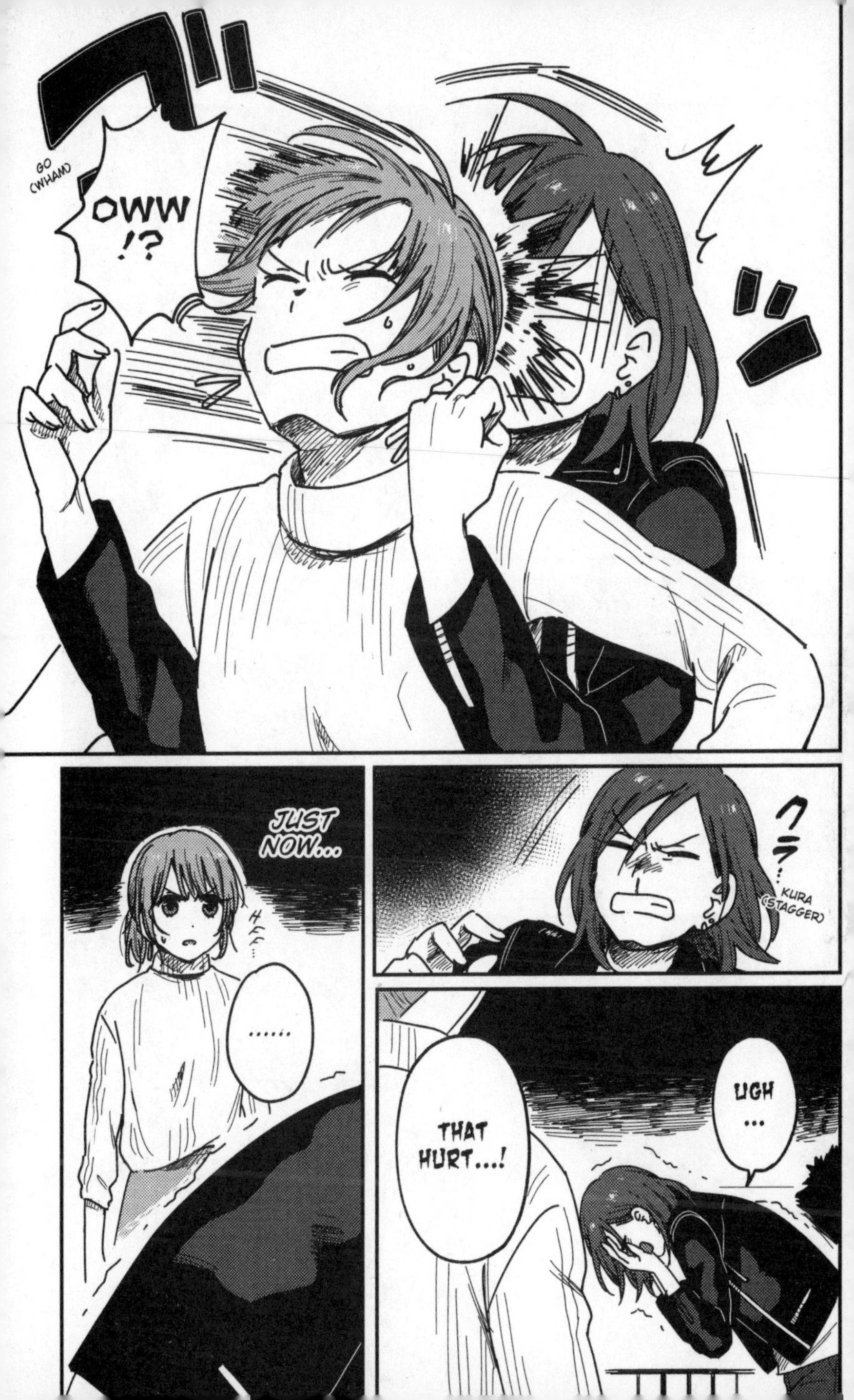
GO (WHAM)
OWW!?
KURA (STAGGER)
JUST NOW...
......
UGH...
THAT HURT...!

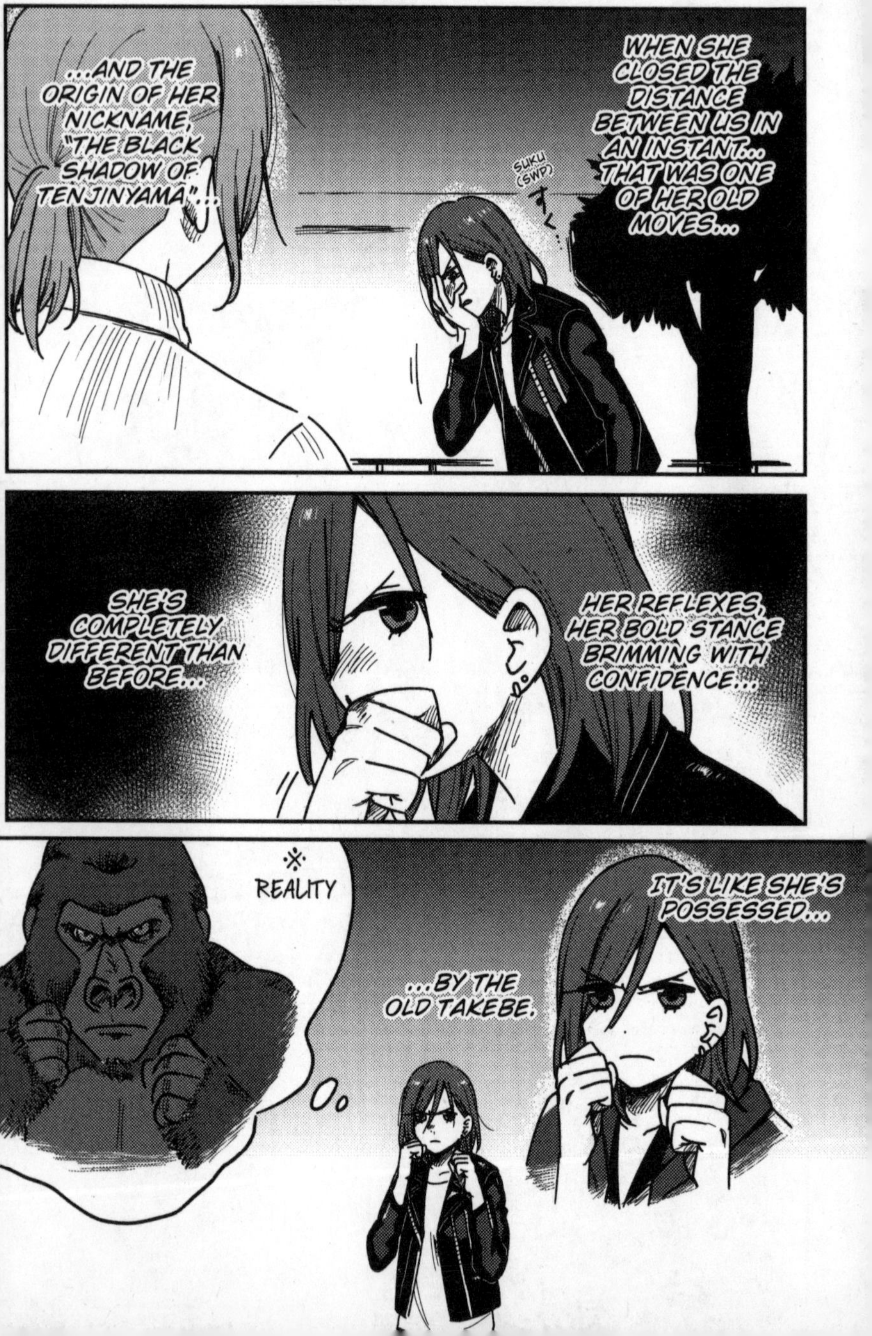
WHEN SHE CLOSED THE DISTANCE BETWEEN US IN AN INSTANT... THAT WAS ONE OF HER OLD MOVES...
SUKU (SWP)
...AND THE ORIGIN OF HER NICKNAME, "THE BLACK SHADOW OF TENJINYAMA"...
HER REFLEXES, HER BOLD STANCE BRIMMING WITH CONFIDENCE...
SHE'S COMPLETELY DIFFERENT THAN BEFORE...
IT'S LIKE SHE'S POSSESSED...
...BY THE OLD TAKEBE.
※ REALITY

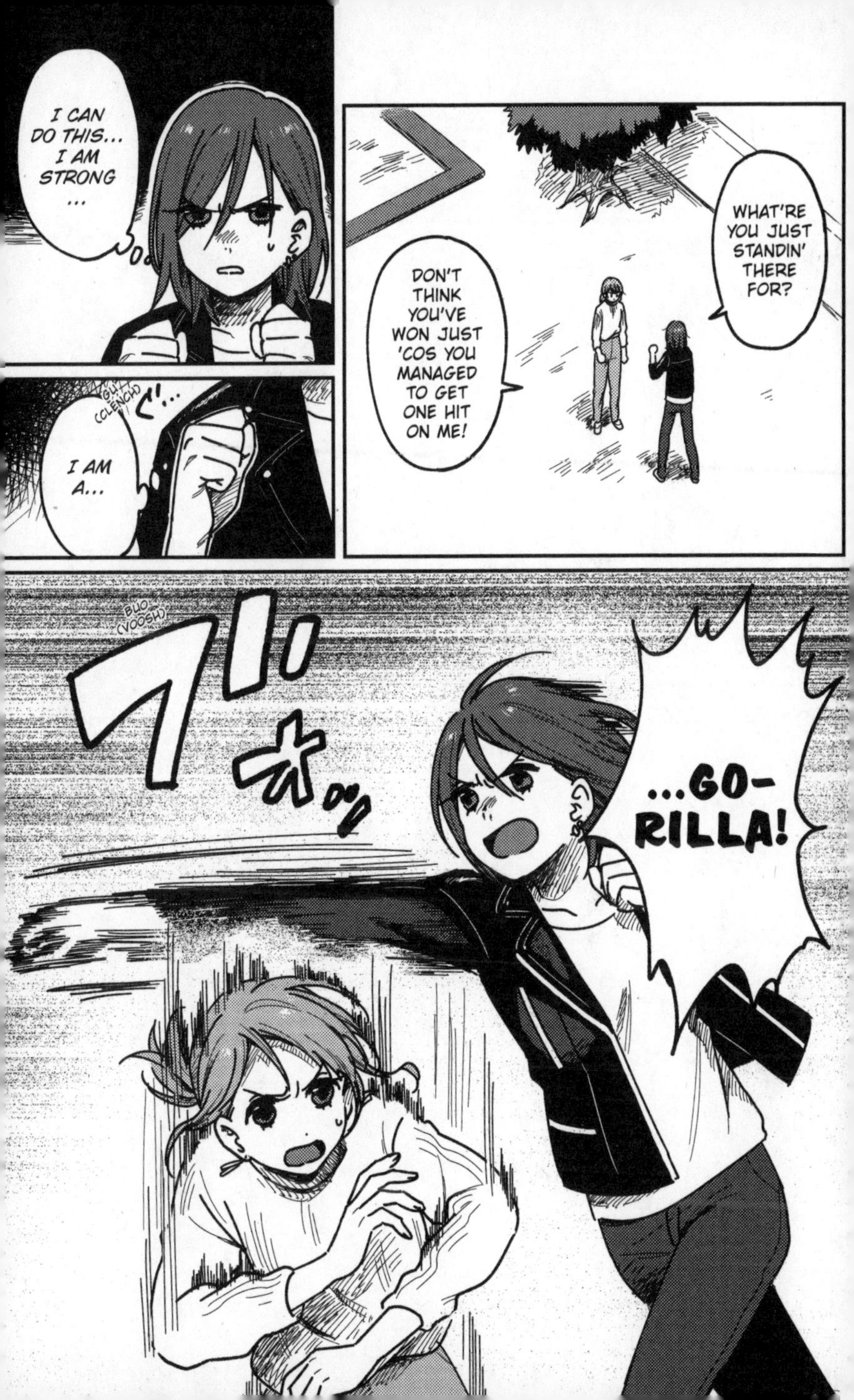
WHAT'RE YOU JUST STANDIN' THERE FOR?
DON'T THINK YOU'VE WON JUST 'COS YOU MANAGED TO GET ONE HIT ON ME!
I CAN DO THIS... I AM STRONG ...
GU (CLENCH)
I AM A...
BUO (VOOSH)
...GO-RILLA!

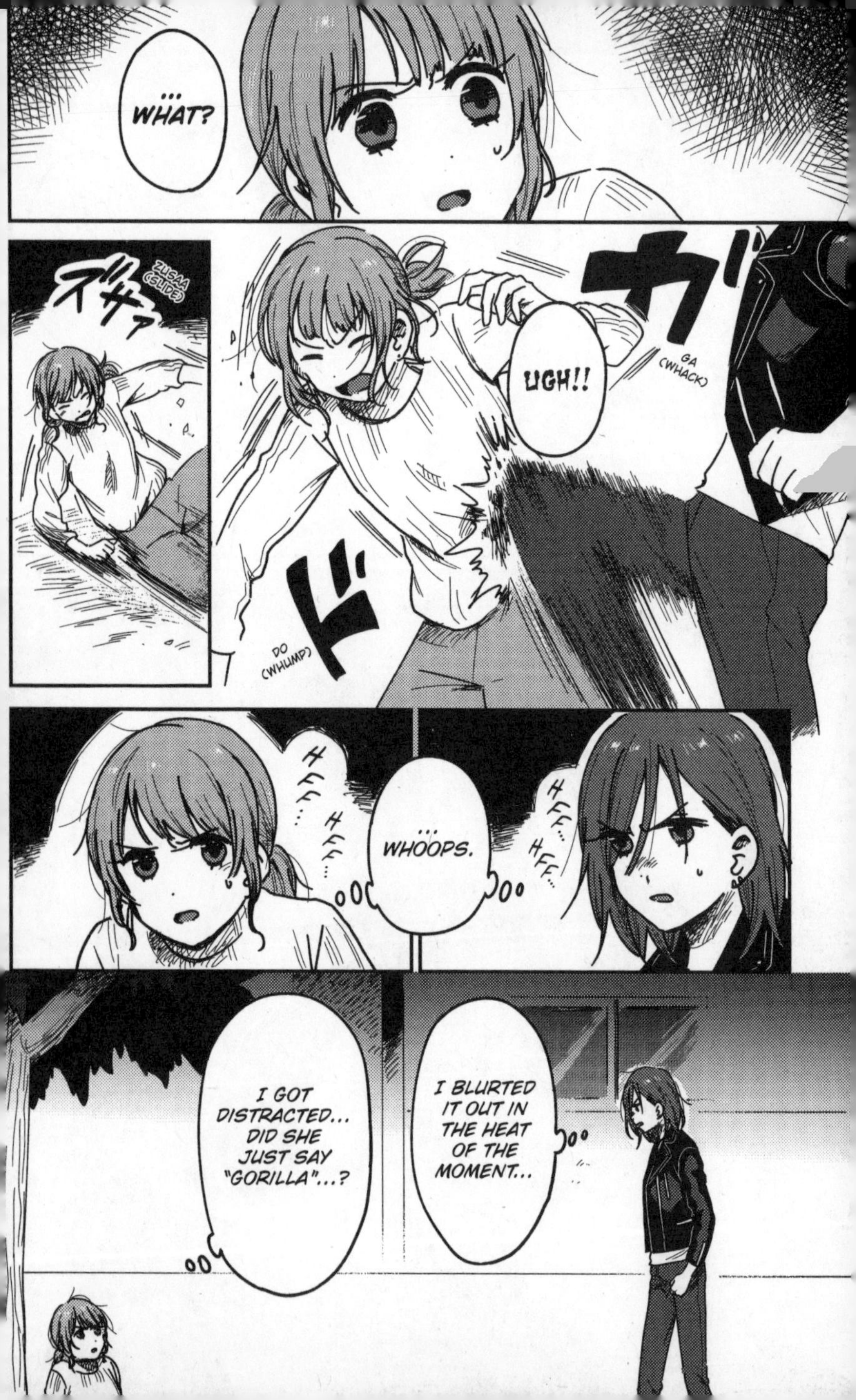
...WHAT?
GA (WHACK)
UGH!!
DO (WHUMP)
ZUSAA (SLIDE)
HFF... HFF...
...WHOOPS.
HFF... HFF...
I BLURTED IT OUT IN THE HEAT OF THE MOMENT...
I GOT DISTRACTED... DID SHE JUST SAY "GORILLA"...?

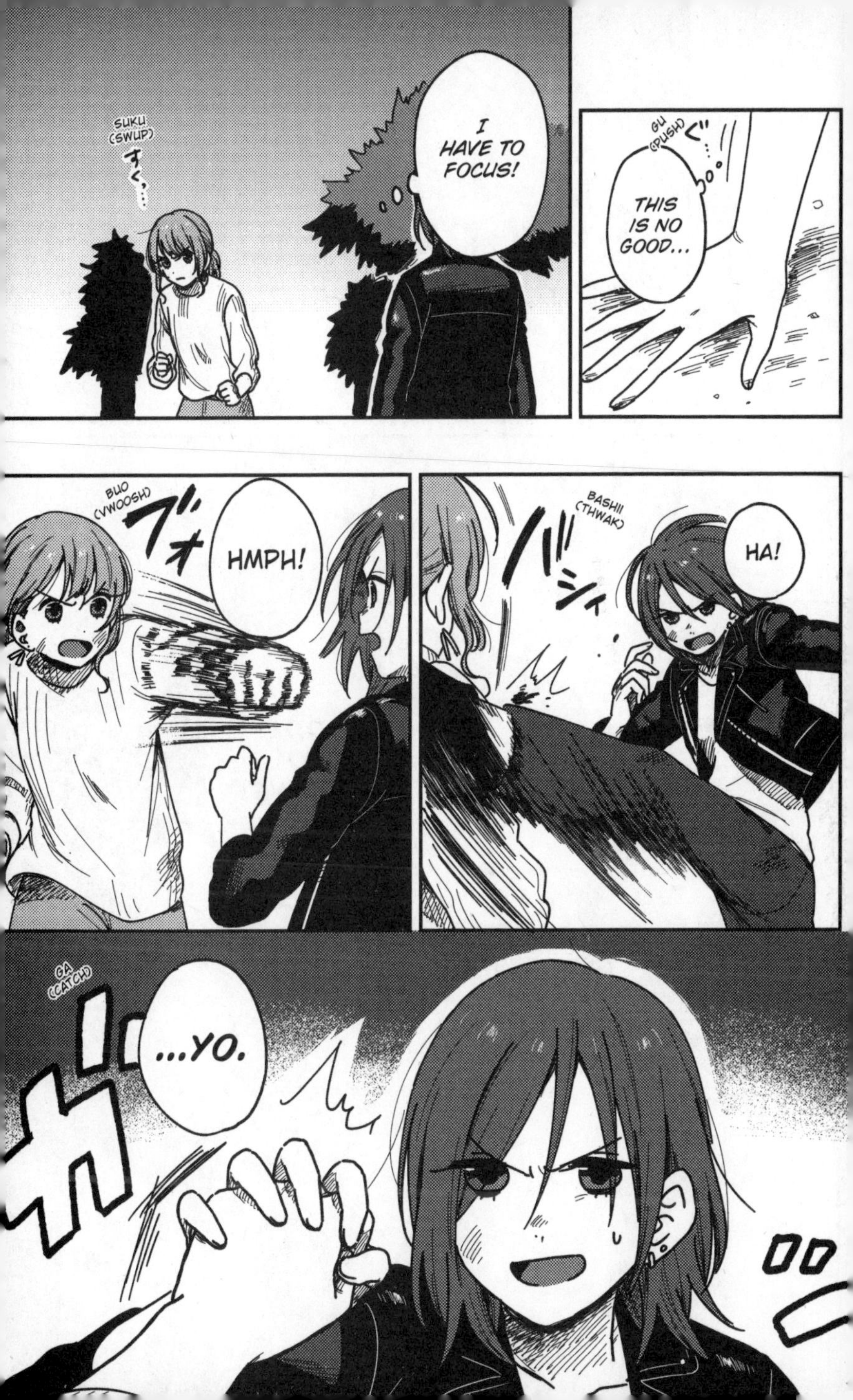
GU (PUSH)
ぐ…
THIS IS NO GOOD...
I HAVE TO FOCUS!
SUKU (SWUP)
すく…
HA!
BASHII (THWAK)
バシィ
HMPH!
BUO (VWOOSH)
ブォ
...YO.
GA (CATCH)
ガッ

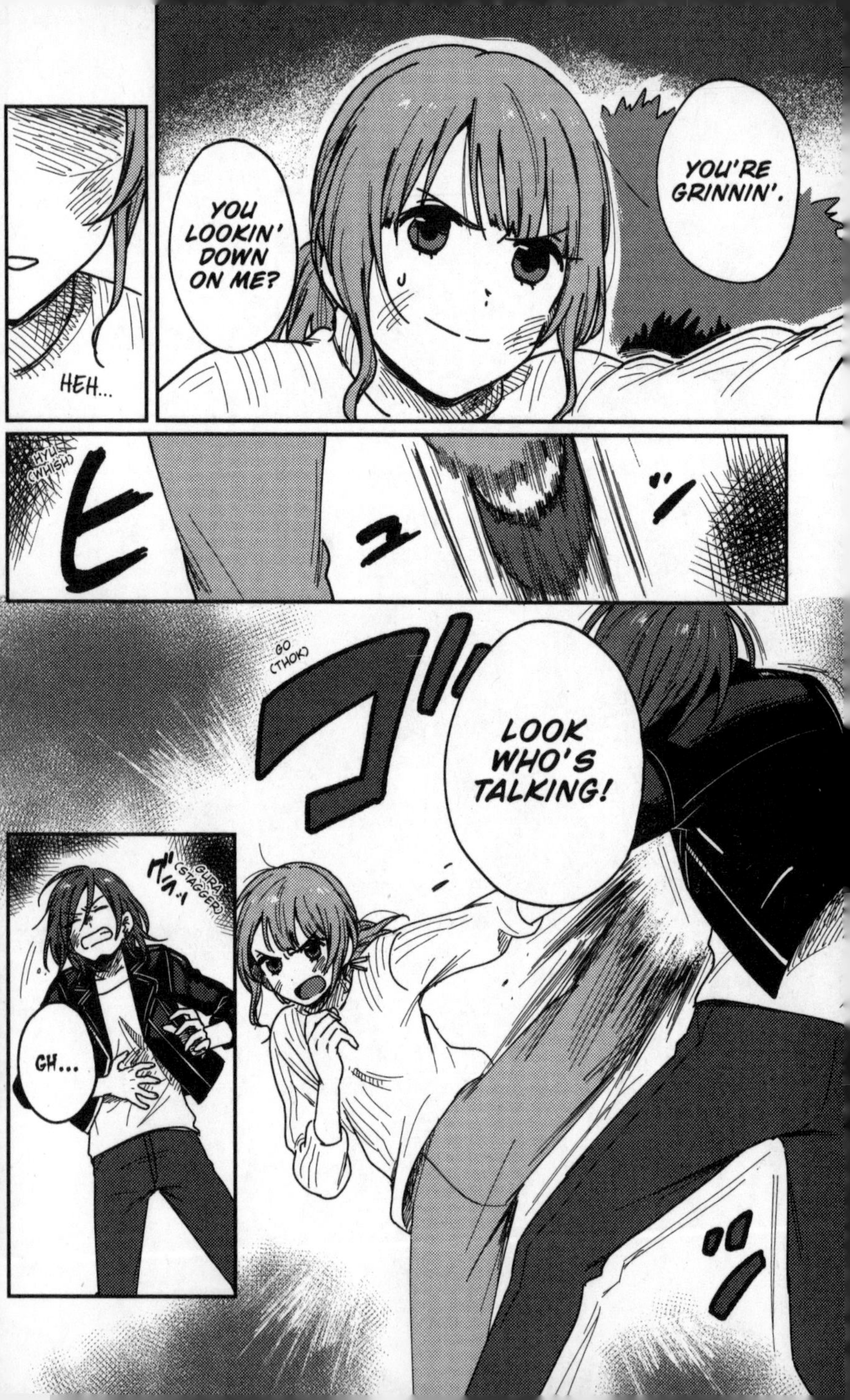
YOU'RE GRINNIN'.
YOU LOOKIN' DOWN ON ME?
HEH...
HYU (WHISH)
GO (THOK)
LOOK WHO'S TALKING!
GURA (STAGGER)
GH...

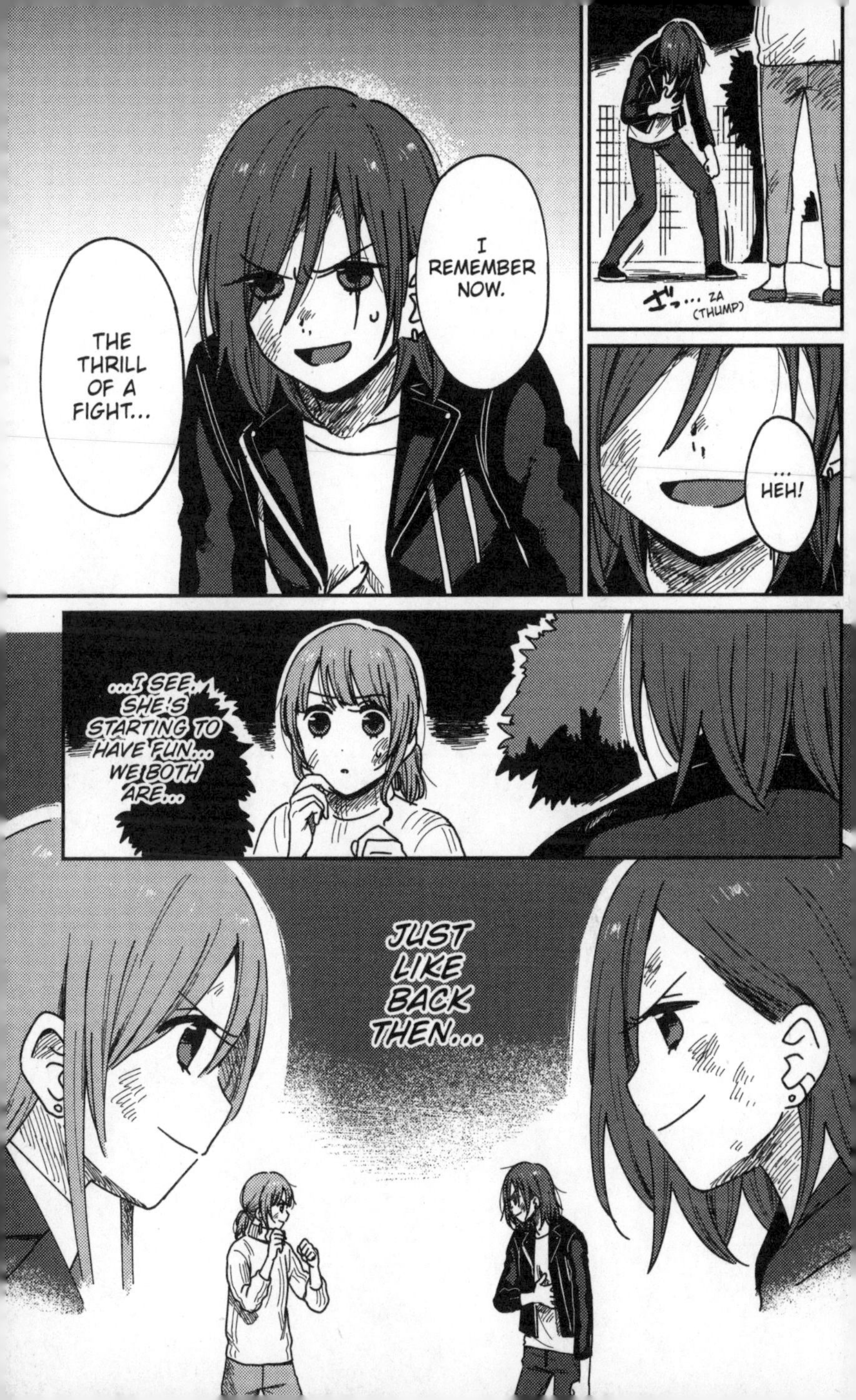
ざっ… ZA (THUMP)
...HEH!
I REMEMBER NOW.
THE THRILL OF A FIGHT...
...I SEE. SHE'S STARTING TO HAVE FUN... WE BOTH ARE...
JUST LIKE BACK THEN...

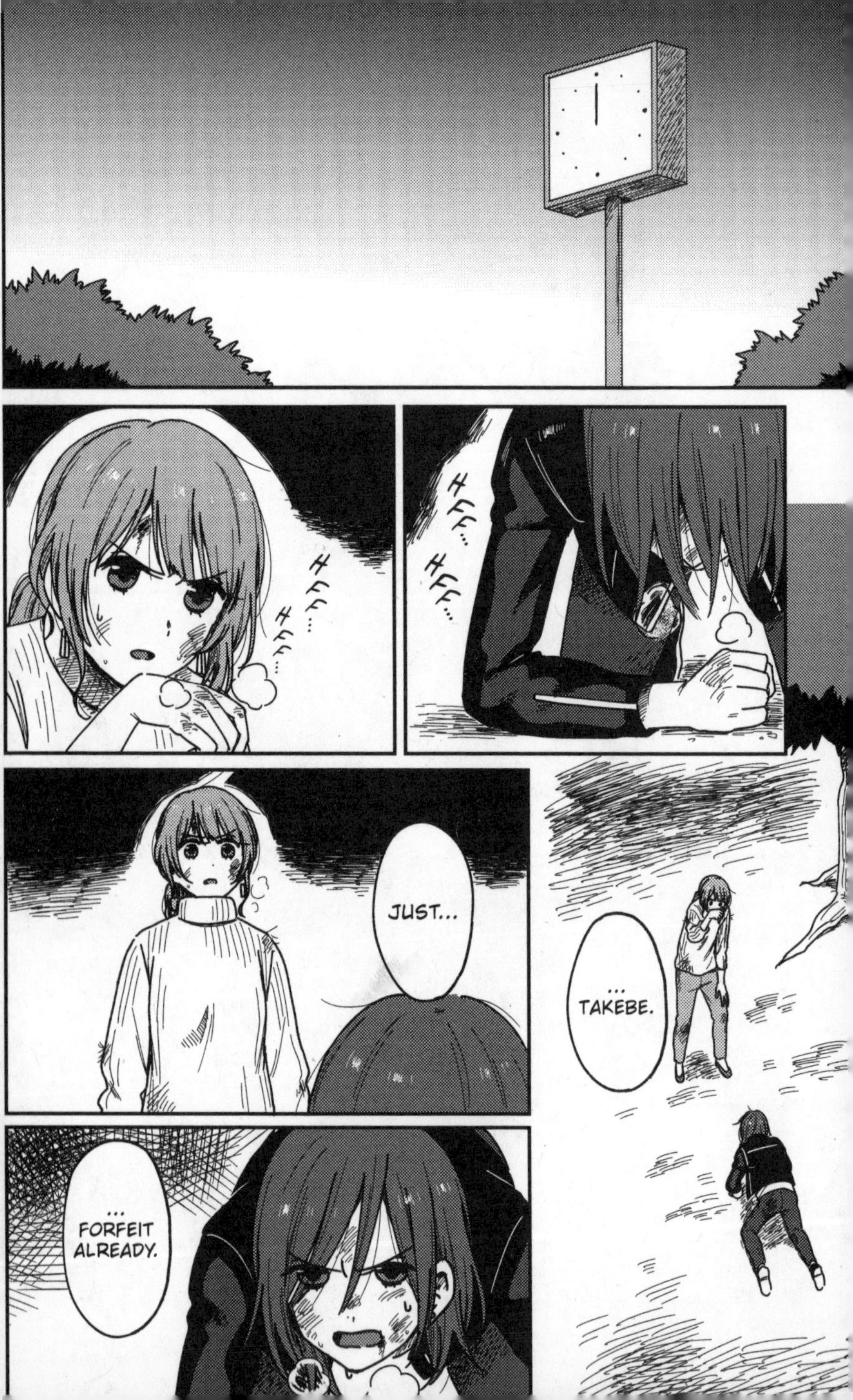
HFF... HFF...
HFF... HFF...
... TAKEBE.
JUST...
... FORFEIT ALREADY.

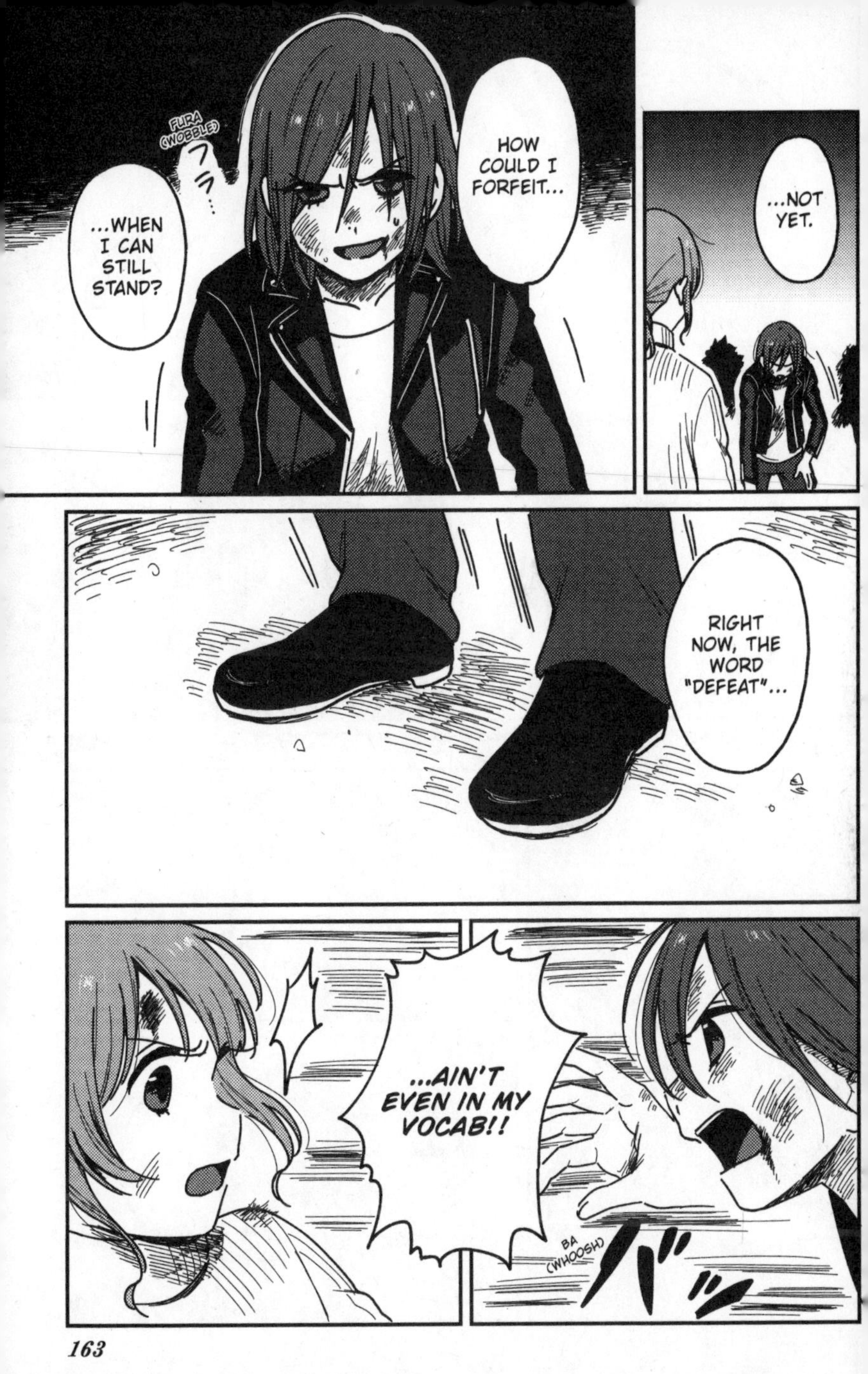
...NOT YET.
HOW COULD I FORFEIT...
FURA (WOBBLE)
フラ…
...WHEN I CAN STILL STAND?
RIGHT NOW, THE WORD "DEFEAT"...
BA (WHOOSH)
...AIN'T EVEN IN MY VOCAB!!

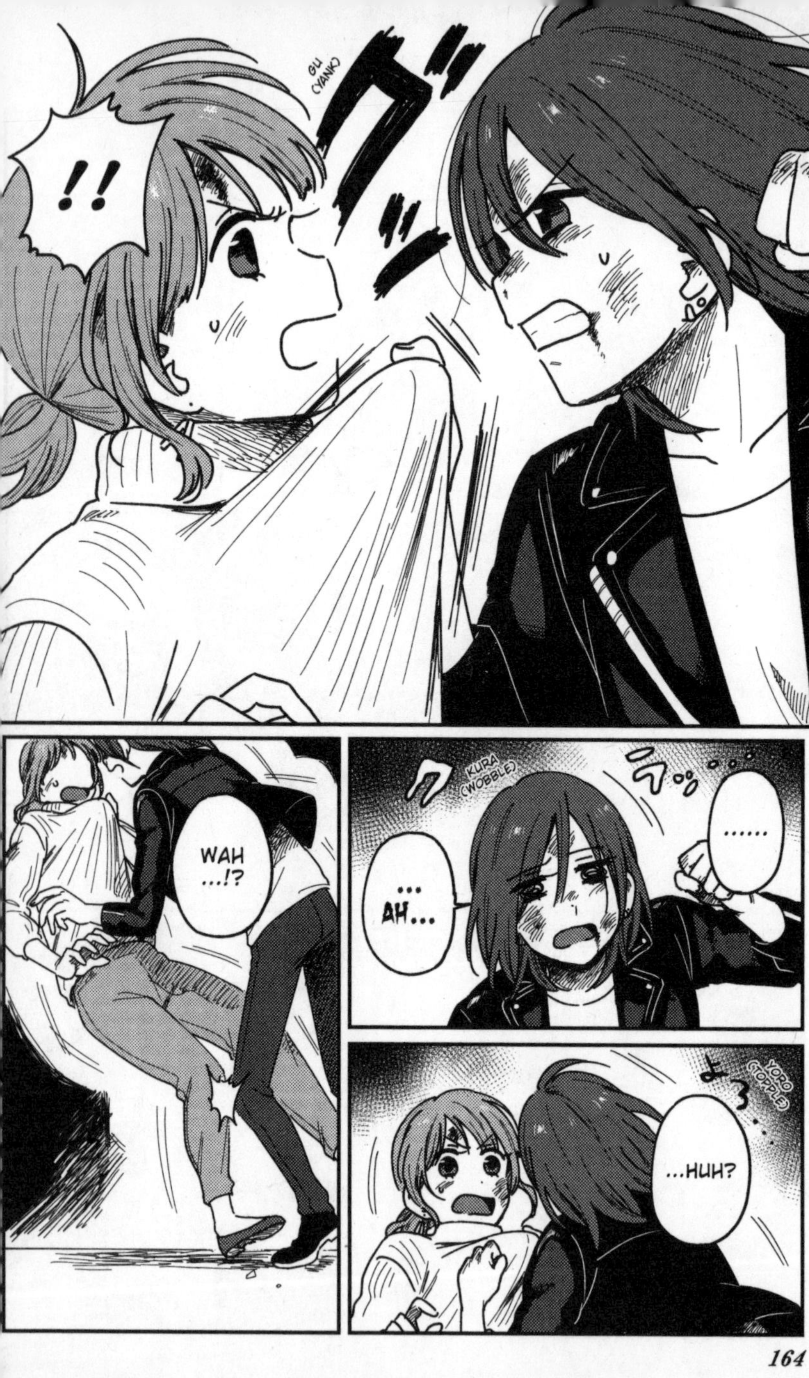
GU (YANK)
!!
KURA (WOBBLE)
......
... AH...
YORO (TOPPLE)
...HUH?
WAH ...!?

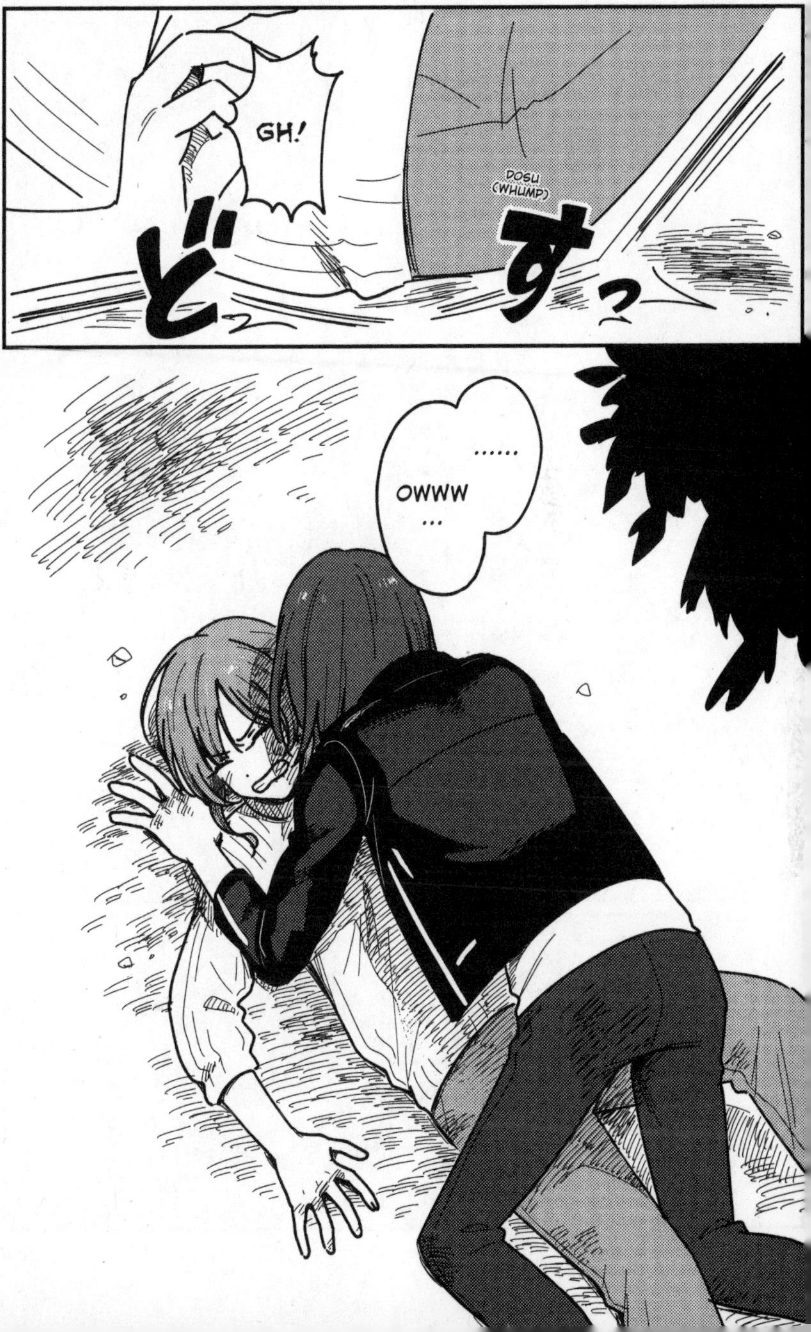
GH!
DOSU (WHUMP)
どすっ
...... OWWW ...

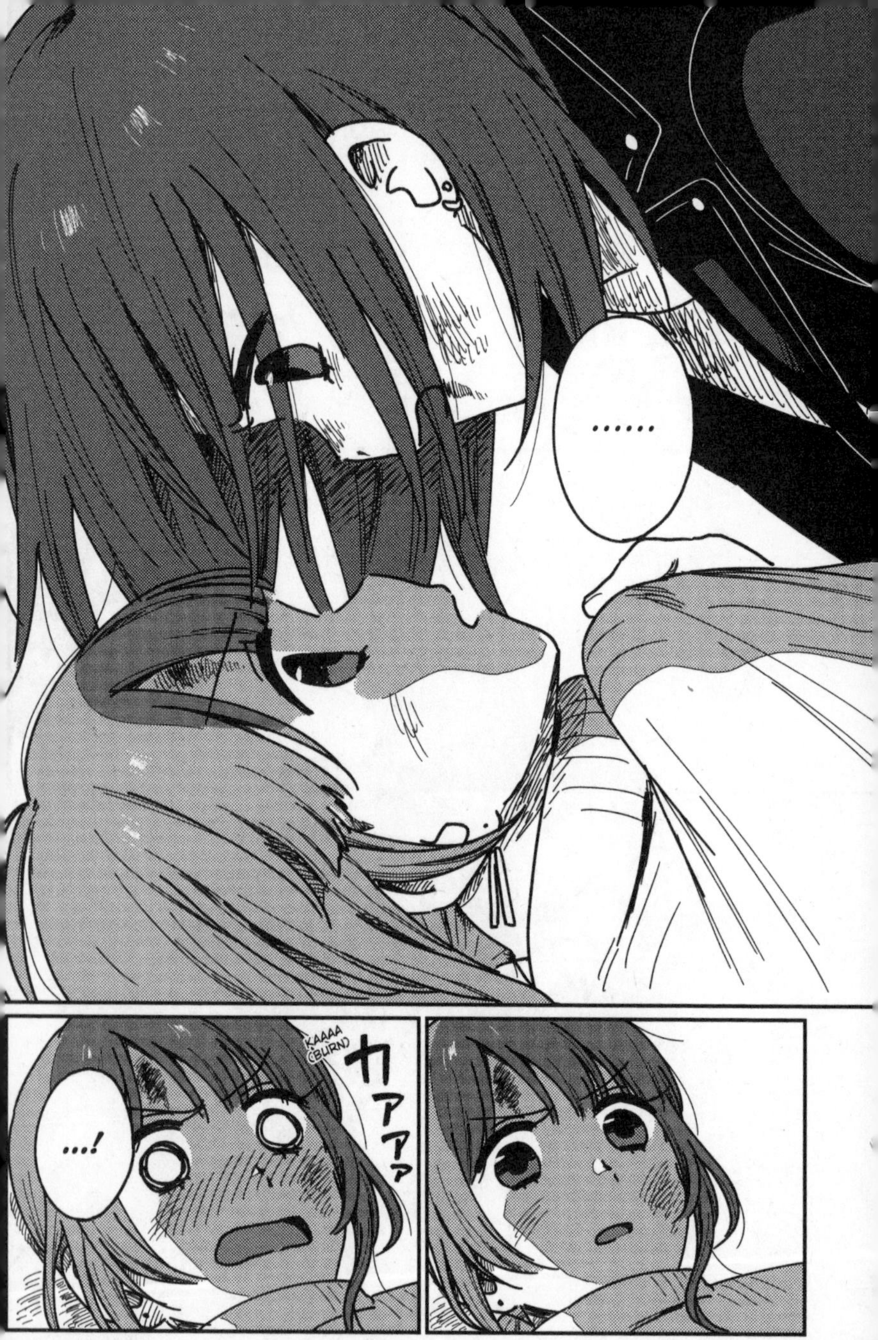
......
KAAAA (BURN)
カアアア
...!

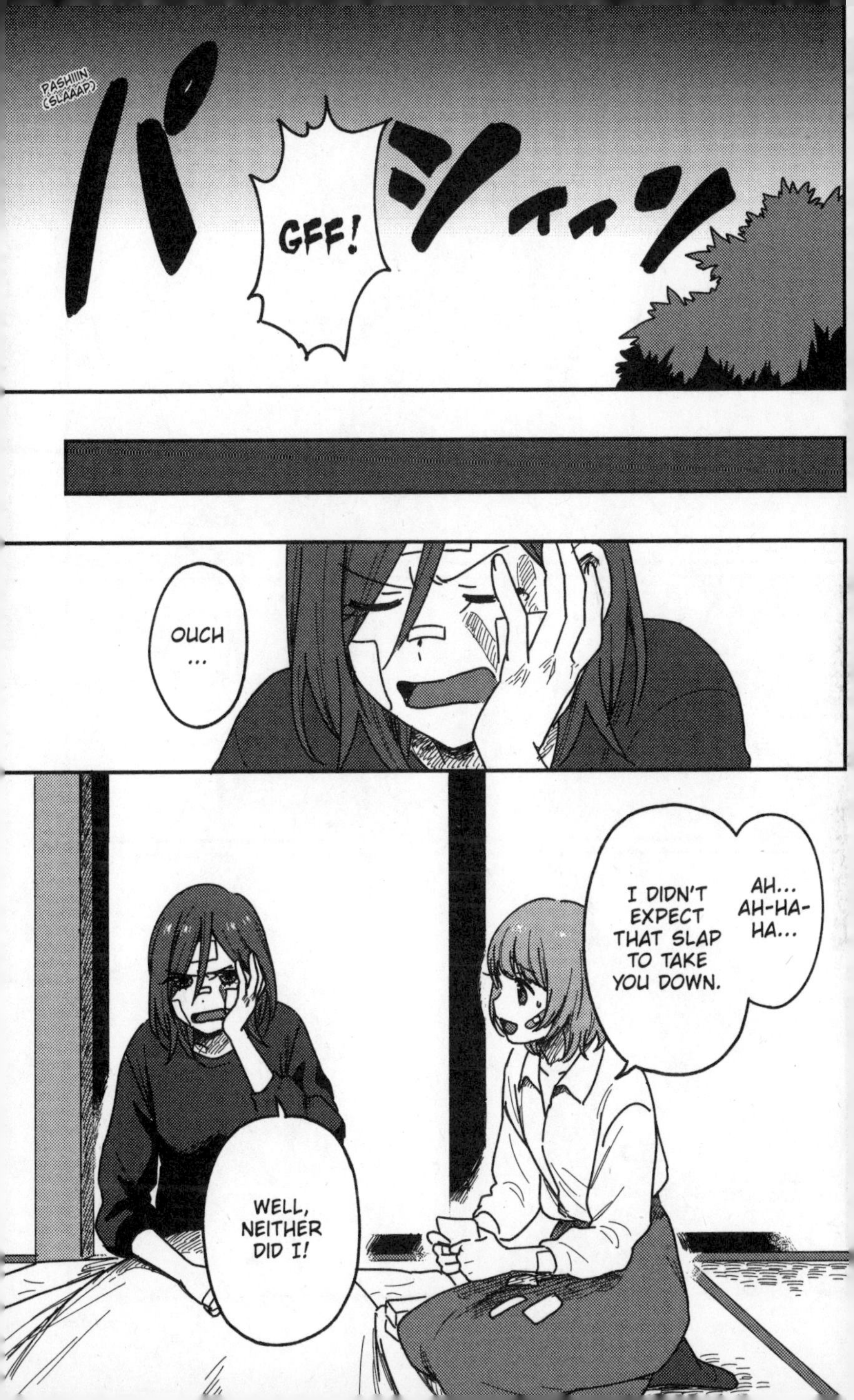
PASHIIIN (SLAAAP)
GFF!
OUCH ...
AH... AH-HA-HA...
I DIDN'T EXPECT THAT SLAP TO TAKE YOU DOWN.
WELL, NEITHER DID I!

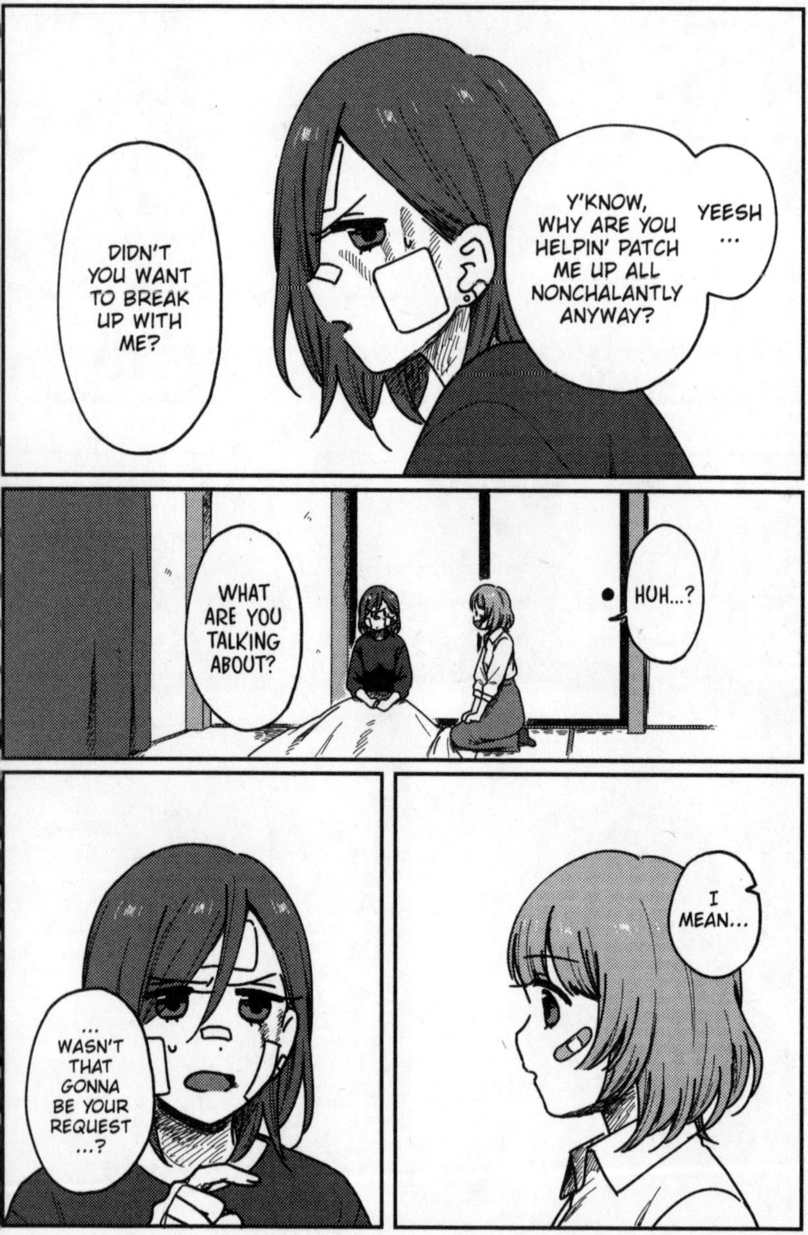
YEESH ...
Y'KNOW, WHY ARE YOU HELPIN' PATCH ME UP ALL NONCHALANTLY ANYWAY?
DIDN'T YOU WANT TO BREAK UP WITH ME?
HUH...?
WHAT ARE YOU TALKING ABOUT?
I MEAN...
... WASN'T THAT GONNA BE YOUR REQUEST ...?

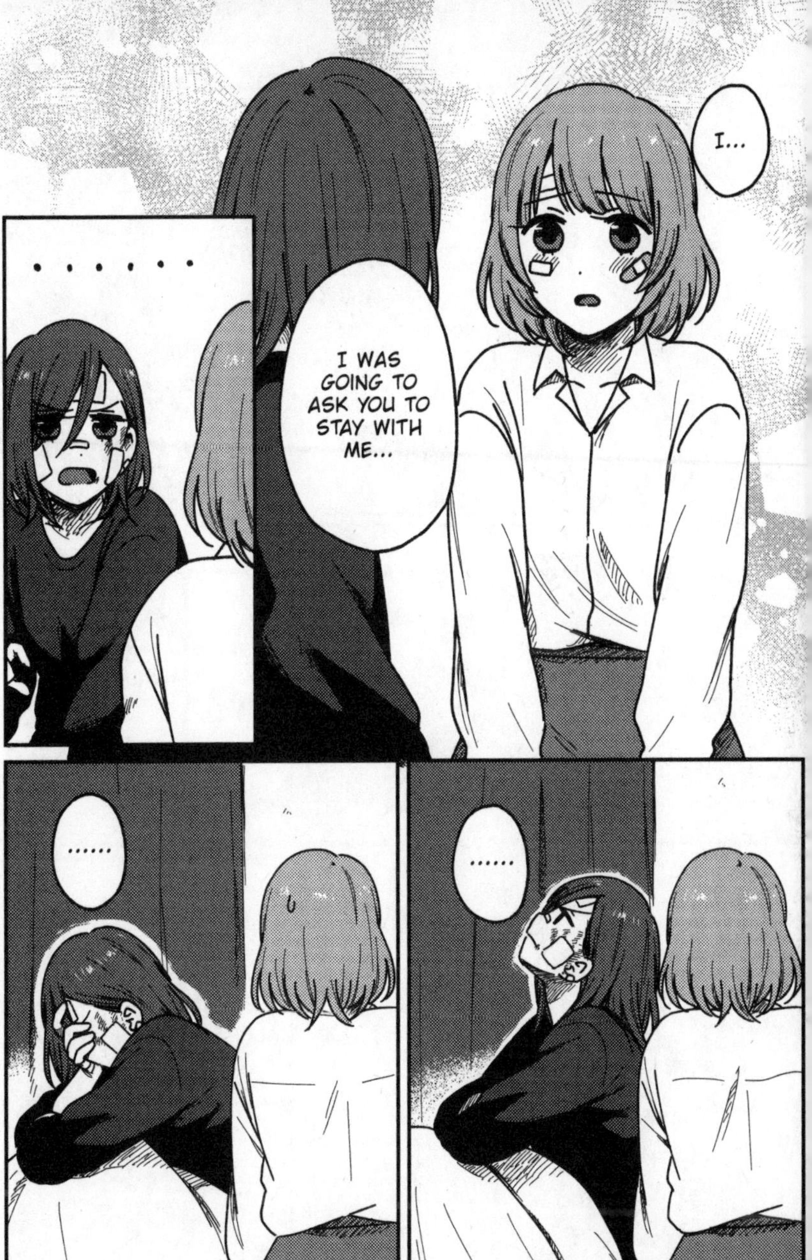
I...
I WAS GOING TO ASK YOU TO STAY WITH ME...
....
......
......

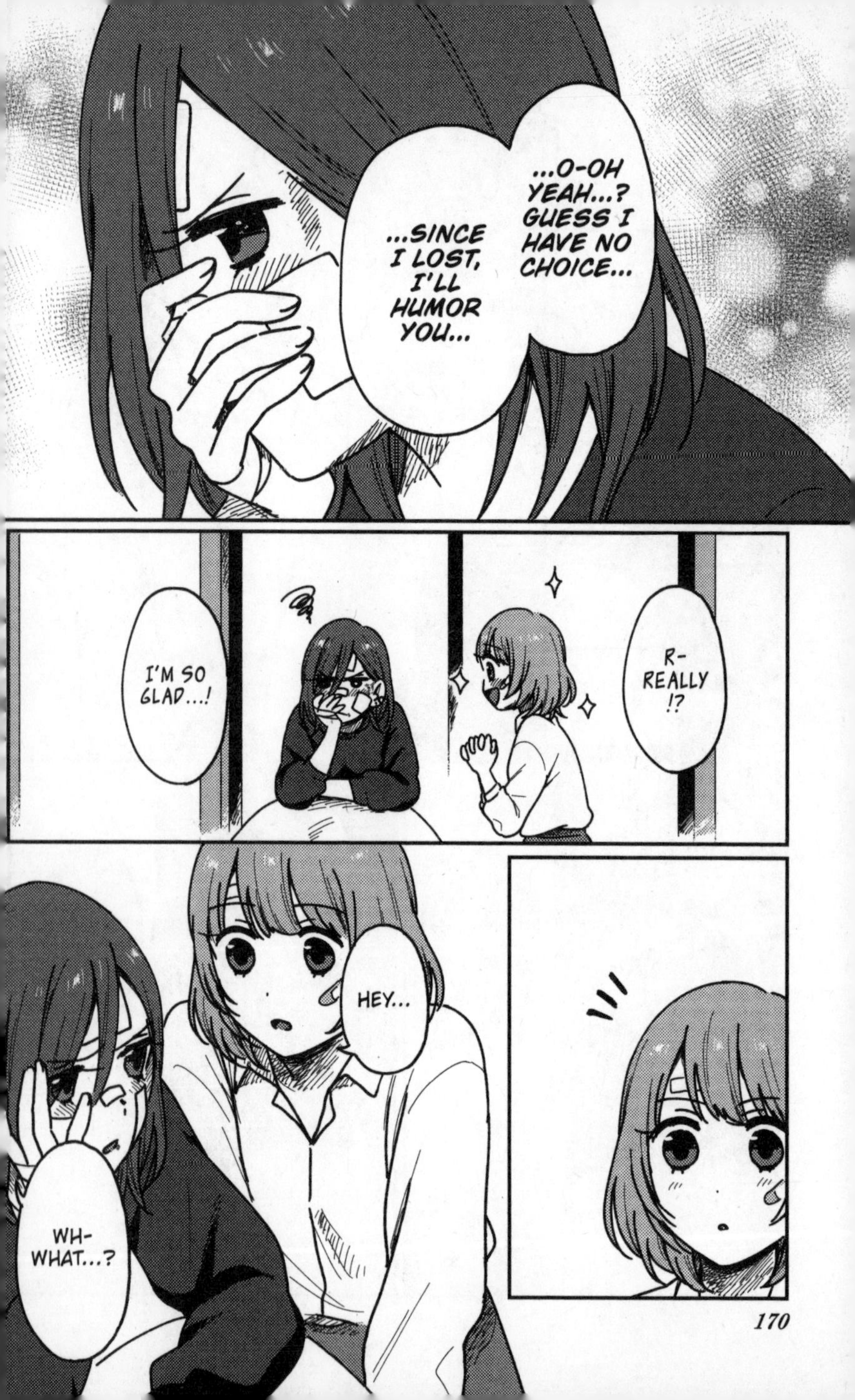
...O-OH YEAH...? GUESS I HAVE NO CHOICE...
...SINCE I LOST, I'LL HUMOR YOU...
R-REALLY!?
I'M SO GLAD...!
HEY...
WH-WHAT...?

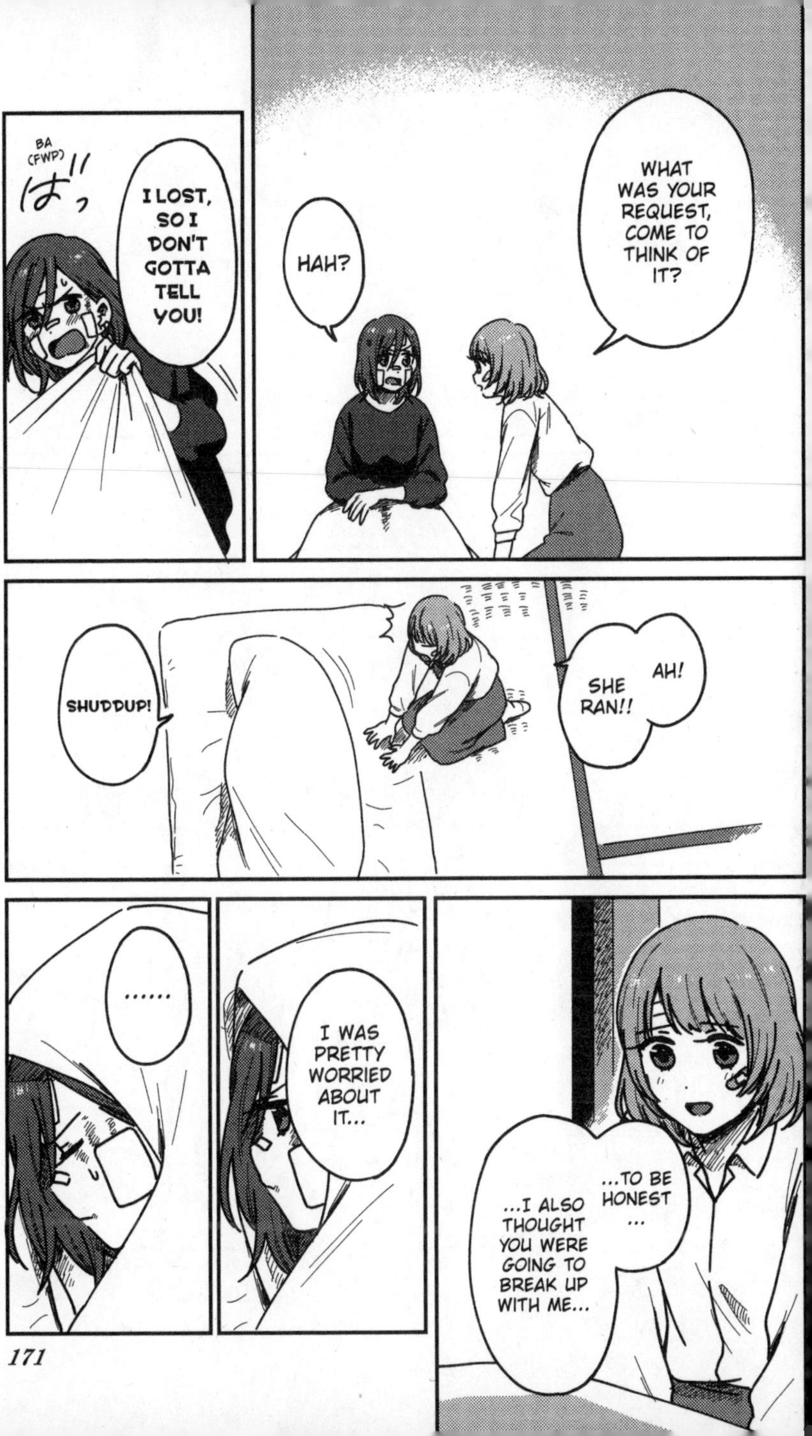
WHAT WAS YOUR REQUEST, COME TO THINK OF IT?
HAH?
BA (FWP)
ばっ
I LOST, SO I DON'T GOTTA TELL YOU!
AH! SHE RAN!!
SHUDDUP!
...TO BE HONEST ...
...I ALSO THOUGHT YOU WERE GOING TO BREAK UP WITH ME...
I WAS PRETTY WORRIED ABOUT IT...
......

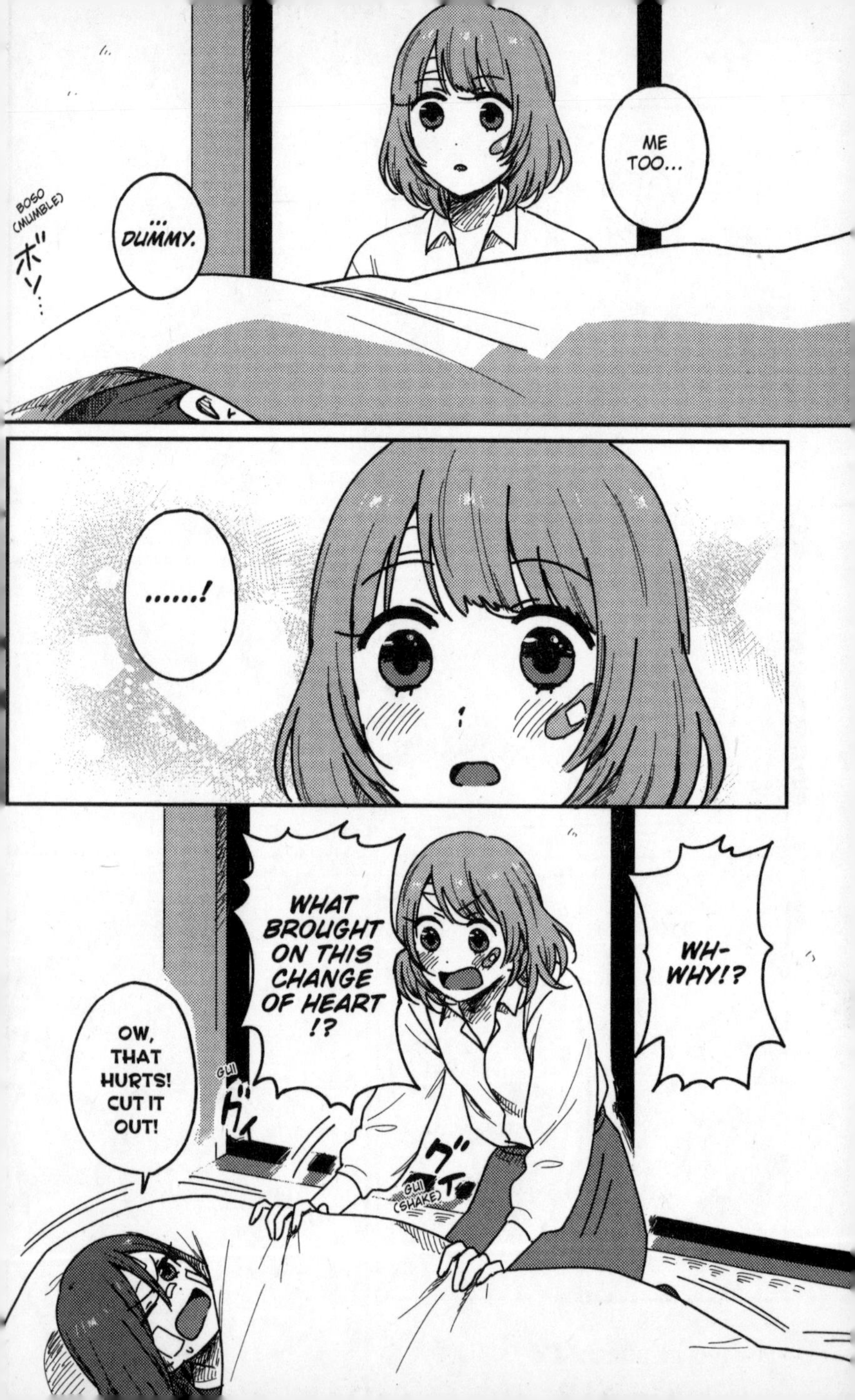
ME TOO...
...DUMMY.
BOSO (MUMBLE)
ボソ…
......!
WH- WHY!?
WHAT BROUGHT ON THIS CHANGE OF HEART!?
グイ
GUI (SHAKE)
グイ
GUI
OW, THAT HURTS! CUT IT OUT!

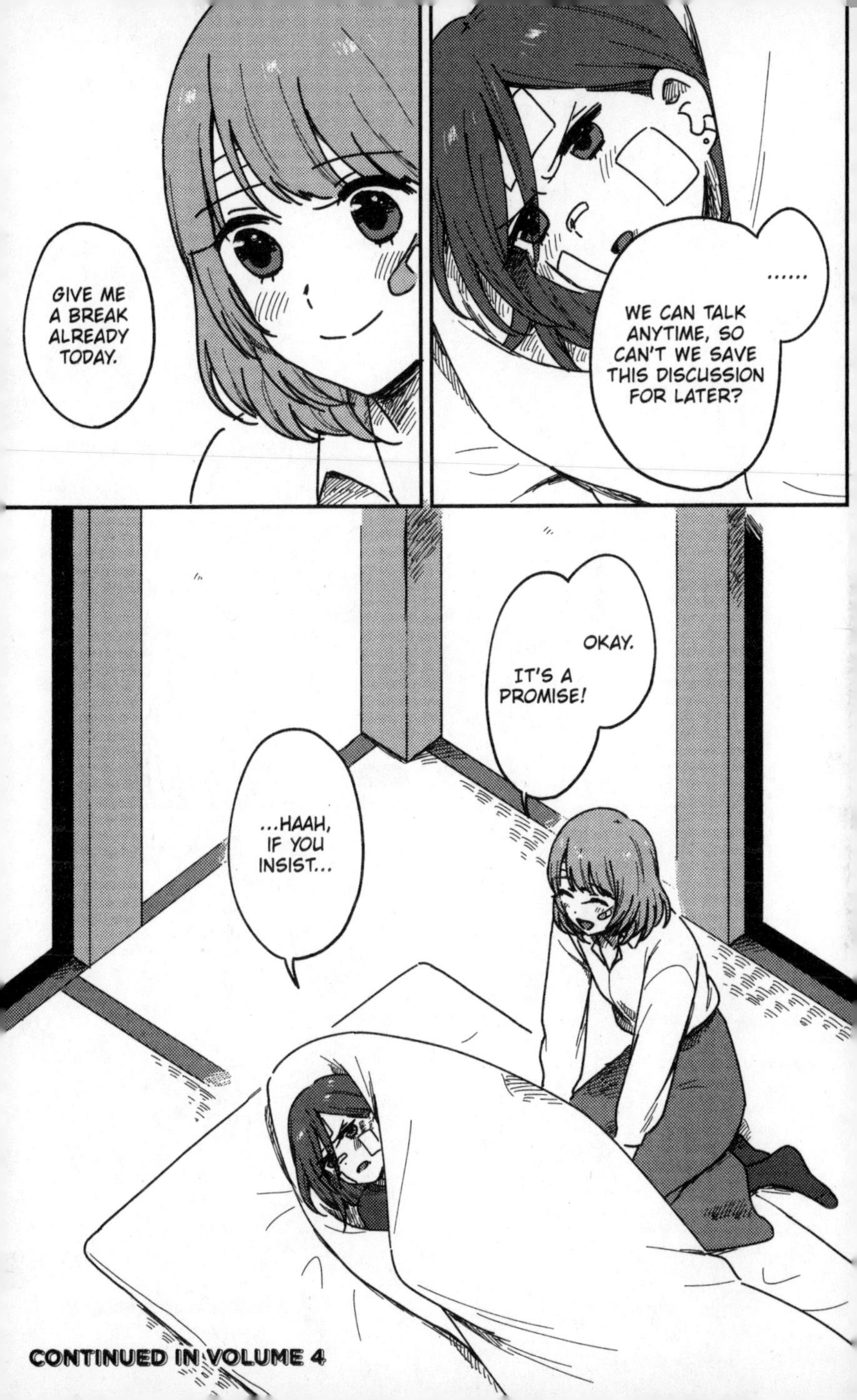
...... WE CAN TALK ANYTIME, SO CAN'T WE SAVE THIS DISCUSSION FOR LATER?
GIVE ME A BREAK ALREADY TODAY.
OKAY. IT'S A PROMISE!
...HAAH, IF YOU INSIST...

CONTINUED IN VOLUME 4

HAPPY

Catch These Hands!

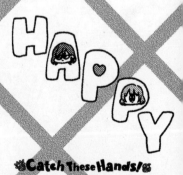

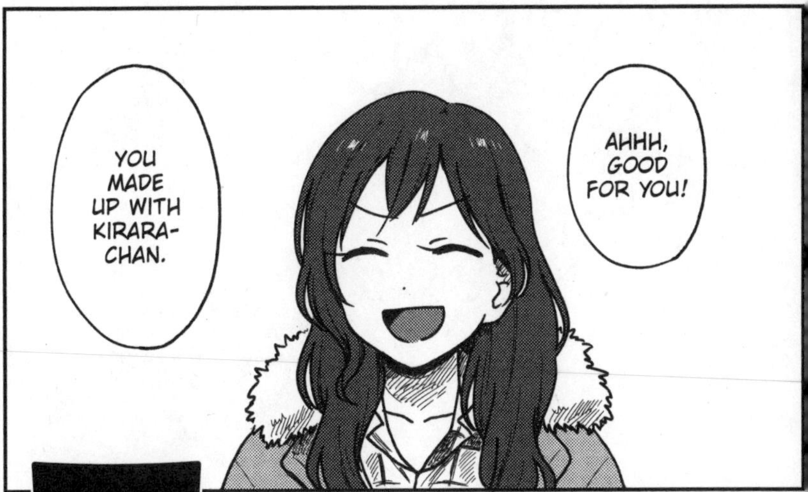
AHHH, GOOD FOR YOU!
YOU MADE UP WITH KIRARA-CHAN.

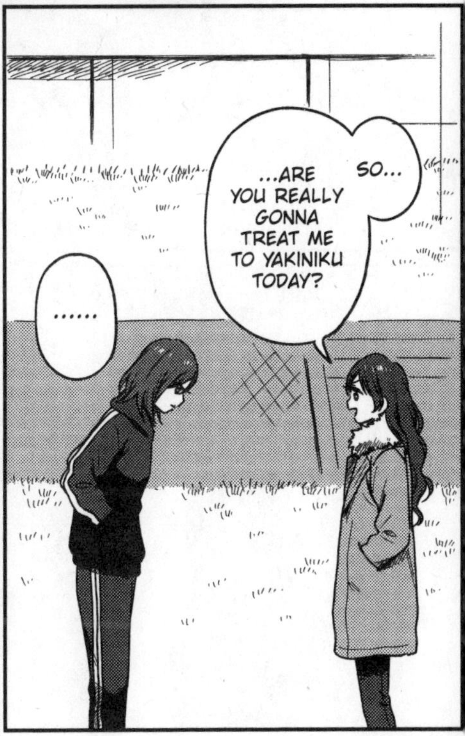
SO...
...ARE YOU REALLY GONNA TREAT ME TO YAKINIKU TODAY?
......

BONUS STORY 3

Catch These Hands!

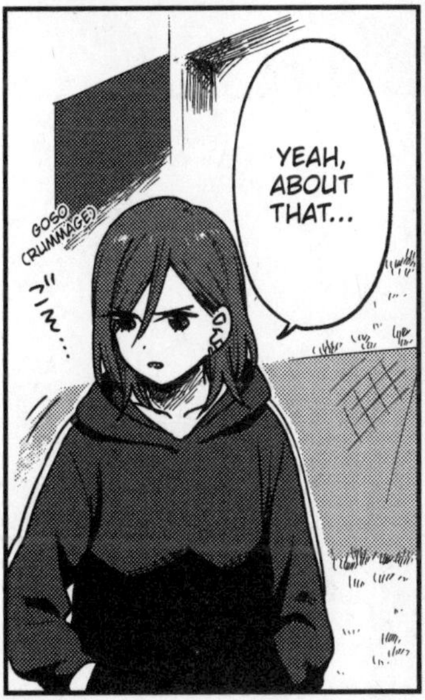
YEAH, ABOUT THAT...
GOSO (RUMMAGE)

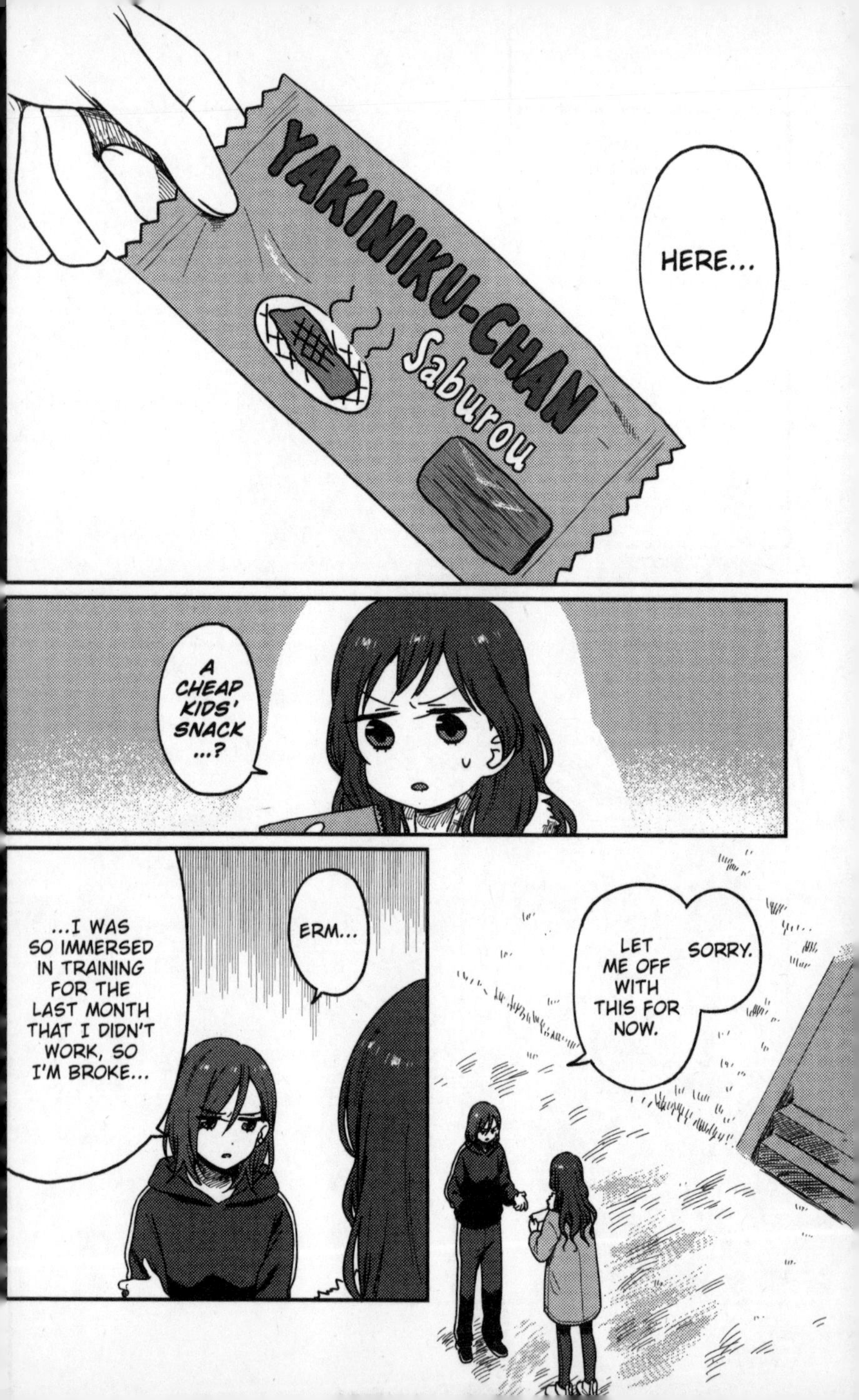
HERE...
YAKINIKU-CHAN
Saburou
A CHEAP KIDS' SNACK ...?
SORRY.
LET ME OFF WITH THIS FOR NOW.
ERM...
...I WAS SO IMMERSED IN TRAINING FOR THE LAST MONTH THAT I DIDN'T WORK, SO I'M BROKE...

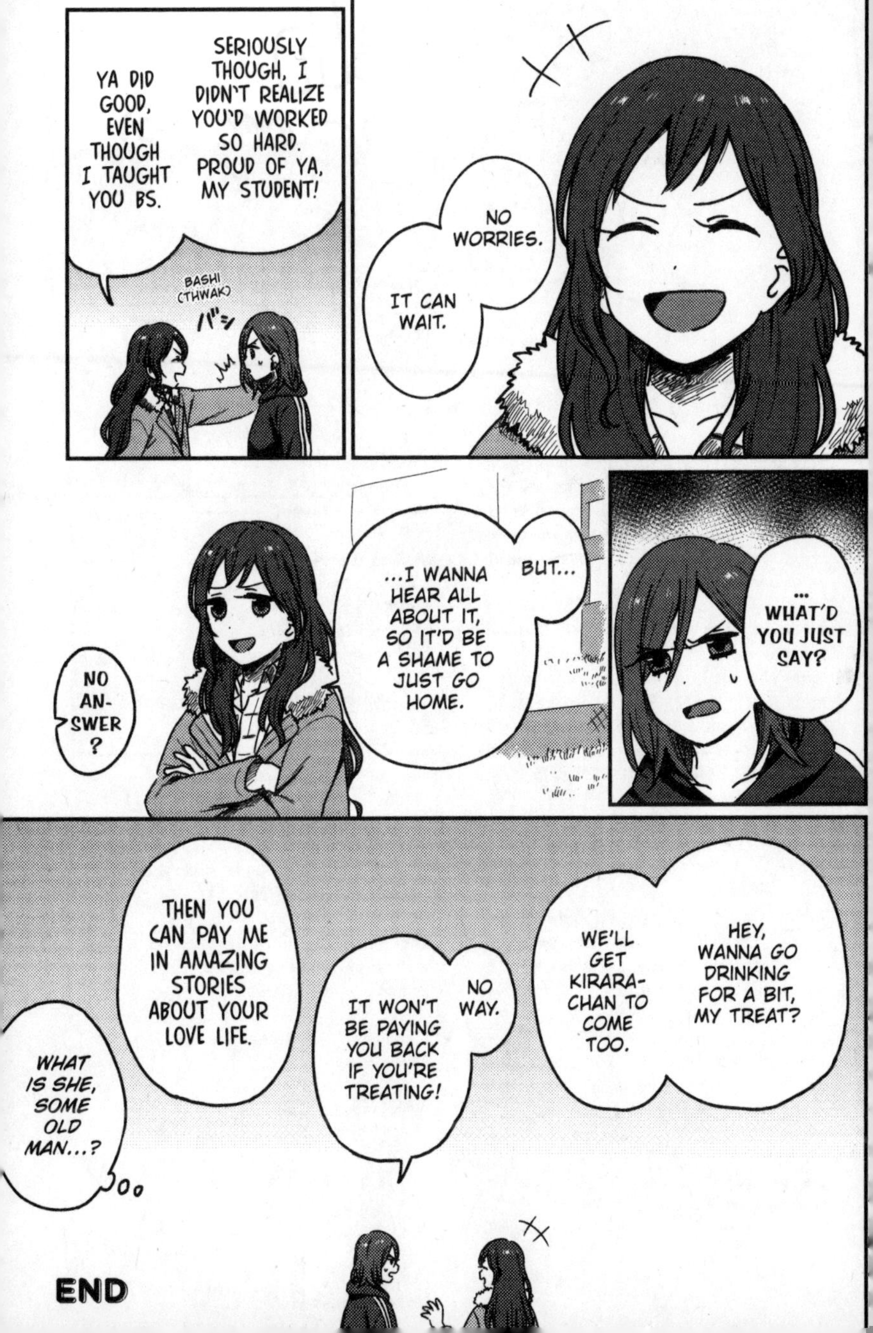
NO WORRIES.
IT CAN WAIT.
SERIOUSLY THOUGH, I DIDN'T REALIZE YOU'D WORKED SO HARD. PROUD OF YA, MY STUDENT!
YA DID GOOD, EVEN THOUGH I TAUGHT YOU BS.
BASHI (THWAK)
...WHAT'D YOU JUST SAY?
BUT...
...I WANNA HEAR ALL ABOUT IT, SO IT'D BE A SHAME TO JUST GO HOME.
NO AN-SWER?
HEY, WANNA GO DRINKING FOR A BIT, MY TREAT?
WE'LL GET KIRARA-CHAN TO COME TOO.
NO WAY.
IT WON'T BE PAYING YOU BACK IF YOU'RE TREATING!
THEN YOU CAN PAY ME IN AMAZING STORIES ABOUT YOUR LOVE LIFE.
WHAT IS SHE, SOME OLD MAN...?

END

Catch These Hands!

murata

Translation: AMANDA HALEY ✖ Lettering: BIANCA PISTILLO

WATASHI NO KOBUSHI WO UKETOMETE! Vol. 3
©murata 2019
First published in Japan in 2019 by KADOKAWA CORPORATION, Tokyo.
English translation rights arranged with KADOKAWA CORPORATION, Tokyo through TUTTLE-MORI AGENCY, INC., Tokyo.

English translation © 2022 by Yen Press, LLC

Yen Press
150 West 30th Street, 19th Floor
New York, NY 10001

Visit us at yenpress.com
facebook.com/yenpress
twitter.com/yenpress
yenpress.tumblr.com
instagram.com/yenpress

First Yen Press Edition: November 2022
Edited by Yen Press Editorial:
Jacquelyn Li, Carl Li
Designed by Yen Press Design:
Wendy Chan

Yen Press is an imprint of Yen Press, LLC. The Yen Press name and logo are trademarks of Yen Press, LLC.

The publisher is not responsible for websites (or their content) that are not owned by the publisher.

Library of Congress Control Number: 2021950487

ISBNs: 978-1-9753-4017-9 (paperback)
        978-1-9753-4018-6 (ebook)

10 9 8 7 6 5 4 3 2 1

WOR

Printed in the
United States of America